CHAT WITH A PRAIRIE CHICKEN

Most Of My Life In Pictures and Words

Sarah (Baker) Sergius

SARAH A H SERGIUS

CONTENTS

ACKNOWLEDGMENTS

If it were not for all the great people I met in my lifetime I would have experienced nothing, done little, and had dreadful life with to say here. As it is I had a normal life with some happy and sad times, some struggle and some rejoicing, so I want to thank all of these wonderful people for helping to create this story. I want also to thank Penny Greenslade who read early versions of this book. Frank Mesich deserves a great thank you for cooking allowing Glenn and I to work. I thank Glenn for making notes, taking dictation, and as is his nature, asking a lot of questions.

ISBN:

ISBN-13:

DEDICATION

I dedicate this book: to all people who can identify with the stories and feelings found between these covers; to all those who want to know more about the life of an average Canadian woman in this time; to my family past, present, and future; and to all those friends and acquaintances who I have met, liked, and loved, and have helped make my life more meaningful and more enjoyable. Thank You.

Family and Emigration: My Parents, Relatives and My Early Days

I could have been dead a long time ago. I have courted death a few times. Sometimes it was unknowingly. As a baby, I could easily have died from an assortment of fevers that took my brother and many others. Silently, I could have drowned as a kid in a boating accident because of my own irresponsible stupidity. Dramatically I could easily have met death in a plane crash into a lake amid a horrendous wind and electric storm. Instead, I thrived, clung hard to a boat, and the plane bounced across the water.

Perhaps because of my own folly, I could have been trodden to death by a crazed cow chasing me, but Ruby's intervening actions saved me. Strangely the good judgement of a wild bronco, something one does not expect, is my first recollection of somehow avoiding early death at age 4 or 5.

As a child, I was not to be sitting in the narrow pasture between the fence and the barn. I was never to be there at all. Especially I should not have been there right at that moment. I had squeezed under the fence and into danger. An escaping wild bronco with trampling, killing, hooves was galloping towards me. Untamed, unpredictable, and unfriendly, it rounded the barn and raced towards me. I remember the huge beast coming towards me. I still hear my frantic father yelling "Sarah". Even now I can see the bronco's shadow as it jumped and its killing hooves and body flew over me, and again I hear my father calling to me "Sarah".

With that bit of luck, I lived, at least until now, 93 years later. I was given another stern direction not to go near the pasture at all. I remember the importance of the warning, but I do not remember being afraid at the time. I remember my parents had a serious discussion about being more careful and keeping me away from the pasture. It turns out that the need to stay away from the pasture and away from farm animals, at that age had some long range effects on my life.

My parents were just beginning to make a decent living farming. They had not been in Canada all that long. To make ends meet my father did more than just farm. Capturing wild horses in the south of Saskatchewan and breaking them for farm work as well as blacksmith work were two other avenues my father used to increase our meagre family income.

I liked to help while my father worked at his blacksmith forge. Standing on a wooden box I turned the handle on the air blower and gazed happily as the fire roared up in heat. It seems perhaps a wonder, but I never remember being burned.

From my early childhood, I have memories and visions of bedtime. At night, I wanted my mother to lie beside me. I would call out something like "Mam, come lay beside me". Mam was my mother. All her children called her that but I cannot remember what my father called her when their family was around. I think the term was customary for the people from Yorkshire to use with their mother. It was not a term my own children used with me. I never wanted that name. To my own kids, I was always Mom, or Mother, but my mother was Mam.

R. M. S. TUNISIAN.

Remembering my childhood, I see Mam, beside me on the bed, and with entangled hands making shadows of animals and things on the wall until I fell asleep. As I grew, she told me of her life before the Canadian prairies.

Mom, Mam, Harriet Baker, nee Harriet Corney, told me more than once that in the first years after they emigrated life was hard. She would have liked to have gone back to England where they used flush toilets. She would have walked back had there not been so much water in between Canada and England. Perhaps that feeling tells us just how hard that the steerage class journey and the first years in Canada were to immigrants. She wanted to walk rather than sail back to England, and she preferred to leave Canada rather than stay.

From my perspective, life in England at the time was not very easy either. I guess for many, life was in some ways better on the great western plains and to others it was not. One way or the other the distance set my mother's mind to staying. As she aged, she never expressed any desire to return to England.

I wish now I had asked more questions and remembered more of what Mam told me of her life story. So many details, events, and insights to a way of life are lost. With that thought in my mind, I have felt compelled to write down some stories of my own life. Some may find it of interest. It may be that some will find them of value at some time in the future. Herein are my recollections and some glimpses into family history, some stories, interesting people, and always the ways of life I have experienced.

My grandfather John Corney, his son Charlie Corney, and my dad Sam Baker came to Canada in 1905. John Corney had been told he needed to quit working in the mines. Sam and Charlie came for work. Certainly, they found work. Life in the west in those days meant working to survive. Life in Canada did not reflect life in England at the time. It was drastically different. It had a different social structure and a different environment. The differences they experienced started as they left England. My mother Harriet Baker and my oldest brother Syd came from England to Canada in 1906. My mother came to Canada on a boat called the *Tunisian* pictured here.

Harriet's mother, Sarah Ellen Corney, came over with some of her children. Two of Sarah Ellen Corney's sons did not come. Neither John her oldest son, who married, and had at least 2 children, nor Walter, who married and adopted one child, ever came from England to Canada. When Walter's wife died, he married his wife's sister. As far as I know, they never had children. John's son did come to Canada, and their family lives in Alberta and Bob Smylie is the relative that I remember there.

My Mam came with her mother Sarah Ellen Corney. Also with Mam came her brothers Harry and Fred, and sisters Ada, Hilda, Gladys and Nell called thus though her real name was Ellen.

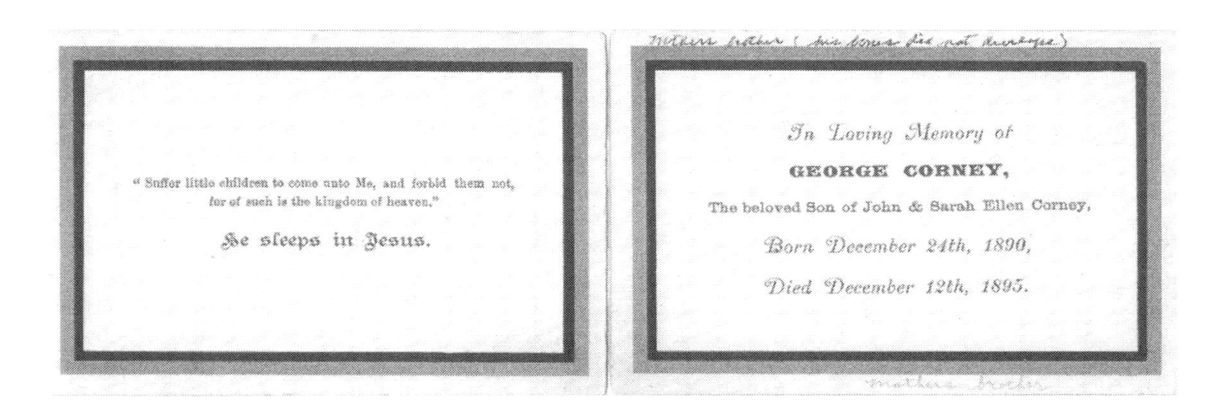
"Suffer little children to come unto Me, and forbid them not, for of such is the kingdom of heaven."

He sleeps in Jesus.

In Loving Memory of

GEORGE CORNEY,

The beloved Son of John & Sarah Ellen Corney,

Born December 24th, 1890,

Died December 12th, 1895.

Sarah Ellen Corney had at least three other children. Caroline Evelyn Corney, died at the age of 4 months, December 22, 1901, and was buried in Conisbrough Cemetery, December 26, 1901. Another daughter that died young but I cannot remember the details.

A third child was a boy called George. My mother told me he had an odd condition where his bones never developed. He had gristle but no bones. He lived in a cradle. Every hour he had to be turned. I am not sure if this meant every hour for 24 hours a day or if it was less frequent at night. He could not chew and they had to feed him soft food he could easily swallow. Though he could smile, he did not talk. It seems a horrible existence without joy.

On December 12 of 1903 Harriet Corney, then still a young girl, but one who worked out of the home for a few days, say 8 to 10 days, and returned home for two or three days, woke early turned George in his cradle, made sure he was warm, and went back to bed. Sarah Ellen Corney got up later, lit the fire by his cradle, and found that he had died sometime after Harriet had turned him. He was born December 24th 1890, and died 12 days before his 5th birthday, and was buried December, in Conisbrough.

A small folded card, each side 3 x 4 ½ was sent out announcing his death. I have this along with other cards for other family members. In the late 1890's mailing cards like this was a way to let family and other people know of a death.

Whenever Mam told me the story of George, she was sad. I could see the images of the story in my mind and it bothered me and could see it bothered her. She explained to me that she did not feel that it was her fault or the fault of anyone. It was easy for me to imagine that she thought it a blessing George died peacefully and that still she missed him.

The back of this class picture says it was taken by E Stockham, School Photographer, 26
Russell Rd, Kensington, and London. The picture is done at the Mount Pleasant School, Conisbrough, near Rotherham, England. Harriet Corney, my mother, in grade 2, is in the front row, a few down to the left from the girl holding the number 2. She is the little girl third from the left whose cuffs of her dress matches what looks like an imitation tie down the front of her dress. Above a barely visible X on the bottom margin indicates Mam.

Harriet went to grade six. She called it standard 6. After this time, she was sent out to work. Mam told me she had a teacher by the name of Miss Dier that she did not really like. Every Monday morning Harriet had to stay home and help her mother Sarah Ellen Corney, do the laundry. When Harriet returned to school every Monday afternoon she got the strap for missing school in the morning. This continued until her mother went to school with clenched fists and made sure it stopped.

Mam told me of the hard life in England at the time. It seems that she was out to work at a relatively young age. She was still a child and working. We consider this child abuse now. Her wages were low she said. This might be termed by some to be child slavery. In those days, it was necessary for children to work for a family to survive.

Harriet went to work as a servant for a few days living away as she worked, and then would come home for a few days. She had more work to do at home. There was not much rest as there was always another baby to help look after. Mother being the second eldest was required to work. There were nine births after her. Both Harriet and her mother Sarah had a lot of work. Her mother would say to Harriet things like:

> *When you're resting, you can sweep the floor, or when you are resting you can do this or that.*

Keeping babies and kids clean is a lot easier today than it was for Sarah Corney. It would be hard to keep things as clean as we have them now with the convenience of washing machines and diaper services. In every previous time, raising kids meant more work than it does today, and today there are different concerns.

Harriet's sister Caroline Evelyn I think died at a few months old. My mother remembered there was some disease around. She said there were many caskets in the streets waiting to be taken for burial all the time. Both adults and children would die.

The long and hard work hours for everyone in the family, the frequent deaths of children, and their poverty, contrasted with the promise of land, and a new hope for a brighter future somewhere else. It seems they had plenty of emotional, physical, and economic reasons, to motivate a move to a country of promise like Canada. Perhaps Canada represented escape as much as it did hope.

About the same time this branch of the family came to Canada, some of the Baker family moved to the Lucknow region of Northern India in the state of Uttar Pradesh, and perhaps they subsequently moved to Australia.

To get to Canada the Corney family, with the now married Harriet Baker, travelled by boat in the steerage class. The living conditions in such transport were horrible. Many people died in steerage class because of the unsanitary, cramped conditions that additionally had no privacy. The stench would have been awful. Mom never mentioned much about it other than to say they were all sick and that it was awful. Syd remembered running around the boat, and spending time eating with the crew because his family was sick.

Stories of steerage class feature bad bathrooms and no bathrooms, and people crammed in like animals, filthy, smelling, and for sure in cranky moods, certainly does not match the picture below taken from the internet. In the picture, here, the religious service in the *Tunisian* steerage, class looks relaxed. I wonder if it were at the start of the voyage as people are well dressed and look clean. It does though give a close view of part of the *Tunisian* but not the dreaded steerage class section.

I imagine when the steerage class arrived in Halifax they were mighty glad to get a breath of fresh air. That I know of, they had no one to meet them upon arrival. They purchased railway tickets from there to Qu'Appelle, Saskatchewan. Mam said the seats were hard and uncomfortable on this journey of several days. In those days' trains made a lot more noise than today. This is partly because the track sections were shorter and the wheels made a much louder and far more frequent clicking noise as they passed from rail to rail. Consider too that the cars were not as solid as they are today and you have a much noisier rail ride.

Sam Baker, my dad, was working for farmers in Saskatchewan while waiting for his family to arrive. When Harriet arrived, she also worked for established farmers and kept Syd with her. They did not yet have their own farm. This was the situation for about 2 years.

After this time, they moved to Woodrow. They took the train from Qu'Appelle to Morse, Saskatchewan. In Morse, they picked up two teams of oxen. It was now that Harriet, a town girl, learned to drive a team of animals. Until this time, she had never had responsibility for animals something I never learned. They drove the oxen to a plot of land 12 miles south of Woodrow. There was no road. They followed a rough prairie trail. There were no fences but there were sloughs of water. Sometimes the oxen would decide they wanted water and head to the sloughs because they had their mind made up and could easily take advantage of a new driver. Harriet had to get off the wagon quickly. The yolk that bound the oxen to the cart had to be unhitched. If she were too slow, the oxen would drag the cart into the slough where it would be stuck in the mud and their few belongings would get wet. Generally, the oxen liked the sloughs so she would have to wade into the water up to her knees to get the oxen out and hitch them to the yolk. I cannot imagine that was too much fun or too easy. Slough water is usually smelly and slimy and the slough bottoms are sticky mud.

My parents moved into a sod shack south of Woodrow. The change from living in England with indoor toilets and stone walls, to living in a shack made of dirt must have been a significant adjustment. I never

heard her complain about it though. Sam had built the sod shack the year before while he waited for the arrival of his family. The sod shack had a pole roof and a wooden floor.

Mam said that the sod house was nice and warm and that she papered the inside walls with newspapers. One problem was that when it got warm insects would drop down from the ceiling. Mam told me this house had a wooden floor. I never saw it, but others that I did see later, used by Romanian immigrants living in Northern Saskatchewan had just hard mud floors. To sweep they would just sprinkle the floor with water and then sweep it. This would smooth and harden the mud surface. I imagine my mother did the same.

Here you see the Harriet Baker that had been in Canada about 7 years. She is about 33 years old in this picture. She is wearing a high collar buttoned blouse tucked into a skirt of the same color.

During the winter in heavy snow and storms, Sam would go to the stables from the sod house with binder twine fastened around his waist. Harriet stood in the house and let the roll of twine out as Sam went to the stables. This gave him a lifeline to follow on his return. Was this necessary? Yes.

In blizzards snow blows around. The visibility gets to be zero or approaching zero, and the temperatures can be a killing -20 to -30. When everything is frozen, and white, one easily loses orientation, as there is no point of reference. Everything is white. This is called a white out. I have experienced this myself and it is not pleasant. It is disconcerting and dangerous. Without protection of fencing or trees or hills, the snow would blow over covering the sod house and it would look like any other snowdrift.

On one occasion a neighbor showed up with a team of horses. The snow had blown up and over the sod house. The team of horses came towards the house. One horse stopped abruptly and uneasily. Sensing there was something wrong with the footing it would not put his foot down. Had the horse put the foot down, it would have gone through the roof of the house to become and unwelcome and distressed house guest ending in disaster. The horse would have been injured and would die. The humans would have lost a house and freeze to death.

Here are my Mam, Harriet Baker with my sister, Ruby holding a pet cat. They stand next to the sod house in the winter. We might think cats are good at keeping down mice populations but apparently, they are not and terriers are better at that task than cats.

Ruby was born in this sod house in 1913. One can see snow caught on some of the sod. Ruby is wearing a plaid skirt and a plaid jacket. The jacket fits tightly around the neck and has a low waist. One can notice Ruby has begun to outgrow the coat with its fancy buttons. Being poor and living in an isolated environment, wearing clothing that was a little bit small was not too big of an issue. Having any clothing to wear was a bigger issue. People wore what they had for longer periods and made repairs to extend the life of the clothing.

Her skirt is pleated and she is wearing leggings. She wears interesting rubbers too as they come up well over her ankles and have eyelets for laces.

From this sod house, they moved to a lumber house my father helped build. This bigger house is pictured later, and about the time we moved out of it. Ruby was about 4 years old in this above picture because Willie was born at home October of 1917 in the lumber house.

The picture here of Ruby Baker on a saddle pony called Bess. The sod house in the back looks deteriorated as you can see spaces between shrunken sod pieces and that it is assembled somewhat like a brick house. The main living area was now the adjacent lumber house. The contrast between the two living areas is

now easier to imagine and quite dramatic. Certainly, for them it would have been a great improvement. Mom curled Ruby's hair wrapping it around rags. Mom said Ruby's hair was always a bit curly but that mine was straight like a yard of pump water.

In the following picture of Syd and our father Sam Baker, Syd looks to be about out 10 or 11 years old dating this picture to somewhere around 1913 to 1914. I would not be around for another 10 years. There are two oxen, Ben and Bright pulling a seeder or a drill. Somehow the machine drilled a small trench, planted a seed, and covered the seed over. You can see Syd is sitting upon a seed box holding a buggy whip in his right hand. The big spoked wheels are about 4 feet high. Notice they both have hats in this case perhaps to protect themselves from the sun but they are hats of an old style. Sam is wearing a vest with buttons and heavy pants.

Syd is wearing knee pants with suspenders. Dad had to be hot wearing this much clothing, if Syd was warm enough in knee pants.

I do not remember seeing Sam Baker without a cloth hat. You can see he is wearing a lot of clothing even though it is in the summer time. Even though it had to be hot dad was always concerned about being kept warm. He probably is not wearing denim. You might wonder why he is not wearing shorts. Well the answer is that none of the Canadian farmers at least wore shorts in those days, even on hot days. Sometimes boys would wear knee pants made generally from tweed, but they had to be to the knees and men never wore knee pants.

I do not know the name of the dog at the far right of the picture. Based on the dog's posture in that it is close to them and sitting they have been in this spot for a while because it would move away from the moving animal and machine and thus not been so close.

My dad also used an ox to pull a one furrow plough. It turned the sod up and my mother threw the potatoes under the sod before it fell back into place. These potatoes were planted somewhere in the year 1908 or 1909 in virgin prairie soil. Before they ploughed the field, only buffalo roamed over it.

Mam said these potatoes were the best they ever had. Perhaps this might also be because of the fertile soil, and perhaps too because they were very glad to get the harvest to eat in the following months. Years after this picture, when we moved north, we brought horses with us, but they ate swamp grass. They were not used to it. Like a lot of other horses that did the same, they got a fever commonly called swamp fever and died.

Pictured here is of my father Sam Baker. He is working on Section 12, Township.7 Range 6, West of the 3rd meridian Saskatchewan. The field seems to go on forever of into the horizon without a tree in sight. There are no signs of habitation or civilization on the horizon. One can just make out that Sam carries a binder whip made from a long bamboo stick with a narrow piece of leather.

The binder is the machine Sam is riding. It cuts the grain stock and gathers the stocks into a bundle. It then expels the bundle out across a binder canvas that is about 3 feet wide. The binder twine went around the straw tied it into a knot and it was expelled. When I look at this picture the machine looks like it is not doing a good job. It looks like it is messy and the string is not tied on to it properly but that is the way flax came off the machine.

The sheaf that you see in the foreground is standing up. It may have come out of the machine and stood up. If you look closely, you can see a string around it. It would take five sheaves to make a stook, a standing pile. The goal was to get the sheaves into a stook so that they would dry out before it rained. Sheaves left on the ground rot fast. The sheaves were propped against each other at the top with splayed bottoms to hold each other upright. When dry, the stooks were picked up and taken to a thrashing machine.

Sam Baker is driving a horse team hitched to a cultivator I think. It appears that the field in the foreground is covered in stubble and the field behind the horses is turned over. Four horses in the team would lessen the work severity and allow the team to get more done in a day. It is summer but again Sam is wearing at least two layers of clothing. He certainly would not catch a draft. Frequently he wore a scarf. At home the windows were always shut to keep out the draft. Mam told me that once a doctor making a house call advised him to open the windows in the house and get some air in. Sam did not like the advice and thought the windows were better closed to keep the drafts out.

My dad's hard work and preference to keep the windows closed did not help keep him from injury. He was laid up unable to work for several weeks one time. The picture below shows him using crutches.

Dad was riding a horse when it stepped in a badger hole or gopher hole. The horse stumbled and fell on Sam's leg breaking it. Here he is with his thick mustache smoking and using crutches. A long time after this picture was taken I rolled him cigarettes using a little machine and remember counting 21 one day. At the end of the day they were all gone. No one thought much about the cancer connection in those days.

Behind Dad are the smaller trees he had received from the experimental farm in Indian Head. When Walter and I visited the area in the 1980's the trees were still there.

While he had a broken leg, Syd had to look after the horses. Syd had the horses roped with the rope wrapped around his hand. The horses jerked the rope tight. All the bones in the back of his left hand broke. He had played the violin in church. He could no longer do the violin fingering after the accident and switched to play the mandolin.

When Dad broke his leg, cousin John Corney was living with his grandparents their names were John and Sarah Ellen she being the lady with the hat in the car. John came to look after the horses and did exactly the same thing to his hand, a repetition of what Syd had done. I do not know who looked after the horses then.

This picture of a threshing crew was taken about 1928. I do not know the name of the man on the far left. Second, is Sam Baker, following then are George Heslop, Harry Russell, and Syd Baker. I think George Heslop wore this hat a lot, as I remember him in it. You can also see the lugs on the metal wheels without rubber. Note the long belt of the tractor to the thrashing machine. This belt powered the threshing machine. The men have pitchforks and there is a two color, short haired, terrier, behind Harry. I do not know where the picture was taken but it shows early western farmers at work with the latest tools. Below, a three wheeled Case brand tractor is the modern tool. The wheel has no rubber

tire. The steering wheel is off to the side. In the background is a thrashing machine that was powered by the tractor connected with a long belt. The backdrop of this picture is nothing but open fields. Sam Baker is looking at a child that I was once told was David Corney, but now I am not so sure that is the correct identity.

In this great picture, the lady in the hat is Sarah Ellen Wilcox Corney. Hiram Houston is on the running board and his mother Lottie Corney is driving. It might be Mary Houston or Ruby Baker standing. I do not know the others in the photograph. Lottie & Charlie Corney would drive Mary to see a chiropractor for treatment a bit south east of Sam and Harriet's farm.

Mary was sometimes there for several days. She used to play with Ruby and confessed to Ruby that the treatments frequently hurt. Later Mary died of TB. It seems that the treatments did not work.

In this picture below, as in the previous three pictures, the remote isolation of farms in the Canadian West during this period is very apparent. It is as if this house does not belong there. It is upright and foreign to the flat environment. It is something, where there is nothing.

Certainly Mrs. William Harcourt seen here feeding her turkeys and chickens has no neighbors to talk with, and of course no phone. There are no other human signs for miles into the background. How very lonely people living like this could be so very isolated! She could scream and yell and no one would hear. Her transportation was the one seated democrat, the thing with 4 wheels to the left of the picture. When hooked up to a horse, it would be for its day, fast transportation, but agonizingly slow for today. These farmers worked, ate, and slept day after day without outside world contact. It was into this world that I was born.

This is the first picture I have of myself. Here I am Sarah Ann Harriet Baker aged about 6 months. Named for my grandmothers and my mother, I wonder if I am like any of them.

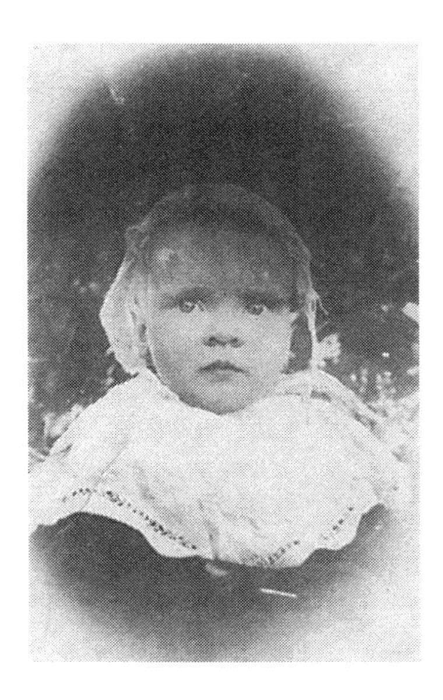

I remember many of things, but not posing for this picture in front of the wind break at about age 2, but I do remember posing for the next one following it on the auto.

Below I am, Sarah Baker, age 7, standing, wearing a hat, with my friend Dorothy Agar age eight sitting. Dorothy and her family moved to Ravenscrag, Saskatchewan and we lost touch with each other. I am neatly dressed and had started to attend the Winnifred School.

This shot is of the Winnifred School where Syd, Ruby, Willie and I all attended school. I was not there at the same time as the older Syd and Ruby, but I was there with Willie. There are two outhouses and a

Winnifred School Site. —

stable as well as a storage shed. The front door of the school was on the left of the part that sticks out. I sat on the other side of the building.
One day while attending this school Willie and his friend Milton Jewel were being teased by a big kid. The two of them held him down took off his pants and put them up a telephone pole perhaps the barely visible one. Then they were called in from recess and the big fellow did not appear. He had to get his pants, and Willie and Milton were reprimanded.

Willie and I would walk home together and he would convince me we should go barefoot stepping between cacti as we crossed the fields. We were not allowed to go barefoot so we had to be careful. I remember Willie teasing me that George Heslop's cows were following us. He would run. Afraid of cows but unable to keep up I would cry. Then Willie would carry my lunch pail to make up to me. I guess it worked as I always remember him fondly.

We walked to the right of the picture to get home. It is a bit flooded in this picture. There is a creek on the far left. It was in this creek that Syd and his friends stuffed a fellow in a gunnysack and hung him in the creek so that his feet were wet. He had been causing problems in the classroom. It is an interesting example of schoolyard justice. Syd said he learned to smoke in this school and quit smoking when he left it.

Clearly my father loved his children. I know he loved me, as he would get me to sing. Christmas concerts were held in the school. I remember singing there before I had even started school. I remember once singing "Away In A Manger" in this school at a concert.

Some boys of the Winnifred school are lined up for a photo. My brother Willie Baker is pictured second from your right wearing a one piece coverall set. You can easily see his distinctive hairline. The sleeves of his clothing are a bit short. Notice the boy's hats hanging above and behind them. They are all smiling as they posed for the picture taken by some unknown person. This picture was taken in the winter or early spring as there is snow on the ground.

This is another picture of the school kids who are not all so happy this time. Ruby is in the front row on the right of the picture wearing a fashionable checkered pinafore. It is interesting to see what the kids wore to school.

It seems to be the whole class as the ages as indicated by size seems to range quite a lot. There seems to be only three girls. Ruby was older than me, and though I never knew her at this age, it is fun to look at her and imagine what she was like. This would be the same type of class I was in but have no pictures to illustrate it so I use this one.

All four seasons we used animals to get around. We rode them, hitched them and led them. They were essential for transportation. The mother and son duo pictured here in this stylish sleigh are my grandmother and my uncle Harry. Like this one, our horses were big, strong, heavy boned animals, and

bred for strength and not speed. Having a horse pull a sleigh was a lot nicer than walking a long distance in the cold and snow.

Sam and Harriet had the very good, and childless, neighbors pictured below, George and Minnie Heslop. Minnie had her own horse and buggy. This immediately gave her independence. Her level of independence, was definitely, not the norm for women at the time. George and Minnie would tell the story that on one voting day, not long after women had been given the responsibility to vote in Canada, George drove to town and left Minnie at home. A while later, and after he had gone, she drove her own buggy to town, and voted for the other party, expressly to kill his vote. I suppose that happens quite a few times in elections but they made it sound funny.

Oddly, Minnie's first husband was killed by a band of monkeys somewhere else in the British Empire. Minnie played the piano. I do not think the two were connected, but I am mentioning this talent, because it was an appreciated talent. It was a time and place where music was not readily accessible to hear and enjoy. In such a remote location, freighting something as big and heavy as a piano would take concerted effort and intent. To be able to own and play a piano was a rare luxury. It would be a warmly remembered attribute. How she kept it in tune I do not remember.

Another time they were milking cows and that developed into another story. They disagreed on some topic, but in turn they both agreed that dumping a pail of milk on the other made them feel better and was deserved. These charming people are both buried in the Woodrow cemetery. They had a good sense of humor.

Something that is not funny is global warming. Let us look at this picture below. Ruby is on the far left inside this boat. Willie is wearing toque sitting facing her. I do not know the other people in the boat. From this shot, it is clear we used the slough for recreation. The name of the boat is Victory. There are other letters after that but I cannot make them out.

Our cows came down to this slough to drink. It was a large slough and an integral part of our family life. Willie and I walked around the edge of this slough and with sticks. We turned prairie chips over to dry in the sun. The cow patties had to dry for several hours on one side before they were turned. Using the wagon that he had made seen in an earlier picture, we would take them back to the house to be burned in the stove. They made a quick, hot, fire.

Now compare this above picture with the color picture below. The color picture following shows what the area of the slough looked like in 1989. The slough is gone. Is it possible the actions of man, global warming, and other things have upset the water table? It is farm land. People would be pictured here on a tractor not in a boat.

In this picture, the woman is Ada Corney my mother's sister, and the two others are Ruby and Syd Baker. Ada was the aunt of Ruby and Syd. She married she became Ada Reynard. They are in front of a bunch of young trees planted by Harriet and Sam Baker. These trees were given to the pioneers for free by the Indian Head Experimental farm. Trees were used to develop a wind break for the fields to stop soil erosion. Soil erosion can be a significant problem for farmers, causing farms to fail and change a way of life. They were caragana, ash, and others. In this picture, it looks like they have just finished planting some new trees, as the trees in the back are taller than the ones up front. I think they planted the trees on the west and north of the yard.

Without these plantings, there would be no trees and only wide open prairie. That is obvious in the color picture below. The picture below is what the wind break looks like in 1989.

Ada on the right was about 2 years younger than her sister Harriet, my Mam. Ruby is about 6 years old in this picture. Ada and Harriet are dressed similarly in skirts and blouse tops.

The following picture is of Ruby and Willie, aged about nine and six and they appear to be dressed and posed for the picture.

Mam and pose I in the grass. Mam has darker hair that had a touch of auburn. I was told it was auburn. I never saw her hair with any color. Taken in about 1925 and I was about 2 years old in this picture. I am wearing a hat, and an apron, and I think we must have been going somewhere for me to be dressed like this. My parents were doing well at farming in Woodrow. Yearly their lives improved, and they prospered and life got better.

In this picture taken beside our house, Willie is looking at the camera. His good friend Eldon Bell is beside him in the yolk looking down. Willie later named his son after Eldon his good friend. Billy Bell is in the cart on the left, and I am on the right. I have not worn hats much for last 80 years and I wonder if it was because as child we always had to wear them as in this picture. Willie had made this cart from supplies around the yard. The car in the background is likely that of the visiting Bell family. We had a similar vehicle. The building behind the car is likely my dad's workshop. The space between the trees on the far

left of the picture is a road on our property. In the far background are the farm buildings belonging to George Heslop. Just behind the small section of trees on the left of the driveway or road is where stood the sod house in which Ruby was born.

On this side of the same trees and on the left of the road was the workshop of my dad, Sam Baker. To the right of the gate out of the picture was a well with plenty of water. To the right of the gate and further back stood a hip roofed barn where my dad would bring wild horses and break them in or train them. It is under this fence to the left of the gate that as a child I crawled under the fence to play in the dirt and had the close near fatal encounter with an escaping bronco. From then on, I was told to be more careful and forbidden to be in the stable yard on my own.

Willie in sits astride a horse in bib overalls, and a soft cap. Our dad cut our hair and you can see the straight firm line of Willie's haircut. The stamp on the back of this picture says July 12, 1929. Willie's shoulders are hunched forward. It seems perhaps a sign of a less than robust, growing boy. He looks thin and fragile. He had chest problems that began from the time he and George were sick and George died.

Though he teased me, he was a good brother and I must have liked the teasing. It would have been his idea to take our shoes off when we walked in Heslop's field on the way home from school. He had longer legs than I did and could more easily void the plentiful cacti. Stepping around these thorns made me go slower. It was to hurry me long that he would tease me saying the cows had seen us and were coming after us.

This picture is likely taken the same day. I am age 6. Willie has his cap removed but his other clothing is the same and seems perhaps to fit him a bit largely. All of us are looking at something other than the camera except perhaps the photogenic horse. I have on a fancy hat with decorations on the back side and t strap shoes

.

Syd is standing with reins in his left hand. Buck and Duke are harnessed but are not hooked to anything. Syd loved horses but I cannot tell if he is finishing or starting some work in this shot. The picture gives us a clue to farm life. He is wearing bib overalls, a vest and a long sleeved shirt, hat and sturdy shoes. One

of Syd's shirtsleeves one rolled up, still they look a bit too short for his size. He is dressed in the normal clothing of a working farm son in a family starting to climb out of poverty. It might be fall as there are some large leaves on the trees and some have no leaves.

There are large wagon wheels in the background. Against the shed are what might be wooden wagon siding. It is possible to make out where the bolts are placed on the boards. The right hand side of the granary has a pole that might have had a windsock as you can see the end of something coming into the picture from the top. The shed is higher off the ground on the left hand side than it is on the right hand side. I wonder why.

It looks like there might be a windsock on the roof of the granary or some other thing certainly fastened well to the pole.

To the right of the picture one can see two sets of wheels the back wheels to the wagons were larger than the front wheels so the wagon is facing to the right. Perhaps Syd was going to hitch the wagon or some other farm implement. The picture below is an enlargement useful to examine the picture.

Seeing the barrel in the above picture, reminded me of an incident involving a barrel quite similar to that seen on the right of the building in the enlarged section below. During the fall threshing time, teams of workers would go from place to place doing the threshing. Usually a threshing team was composed of men from the farms that were to be harvested. There were also itinerant workers on many of the harvest teams. Sometimes these itinerants came from back east looking for work. They travelled in or on freight cars and usually without purchasing tickets. They would ride the rails meaning they would get a free ride on a train car. There would be up to about a dozen people in a team.

I was about three or four running around outside and there were some of the men at our place filling gasoline barrels from a truck with a hose. I cannot remember the truck, but I can remember the men used a hose to fill the barrels such as the one in the center of this picture by the granary. One of the workers picked me up and sat me on a barrel being filled with the hose. An edge of about an inch can be seen around the barrel. There was some kind of leakage, and soon I was sitting in as much gasoline as the lip around the edge could hold. I was taken away and given a bath immediately. I do not remember it burning. I was just being a kid. Accidents happen. That was a small one I remember.

In the enlargement of the picture one can see my mother's Rhode Island Red chickens are under the wagon between the wheels, so the wagon has not moved in a while. Perhaps Syd was going to hitch the horses to the wagon or some other implement. We had this picture for years but it was not until now that we could really examine the whole picture and see all of it.

This picture was taken in a happy time of stability and prosperity. That would soon change.

The Dirty Thirties hit our family as hard as a hammer hitting a blacksmith's anvil. The rain stopped. The farm dried up. The winds blew. The dirt flew around. Everything was dirty, and it was in the 1930's. Thus, came the term the dirty thirties. My parents made the decision to leave this farm and move north where there was rain. Without rain, nothing grew. Their success would continue to be zero. Their climb out of poverty was halted. The dirty 30s changed my life for good at a young age.

In this picture taken in 1932, my dad Sam Baker is driving and facing the front of the tractor. It is not a speedy tractor. He is not driving in heavy traffic requiring his full attention. It is a scene like this that I remember most, in relation to our leaving this farm. I was about eight at the time. It is as if this picture truly represents my dad's attitude and forward thinking. He decision had been made to move he was not looking back or changing his mind. His mind and intent were focused on the future and he was only willing and able to concentrate on the future and moving forward.

Fittingly, Syd's stance on the tractor seems to represent a slightly different attitude. He is looking back towards the farm and camera, seeing the Hare Hills farm south of Woodrow for the last time as he drives off into a different life of the future. He looks back to see it and remembers perhaps the recent death of his good friend Bill Sandor from appendicitis and perhaps the notion he had said goodbye to Grace Frame his girlfriend.

Dad and Syd are on their way to Gravelbourg, Saskatchewan, to the CPR railway. There they would ship the wagon and its load to St Walberg from where Syd would pick it up take it to Pierceland and Dad would drive the tractor home.

Although Syd and my dad had been north to see different farming areas, the decision to move would not have involved Syd, and my mother may have had only a small say. The decision would have been my dad's. He chose the north to be close to water, and to be close to the bush with wood to build with and burn, fish in the water and hunting in the bush. It was where his family could survive. Perhaps there was

no available land close to Mam's parents so, our family joined dozens of others in the trek north.

In the wagon is farm wire, perhaps page wire. Notice on the Rumley tractor wheels there are no rubber tires. There are knobs of steel called lugs. Rubber was not yet commonly used on wheels for large equipment. You can see the way the wheels dug into the ground. The smoke stack on the front of the tractor is quite big. The wagon has huge bigger wheels on the back than the front. This tractor never went to Pierceland. It was left in the yard at Woodrow. It is another hint into the personality of my father and the changing times. My dad refused to take the equipment with him to the new farm in Pierceland because he could not afford to pay for it. The farm machinery company wrote him letters asking him to take it with him but he would not take what was not his. He said if he could not pay for it, he would not take it. So, they came and took it. The steel lug Rumley tractor represented an old life and in this case old technology too. Dad was starting over. I wonder if he had taken the machinery if his life and new farm would have succeeded faster and his life road been different from what was to come.

There were more loads of stuff than just this wagon. We had an organ put into a wooden crate and shipped. I do not remember how my Dad and Mom got the organ. I just remember the organ as part of the family furniture. Ruby would play it a little bit, and I remember improvising, and playing it by ear with one foot to pump the organ.

A couple of years before this picture, in about 1929, we had gone out to a party we called a Shitakwa but was more commonly spelled Chautauqua. It was something like a big picnic located 12 miles south of us. The wind came up, and blew over all the retail booths. I remember being in awe as the candy and chocolate bars were thrown everywhere. Dad got my mother, Ruby, Willie and I into a car that had canvas covers in place of windows. He drove the car up close to a building to be out of the wind. I remember being a bit sad that he would not let us go gather any of the candy blowing around. When the wind stopped blowing there were dozens of cars in the ditches all along the roads because the wind had blown them off the road. When we got home, soil had blown into our house at the windows and doors. For us that was the first hint of the coming depression. It leads into Dad's decision to move.

Years later when Darcy, Glenn, and I were travelling from Lac La Ronge to Winnipeg a storm came up and I remembered this sheltering. I insisted we take shelter behind a building during a wind and hailstorm. We stayed there for about ½ hour as the wind shook the car and the hail thundered down. We were glad to have done it.

Below is a picture of our house at the time of the first windstorm that had blown dirt under the doors. This is the east view of the house. This picture is moving day from the farm South of Woodrow, to Pierceland. Mam and Ruby are pictured at the back entrance to the house. All the junk was not normally there but was accumulating in the preparations to move.

It looks like there are two buildings because the building on the right was a kitchen and it was added at to a building Dad had purchased from someone else. Syd said it had been meant to be a store. The cook stove was inside behind the dog but not against the wall, and you can see the stovepipe out the roof. Further to the right on the end wall there was a shelf that went across the end. On this shelf, Mam had a jar in which she made vinegar.

Right behind Ruby, inside the connecting room on a low stand, was a hand crank, honey extractor. Mam was allergic to bees and honey and would get a rash from it so working with it she had to be careful. My parents sold some honey in jam or syrup pails that were about a 4 pound tin, or about 2 litres.

This is the house in an area referred to as Hare Hills, in which Willie and I were born. Georgie was born and then died of Spanish Flu and Scarlet fever in this house. Willie and Georgie were both ill at the same time. Having two seriously ill children located so far from a hospital would be a horribly stressful time for the family. The boys were wrapped in warm cloths to bring out the fever. Still, Georgie did not survive. When Georgie was buried, Mom was not able to go to the funeral because she had to stay home and look after Willie because he was also still very sick.

Georgie's little body was wrapped in chlorate of lime to make sure the disease had no chance of spreading. Only my dad, my brother Syd and the minister were at the funeral. There was no marking on his grave until years later. Syd went to the local authorities in Woodrow and found the location. Syd and I cooperated to buy a headstone. At the gravesite, Syd told me Georgie died in his arms and took a few steps from me and cried. It was the only time I ever saw Syd cry. It was a horrible thing for a young man to have his brother die in his arms. I felt his pain.

Some 55 years, later Walter and I stopped to and talked to locals who directed us to this building and they called it the Baker Homestead. The general shape of the building is the same, but there are details that are different. I like to think it is the old homestead taken from the other side with renovations and extension and removing of windows.

This is the front door to our family house. The previous 2 pictures are around the corner to the right. Harriet is behind Georgie, Willie, and Ruby. Notice Georgie has a dress on and some leggings. Willie is wearing a long sweater, knee pants, and long stockings while Ruby wears a dress.

A lovely pendulum clock that would have stood inside on the living room behind Willie and Ruby was left behind in our move. We did not use this south facing door all that much. Instead, we used the one in the previous picture. The outer storm door is open and the inside door is shut.

While we lived in this house, Sam and Harriet had a 25th wedding anniversary. At this party, they received some blue trimmed dinnerware, and the bone handled knives that I still use daily some 89 years later.

I remember my Dad used to do blacksmith work when I was 3 or 4 years old. I was not yet in school. I stood on a box of some kind, and watched the fire turn the steel red, then white hot as he hammered it into shape. I got to turn the handle of the blower and blow air onto e fire. How I was never seriously burned I do not know. I guess my dad was careful. Today we might be quite concerned a child being so close to such an intense and dangerous fire, or maybe I just imagine I was that close.

We ate in the larger building just inside the window on the bottom right that was where the living and dining room were located. We had an oak table that is very much like the one I have now in the dining room. Syd and Willie slept upstairs. To get there they climbed a ladder fastened to the wall. I was not allowed to climb the ladder and never did. Ruby and I slept on the main floor to left hand side half way down, on the other side of the house, but in the same wall location as the window on the bottom left of the picture. The west side of the building had two bedrooms, Ruby and I on the south side, and Mom and Dad on the north side.

I forgot a child's ring with a blue stone hanging on the wall that divided our bedroom from our parent's room. We also left a shiny steel decorated heater with mica inserts through which we could see a flicker but not a flame. We did not have room to take these things in the wagon. Puppy, the name of the dog in the picture did not make it to Pierceland either.

There was usually an ash pile where the ashes from the kitchen stove were dumped. Once Ruby was out somewhere when I decided it would be nice to wear her shoes to see if I could make marks around the pile. It worked quite nicely and I made a nice heel track through the ashes. My fun was stopped when my mother caught me and insisted I clean up the mess I had made of Ruby's shoes. I guess I did because I do not remember Ruby being angry with me. I remember I used to put on her shoes and wear them and especially like the ones with a bit of a higher heel. She caught me a few times too but never really scolded me.

Ruby was kind to me as a child. Someone, perhaps a relative gave me a frilly, little girl's, sleeveless dress. My father did not approve because it had no sleeves and could not keep anyone warm. Gift or not Dad thought I was not to wear this pretty dress. Ruby had other plans regarding my frilly dress and me. To attend some school function, she dressed me in some warm felt dress of which our Dad would approve, and hid the frilly dress when we left the house. Down the road, she helped me change into the nice frilly dress. On the way home, she helped me change back into the felt dress. Dad never became aware of our little treachery. I was able to look cute in a pretty dress, and I do not remember feeling cold in it.

In the picture following, Willie is on the left and Syd is on the right. They are dressed with veils to check the frames for honey. They are standing in front of the windbreak the family had planted a few years earlier. The rocks are on the bee hives to hold down the lids I guess. To get the honey extracted they cut the wax off with a hot wire. With the honey thus exposed the frames inside were placed into an extractor, a tool that resembles a barrel with a twirling apparatus inside to hold the frames upright. The frames twirl around and the honey flies out of the combs to the sides of the barrel and runs to the bottom of the barrel. A tap on the bottom of the barrel permits smaller containers to be filled.

This picture following is isolated from the larger crowd picture below. Harriet Baker is the third lady from the right with her hands folded in her lap. Sam Baker is second from the right in the back row with wearing a soft cap. It is the 25th wedding anniversary party of Mr and Mrs Harry and Louisa Russell. She wears a corsage and he is sitting on the right wearing a white shirt. The Russell's invited all the neighbors to a party and served a nice meal. The Russells had no children. The Russells befriended bachelors and others that needed help and were very kind people.

When I was about five the Russells gave me a cut glass cream and sugar bowl. On a visit, I had stood and admired all the nice things in a cabinet. I still have them, and use them on special occasions and remember their kindness. In this picture below they sit on a doily I crocheted.

Sam Baker and family, pioneers of the Winnifred district, southwest of here, were tendered a farewell party Friday night in the school, as they were leaving soon for the Cold Lake district, north of Peace River, by the people of the community. Mr. and Mrs. Baker were given miscellaneous presents, consisting mostly of linen. The young son and young daughter were each given a purse.—Miss Jessie Crawford, who has been the teacher of the primary room of the public school a couple of years, has

This newspaper clipping from June 1932 is about my family when they left the Woodrow area. It is nice to know my family made comment in the paper but the clipping is not accurate. We went to Pierceland and that is of course not near or north of Peace River. I do not know the linen my parents got. The young son and daughter must have been Syd and Ruby and the purse they got must mean a small amount of money because Willie and I were at a party. I remember there was a going away party for us kids. It was at the home Mrs Hoof who had a daughter named Gladys Hoof a similar age to me. Milton Jewel, close in age to Willie, was a son of Mrs Hoof from a previous marriage. After we moved we were never again in contact until December 2016 when Gladys and I spoke on the phone.

My grandparents living perhaps 289 miles away were not so severely impacted by the dirty thirties, as were we. Their farms continued to prosper and do well for years. Location and weather interact in farming determining success. The picture above is an enlarged portion of another picture. It allows us to see the faces: of my Grandfather John Corney on the left, his daughter Hilda who is holding onto his arm, the next person is my Grandmother Sarah Ellen Corney, and next to her is Bert May the husband of Gladys Corney sister to Hilda in the picture, perhaps it is the shadow of Gladys in the picture. Bert and Gladys farmed near Indian Head, Saskatchewan. I do not know when the picture was taken.

The picture above and the picture below are the same house taken a few years apart. The house is interesting because it is a house ordered from a T Eaton Company Catalogue. It came from back east in bundles on the train and was assembled on location. I am told my Uncle Jim Reynard helped to assemble it for my grandparents, John and Sarah Ellen Corney. I do not know everyone in this picture. Enlarging the picture reveals more details. On the far right is one my aunts I think holding on to my grandmother Sarah Ellen Corney. The woman on the left is unknown but she may have been either a neighbor or a hired hand. In the background near the plant is perhaps my cousin Winnie Pelky daughter of Ada Corney. Ada married James Reynard.

Below you see Ada and Harriet my Mam, in the early 1930's. You can see that John and Sarah Ellen had house plants in the window. The storm door is open and you can see that it is a simple door.

At the bottom, right of the picture, is a pile of wood to be burned in the stove. I was in this house very briefly and cannot remember what it was like. At the time of this picture their mother had just died. Harriet had been home to look after her mother for a few weeks and then Ada joined her.

My grandmother Sarah Ellen Corney poses here at the back steps of her house. She is wearing a crocheted lace collar over this top. This type of lace collar was a separate thing and could be used on different garments. There appears to be a large embroidered flower on her dress. Her velvet hat has a satin band around it. Looking closely at the dress you can see there is wide elastic sewn into the waste of the skirt. The top has long sleeves the cuffs of which have some decorations. It is interesting fashion.

The hay piled up around the bottom of the house is there to prevent draft blowing under the house. There are storm windows on the windows as indicated by the three air holes on the bottom of the window. On the left side of the picture it appears there is some chicken wire so perhaps they kept chickens. I remember my mother telling me that my grandmother Sarah Ellen had a skin problem and she had to put something black on her face. The black product was something to do with coal and tar. Perhaps she had eczema.

Sarah Ellen had reddish hair. My Mam told me many times that her own Mam would always have work for her to do at home. It seems something that carried on from early in life. This is the newspaper clipping published when my grandmother died.

MRS. SARAH E. CORNEY DIES AT QU'APPELLE 1937

QU'APPELLE, Sask., Feb. 6. — There died at her farm home near Qu'Appelle on Monday, Feb. 1, Mrs. Sarah Ellen Corney, having just completed her 78th year. She came to Qu'Appelle with her husband and family in 1906 from Yorkshire, England. Her husband died in August, 1921. She leaves to mourn her, three sons and five daughters, Charles, at Alsask, Sask.; Walter, Yorkshire, England; Harry, at home; Mrs. S. Baker, Pierceland, Sask., who has been nursing her mother for the past two weeks; Mrs. J. Reynard, on a farm near home; Mrs. C. Stephens, Tugaske, Sask.; Gladys, at home, and Mrs. J. Desrochers, Newport, Vermont, U.S.A. Two sons were lost in the Great War.

Burial services were held at St. Peter's pro-Cathedral, conducted by Rev. L. C. Scott, and burial was made in Qu'Appelle cemetery. The chief mourners were Harry Corney, son; Mrs. S. Baker, daughter; Mr. and Mrs. J. Reynard and family, daughter; Gladys Corney, daughter; Mr. and Mrs. J. Corney, of Regina, grandson. Floral tributes were sent by a large number of friends.

Pallbearers were R. Skinner, J. Hamblin, B. Madeley, H. McGillivray, F. Hepley and T. Bunn.

Before I was born, my grandmother came from Qu'Appelle for a visit to my parent's Hare Hills farm just south of Woodrow. The two places were about 280 miles apart. Today it is about a 3 hour drive from one place to the other. At the time of the visit, it would have been an all day trip that one had to plan. Travel years ago, was not as affordable or as common as it is today partly because of the great amount of time needed to be able to travel what we consider short distances. On the way, she stopped off to visit her son, my Uncle Charlie Corney, his wife my Aunt Lottie, Hirman, and Dave. Dave remembered the visit and told me a funny story at which we both laughed. Our grandmother brought with her a bag of oranges, a real treat in those days. She brought out the bag of oranges and they enjoyed them. When someone asked if she were not saving any to share with Harriet and Sam she replied, "No, they will just eat them anyway." I am not sure my mother ever heard the story but she would have laughed at it.

The picture above is of a butcher shop, in Tugaski, Saskatchewan, circa 1930. The store is owned by Charles Stevens, my Uncle as he was married to my mother's sister Nell. It is not a good picture but it is interesting to study. It shows a wood or coal stove on the side, a roll of paper on the counter and a scale. The meat is displayed hanging around the room and on a counter in front of the window. The meat chopping block, the dark portion of the picture, seems to stand in front of the counter rather than behind the counter.

Mam's brother Harry lived not far away, and had taken over my grandparent's farm. Below my mother is pictured on this farm. She is the shorter of the two women beside the horses. The picture was taken around 1937 and the team of horses hitched to a wagon, look big and strong and appear to be watching the two women. In the background is a pile of split wood blocks for the wood stoves, and a way in the back is a 4 wheeled democrat, but the most interesting thing of this picture might be the woman with her arm around Mam. She is Delena Lambkin.

Harry was single. Delena came in answer to a newspaper ad Harry placed looking for a housekeeper. The two seemed to get along well and Delena soon became his wife. That sounds like a nice romantic story so far. Soon the couple adopted a boy.

It seems that Delena was sickly. Somehow, she frequently seemed to need to go to the United States for treatment. She would leave for weeks at a time and return to the farm. On one trip, she left, and never came back. It was later discovered that she was a bigamist and had a family elsewhere.

Harry a handsome man, raised his son alone, an awkward thing to do for a single man with a farm. Gordon would be taken to the Orange Hall for baby-sitting. Harry did marry a widow with a family a few years later. Harry did very well farming and was a success. I have been unable to contact my adopted cousin Gordon.

Sarah Ellen (Wilcox), and John Corney, are seated with some of their 11 children. The back row from the left is Harry, Fred, Hilda, and Charles. Children missing from the photo are: Gladys, Ada, Harriet, Ellen (Nell), John, Walter, and Georgie. Fred, second from the left above, was conscripted into the Canadian army for WW1 but was sick and had to go anyway. Harry, on the far left above, volunteered to take his place but the military refused to allow the substitution. Fred left the farm to follow orders. Fred on military parade in Regina collapsed on the street. Sent to England he died of the flu aged 21. Below are two pictures of Fred and his last letter home. In one he is just an innocent farm boy and in the other a military man. Together they show a glimpse into the events that happen in war.

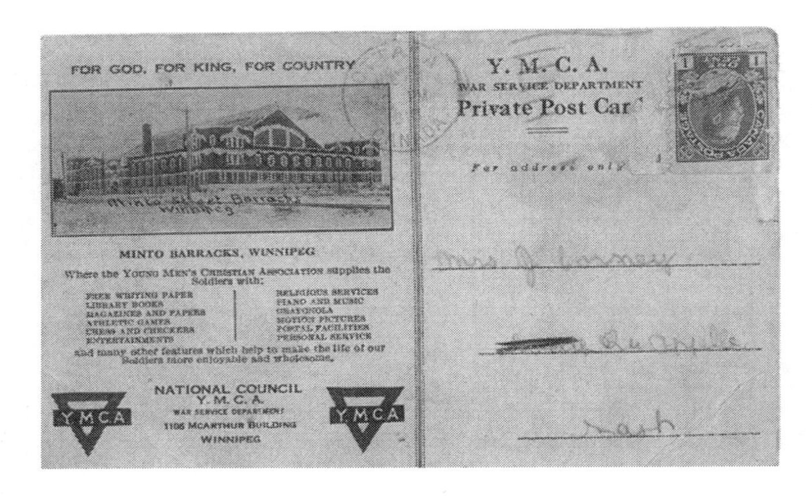

FOR GOD, FOR KING, FOR COUNTRY

MINTO BARRACKS, WINNIPEG

Where the YOUNG MEN'S CHRISTIAN ASSOCIATION supplies the Soldiers with:

FREE WRITING PAPER	RELIGIOUS SERVICES
LIBRARY BOOKS	PIANO AND MUSIC
MAGAZINES AND PAPERS	GRAFONOLA
ATHLETIC GAMES	MOTION PICTURES
CHESS AND CHECKERS	POSTAL FACILITIES
ENTERTAINMENTS	PERSONAL SERVICE

and many other features which help to make the life of our Soldiers more enjoyable and wholesome.

NATIONAL COUNCIL
Y. M. C. A.
WAR SERVICE DEPARTMENT
1106 MCARTHUR BUILDING
WINNIPEG

Y. M. C. A.
WAR SERVICE DEPARTMENT
Private Post Card

For address only

Mrs J. Forsey

[illegible]

Sask

Sunday July 28th

Dear Mother,

Still alive and kicking but getting sick of train life. This will be the 4 day that we have just come through North Bay Ont. and still have quite a long way to go, and pretty near broke. But I should worry, Harry. We have been two days [illegible] seeing nothing but rocks and evergreen trees and water. Well this is all this time so goodbye.

[illegible]
Fred.

Find the pony yet, Harry

Pte F. W. Forsey #277729
No 2 Coy. 106 [illegible]

In Regina Fred bought his mother two small white bowls with lace edges that are printed with "Souvenir of Regina-Canada" and brought them home before he left for England. I have them in the china cabinet to this day, though one has a small chip.

The oldest of Mam's brothers, John Corney, never came to Canada, and was in the British army. He served in the Boer war at age 18. He lived through it without incident. He is shown here in uniform without a hat. A few years later he was called up for the First World War, and was given the same uniform he had worn in the Boer War. He could not fit it as he had grown. In the first battle of the First World War, in the battle of St Julien, France, 21st of October 1914, he was blown up. Gruesomely, his family was told afterwards that his remains were picked up in a scoop shovel. He was 34.

My grandparents had 11 children. It seems a few too many to my eyes. My grandmother always worked in the home raising kids. After my grandfather died, Harry lived with her until she died.

It is perhaps not appropriate for me to say whether it was or it was not a wise move leaving England. My parents and grandparent did move and I am glad they did, and I am glad to have been born here. My grandparents seemed to have a better life in Canada than in England, even though my grandfather died early at age 59. I wonder if he would have lived longer had he left the mines earlier. I wish I had known my grandparents.

My father died early and I wonder if he had left England earlier would he have enjoyed life more and lived longer. I feel sure my mother came to enjoy life in Canada even though there was a pretty significant culture shock upon first arrival handling life on the frontier. They felt the effects of the wars, but living in Canada allowed them to miss the direct bombing results that happened in England, and that alone is a blessing. It seems easy for me to think that, I think it was good and wise move for my Corney ancestors to come to Canada.

That is one side of my family. What of the Baker side? Information regarding this family is more difficult to find. Just now in 2017 I am getting some connections to learn more of it.

Pierceland: A New Location and New Life

Our move happened in two stages. I am sure as a young girl I did not understand the move orchestration, but I think I must have wondered where we would live, in what kind of a house, and how long it would take to get there. I may not have wondered how it would change my life and that of my family, and probably I would have been more involved in the adventure taking place. Surely the minds of my parents would have focused upon how the move would change their lives. With hopes for improved prosperity, they would have also had wonders and worries. Would this move affect the family as much as their earlier emigration? I know now that the move was a bigger concern for my parents and older siblings than it was for me. I was too young to have too many such ideas. I remember seeing more bush than I had ever seen before and thinking that was interesting. Still there is the question of how this move altered my life and that of the rest of my family?

Syd with horses, cattle, and machinery, took the train from Gravelbourg, to St Walberg. When the train with Syd and the animals stopped at Avonlea, pictured twice below, my dog Puppy, disappeared. Syd told me that he got off for a run and did not get back before the train pulled out. I imagine in a town this big he found a home. Puppy had no name. He was just called Puppy. Pictured earlier, he was the short haired white dog with brown spots, sort of a terrier type pictured earlier. I missed him.

I think Syd took this picture above of Avonlea. It was a small prairie town like most others of the time with dirt roads in the 1930's. All buildings seem to be wooden. In the front lower left is what appears to be an outdoor toilet.

While Syd was on train the rest of the family looked like the TV show The Beverly Hillbillies in an overloaded vehicle. We travelled in a very narrow truck, perhaps a Ford, piled high with our belongings. One could not travel today's highways in Saskatchewan with a vehicle thus loaded. Just behind the cab on top of the load there was a nest like place for Willie and Ruby. They had a great adventurous ride for the ten days it took us to go the approximately 830 km. I bounced along in the cab with my Dad and Mom. The roads were narrow and bumpy and not as smooth and wide, and not as direct as today to drive Woodrow to Pierceland. We had to take a circuitous route into Alberta and back into Saskatchewan, going past the edges of places like Rosetown, Biggar, Battleford, Lloydminster, Kiscoty, Onion Lake, Frog Lake and through Beaver Crossing to Pierceland. I do not remember the nighttime. I do not know where we stayed but we did have a tent with us. I recall stopping to eat picnic style along the edge of the road.

I do not know if the vehicle was ours or borrowed. There was some mechanical problem with the vehicle. I do not know what, but my Dad would ask my Mom to reach over and hold in place the gear shift that had a knob on the end of it. That kept the engine in gear and braked the vehicle. When we got to the edge of the Saskatchewan River valley, ahead of us lay a long winding road descending to the river. My father made us all get out of the truck and walk to the bottom of the hill. He was aware of some mechanical troubles with the vehicle and took the truck ahead of us down the hill. It sounds like brakes were part of the problem.

The incline of the road was dangerous if the brakes were not very good. When we reached the bottom of the hill, we saw my dad with the truck sideways parallel to the river and the ferry. Luckily, he had made it to the bottom and close to the river without driving into the river, and this is where the vehicle ran out of gas. We crossed the river on a small ferry not much bigger than the truck. I remember passing the Onion Lake Indian Reserve and crossing a river at Beaver Crossing just south of Cold Lake, Alberta. Here we stopped at a little house and had a meal at Mrs Elliott's. I cannot remember what the meal was then, but later I remember stopping there again with my Mom and Dad. Mrs Elliott was such a nice lady. I remember eating at a table but not what the house looked like on the inside.

Mrs Elliott's house pictured here was still standing a few years ago, on the left side of the road as it bends towards Pierceland, and later north to Cold Lake, Alberta. We took this narrow, winding road to the end, and then climbed up onto a gravel railway grade without tracks yet, and drove on that for about 1 mile.

We went to an opening in the poplar trees and a one room shack with a hard mud floor about 3 miles outside of Pierceland. Ruby and I slept on the top bunk and my Mom and Dad slept on the bottom bunk. Syd and Willie had a bunk where their feet met the foot of my parent's bunk. We filled the beds with hay until our mattresses came. We stayed in this house for a winter.

I remember my father would go hunting rabbits with a pitch fork around the hay stack. We ate a lot of rabbit that winter because we were very poor. I do not much care to eat rabbit now.

In this picture above Willie and I are holding fish. I remember having to be coaxed to put my finger into the fish's mouth. This tent is beside our log house that we used when we first moved to the farm outside Pierceland. Willie slept in the tent rather than the house. You can see Willie is wearing a long sleeved shirt and his bib overalls. We both wear hats and I have open sandal type shoes.

Around about the same time this picture was taken of my future husband Walter. Walter was about 13. I think the picture was on his parent's farm also in Saskatchewan about 40 miles away. In the background is the building for which he and his mother made the shingles by hand from wood blocks. They chopped log sections into shingles.

Walter is all dressed up with a tie on and is wearing a vest. What is he doing with his hands? I am not sure. It looks like he may be posing with a gun the base of which is standing on the ground. His left hand is up closer to his head and it looks like he has perhaps a stick or something in his hand and he is holding some prize. It seems unusual he would be wearing a tie unless he did so to pose for the picture with a chicken he had shot. The rest of the picture is rather dark but his family appears to be dressed up as if they had just come from church. Perhaps he shot this animal for their dinner on the way home from church.

The log home picture below is what my dad was having built for our home. My brother Syd was building it with help. It appears we had visitors, perhaps the RCMP, and there are 6 working men in the picture. My dad was not as involved as he should have been. During construction, my father was having significant trouble with alcohol. It was a problem. Clearly, the stresses of his financial woes were influencing his mind and behavior. This was the second big move and change in his life and he had to be worried about succeeding and completely starting over again in the northern bush.

Ruby, now about 20, left home telling my mother she was going to a neighbor's house, Mrs Orcot, one or two miles away. Ruby stayed a while, perhaps one or two days and then came home. She could not stand the constant troubles of our father Sam Baker. He was physically abusive and hitting his family and the ones he hit were Ruby and his wife Harriet. I remember Ruby running away from the Dad's drinking buddy, the dentist. He chased her around the well and through the yard at Woodrow. Ruby was afraid of both her Dad and the dentist. I do not blame Ruby for leaving.

John Stonehocker Senior came over to our house. I am not sure why he came, but he came over. He found my father cleaning a gun, sitting on a stump talking about going hunting for rabbits or something. John Stonehocker stayed and chatted a bit.

Just as Mr. Stonehocker was arriving, Willie took me by the arm and dragged me to some taller weeds. We lay down to hide. I do not remember much after that on that day. I am not sure how long we stayed there. I guess nothing else happened.

The police came the next day and took my dad away. As he left, Willie and I were standing side by side. The police were opposite to us. Dad gave Willie something. He gave me a dollar and Dad told us he would see us later. I am not sure he ever did see either of us again. I do not think Willie went to see him, and I wonder if I saw him.

When dad went away for treatment, my mother went for a holiday rest to Lac Des Isles staying with a forest ranger and his wife for a week or 10 days. I had missed a lot of school with Dad acting up and then missed an exam as I was in Lac Des Isles with my mom. Ruby and Willie stayed at home with Syd. So, whatever grade I was in I had to take it again. Today they would not make you repeat the grade, but in that was a time when they took such an action. I had started school at age 7 and this happened when I was 9 or 10. At school, I had this feeling that different kids knew my father was taken away as they all had dads around and I did not. Of course, they all knew. They teased in a roundabout manner.

At that time, in the bush and prairies, many people drank heavily and drank home brew because they could not afford to buy alcohol but could make it. A lot of heavy drinking happened in isolated areas. It still does. It is a way to handle both stress and boredom.

I am not sure how the home brew affected people's health. The harmless quality of this brew was not assured. Impurities, and poison, with this alcohol are possible, and likely. I am sure it caused physical and mental problems to a lot of people. Perhaps this affected my dad.

Later, Syd would sign the papers that would commit our father to the hospital to get treatment for alcoholism. He went to the only place that could take him, the North Battleford institution for the mentally ill. He died there June 15, 1942, eight years later. He might have made it home if the treatments of today were then available.

People from Pierceland visited dad in North Battleford. He recovered enough to be able to have freedom to go about and visit in the town. He perhaps saw people from Pierceland in the local bus depot. He was in communication with his brother Robert in England. It was Dad's plan was to go back to England for a visit after the war was over.

I never heard if my mom and my dad were in communication while Dad was in hospital. I know that my mom, Ruby, and Mrs Matt had a service in Mom's living room for Dad after he died. I do not know if there were other people present. I learned of Dad's death in a letter from my mother while living in Winnipeg. I was shocked even though I did not really know him.

A few months earlier than June 1942, on the way to Winnipeg I thought I might have seen him in the bus depot of North Battleford. I was with Walter. Though I thought it was my dad, and though Walter encouraged me to go talk to the man staring at us, at an angle across the room, I was shy. I was perhaps still too afraid to talk to him. I thought it looked like my dad. I was very unsure.

How do you go ask a stranger if he is your father? It is sort of a foolish question. It makes you look stupid. I did not ask. He watched us from across room about 20 feet away. He never spoke. Why? Maybe he too was unsure of himself. Perhaps he did not understand whether he should speak. It was a moment lost. We left the building and walked up the road. He followed, behind and across the street. He looked at us every now and then. Was he just walking home? Did he imagine I resembled someone he might know? Did he wonder if it was his daughter? How could he tell?

We turned and went back to the station. He did not follow. If this was my father, I never saw him again.

I am sure now, all these years later, that it was Dad. I have no other information to bend my mind on the matter but I try to remember the incident and am now sure. Regretfully, I did not speak, but for some reason I just was not yet ready to speak to a stranger that may or may not have been my father. Of course, now I wish I had spoken. Were it to have happened a few years later when I was more experienced with the world, I would just have gone over, talked to him, and asked if he were my dad. I would explain the situation and risk rejection.

At that time, I was just too inexperienced and young to have the nerve to do it. This was my first trip away from a small town and I was learning to see the world. I was not assured and self confident. Neither was he. Certainly, I did not know he was going to die so soon.

Years later, I was surprised to be able to see my dad's grave site. I had wanted to see this for years. For years spent some time wondering where it was located and if anyone knew where he was buried. When I finally did see it, there was no grave stone. All I had to place on his grave was an artificial yellow daffodil. Then later, in the chapel, I played a tune for my father on the organ. He would have liked that. I played the song "Faith of Our Fathers".

I missed my dad as I grew up, and have missed remembering more of him all these years since. Memories of my dad are few in number, and less clear than I would like them to be because Dad was gone for rehabilitation. I remember him as a mustached man, and not a particularly light or heavy man, but one kept trim from hard farm work. I do not remember any personality quirks except he smoked and drank too much. He used to wear a cap and a leather coat. I would touch the folds in the arms of the coat watching them collapse. He would smile and say to me, "Go tell your mother bugger". When I did repeat the words, Mam would tell me not to talk like that. These are small remembrances but they become more significant without others.

Roseanne Able, my niece who took me to the cemetery and I agreed that there should be a stone marker. Ruth Lebadoff, her sister, organized the Baker family. They purchased a stone marker and had it placed on the grave. On my 90th birthday, they presented me with a photograph of the stone marker. I was surprised. I think it was a wonderful 90th birthday gift. Making another visit is complicated by the barbed wire fence I would have to climb through and rough terrain I would have to cross to get there.

Life continued even after my father left, but things were economically hard. I was able to get to school more regularly. All the schools that I went to had a few things in common. All of them were one room schools. All had outdoor toilets, one for girls, and one for boys. They all had catalogues for toilet paper thus many of us brought our own personal packet of papers. Sometimes for paper, the toilets had the flattened papers used for fruit wrappings such as for apples. These would be stuck on a nail in the outhouse. Never was there a bit of soft paper. I do not think I saw a roll of soft toilet paper until the late 1930's. My first three schools were all long walks from home. Ironically, it was when I was youngest that I had to walk the furthest.

All but one school was heated with stoves made from 45 gallon drums laid on their sides with sturdy legs attached. The schools were cold. Each morning we shivered until the fire had been going long enough to chase away the cold. In the winter, older students could help add wood to the fires.

Our tin lunch pails, perhaps from lard, or Rogers Golden Syrup, with push down lids, and narrow handles, were always kept at the back of the room. In the winter the lunch froze. We had walked through the below zero cold weather and the back of the school was cold. We would take the lids off before lunch time and hope the contents would thaw out before lunch.

The first school I attended was the Winifred school. My dad was one of the residents who petitioned the government to get the school. We lived 12 miles from Woodrow. This school was out in the country. This school walk was where I went through the pasture with Willie barefoot, he sometimes teased me by running ahead, and I would be afraid of being left alone.

Pictured here is a copy of the petition my father signed to get the school. When I look at the signature, I feel a strange kind of awe and yet like to look at it. I see in my brother Syd's book, where I got this document, that there are a few more times Dad has signed as he went to the first meeting of the school board and he nominated people. It shows me he was a real person. It shows he could interact and be normal and that he did something for the area. It shows he wanted the best for his sons and daughters. I am proud to see his name and signatures. I wish I had known more about him other than that he liked music.

(Form C)

Proposed School District of Saskatchewan

The undersigned severally declare each for himself that he is of the full age of twenty one years, that he actually resides within the above named proposed school district and that he has resided therein and owned or been the occupant of assessable property therein for a period of at least two months immediately prior to this date.

Names	Property owned or occupied
George Hauser	[illegible]
Sydney P. Hooff	[illegible]
J. Baker	[illegible]
W. V. Harcourt	SE 1/4 S 14 T 7 R 6 W 3rd
Wm Curry	SE 1/4 S 13 T 7 R 6

Witnesses to the above signatures:
George Hauser Chairman
Sydney P. Hooff Secretary
Dated the Nov 11 day of November, 1912

Page 7

The second school I attended was when I lived on the homestead outside Pierceland. I walked along the railway grade to get there. Locating the school here was a temporary measure. It was the Red Cross School pictured below.

I attended school here for one year. I do not remember the name of this school. It may have used the Chocolate Valley name. We used the main floor as a school. In this school in the fall of 1932, I had started grade 3. The teacher was Lois Bates was the only teacher for around 40-50 kids in the one room. We only used the main floor. The school moved the next year and this building was turned back into a hospital.

The third school I attended was for sure called the Chocolate Valley School. I am not certain how it got this name. Certainly, it did not get the name because there were chocolates. There were no chocolates around at that time. Chocolate was an expensive treat in those days. I think the first time I had a chocolate bar I was married with two kids living in Golden Ridge.

I attended this school even though I still lived on the homestead. This school was a log building, in an opening in the bush between farms and in the opposite direction towards the south east. I was there for grades 4 and 5 and had to walk about 3 miles to school, a 6 mile return trip regardless of the weather.

Even though walking through the bush meant a shorter more direct route to school, I was afraid to walk alone. In those days, the bush perhaps more wild than it is now. There could easily have been all kinds of wild animals to surprise, chase, scare, and eat young girls. In my imagination, I was being watched from the bush by the likes of bears, moose, deer, wolves, coyotes, skunks, racoons, and perhaps even strange people.

Instead of the bush route, I back tracked a bit, walking in a somewhat L shaped route to go past the Romanian, Rewega family, and walked to school with Sandy, Dora, and Helen. Rosie Rewega was younger and could not speak English at that time. While Rosie and I played together, she learned English.

Rosie married and moved to Seattle. She was in an airplane that crashed into the Pacific Ocean near Seattle and drowned. It was the rumor at the time that Rosie died but her husband and another woman made it out alive, but I never learned truthfully if any survived the accident or any other details of it. Tom McEvoy the brother-in-law of my brother Syd, married Rosie's sister, Alice.

Then we moved into town and I still had to walk out to the school in the country. When the school moved to Pierceland, it was still called Chocolate Valley School but now it was an easier walk. This school was in what was originally the Legion Hall.

Beatrice Hewlett lived perhaps a quarter mile to the back and east of the school, to the left on this page. I think her father Joe Hewlett gave this property to the town to build the hospital. Joe Hewlett would come to eat at Mam's, saying, "I like to come here because I always get a good cup of tea in a nice clean cup".

The last school and school teacher I had, was back in Pierceland. I had passed into grade 9 and the grade 8 teacher had been Miss Spears. Every morning we had to stand by our desks and say, "good morning Miss Spears", and then sing the anthems " O' Canada", and "God Save The King".

One morning Miss Spears came in blushing. She interrupted our usual morning routine and told us that from now on we were to call her Mrs Elliot as she had been married over the weekend. She was a nice person and I liked her as a teacher. She got the flu just before Christmas and my friend Doris and I took over arranging the concert for her and were pleased when it worked out perfectly fine.

Fifty years later when we lived in Winnipeg I found out from my nephew Danny Sergew that she lived in Meadow Lake. Walter and I went to visit her at her home and Walter took the picture below of the two of us. I was very pleased to see her again. She remembered me and we were happy to see each other again.

Below is my report card from the end of grade 8 with her signature on it.

consolidated

Name....Sarah Baker....

School..Chocolate Valley..

Grade.....VIII...............

Subjects	Marks.
Arithmetic	71
Literature	69
Reading	
Language	68
History	62
Geography	60
Home Economics	74
Nature Science	
Citizenship	
Health	
Music	64
Art	

No. in Class..2...Rank...2....

Is promoted from Grade..VIII....

To Grade..IX.....

Remarks.

(Mrs) Dorothy Elliott.

Overall, I did not really like school all that much, but not because I did not like the subjects and the content we learned. That I liked. What bothered me was the weather. Getting to school was always a challenge. It was a long way to go back and forth. I did not have the clothing and was frequently cold both at school and going to and from school. Girls did not wear slacks or jeans. I had to wear dresses and they were cold. I recall wearing my brother Willy's shorts under my dress. Willie had been given the shorts by our cousin David Corney, so I was at least the 3rd person to get use of the shorts. I got chillblaines, or chill burns, on my feet, from the cold and the itch was awful. At night my feet thrash around with the itch. At the time I had to share a bed with my mother and she told me how I had ruined sheets with my legs thrashing about. The only cure for this condition is to keep warm. It was hard to do without proper footwear and clothing.

I remember the teacher the first year in the country located Chocolate valley school. He was a nice fellow by the name of Archie Barton who later married Edith Foss from Beacon Hill. A few years later, in Pierceland, Archie Barton taught my son David in grade one.

After Mr Barton, I had two teachers that were brothers. I liked Paul Hogan a tall skinny man that could sing well, but did not like his brother Eddie Hogan and I am sure he did not like me. I think he knew that my father was an alcoholic and away recovering, and thus did not like me.

Some sixty years later, my brother Syd told me how angry he was with Eddie Hogan. Eddie Hogan took me to the side room to check to see if I had head lice. Syd thought that this was an unnecessary way to pick on me. I did not have head lice, but it was a common thing to do to check kids for head lice at school.

Mrs Rewega of the Romanian family that I walked to school with had a large outside clay oven. She would bake many loaves of bread in this oven at the same time. I remember eating it and it was good. Mrs Rewega was also a wonderful seamstress. She made her girls dresses. The girls would get the Eaton's catalogue out and point at the pictures of materials. The material would come by post in huge parcels. I would be shown the cloth from which the girls would be getting dresses made. It was exciting to imagine how it would look. I rarely had such an opportunity to get new clothing. Mine were generally handed down from someone else and altered to fit me.

This section of the road is between Black Raven Romanian Church and Chocolate Valley School. I think I took this picture when I was with Roseanne, my niece, who made a special effort to drive around and let me see places from my youth. This is now a decent gravel road. It was not like this when I walked on it to school. In my youth, back roads like this had no gravel. The road was dirt and mud, and narrower. The trees where wild animals roamed closed in tightly upon the road.

On one trip home from school when I was almost home I was chased by a neighbor's bull that was loose on the road. As I ran to the house, but the bull was gaining on me. Ruby came out of the house and yelled at it. The bull stopped. It would have trampled me but I was saved. So, I grew up on a farm and never came near cows or horses and was always afraid of animals with horns.

This picture of Pierceland was taken perhaps in the 1960's. I think now that I am damn glad I am not there, and would not want to go back and live like those times again. The dirt road seems to be leveled a bit as the rise on the near end seemed higher when I lived there perhaps it was a gravel road then. Elmer Little liked to hang on to the back of vehicles and let the vehicles pull him as he slid down the hill

both in the snow and in the dirt of the summer. It was dangerous but people laughed at him at the time.

The school in the picture is one I attended. The heater was a 45 gallon drum laid sideways with a hole cut in the end to load firewood, and the stove pipes went up out the roof. That was the heater. I would go to the school early and start the heater fire to get the building warmed up. I cannot remember much about what the school room looked like on the inside.

I did the janitor work in the school. I was paid but I cannot remember how much. It was not a lot of money. This was the last school I attended. There was one teaching position in the school and 60 students. It is a good picture of the Pierceland downtown and seemed a good picture for this portion of my story.

At the far end of town past the bushes at the end was a slough. It is no longer there. In that slough, Willie made a raft. Willie and I went out into the middle of the slough. He jumped off the raft and ran to the shore. I was about 12 and too scared to get off the raft. Had I fallen off I could have drowned. Eventually after a lot of complaining Willie had to come and get me.

Above you can see the somewhat square like hotel to the left of the school and the building on the left of the hotel was the Co-op store. Mervin Curry used to work as a clerk in the store. After Norman was born when I was 11, Mervin started to tease and call me Aunt Sarah. I began to want to avoid the store when Mervin was there. I did not want to be called Aunt Sarah because Aunts were old. I began to not like Mervin Curry. For the same reason, I later refused to let Norman call me Aunt Sarah. He never did except later he might introduce me as his aunt but always called me Sarah.

This picture shows the school after it had been used for a church service. We were happy because we did not get to go to church every Sunday. We had more church services in the summer. That is when theological students would travel the country getting into small remote towns. We were a happy bunch to have this picture taken. I cannot find Betty Baker in this picture so she may have taken the picture. I also cannot see reverend Wright either, the United Church minister who had led the service that day.

On the left, the man with the hat is Otto Sager my brother-in-law, in front of him is his son Norman. The woman in the hat beside Otto is my sister Ruby and I am right next to her wearing a scarf band. In front of me is Ruth Stonehocker who went and did missionary work for the United Church and died at a fairly young age. In front of the window in the back row wearing a hat with a white circle in the front of it is Mrs Rawlake, to her left wearing a hat is, I think, Mrs McEvoy my brother Syd's mother in law, and to her left the man at the back without a hat is my brother Syd.

My mother, Harriet is only partially visible. She is wearing a hat with a lighter colored band and only a portion of her face can be seen right in the middle of the picture. Behind her at the back wearing a black hat and glasses is Mam's good friend Mrs Matt.

You can easily see the wooden shingles on the side of the building and the pile of wood used for heat in the building. I would split this wood as part of my job as janitor. Later, at the farm, working with Walter and a machine powered buzz saw, I would grab the cut wood blocks as they were being cut and before they fell on the ground. I held on to the block of wood as soon as the whirling blade cut it half way through. Being dangerously close to the high speed, cutting blade, it necessitated one being very careful. One had to watch and know exactly what was happening being mindful of the person feeding the log into the saw. Then I would pitch the blocks to the side in a pile far enough away as to be out of the way. One had to keep up with the cutting so that a pile did not develop under the turning blade. The slightest mistake could cost a person a hand.

Verna Laird and I were friends and we are pictured here. One winter day we were taking turns skating and pulling each other on a sleigh across the ice in a ditch. When it was my turn, I kneeled on the sleigh.

Verna accidentally hit a willow stump. I went head first over the front of the sleigh and tore my upper lip. It hurt quite badly. There was a lot of blood. I had to walk about a quarter of a mile to get home. When I got home, Ruby pushed it together and bandaged me the best she could. We were a long way from a doctor, so that was all the medical attention I got. I have the scar on my upper lip from this accident. Verna and I are pictured at her home. I am standing and she is behind me. Verna and I would put strings on sticks and call them horses. We had races and all the stick horses named. Later Verna became a veterinarian and worked in Weyburn Saskatchewan.

One day coming home from playing with Rosie Rewega I was walking along the grade for the unfinished railroad originally started in the time of Prime Minister RB Bennett. We used the raised grade as a road. I came across my parents and Ruby on the side of the road pulling on a rope. The other side of the road was a swamp. Our gentle cow Nancy had wondered into the swamp. The only thing showing of her was her neck, head, and horns. My father had lassoed Nancy's horns and they were pulling her out of the swamp that was sucking her down to disappear and death. Eventually, they succeeded.

Ruby and her friend Dorothy Mehalcheon who later became Dorothy Hauka are pictured next. Dorothy's husband was Steve Hauka are picture here beside a store as perhaps indicated by a sign for Coke but they are standing in front of residential windows. Perhaps it is store in front and their home in back of the building. I went to school with Dorothy's half sister Mary. Mary Yurko has a different last name than Dorothy because Dorothy's father had died and her mother remarried to Bill Yurko. Yurko is also a Romanian immigrant name. Dorothy had a brother George that was a friend of my brother Syd. George married Marguerite or, Margaret L'Heureux, a Roman Catholic. Margaret and my sister in law Betty were good friends in these years.

Years later Margaret went to live in a nursing home in Cold Lake, Alberta. When Betty entered a nursing home, it was the same one. These two women were good friends for years. It was during their years together in the nursing home that Betty reverted to her original denomination and became again, Roman Catholic.

When Mary Yurko married, she took her husband's last name Ingram, and she changed her first name to Marian. I do not know why she changed her first name other than she preferred it. There were many Yurko children: Nick and Merton were older than the rest, but I went to school with Jack, Mike, Mary, and Annie. Verna and Hazel Laird went to the same school. I would begin my journey to school, walking past the Laird's and then on past the Yurko's and sometimes there would be a group of seven of us all going to school. Many times, there were two, three, or more members of the same families all in the school at the same time. I for the most part went to school alone without brothers or sisters. This made me feel like the odd one out a lot of the time, a feeling that was compounded because I was not a Roman Catholic.

Now that I think of it, there were a few female name changes in addition to the Mary to Marian. Magdalena Gelowitz was known as Lena in school, and then later I heard she changed it to Lynn. Elizabeth Gelowitz was known as Lizzy in school and she later changed it to Beth. Sanda Rewaga changed her name to Sadie. There were a few others named Mary that changed their names. It may have been a desire to make the names sound more modern but I am not sure. Ruby never considered changing her name and, I certainly never considered changing Sarah to anything else.

Before we moved into Pierceland, I would walk to and from school with Verna Laird. We walked along the old railway grade that never did get any railway tracks, and was always used as a road. It was on this road that I had seen an owl in a tree. I was afraid. I told my dad about it when I got home. I remember him telling me that I need not ever be afraid of an owl because all I had to do was walk around the tree. Since the owl would keep turning its head to watch me eventually its head would fall off. Such nonsense. He was just trying to reassure me against a remote threat.

On one occasion, I remember walking home from school along this railway grade and Otto was walking out to see Ruby. Otto carried my lunch pail and I showed him how to do summersaults down the grade of the road. It made us laugh years later. Otto Sager had lived in Pierceland for a couple of years before we did. He worked for Joe Hewlett, and worked around the store and did other things. I think that might be how he met Ruby.

Otto had a coupe car with a single bench seat under the canvas roof over the cab. The back window was just a hole without glass. There was a space that might have had a lid at some point and perhaps had been a small trunk. Otto came out to pick up Ruby. As they sat on the seat, I had my head through the window hole and jabbered away. I am sure they would have liked me to have vanished, but I liked Otto, and was a kid so I never clued in. Ruby was of course very tolerant of her little sister. Ruby and Otto were married in 1934, in Bonneville, Alberta, in a United Church. Orie, or Ora, Orcutt, and his wife Daisy were part of the wedding party. I am not sure of the spelling of Orcutt and I do not know the name of the minister. Ruby was 21 when she got married, and Otto was 9 years older. No one could afford a wedding in those days. Our poverty was awful. I knew we were poor but I never knew anything else. Now, I know how poor we really were. Mam knew they planned to get married, so Ruby and Otto made their marriage arrangements.

Ruby and Otto lived with Mom and me for a week or so until they got a house of their own. Mam was fond of Otto. Years later when she lived with Ruby and Otto it was Otto that would daily give Mam her diabetic injection just above the knee because Ruby could not stick a needle in her mother. It was Mam's fashion to wear dresses below her knee, as it was not a lady like thing to show her knees. So, she was often kidded about showing her knee for an injection.

This picture of Ruby and Otto is in front of a building that I think Otto was building. He was a Swiss finishing carpenter and did a lot of work for people. He was recognized as being very good at his job. Otto, Willie and Syd built the house for Mam in which we lived, and I was married. In this picture, they stand in front of a barn. I think the barn could be for Joe Hewlett or someone else. They are standing at the back end of a wagon because the big wheels were always at the back of the wagon. In the background against the building are some runners for a sleigh.

Below, this winter picture is of my brother Willie, aged about 16. You can see here he is thin. He grew after this picture was taken as I think he was about 5ft 10 or 11. He is smiling, though I do not think he is dressed all that warmly to be waking two or three miles in the cold. This animal came up with us from Woodrow. Three of the seven horses we had died of swamp fever from eating grass from the swamps. This is not Nancy.

Willie had led this rusty red heifer to Pierceland. Everything we needed from town had to be carried. He was getting 98 pounds of flour in a cloth bag. On the far left, part of a sled that he may have made himself. The flour bag would be saved and made into sheets. It took five, 98-pound flour bags, to make a bed sheet. Sometimes the dye was hard to get out of the bags. Tea towels, table cloths, and pillow cases were also made from these bags. We would embroider on these bags. We would use transfer pictures of flowers to get a design to follow. The transfers were perhaps waxen and were iron on transfers.

Sugar bags were of a different weave and better for table cloths because they were a bit harsher. We made aprons from both sugar and flour bags. Some people had dresses made from these bags.

We had to make many things we needed because we could not afford to buy them. Willie and Syd made charcoal to burn in the blacksmith shop. They had to make their own, as it would be difficult and expensive to buy and transport. They cut pine trees, or perhaps poplar and other trees from the local bush. After digging a hole around 20 x 20 they piled the cut trees into the hole, set it on fire covered it with sod leaving an air hole and made the trees into charcoal. This they used in their welding. Years later, Eldon, Willie's son would make a good living selling welding supplies but charcoal was not one of the things he sold, but it is a related industry.

In the background is Hewlett's general store that also housed the post office. Mrs Fanny Hewlett was a friend of my mother's. The Hewletts had a farm joining the town edge.

Notice the sign is painted but the buildings, like most in the day, are not painted. In this store, they sold hardware such as scissors, screw drivers, nails, socks, moccasin rubbers, felt soles, food such as salt, baking soda, chocolate bars, and soap and a few things one might get in a pharmacy nowadays. There were not as many patent medicines, or ready made, packaged medications, as there are now. They sold tinned meat, and some bulk meat like bacon and bologna that would be weighed out on a scale. People would buy a pound or half a pound for 25¢ or 50¢ and take it home in paper bags.

At 13, I was bridesmaid at Syd and Betty's wedding. The picture was taken in Agnes McEvoy's garden on their farm about three miles outside Pierceland. I do not remember how Betty asked me to be bride's maid. I do remember thinking that I did not want to wear a long dress. I thought those sloppy things were for older people.

Betty said of me at the time, that you could always find Sarah because there was always a bunch of young kids following her around. In those days, we did not have organized events and playgrounds as there are now. I guess the kids liked me and I liked them.

Betty and her family came to Pierceland to get their mail about once a week. On these occasions, they would visit my mother. When Syd and Betty were courting, I was 12 and 13 and Syd was a wonderful older brother and more like a father to me. From the age of a very young girl, he would tell me to sit on his knee. We would talk and teasingly he would give me a whisker rub from his chin. On one visit, Betty and her family were in the house and I was sitting on Syd's knee with my arm around his neck. I looked at Betty and said, "don't you wish you could do this?" I had forgotten about this incident. Betty told me the story later saying at the time she did wish she could have sat there on Syd's knee, and she thought about what she would have liked to have done to me for boasting what I could do at that time. We had a good chuckle.

In this garden picture below, I am standing on the far left and beside me is Joan McEvoy who was a couple of years older than me, Betty McEvoy the bride, the minister Reverend Deering from Loon Lake, the groom my brother Syd Baker, Willie Baker and Mam. In the front row, the smallest boy is Tom McEvoy, who had the nick name, Tuckie. John McEvoy is the other boy.

I do not remember Betty's father. I met him, but, cannot remember what he looked like. Mam went out to stay with Betty's mother Agnes McEvoy for a few days to look after Mr McEvoy when he was dying. Mr. McEvoy died from some type of cancer. He had at one time been a policeman. He was Roman Catholic. When he died, the priest came to see him as he died. This priest was a French Canadian and very nice fellow. Another RC priest had visited, but had encouraged, and harped at Agnes to have more kids. Agnes said they could only afford to feed the four that they already had, and in a tiff left the RC church. When Mr McEvoy died, Agnes contacted the local Anglican minister and had Betty and Joan confirmed in the Anglican Church. In Betty's case, the conversion was not permanent.

Tom McEvoy was comical as a boy. When asked to draw a picture of a rabbit by a teacher he drew a black circle on the page. The teacher asked him where the rabbit was and his answer was just inside that black hole. Another day he put a skunk on the school step. One day sometime after I had left home, Mam hired Tom to do odd jobs such as split wood and other things. I came home for a visit and Tom seemed a bit annoyed with me. He thought I was home to stay and thus he would lose his job. Things were fine after he learned I was just visiting. Tom died in or near Prince George in a vehicle accident. I think in the early 1980's. Tom was survived by his wife and three sons.

Joan McEvoy died in child birth in her 40's. She already had two children. She was a good friend, and when I was in Saskatchewan a few years ago, I went to her gravesite and placed a flower on it.

John McEvoy died somewhere in Alberta. He was married but at the time was living on his own. Years ago, I was told that John was always a neat person. He was found dead in his house with a mess of dishes in the sink and on the table etc, and there were a few used ashtrays and several other dirty glasses. I do not know how he died. Certainly, everyone thought it was odd.
Agnes McEvoy died around the same time as her two boys and daughter. Betty lost all her family within a period of a few years. She said to me at the time, "I am the only one left in the family." I felt sorry for her because she had lost everyone in her family. I know now it is hard.

At Syd and Betty's wedding there was a lot of food. Betty was not allowed to get married until she was 21 years old. So, on August 21, she turned 21, and August 22nd she was married to Syd by Reverend Deering. Years later my middle son Lyle would marry on the same date in August.

Pictured here standing side by side my two older brothers had similarities and differences that I even noticed at a young age. Both enjoyed music. Both were affectionate and teasing with Mam, as they would tie her apron strings to chairs as a little prank. Willy was more apt to speak his mind on a subject, but Syd would perhaps keep his own counsel. Both were mechanically minded and close to the same height, Willie was a bit taller and I think tended to enjoy school more than Syd. Where Willy had thick dark hair and a widow's peak, Syd's auburn hair always tended towards frizzy with a curl. Syd was healthy and widely known for being a helpful, caring man and was very well respected and lived longer. Willy was not as healthy and died young. Syd lived to be 86, more than twice Willy's life span.

The picture is taken outside and against the wall of McEvoy's house. You can see the logs and the mud plaster white washed over in between the logs in the background. You can see the cake is quite elaborately decorated with swirls and there are fresh flowers in a milk bottle, and a quart jar.
The picture is taken outside and against the wall of McEvoy's house. You can see the logs and the mud plaster white washed over in between the logs in the background. You can see the cake is quite elaborately decorated with swirls and there are fresh flowers in a milk bottle, and a quart jar.

Syd and Betty drove off in an old car with a lot of writing on the side, a just married sign on the back of the car and only a few dollars in their pockets. They headed towards
Alberta. Betty later told me they were happy even though they had a lot of flat tires starting somewhere around Lloydminster. Luckily, they were not going anywhere in particular.

Bride and Bridesmaids in the poplars would be a suitable name for this picture Joan McEvoy, Betty the bride Baker and I, are pictured here in front of the McEvoy house. This is the dress that I really did not want to wear. Now I look back remembering that silly thought. Still it was fun to be a bridesmaid. Perhaps Betty made the dress because she was a good seamstress. Joan's dress has two different colors and a lot in those days would be three colors. She is not wearing a white apron. Joan and I are wearing celluloid head bands decorated with real flowers from the garden. It is the only time I ever wore a head band. Betty was very good at making things like this and it is likely she made them.

The McEvoy house is in the background with white washed mud plaster between the logs. The ladder

mounted on the roof gave easy access to the chimney to clean it out because without cleaning the pipes were prone to catching fire. When green or fresh cut wood was burned, problems could occur because the wood contains too much pitch that leaves a flammable layer inside the stove pipes. Regular cleaning was required to strip the layer of soot from the stove pipes.

This is a picture of me when I was about 16. I am at the side of Syd's house in Pierceland. This was a new house at the time. These were poorer days, and because of that, the building is not painted and you can

see tar paper around the edges of the window. You can see frost on the windows. In those days, most every home had frosty windows.

Some of the other girls that were my friends, such as the Gelowitz girls, had the stylish new jumpers, and I wanted one. A new jumper, or any new, never before worn, clothing, was for me, indeed, very rare. Mrs. Mary Chornopesky, or as we called her a shorter name Mrs Matt, made this dress for me. I was thrilled. It was brown and the blouse is ruffled and beige colored. Mrs Matt also made the blouse to match. My overshoe boots went over my shoes and had fur around the top of them. We always wore dresses. Pants and pant suits were not in fashion in those days. To be honest I do not think I had even seen a pant suit until many years later.

Mrs Matt made a lot of clothing for me using discarded or donated clothing from other people. That is why this new jumper was so nice and special. It was not a reworked dress. It was not a coat previously worn by someone else. It was made new from new brown unused material. Such a special occasion warranted a picture. I cannot remember who took the picture, but since it is in front of Syd and Betty's house it may have been one of them, and they gave me the picture.

I note my hair is different. The forehead curls look gelled. I must have fixed it up for this picture. My mother taught us to boil flax and strain the liquid. After sitting, it became a gel. We used this gel to style our hair. We would make up a batch and keep it in a jar. It did not smell but neither did it have the perfumes of the gel sold today. We girls did each other's hair. There was no hairdresser for miles around. When I was a little girl, I remember my father cut my hair. Once he accidentally cut my ear a tiny bit. It was not serious but I probably howled at the sight of the blood.

Pictured here is the wonderful, Mrs Matt. Her maiden name was Porter or her first husband's name was Porter. She came to Canada after her first husband died. She then married Matt Chornopesky, thus the name Mrs. Matt. They had a son by the name of Jack.

Mrs Matt lived alone with Jack. Her husband had helped neighbors, Mr and Mrs Rust, move to Pierceland from the Fir Mountain region of Southern Saskatchewan. The Rusts had three or four kids and I was a friend of one of their daughters, Mable or Lydia, but I cannot recall which. Not too long after the Rust's moved to town, Matt Chornopesky, and Mrs Rust, disappeared at the same time, and were never heard of again. After this, Mrs Matt moved to Pierceland with her son Jack who started a garage. In the picture, Mrs Matt is standing in front of my mother's house covered by an ivy vine that grew up strings every year. You can see through the window that Mam always had nice frilly curtains on the windows. This window was usually full of house plants all year round and you can see there is something in a pot near the window. The house had an open plan and this bay window looked out from the combined living and dining room. A few years later in the winter, my own wedding picture was taken in front of this window. David was baptized in 1943 just through the window in the middle of the room, and by the same man that married Walter and I, Reverend Ashmore, from Loon Lake, Saskatchewan.

Mrs Matt is wearing good sensible shoes, stockings and holding a flower. Her dress that she may have made herself is of fine material and quite stylish. In the old printed picture, it is possible to see her arms through the fine material of the dress, and her slip that did not come all the way to the bottom of the dress. Years after this picture was taken Jack came to visit my brother Syd and Betty. Sadly, a short time after Jack left them he committed suicide.

Above three of us stand at the end of Mom's veranda. I am standing between my mother and the tall thin Mrs Matt who are both wearing aprons. I am wearing a pretty fancy dress that I must have received from the church bundle of clothing.

Mrs Matt and my mother were good friends. Mrs Matt came to our house almost daily. Other than her son, she had no other family. Mam and Mrs Matt never called each other by their first names. To Mom Mrs. Chornopesky was always Mrs Matt, and to Mrs Matt my mother was always Mam. People would teasingly call Mam and Mrs Matt, Mutt and Jeff when they walked together because Mrs Matt was tall and skinny and Mam was short and plump.

Mrs Matt could sing beautifully and had a louder stronger voice than Mam. Mam also sang beautifully but not loudly. Mam did not talk in a loud voice. She was soft voiced. Calling me to come in was a problem. I could not hear her. When I was away somewhere and Mam wanted me to come in for some reason, Mrs Matt would tell her no one could hear that volume, and so Mrs Matt with her loud voice would call me, "Sa raha". I could hear that, and so could everyone else in Saskatchewan. Mrs Matt died in Lafleche, Saskatchewan, and I have a picture of her grave. She was a good friend and neighbor.

The picture below was taken Monday, May 6, 1940 in an empty lot not far from my mother's house. Bishop Martin is the man in the back on the far left. Beatrice Hewlett and I are in white. Beatrice with a birthday January 3, 1925, is on the left, her brother Alfred a bit older, and with a birthday September 1st, is in the front row between Beatrice and me. I am in white on the right. It was tradition we wear white. It is our confirmation in the Anglican Church. Reverend Deering is in the middle, and I do not know the identity of the barely visible person behind me.

For this event Reverend Deering, the visiting parish priest, came from Loon Lake where he was living in a house I would later have dinner in, near the hospital. I do not know where Bishop Martin came from, but he and Deering came together. The confirmation may have taken place in my mother's living room or perhaps the school. There was no big dinner after the event but I feel certain we would have had tea in Mam's living room.

The rules on the back of the Confirmation Certificate are enlarged here on purpose. I think they were important, and overall, I hope they have guided my life as much as I wanted them to at the time of my confirmation. Some I think reflect more of my values. Rules 3,4,5,8 and 9 are important in more than just the church and apply to all of life. It is certainly true that we should not expect life to be easy. We should be charitable in judging others, as there is no heavenly perfection anywhere on earth. We can all do our part, and if we are part of something, we should try to make it good.

This is to Certify that

Sarah Ann Harriet Baker.

was confirmed

at Pierceland, Sask.

on Monday, May 6th 1940

by me Henry D. Martin

Lord Bishop of Saskatchewan

Presented by Rev. H. R. Dewing

Loon Lake, Sask.

First Communion Sun June 16th '40: 11 am

Legion Hall, Pierceland Sask.

O JESUS, I have promised
To serve Thee to the end;
Be Thou for ever near me,
My Master and my Friend;
I shall not fear the battle
If Thou art by my side,
Nor wander from the pathway
If Thou wilt be my Guide.

The Vigil

In olden times, on the eve of receiving his Knighthood, the Knight spent the hours from darkness until dawn in prayer and meditation before the altar, that his spirit too might rise to the new life before him unspotted and unafraid.

Bread of Thy Body give me for my eating,
Give me to drink Thy Sacred Blood for wine,
While there are wrongs that need me for the righting,
While there is warfare splendid and divine.

Rules

In a large degree Life is a following of lines of habit. These lines were started originally by the observance of rules of some kind. The following are herewith suggested:

1. Make a point of attending Holy Communion at least once a month, at a certain fixed time, e.g., the first Sunday.
2. Be as particular in your religious duties—such as Church attendance—as you are in your business or household duties. Why should you not be?
3. Remember that this is your Church, not your Rector's, and that if things are not right, it is partly your fault.
4. Remember that every Church member has certain services that he can and should render.
5. Do not expect to find any heavenly perfection in the Church or in the Church membership. Be prepared to tolerate and understand. Above all do not grumble and find fault. Try to improve things.
6. Read your Bible regularly and intelligently. Do not read too much at one time. With the assistance of a Commentary read and meditate.
7. Pray regularly and at set times—early morning and at night—and do not give up praying. Jesus Himself found it necessary for His soul's health.
8. Be charitable in your judgment of others; slow to express or pass on critical judgment; ready to see the good which is in most people.
9. Don't expect life to be easy. It will have many discouragements and heartaches. These are what make moral muscle, and God will be with you through them all, turning the darkness into a ministry of grace.

Confirmation Certificate

"Remembering that hereafter he shall not be ashamed to confess the faith of Christ crucified, and manfully to fight under his banner against sin, the world, and the devil, and to continue Christ's faithful soldier and servant unto his life's end."

"May he continue Thine forever, and daily increase in Thy Holy Spirit more and more until he come unto Thy Everlasting Kingdom."

Hywel Jones a preacher boarded at my mother's house and kindly gave me a pen for my 16th birthday. I remember him acting comically and joking pretending to be the local Catholic priest. He made us laugh. This picture was taken around my birthday in September. It is in front of my mother's house.

Later two bedrooms were added to the house so Mom could have boarders to earn a living. Willie had the front bedroom off the living room. Mom and I shared a bedroom on the other side.

Mom charged 25¢ cents a meal and some people boarded for a few days to a month at a time. Sometimes people would not have money so they would bring a chicken as payment.

Those who could not pay Syd for blacksmith work would try to pay with home brew.

Mam had school teachers Irene Weston and Rae Swellick renting in 1942 and 1943. They were excited waiting for David to be born. Irene came from Macrorie in south Saskatchewan and was dreaming of marrying her boyfriend. I remember her saying that she was going to decorate some of her bedroom and other rooms in mauve and green. I have a picture of Irene playing the accordion. That winter a retired school teacher Mr. Monahan, and his little white dog stayed with us too. The winter of February 1943, the girls would have to go out to the toilet outside. Everyone would wait for Irene to go to the bathroom first so she would have to clear the path.

Norman Sager and I are standing in the snow. In the background is Mrs. Flagel's house. Her husband had died and left her with 5 children to raise: Appolonia, Lena, Annie, Jackie, and Freddie. Mrs. Flagel did not keep the store after he died. They had lived next door to us and she was there after he had died. I think that this is the end portion of their house pictured.

Norman and I were close. He was like a little brother to me as we were only 11 years apart in age. That is why years later he came to visit when he ran into some problems. He came to someone like an older sister and someone he could trust and wanted only the best for him. It was not a secret and we all knew he wanted to change. We remained close until he died, on his daughter, Merilee's birthday.

Once, Ruby had Norman all dressed for church. He looked cute in a newly made blue velvet suit with white fur trim and white buttons, looking all proper and tidy. During the short time, it took Ruby to get ready for church, Norman got into the mud and could not wear his new specially made clothing. Another time Norman was sent to Sunday School with a 5 cent piece to put into the collection plate, but when he returned home, he still had the money. Ruby questioned him wondering why he still had the money. Norman said he had the money with him, but when the collection plate came around, he looked inside, and since they had enough, he kept his.

In the picture above am wearing a coat with an imitation fur collar. I got the coat from a box of donations at the church that had come from Winnipeg or Toronto. The coat was black cloth and the collar light colored fur or imitation fur.

One winter a box of clothing came from back east. In it was a real muskrat fur, brown coat with a satin lining. It was princess style being a little narrow in the middle. It fit me perfectly. My mother bought it for some amount and I was so pleased because it was a very stylish coat but I would not wear it. No other girls had such a coat. A group of girls new to the area came to Mam's place and bought a meal. One of the girls whose last name was Robie was not dressed very well for the cold. I gave her the coat telling her not to put it on the bed as a blanket but to hang it up when she was not wearing it. Years later, I was visiting Edmonton and I went to visit my friend Beatrice. Beatrice got a phone call from a friend. Beatrice told her that I was visiting. The woman on the phone said tell Sarah that I remember her giving me a fur coat and telling me to hang it up and not lay it on the bed. We had not seen each other for years and it was a good feeling to know she remembered the fabulous coat.

Another little girl, Audrey Hayward came with her parents to eat at my Mom's place. She and her family lived out in the country. They would come in to town with horses. Some customers became regulars and we kind of knew whom to expect on certain days. Audrey and her parents were regular customers. Audrey and I became friends.

Audrey died very suddenly. I think her death came from appendix problems. I was one of the girls that helped carry her to her last resting place as a pall bearer. I have often thought of the little girl. They had other older children but Audrey most frequently came with her parents. She was a nice girl.
Some 50 years later, I mentioned Audrey to Matilda Baker. Matilda found the grave and took a picture of a memorial that was put up when the cemetery was closed and I saw Audrey's name on the plaque. I think of Audrey with fondness and it leaves a strange empty feeling because you do not lose many friends in childhood. I wonder now how our friendship would have lasted over the years and the fun we never got to have.
Pierceland had an outdoor skating rink on the edge of town. It did not look like what rinks look like today, no illuminating lights, and no ice machines and certainly no rows of seating. This rink had a wooden slab fence around it, and a wooden shack with an air tight heater. We would all gather in this shack to warm up. It could get pretty hot in that shack and with a few kids and our efforts keeping the fire going. It was dangerous. That heater could easily have over heated and we all would have been in the fire. I heard that it eventually did burn down.

Beatrice and I would go to the rink to skate if the moon light was good enough and it was not too terribly cold. Frequently we stopped at the Ewert household to pick up their daughter of 5 or 6, and take her skating. I cannot remember the kid's real name, but her nick name was Bubbles Ewert. Bubbles was always dressed like a toy doll wearing pretty outfits. Bubbles was protected by her parents quite a lot. Still they allowed us to take her skating. It was like a playing dolly skating party. There is not much more of a story here, I just remember the cute little, doll like, girl and her nick name. I do not even remember if she could skate or we just dragged her around holding on to her.

On this rink, we played the game crack the whip, on skates. Everyone joins hands to make a long line, skating around the rink. When the leader makes a sharp turn, everyone turns. The person on the end gets an extra push of inertia and usually the one on the end flies off in a burst of speed. It was fun. One time playing this game Alfred Hewlett and I skated into each other. I was knocked out. I woke up on the ice. Alfred was fine. This is the same Alfred as pictured in the confirmation picture.

Two fellows volunteered to teach Willie to skate. They were mostly into being mischievous, rather than interested in teaching Willie to skate. Each fellow took one of his arms and they skated towards the end of the rink quickly and let him go. Willie went straight forward and hit the boards. Willie took off his skates and never tried to skate again. It was a mean thing to do. Willie was not robust for his age. I was healthier, and though I fell in learning to skate I never gave up and it was something I always loved to do.

Below is a picture of a store in town from when I was young. The road is gravel and there seems no differentiating mark between road and store yard. The wooden step into the store is raised up on 2x 4s, and the building does not seem to be painted. Ruby and Otto owned this store. They sold hardware and groceries. The sign above the door is for Royal Household Flour a brand sold by Ogilvie that is now gone. The lower sign is for Orange Crush. Through the store, Otto bought hides from local trappers and shipped them back east. Seneca root, also known as snake root, and Seneca snake root, was another thing Otto bought and sent back east perhaps to Winnipeg. If the roots were dried, he paid more money for them than if they were fresh and green. Fresh Seneca would take a couple of weeks to dry.

I got my first hair home permanent a brand called a Prom from money earned getting Seneca root. Walter helped me dig the root. Walter made a Seneca digging tool. It was a pointed digger with foot placements along the handle to step on and sink it into the ground. I worked hard to get that Prom.

I kind of remember that dried Seneca root was $0.60 and green root $0.40 a pound. Although I am not sure of the price, I know one had to dig a lot of Seneca to make a pound. On the internet, I learned that when dried it weighs less than half what if weighs green and that in 1999 a company was selling it for $14 a pound. Seneca was then, and is still now, used to make a cold medicine. Seneca can be used for treating inflammation, convulsions, cold remedies, and many other things.

Otto also did carpentry work, as well as running the store. The store sold gas. There is a gas pump on the left of the picture. It may be that the gas came in the drums right beside the pump. Otto was always busy doing work of some sort. Notice the moveable accordion type grating inside the windows and the plants in the other window. Since they lived in the back of the store, Ruby tried to keep the store looking fresh and friendly.

Ruby did not mind washing clothes but she was not fond of ironing. I would come over and help her out by doing her ironing. I liked to iron. One day while I was ironing and hanging things up Ruby came into the room to tell me she had already ironed everything I was ironing. I could not tell. We both laughed. She was fun to be around and we did a lot of laughing.

I cannot remember why we all lined up like this in the picture below, but it would probably have been either Syd or Willies idea. In this picture from the left are Syd Baker, Joan McEvoy, me, Doris Rawlake my school friend, and my brother Willie Baker. On close examination, one can see that all of us had nails in our shoes from having had them resoled or re nailed. The picture is under Willie's bedroom window on the south side of the house. We all look young and healthy despite being poor. Doris's dress had all the fancy white trim on it. I was wearing a short sweater tucked into a skirt and I think the sweater was red or maroon colored. Notice there is no paint on the house.

This picture following commemorates the visits of the Sunday School By Post, Van Girls. The van is what they used to get around and it is a style not seen much even in old movies. In the van, they brought us the Anglican Church. We were always glad to see the van appear. Miss Herne, the tall woman with the fancy hat in the middle of the picture was one of the Sunday School By Post girls. Miss Hearn later married Reverend Deering.

Also in the picture is Mrs Matt on the far left, then my mother, Mam, Harriett or Granny Baker, then Ruby and Otto Sager with their son Norman aged 7 or 8. Taken in about 1939 the van in the background contained camping gear, food, and numerous copies of Sunday School By Post. These lessons were printed on paper. There would be a story and a few questions at the end of the story. Sometimes the questions required more paper to answer. The lessons were mailed to Prince Albert, and new lessons were mailed out. The purpose of the girls' visit was to deliver Christian life lessons to remote and isolated farm families.

There were always two van girls per truck. They always came in the summer time, and always drove north into as remote a location to which they could drive. Miss Hazel and Miss Sale were a pair that came to our house. To remember their names, they told Mom she just had to remember the phrase "hazel nuts for sale".

Here I am, a smiling teenager, standing with bare feet in Trout Lake. It was 9 miles from Pierceland. Standing on the edge is about as much as I ever wanted to do in any lake, other than sit with Walter in a boat. It seems in my life I spent a lot of time with Walter on the water. Neither of us could swim. I think Willie took this picture.

Walter and I are sitting in a boat in Pierce Lake. Everyone also called it Trout Lake. The lake was about 9 miles from Pierceland and we only went to this lake once or twice year. Then, and in that part of the country, that 9 mile drive, was a big drive. It is a good sized lake. We were at the lake with a few people. I had known Walter for about 6 months at the time of this picture. We likely had a picnic there this day but I cannot be certain. We were not engaged but in love in this picture.

I can remember when for the first time I realized I was in love with Walter. Walter, Willie and I were in front of our house. Walter and I had an argument. Walter walked away towards his shop then turned and came back. Willie said something to me as Walter approached but I cannot remember what he said.

I do not know the topic of the obviously frivolous argument. However, when Walter came back, that was the end of the argument. I knew then and realized more in the days following that I was in love. As I relate this story, not one I have told often, it is a strange feeling to use my Brother Willie's name these 66 years since his death. Perhaps because he has been gone for so much longer than Walter has been gone that it makes for a strange feeling, and perhaps it is because I still feel Walter's presence stronger.

Still, now almost every day, I think of someone in my family that has died. I knew them. I see their face and name and think of them. When I think of Willie, I think of him sitting straight upon his bed after being sick, or as he worked on a charcoal pit vent, and Mam sending me to take him a snack of cocoa and sugar.

I seems that there are some stories I do not really believe could happen. People tell them. My Mam told me that after my brother Georgie died he came to her shoulder and said that he was fine and did not hurt anymore. She said it lifted a weight off her shoulders.

I think of my mother. Even though I never saw her drive oxen on the open prairie, I sometimes see her in my mind driving oxen. Ruby said after our Mam died, that Mam came to her, and told her not to feel so sad and that she was not in pain, and was fine. I was glad to hear it as Ruby was stressed.
I do not really think those things could happen. Yet sometimes I am not so sure. Still I feel certain that after Walter died that I looked up to see him come through the outer bedroom wall right where a clock hangs. He wore the suit he was buried in, and he came to the foot of the bed and smiled. As I reached up to touch him, he backed away through the wall and disappeared. How can I rationalize the issue when I do not believe what I know I saw?

The day I met Walter, I was with my sister-in- law Betty. We were walking on the side of the gravel street. We were not too far from the front of Syd and Betty's house. This fellow came up over the hill towards us wearing a black shirt with white buttons. Betty asked me if I knew the man coming towards us. I of course said I did not know who it was. She said that it was the new blacksmith in town. Betty did not really know him either. We did not stand and chat and just said hello in passing. Betty and I made comments to each other saying that he was a good looking man. Years later Walter told me that as he approached us and said hello, he knew right then that I was going to be his wife.

Walter had been working in Calgary and accidentally cut his arm. He returned home to his parent's house near Golden Ridge. For a while he worked in Meadow Lake, and stayed there most of the time. Somehow, he heard there was an opening in Pierceland to start a blacksmith's shop. Syd had been the blacksmith but wanted to quit and farm. When Syd quit, the word got out that a blacksmith was needed in Pierceland. Walter came to town and started to work in a garage owned by Mrs Matt's son Jack. My brother Willie worked in that garage too and met Walter. Walter worked there for a couple months then built his own shop not too far from the post office. It was a small place. Walter lived for a short time with Johnny Wendish, one of a few Sudeten Germans that had come to the area. Also single, Johnny was starting a bake shop in the front of his living quarters. Walter and Johnny made their own food of sorts, and once in a while ate at Lee Kong's restaurant.

Lee Kong ran a cafe and gambling establishment. People would hang around and play cards. Willie would go there and gamble. Walter was not much of a gambler and stayed away. Soon Willie would learn a lesson and that led him to give up gambling too. In a series of card games Willie won all of one man's money. The man had stopped in at Lee Kong's restaurant after delivering a load of pigs to a rail head at perhaps Beaver Crossing. He had a large family and many kids. Willie had been lucky and once he had the money but felt terribly guilty and gave the money back. Willie quit gambling and never ever gambled again.

There were already many Russian Germans in town. There was not really friction between the ethnic groups but there was tension between Jehovah Witness, Catholic, and Protestant, Christian denominations. Walter never really went to church in Pierceland. Later when the war broke out there was friction but more with kids than between adults. Adults never really had time to visit. My mother for example would visit with the Hewletts and Mrs Matt but she never had much time to visit others except when she would go to help pregnant women give birth.

Across the street from my mother's house was the community hall. From the bay window in the house, we could see through the open door and hear the music. From the time I was 15 or 16, I would go to the hall and help play if the musician Lena Gelowitz wanted a break from playing so she could dance. I learned to play guitar in what we called Hawaiian style using a metal bar to make chords and strum in time. I was just learning music.

My family liked music and I always remember being interested in music. My mother sang around the house. Sometimes we would sing together and she would teach me songs she knew as a kid. Her soft voice was never loud but nice.

We had an organ around the house. As I grew up, I would stand on one foot and pump the organ with the other playing tunes. Later I learned to sit down and play with two hands playing by ear. Ruby played a very small amount, and I played it with one hand. My brother Syd played the violin at home and in church, and later he played the mandolin. My musical ear was always encouraged by everyone in the family and I could at one time hear a song once, and then be able, to almost, play it all the way through, by ear.

I must say that I do not like much of today's music. The last ten years there seems to have been a shift in music. It is all too choppy and a lot of talk without much of a melody. I do not remember my mother making any such a comment of music as she grew older. Neither do I remember thinking that any music in the past was quite so bad.

As a teen, I baby sat for Jake and Edna York. Jake had a piano accordion. Jake allowed me to try this instrument and encouraged me. Then Walter came into my life, he sang so beautifully, and so did his parents and his sister Minnie. Walter was always happy to have me play the accordion. Walter and I played together. He played the mouth organ and sang. In Golden Ridge, one of the Wagman boys would come play the guitar with us and we had a trio. I had a guitar for a while but I do not know what happened to it. In later years in Winnipeg and Vancouver Walter played the mouth organ and sang as I played the piano or accordion and Glenn strummed his guitar.

I have always loved music and think perhaps along with Walter we have influenced Glenn and grown his love of music. He has more of an ear for music than his two older brothers who listen and do not attempt to make any music. Even when I tried to take Lyle and David to the choir in Lac La Ronge, it did not seem to help their interest. When this book is done, I hope to have more time to play the accordion and have Glenn accompany me on the guitar again.

My Dad did not play. When he drank, he clog danced, but I never remember him singing. My dad could fix guitars and violins. I watched him take the instruments apart on the dining room table. He would take the back off, scrape them, and put them back together. It was detailed, intricate, careful work. It is odd he could not play or tune the instruments, or even actually tune in a radio without it being all static and fuzzy. Still, he always encouraged me to sing and I remember him taking me to the Christmas concert in the Winnifred School when I was 6, a year before I had started school. I sang, "Away In A Manger" in front of a crowd. Always, at school, Dad made sure I sang.

I one time asked my mother how she and my dad would date before marriage. Did they make dates? How would they know to meet? She told me that he used to whistle at the gate. It seems he could and did whistle, but never sang, or played an instrument.

The day I really met Walter, and was introduced to him, I was at a dance across the street from our house. I was as dressed up as I could be in hand me downs. I probably had applied my free Tangee lipstick, and maybe had on some kind of face powder. In those days, monthly magazines with glossy paper had small classified ads offering free samples of lipstick. All us young girls would clip the ad, fill it in, and mail it off. A small inch high, lipstick tube, as big around as a pencil would arrive in the mail. The colors were usually some kind of red. We never got to ask for a certain color. We wore what we got. I never had money to buy anything like lipstick. I am sure I had gone hoping to meet someone and probably wanted to meet the handsome young man Betty and I had greeted on the road. I am sure I would have wanted to look my best.

At the hall, Willie introduced me to Walter. Yes, he asked me to dance. We had a few dances. I remember thinking he was a friendly, nice looking man, and we had a good time dancing. Walter danced with my friends who were also all dressed up wearing Tangee. I danced with Willie who was a good dancer. There were so many dance varieties: one step, two step, schottische, waltz, fox trot, and polka. Walter would do them all except the schottische and I cannot remember the reason why not.

These dances were well attended by the community and sometimes they were held in schools. Young singles attended, and parents would be there with their kids. I remember going to dances with my boys, and had Glenn as a baby sleeping on the teacher's desk.

Frequently a bunch of people would go to an event or to the lake together standing in the box of a truck. Road traffic was limited in those days in these isolated spots and not everyone had a vehicle. All ages mixed on these outings. Such things would not too likely happen now. On one such occasion, Mrs McEvoy came along and was sitting on some pail, stool, or something, and could not see over the top edge of the wooden box. Buster Ingram said something like oh look at that over there. Mrs. McEvoy jumped up to see what he was talking about and looked. Buster Ingram then yelled "rubber neck, rubber neck". Mrs. McEvoy was ticked off though not for long. She enjoyed the joke too. "Rubber neck" was a funny saying of the time that you no longer hear. I suppose it meant I caught you looking.

Part way through a dance we would have a lunch. People brought their own lunch and sometimes there would be pie socials or lunch box socials. The girls would decorate lunch boxes. These boxes would be auctioned off to raise money for the hall or some organization. I participated. I remember telling Walter which box to bid on, so we could snack on what I had made.

Walter began to come to Mam's to eat. He would usually come for lunch and dinner but sometimes he came for breakfast. The fruit we would be able get were oranges, apples, and lemons. For breakfast, Walter would have a cup of coffee and a lemon. Mom would ask him to eat something else but he was resolute. He was never a big eater even later in life he never ate a lot at once, but sometimes he ate too many times in a day.

Slowly Walter and I saw more of each other. We went to ball games and dances or just walked around. Occasionally we went to the lakes. We would buy a small bottle of pop to share. Usually it was Orange Crush.

One day in the heat of the summer, Mam made a pitcher of lemonade. She gave me the pitcher and told me to take it down to Walter because she thought he would need it. He was working in his own shop.

Willie would sometimes come into this shop to work. Frequently in the past, I had taken a similar drink down to Willie and Syd when they had their blacksmith shop. Walter was so pleased and very happy that Granny had thought of him. He later said how much that impressed him and wondered if his own mother would have thought so kindly to do such a thing. It seemed that Walter and my mother liked each other. Sometimes Walter and I would go to dances with Tony Gelowitz and Rosie Gross, meeting them outside before we went in. On other occasions, Walter and I would go together to Syd and Betty's home and look after Bob so his parents could go out. For a short time, Betty's sister Joan McEvoy and her boyfriend Jimmy Day would join us. The four of us would look after Bob and socialize. This baby sitting foursome did not last long. Mrs. McEvoy did not want Joan to take the responsibility of chaperoning me and Walter. She would not let Joan come. I thought for a while Joan would marry Jimmy Day but she did not.

Although we went to dances, we also used to sing together in groups to create our own fun. My friends Beatrice and Alfred Hewlett and Mike Yurko, Jimmy Simms, and others, would come over, and sing and play table games such as rummy. I do not remember Walter singing with my mother or dancing with her because my mother never went to the dances though she would wait for me at the door. Being just across the street from the hall Mam listened to the music through the open window. I do remember Walter and his parents singing together and it was beautiful. Walter had a beautiful voice and so did his parents. His parents were frequently asked to sing together at dances in the old country.

Walter and his friend Syd Waggle as teenagers would go to dances. The Catholic priest would come and drag them out of the hall feeling dances were not places for young teenage boys. Syd and Walter of course would leave temporarily as they ran around the building and climbed in a window to stay at the dance. Bathrooms for these events were traditional outdoor toilets with holes cut in the seats, so it was not a bathroom window they would climb through to defy the priest but a window on the side of the building. I think they would sneak in through the door too if they could. It did not leave a good taste in Walter's mouth for the influence of these domineering priests.

Here, Walter and his brother John are posing leaning on the back of Willie's car. It is parked just outside of my mother's house. Walter liked to wear a vest a lot in those days and John was much taller and slim. It is about the summer of 1941. John had just come up to visit Walter.

Below is a picture of the same car and me. I am not sure of the color of the car but it was a darker color. The top of the car was canvas and you can see where there is a canvas repair about at my shoulder height. The windows were of mica and not glass. I am wearing an apron that I think I made from either sugar or flour bags and had embroidered. Mom taught me to sew and she used the same machine she had sewed diapers for me to wear. Now Lyle and Gwen have the machine.

In this picture taken in front of my mother's house Norman is in front of me and is holding my dog Tiny, so I know it is from the fall of 1941. sometime after I got Tiny back.

You can see the curtains Mam always had on the windows of her house. I remember ironing the frilly parts. Granny is holding a large cabbage from her garden. She liked her garden but never had one as large as Walter's parents. Betty is holding the twins Ron and Rita, and in front of Betty is Bob, Syd and Willie are in the back row. I am beside my mother and then it is Otto Sager and Ruby.

The day Rita and Ron were born Betty did not want to go to the hospital in Cold Lake. Syd came and got Granny because the baby was about to arrive and Granny had delivered many local babies. Betty's mother was also present for the delivery. Syd and Betty lived in town not too far away, so he walked over to get Mam.

Mam got to Betty's bedside about midnight and came back in the morning. Willie and I were at the front door waiting her return. When we greeted her asking did we have a niece or a nephew, Granny looked a bit surprised and said "Both". Betty had a bit of an idea that she might be having twins but she had not told anyone. They liked the names Rita and Ronnie so after they named these two after having had Robert or Bob already, they decided they would name all their kids with the letter R, and they had four more, Raymond, Roger Roseanne, and Ruth. It was unusual even for that time.

In 1941, about September, Walter took me, Syd and Betty to visit his parents. From the left those in the picture are August, John, two brothers of Walter, then my brother Syd in front of him Bob, then Betty and me and in front of me is Walter's sister Minnie, and finally Johanna, Walter's mother.

I am not sure who took the picture. Both Walter and his dad are missing. I never remember his father using a camera. Thus, I think Walter took the picture. My family was getting to know Walter's family. It was a happy time. I am not too sure Walter's mother liked the idea he was involved with someone not Roman Catholic.

Walter's mother always had the most beautiful gardens and gave a lot away to the church. They were successful farmers. She grew many potatoes, carrots, cabbages and made a lot of sauerkraut into which she would put crab apples. I do not remember if she cored the apples. I helped her make this a few times hammering down the cabbage with salt. They had many of their own vegetables for the winter stored in the cellar of their log houses. The cellar door was on the floor between the kitchen stove and the kitchen sink. Walter's mom liked to put plants in pictures. If you were going to take her picture, she would try to place a plant in the scene or be near a plant in the plant in the picture. She was proud of this garden and had every reason to be as she had beautiful weed less gardens. I think she must have been giving us vegetables to take home in the box.

Walter's parents and Minnie stand in the beautiful garden. I always remember my mother-in-law as plump, standing about 5ft 2inches. I never saw her otherwise. She was a hard working, resourceful woman, that escaped from an early life of constant war or rebellion. She sang beautifully, alone and in choirs, was multilingual, and had a large circle of friends and acquaintances. Johanna was a telegraph operator and worked in the railway station and they lived in a railway house before they came to Canada. Walter looked after sheep keeping them off the tracks. Johanna and her parents were not poor people but I cannot say what wealth they had.

Walter told me his maternal grandmother was a slim woman. She helped hide Johanna, Sergei, and their 3 boys so they could escape tumultuous Romania. Taking trains, they zigzagged across Europe. Somewhere they caught a boat and eventually waited on board in the English Channel until it left for Canada.

Walter's father was a train engineer and drove the train from Romania into Russia. He was about 5ft 8, or 9, physically fit, and for most of his life he had a moustache. He was multilingual too but spoke little English other than "eat Sarah", and used to sing beautifully quite a lot with Johanna. All the time that I knew him, he was afraid of the Bolsheviks. His time in Europe made a huge negative impact on his life.

On the day, that Syd, Betty, and I went to visit Walter's family this picture was taken in front of the raspberry bushes.

Walter and I posed for the following picture when we were visiting his parents farm. Over my left shoulder, through the trees, were located a pig pen, and another part of a big garden. There was a gate between this yard and the rest of the farm. Like all gates on his parents' farm, it hung crooked. I was always wary of the gate because Johanna, Walter's mom, kept geese and the gander would always chase people. I was afraid of it because I had not been raised around geese.

Walter's mother grew huge onions. Walter's brother John took advantage of their large sizes and used to eat onions from the garden the size of a small apple just as if he were eating an apple. I always wondered how he could manage that kind of eating.

Walter and I have Bob and Minnie in front of us. We were happy, but Minnie was still not too sure about us getting married. She thought I was stealing her brother. I remember that in this picture I had on a blue dress. Walter has a pocket pouch for pens in his shirt pocket.

For years Walter always had a carpenter pencil, a piece of soap chalk and a led pencil in his left shirt pocket and suspenders on his pants. Walter had a thin waist. We were both thin. We got these tickets below from a fun weigh scale in Winnipeg in a Woolworth store that gave your weight and personality. Walter's weight was 161, and he had tact in his personality, while I was 123, and should avoid financial transactions on Thursdays. I guess we had a laugh then too. The tickets vouch for the fact I was once nice and slim.

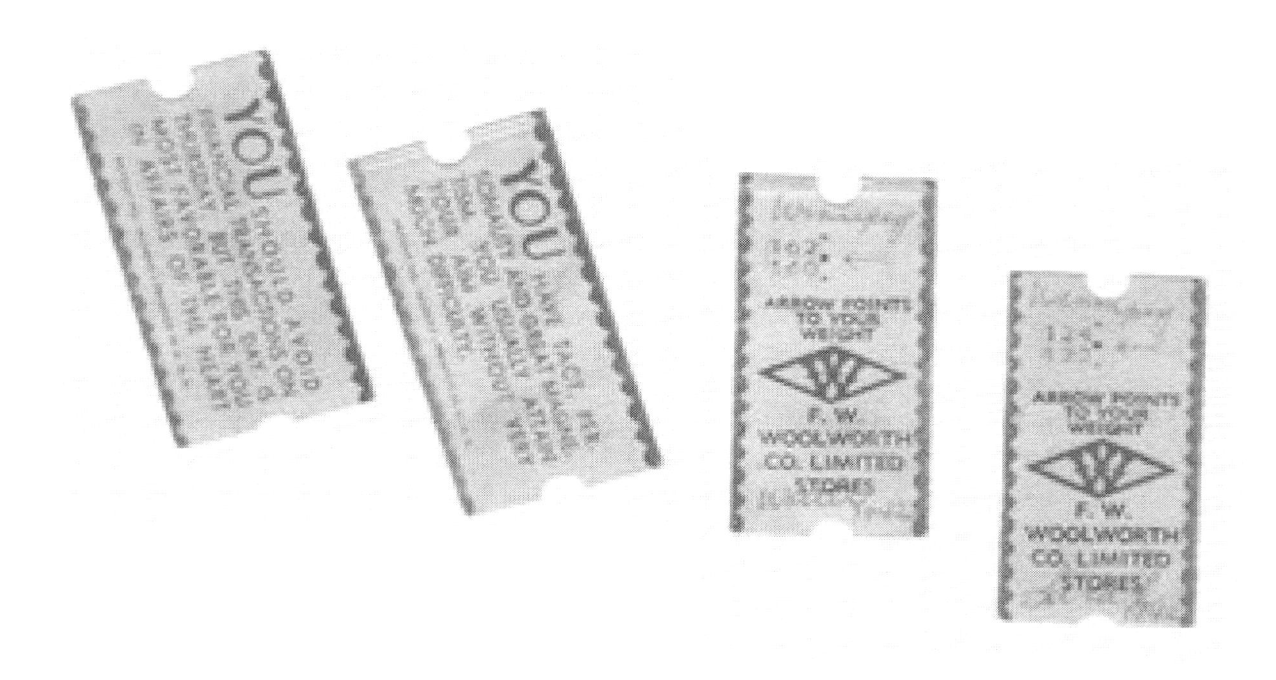

Below Bob Baker is sitting on my knee, on the visit to my future in laws farm. I am wearing the blue dress and, beige long cotton or lisle stockings, held up with garters. Bob looks happy. I was enjoying being an aunt. Bob was a pretty good kid even though he once hid in an air tight heater the summer after this picture was taken. Betty spent a couple of hours looking for him.

My brother Syd had our father's threshing machine brought up to Pierceland from Woodrow. It had been left on the farm at the time of the move. This machine is also called a separator. I do not know who the three workmen are in the picture but this is on a neighbor's farm. Perhaps Bill Cooks farm. I remember the name but not much about the man or family.

To the right, at the end of the belt, would be the crew. This machine made a lot of noise because there were sharp cutting blades, perhaps a meter long, moving back and forth and up and down at the same time, cutting the straw into small pieces. The fellow on the wagon loading the sheaves into the gapping mouth of the machine, had to have a firm grip on the pitch fork so as not to jamb the machine with the fork. This machine also separated the grain from the straw. You can see the spout taking the grain into the granary high up on the wall. You can also see the straw being blown into a big pile behind the machine to the left. The spoked wheels of the machine are steel and count the number of pulleys visible. I remember the machine was a kind of a grey color.

The three children in the front row are left to right Bob, Rita, and Ron standing in front of their mother Betty Baker. Then Walter stands looking handsome in his army uniform. I am wearing a hat with a fancy S in the brim of my hat.

Walter's father had a similar machine to this one pictured. He used to thresh for the neighbors. One time they stopped at Mr and Mrs Fralic's place. Mrs Fralic did not believe in working on Sunday. She did not like the idea that her husband had agreed to have the machine arrive on this day and other people would be working on that day. She decided to make it really clear how she felt. She had made pies the day before and hit her husband over the head with a pie as she was mad at him for the Sunday work arrangement.

The crew came to our place. I cooked for them that day. There was no phone or way of letting me know and I did not know they were coming until they had arrived to eat. The crew had to travel about 2 ½ miles to get to our place. I had to scramble and get something cooked. I did, but cannot tell you what it was.

Everyone in the picture is wearing a hat, except Betty. More people wore hats in those days. Looking at the picture one can see people are wearing a lot even though it could not be too cold as it is in September and it is on a sunny day. Everyone is wearing more than today. The beige coat I am wearing was lightly lined and I think the hat may have been black.

The picture of this grave stone is of no one I know. I include it because my brother Syd said that this man and wife were the first ones in the area or on the prairies to own a combine, a machine that cuts the grain off and thrashes the grain from the heads. They should be remembered.

My brother Willie and Dorothy are pictured in 1942 in in the warmth of late summer. Again, it is another photo by the window in Mam's house. Dorothy from Bonneville had come to Pierceland to work in the Co-op store. They were married just 5 years when Willie died. Dorothy took Eldon and moved to Calgary, eventually marrying Bill Fitzpatrick a man she had known before in Bonneville.

Nothing, in this picture of Dorothy and Willie indicates anything other than love and happiness. It is a romantic picture. Nothing shows poverty, sickness, that there is a war raging, or that Willie is actually sick. Yet Willie soon died, and the war went on for 3 more years, and both these things made us sad.

The following picture taken a couple of months later shows some of the technology of farming of the time. In 1944, Syd & Betty had this team of mules pictured below. Though the war was ending, times were modernizing; many farms still utilized horses daily. I never did see this team but in the picture below you see the mule team and Bob Baker on the pump and his sister Rita and brother Ronnie on their farm, 1 mile out of Pierceland. The mules are in front of a trough of water caked in ice. The trough would have to be broken open with an axe to allow the animals water to drink. To use the pump that Bob is hanging on to it would have to be primed with hot water.

Behind the mules in the trees, one can just make out the house of the Lillico family. The men, two brothers worked away from home in the lumber industry and ranching. One of the men's wives died and all the kids were raised by the one woman who was mother in practise to all, but birth mother to some and aunt to the others. There were eight or nine children and that was a lot of work for the mother. I went to school with this family. At the time, I had a hard time remembering which ones were sisters, and which were cousins. Gladys Lillico married and became Gladys Erikson. I spoke with her many years later around 2000 when she was in Victoria. It was a good conversation, and then a bit later she died.

In the trees at the back of the horses, there is a road running left to right. The McEvoy family lived to the left where there was a junction in the road and a large tree. When I attended the Chocolate Valley School I would come from Pierceland to the right of the picture, walk down this road and right, up over the hill in the background to get to the Chocolate Valley School. Audrey Haywood my little friend is buried on top of this hill in a now closed cemetery.

In 1954, Charlie Corney came to Pierceland to visit his sister Harriett. She was 73 years old when this picture was taken of these two behind a car in front of Syd's house. In this picture, she wears a tweed coat and was wearing felt boots and cotton stockings. I do not think she ever wore trousers. My Uncle Charley was good to his sister. Their personalities were similar in that they were both good natured. Charlie Corney was a tolerant man with a good singing voice. It is possible to see Mam has no teeth. I never knew my mother with teeth. I never asked her when she lost her teeth. She was 42 when I was born.

In the picture below, Mam, then 83, is wearing a blue shawl that I crocheted for her. She used to wear it a lot. She sits in her rocking chair in Syd and Betty's house. I think Bob Baker now has her chair. I again have the shawl.

When David was a baby, I was visiting Mam. I was rocking David to sleep sitting in the chair. Syd came to the house. He said something like, "You don't want to make a habit of that because you will end up having to do it all the time." It did not work that way and I did not have to do it all the time, and never had a rocking chair in our house. When Mam moved to Edmonton, the rocking chair was used years later by Syd, and he rocked his grandchildren to sleep in it. Syd and I both laughed at the situation.

Mam is sitting with an apron on. She had two aprons a day in case she needed to do something and she needed to be clean. One time Dave Corney had to tell her to remove her apron for a picture when she was in Prince Albert for a visit. Pictured here she was just wearing an apron out of habit and fashion for her age.

I remember my mother losing her eye sight and still liking to listen to the TV and hear Elvis Presley. Walter thought a lot of Mam. Walter carried the picture in his wallet for years. He folded it and that is why it got this shape and the crease.

Mam and her brother harry Corney sit together in this picture above taken in 1964. She is much smaller than her brother. Harry is visiting her in Edmonton when she was living at Ruby and Otto's place. On this day, Harry told Mam that her brother Charlie had died a few months previously. It was something we had not told Mam because we knew it would sadden her a lot. He said it was his duty to tell her. He was abrupt and determined. It made Mam sad but I imagine she was expecting the news.

Mam's reputation and physical appearance were opposites. As a caring nurse, midwife, and gentle person, her reputation was large. People for miles around knew of her and sought her out as a caregiver. In later years, she was known widely as Granny Baker. This diminutive woman with a truly compassionate heart, helped many babies into the world, and eased many fears. Widely known for her natural nursing nature, during sickness she was often the first sent for. Yet in person, she was just about 5 feet tall. As a young girl, I soon was her height. Her soft voice was never loud but rather sweet. Mam was 42 when I was born and I wish I had seen her reddish brown hair. It was always grey when I saw it, long, and gathered into a bun on the back of her head. In the picture above, Mam had finally cut her hair short at about age 70.

Somewhere around March 5, 1966, I took the train to Edmonton from Winnipeg where we had moved. Mam was sick. I stayed with my sister Ruby. Syd was also there from Pierceland. Mam was not doing well. Diabetes was causing her many problems and they were considering removing her leg. Syd, Ruby, and I decided we did not want her to be put through the pain of having her leg removed. She had been in the hospital for about 10 days. We knew she would not live too long. We just wanted her comfortable. The hospital agreed and kept her comfortable until she died, March 9th, 1966, and her funeral was the 12th in Pierceland.

My Mam was brought home and spent a night in Syd's garage one night. Syd took us out to the garage to see her in her coffin. When we opened the coffin, I could hardly believe it was Mam. She looked like a younger woman again not in pain and hurting. Ruby would not go look. I am glad I went to look and see her one more time. It was the last time I saw my Mam.

At the grave site, it was March and the snow was melting. I watched sadly thinking goodbye Mam. I remember a drop of water flattened and lay on her gray coffin. I wondered how long the water would be like that. It was not long. A few seconds later, as we all stepped away the outer wooden box lid was nailed on the outer surrounding coffin. I did not like that happening. Mam was special and that wooden lid was junky. It seemed too close, and too similar, to getting rid of a box of junk and Mam was a fine loving woman. That is why I want to be cremated. Mam was a good mother to all her children and I think of her every day.

After the funeral, this picture of Syd, Ruby and I was taken in Syd and Betty's yard. A few minutes after this Otto, Ruby and I went by car back to Edmonton. Otto drove.

Although it does not look like it in this picture, Ruby was about 5ft 2 inches and shorter than me by about 2 inches. Ruby was kind person and had some characteristics quite similar to those of Mam. Both had a natural nursing instinct. That is why Mam moved to Edmonton to be with Ruby as she had space and the time to give to Mam's care. Ruby would have liked to become a nurse. Moving to the remote north ended that desire. I am sure she would have overcome her fear of using a needle just as many others have done, and been a great nurse.

The following newspaper clipping is from the Grand Center paper and talks about Mam, illustrating that she was a well known lady of the area.

SS March 20, 1965

Mrs. Harriet Baker, Pierceland Pioneer, Dies In Edmonton

GRAND CENTRE—Mrs. Harriet Baker, a pioneer resident of Pierceland, passed away in the University Hospital in Edmonton. Mrs. Baker was 83 years of age.

The Rev. Mr. Parker, Anglican minister from Leon Lake, officiated at the service in the Pierceland Community Hall.

Mrs. Baker leaves to mourn her loss, one son, Sydney Baker, of Pierceland, Sask., two daughters, Mrs. Ruby Sager of Edmonton and Mrs. Sarah Serguis of Winnipeg; 12 grandchildren; nine great-grandchildren; two brothers and four sisters.

Pallbearers at the funeral were John McEvoy, Tom McEvoy, Buster Ingram, Roy Farris, Alfred Hewlett and John Rule.

Funeral managers were: Roy Johnson, Stanley Erickson, George Mehalcheon and George Little.

Mrs. A. M. McEvoy was the organist.

Interment was in the Pierceland United Church Cemetery.

My life in Pierceland as I grew up was more civilized, more social, and happier than some future times I would experience. Electricity and other technological advances and niceties of more populated urban areas came to rural towns and farms slowly. In general life was harder, more frontier and primitive like, and less affluent than in urban communities. This seemed to be an accepted fact because knowing this, urban areas of the country sent boxes of used clothing to rural Canada. We all appreciated it. We had no shopping malls and large clothing stores in which to shop. We had few if any options or selections even if we had money to spend. Life in Pierceland was really the only life I knew.

When I returned to Pierceland from Winnipeg a bit after our marriage, I also knew that I did not like the place and that I wanted to leave. Pierceland had a huge effect on our family especially my father. Some of my parents' fears became true. Had they wondered if they would succeed as farmers, they got a clear answer. No, they would not. Dad could not handle the strain, he drank, was removed from the family to dry out, got TB, and died. The rest of us struggled.

I did not know and understand the bigger picture of society. I was not timid and shy in Pierceland, but the outside world was a mystery to me. I yearned to know more of the world. Soon I would begin to know a lot more about life, living, and the rest of the world.

Wedding, Winnipeg, Sardis: Army Bride, Life Begins With Walter

The War took Walter away. It stepped in through the government and altered people's lives forever. I did not know when I would ever see him again or if I would ever see him again. I only hoped. I did not know if I would ever hear from him again. There was a good possibility I would never hear from him again and never see him again. One did not know if he would also be sacrificed to the war effort. It was a stressful time.

Delightfully, a much anticipated, letter arrived from Walter during his first few weeks of military training in a camp in Regina, Saskatchewan. Walter decorated the letterhead with a pen. It is I think the drawing is of a boat, perhaps a love boat, incorporating the title of a song they were singing and the letter included the words of the song.

I cherished and saved these letters for about 75 years. Now I and share them with you here. The big space following is to allow the letters to be inserted.

Thiy. Say. That. in. Camp. you.
Can. have. a. swell. Time
We. ve. heard. it. all. Before
Five. in. The Morning. were. kicked.
aut. of. bed.
To. scub. up The barreck. room. Floor.
a. private. has. realy. No. privatey. Now.
We. re. all. behind. The eeyht. baall.
✶ No. ice. Cram. and. Cookies. For.
Flat. Footed. rookies.
So. cheer. up. my. Frund bless Them
chorus all. bless. em. all. bless. em. all
The Long. and. The. Short. and. the. small.
Bless. all. The. sergant. The. saur
puss. ones.
bless. all. The. Corprals. and. Therr. dopy. sons
Caus. werre. saying. Good. bay
To. Them. all.
As. back. To. The. barracks. The. Crawl.
No. ice. cream. &. Cookees. For. Flat. Footies.
Rookies.
So. cheer. up. my. Frunds. bless. Them. all
2 bless. em. all. bless em. all.

A 4, R.C.A. TRAINING CENTRE
FORT BRANDON BARRACKS
BRANDON, MAN.

1

Good. morning. Sergant major

Good morning. Sergant. major
How. do. you. do. you. do.
We. Love, you. Sergant. major. We. do We. do. We. do.
and Whin. We. Get. up. Early
an. a cold. and Forsty morn.
~~and the~~ We. bliss. you Sergant major
and. the. day When. you. WERe. born.
you. are. The. armees. Littel Sweethart
What. a. Sweethart. What. a. Friend.
We. re. Going. Too. miss. you. Littel
Sweethart. When. This. Wor. comms. Too a End.
da da da do re.
Whin. we. Leave. The. army
you'll, hear. Good. morning.
Sergant. major. Good. bay. & Toodle. Loo.

2

No. more. we'LL. get. up. Early
No. more. Raute, marches. Too.
your. Tummees. is getting. Larger
your. Nose. is. Getting. bLue.
So. Kess. me. SerGant. Major
BeFor. I Say. I. ā duy

and. When. I. get. my. Civis
I'LL sing. This. sang. To you.
We. want. you sergant. major.
I. don't. Know. What. To. do.
and. When. I. GeT. my. pension.
I'LL. always. Think. of. you

A short time later he was shipped off to Brandon, Manitoba for artillery training, a needed skill on the front line. We expected that his next move would most likely be an overseas trip to the deadly front lines. On the day the picture below was taken his troupe had marched about 35 miles. Walter was being trained to be a gunner to operate mobile long range guns a high casualty position in the army. He is a handsome man in uniform.

This is the type of gun Walter was being trained to operate, in Shilo, just outside Brandon.

A more interesting letter is included here from May 25, 1943.

May. 25. 1943.
6A. CETC. and vg
Breeding area.
Chilliwack B.C.

My. Dear Sarah.

Hello. my littel appel Blasemma.

I receved your letter and was glad to her. from. you. I sapuus. you ar ram to go. I hop. Will the sooner you com the batter for boht of aus. I m geting very axsatet about you comming I can hardely. What an tell you get her. I sapaus. you got the theat hav you

I hap and. I am. very. glad. you ar. traying

I love you Sarah My xxx

to be brav. I know
you well. I know
you. will have it hard
but you know hany it
will. be not so hard afther
you get stardet on your
why. and I will be so happy
when you get her.
Well dear I havent mach to
say. but in my hart I
mean a lot and love you
very mach. and I allwes
will. how is Dearved-
Well dear I will be
whetting for you very
pashently. good night
dear. see you soon my
dear. love and kisses
from your hasbant waller
give me love to [illegible]

Walter did not know English well but that would not stop him from writing me a letter. I was thrilled then to get this love letter, and as I look at it now it still fills me with pleasure.

Walter needed to arrange leave time to be married. We had not set the date. We had no phone communications and talking about arrangements was impossible. All arrangements had to be made by letter and word of mouth. Communications were so much more difficult in those years outside of big urban areas. In small towns and rural areas personal messages were also used to communicate. A person going somewhere, would take a message from one person to another or maybe deliver a letter. I knew Walter would be home around the end of December, but I did not really know the date until the last. So, the actual time of our marriage was in the hands of the army. On our wedding day, the minister drove to Pierceland from Loon Lake, and returned the same day.

Walter was in the Shilo army camp and the closest larger town was Brandon. People would refer to the military in Brandon, but they really meant Shilo. In Brandon, he bought me an engagement ring, and both our wedding rings. The engagement ring he mailed to me. On the day that it arrived I entered the post office to see Mrs McEvoy was running the post office. I went to the wicket and she handed me a very small package with my name on it. It was such a small packet in amongst the rest of the mail it is a wonder it was not lost. I had been helping Ruby and I took the package with me back to her store to open it. Ruby was with me when I opened the box. We were both excited knowing what was inside but not knowing what it looked like. The ring had a pattern carved into it but it has long ago worn away. Everyone knew we were going to get married. It was no secret what was inside the small box and soon the whole town knew I had received it.

I remember the day Walter asked if I would marry him. It was not a surprise. Yes, it was a great feeling, kind of like winning the lottery. It was late summer. We were not in town or at Mam's. We were out walking. We had gone down the road to a creek west of Pierceland. We were standing in the middle of the bridge over the creek. I cannot remember the exact words we spoke to each other. I remember replying that I had to ask my mother if I could marry and that I would think about it and ask her, as at the time I was 17. Walter had just started his business and he was working hard. Walter walked me home and waited.

I remember Mam saying she would give permission because she knew I would marry Walter as soon as I was of age anyway. She thought Walter was a nice person, and liked him. Like everyone else she could see that he was a hard worker. She asked where we would get married. She knew where we would marry might be an issue because Walter had been raised Roman Catholic. I think I gave Walter my answer yes, the same day he asked.

Although Walter knew Mam, our families did not know each other. One day, a Mr Anderson, a family friend I do not remember all that well, drove Mam, Walter, and I to see Walter's parents. Walter took the picture below, Mr. Anderson is wearing the hat hugging Ruby. I think he lived near Beaver River but I do not remember much else or anything about the car ride.

The group stands in front of the first house Walter's family built on their farm with the h shingles the shingles Walter and his mother made by hand using axes. You can see the plaster on the log walls of the house. Walter's parents are on the far left and a dog is behind Johanna. Interestingly, Johanna got her name because her father was named Johan and she was named after her father. Sergei is behind her, Mam, then Ruby and Mr Anderson. Walter's sister Minnie is beside me standing on the right side of this picture. For a short time, Walter had another sister Helen who lived only a few months. She was between John and August and she was born and died in Romania.

Walter's parents and Mam got on well and you can see the happy faces in the picture. Though Walter's mother spoke five languages and worked doing Morse code in Romania her English was not great at this point, but I knew some German from my associations at school, and could help explain things to Mam. I have since forgotten, nearly all the German language I once knew. Walter's father was more silent than his mother, and spoke little English.

A few months before we met Walter had tried to join the army. He was working in Calgary and had an arm injury. The army would not accept him. Sometime after we had decided to get married, and before the middle of September, both my brother Willie, and Walter, got letters on the same day directing them to report to Meadow Lake for an army medical exam. Walter passed the exam and Willie failed. Although a man was expected to join the army, it was possible to avoid joining. Walter signed up immediately. He was given a date to report to Regina. There was nothing to be done. I felt badly. I worried and I felt we would be married sometime but I did not know when. In Walter's family, only he joined the army. I never heard how his parents interpreted his joining the army.

Entering the army, Walter had to close his business and sell his equipment. He was at the time very busy and had developed a good customer base. I remember a man by the first name of Johnny somebody bought Walter's trip hammer but never paid for it. After the war, Walter tried to find it and get it back but failed.

Walter was not around when I had to solve the problem of who would marry us. Mam encouraged me to talk to the Roman Catholic, RC priest. I am sure Mam knew what the priest's answer would be but we wanted to try to get along. There was a significant religious divide in the community. It sometimes became a factor in determining your friendships. Religious leaders exerted pressures on people to keep friends primarily within their own religion. Their control was based upon exclusion and discrimination.

Our marriage was a big issue for gossip. We came from two different religious denominations. To many in the community, it seemed an unnatural act for us to get married. It was discussed and commented upon in the small community. Everyone had an opinion. A lot thought it was a marriage doomed and one that should not happen. Others just thought it was wrong. I suppose that they really were short on conversation topics and when they were talking about us they were leaving someone else alone.

Church and religion are perhaps more Christian today than in those days because now people are more accepting of each other's religions. All throughout our marriage Walter and I would disagree on this and that topic like every couple, but we never argued about religion.

When the RC priest was in Pierceland, his presence changed the whole atmosphere of the town. It was not a positive change. It should not have led to social distance but it did. Like a poison, his presence changed things, and as he left, things got better. His presence segmented the community into groups of we, and them, bringing a divisive type of self righteous atmosphere. Some kids you played with acted distantly when the RC priest arrived.

When the RC priest, Father Shultz, was in town, he first stayed with the Gelowtiz family. I would be sent to their place to buy milk. When Father Shultz was around the kids would solemnly and politely fill the jar but not chat and be friendly because the priest would be watching what we did. He did not want his flock to have too much association with heathen Protestants. Shultz would stand closely by looking down his nose disapprovingly at everything in the purchase and sale transaction but say not a word. He seemed to say that making a profit from a protestant was allowed, but it was not allowed to be friendly to a protestant.

Shultz later came into our lives after we were married for about 2 months. Walter came home from an emergency operation dealing with his burst appendix. He came home to stay about a month or so with his parents and I went there to be with him. On one of these days, I was sitting on the edge of our bed and we were talking when Father Shultz arrived at the kitchen. Walter's mother and the priest had a discussion. Soon Johanna came into the bedroom and said that Father Shultz was requesting, perhaps insisting, that we have a Roman Catholic ceremony and marry us for real in the RC church, because we were not really married if married by a protestant minister. Walter said no that it was a bit too late for that as we were married already. I agreed but said little. A few seconds later when Johanna returned to the kitchen there was a lot of excited talk in German. Shultz received the news badly. Had this situation happened a few years later, or now, I would have been more vocal with my thoughts about Shultz's opinionated, self-righteous attitude.

Shultz was not the Roman Catholic priest I had asked about marrying us. It was a different one that now lived not far away from the church. So, at the time I had walked up the street. Inside his office, we sat down to talk and I asked the big question. The answer was yes, he could marry us, but I would have to take classes to be able to keep my promise to raise all our children as Roman Catholic. I said I was not going to raise my children RC because I was an Anglican. He said that he could not marry us. My answer was that I would go somewhere else and someone else would marry us.

The importance of religion cutting through communities, sometimes dividing it, and the influence of priests, wrapped up in their own faith and self importance, became evident when he told me "but you won't be married then". I was not pleased with his comment and it upset me. I stood up, walked out, and went straight home to my Mam.

Mam assured me that everything would work out fine. She would arrange for the Anglican minister to marry us. Walter heard by mail that the Roman Catholic priest would not marry us. I told him that we would be married by the Anglican minister from Loon Lake. He did not really care and I do not even remember his response.

We were married in my mother's house. His parents attended. They drove about 25 miles in the winter in an open sleigh. This would have taken them nearly a day to drive that far. They arrived the day before and stayed in Mam's house. They never complained about the marriage to me, though I do not think they were very pleased about Walter marrying someone that was not Roman Catholic, and that the ceremony was not held in a church. They may have said something to Walter but he never mentioned it to me. Later his parents got their wishes as Walter's two brothers were married to Roman Catholics in churches but sadly, the Roman Catholic Church did not guarantee them a long and happy marriage.

My own family never said a negative word. A few days before the wedding Syd did comment about Walter and the wedding saying something like "He is a good worker so at least she won't starve."

Ruby, Willie and Syd were all present as witnesses. There were no maid of honor and no best man in our small wedding. The ceremony was about 2 in the afternoon.

Walter and I stand between tire marks in the snow a day after being married at about 2 in the afternoon on Tuesday, the 23rd of December 1941, and 75 years later as I work on this, I still consider myself married to Walter even though he is no longer here with me.

Mam and Ruby helped me pick out the dress in an Eaton's catalogue and it was $2.98, the veil was extra as were long white stockings and leather gloves. I still have it. Below is a picture of the dress some 75 years later. A blue flower from my mother's wedding dress is on the veil. "Full Fashion" was printed on the white stockings that I did not like, I think because they were white. On the sole was printed, "Mercerized Cotton, Three Ply Sole, Made In Canada.

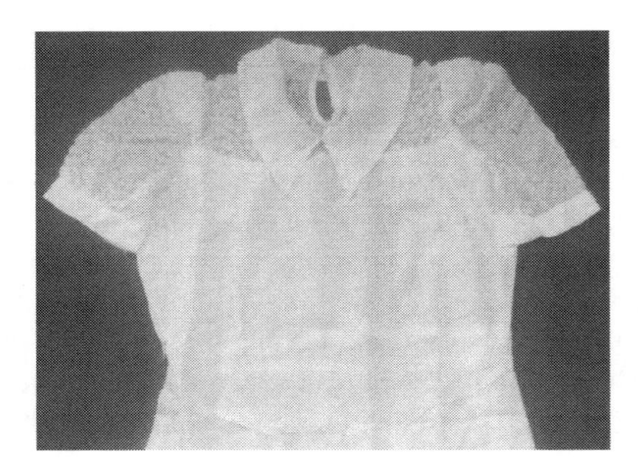

Across the shoulders, the dress was a stylish and delicate crocheted pattern. The collar was small and not reinforced. I still have this dress folded neatly in a cedar chest. It is seen here photographed on my dining room table.

The actual marriage ceremony is a little sketchy in my mind perhaps because it was not a big production like modern weddings. It was a poor people's war wedding. The venue was small and crowded. There were not a lot of guests and witnesses. The walk down the aisle for me was a few steps from my bedroom to stand beside Walter in front of the organ in Mam's living room. Our families were present. Walter had no friends present but I had a couple. Mrs McEvoy played the organ. Syd and Betty were there with Bob and the twins Ronnie and Rita. During the marriage, Rita pulled on my veil. There was no room for anyone else.

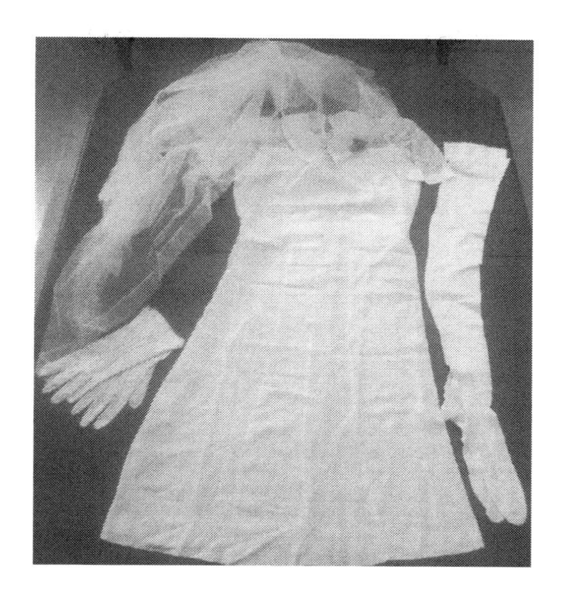

After the ceremony, the table was moved back into the middle of the room and food started to come from the kitchen. Walter's Dad, and my brother Syd, had a bit of fun after drinking some wine, and as the food came from the kitchen to the table, they hid it amongst the plants in the bay window. Both our mothers worked in the kitchen to get the celebratory food ready. Walter's father did not speak much English but always understood, and in later years it seemed obvious he understood more than what he admitted to knowing.

To take this wedding picture in the snow we needed sunlight and had to go onto the road near the back of the house. It is Mam's house in the background surrounded by the slab wood fence. It was a very cold day. On the wedding day, I had long, thigh high white stockings on, but in the picture above, taken the next afternoon, I wore Lyell stockings because I did not like the old fashioned white thigh high versions.

On Boxing Day 1941, three days after we were married Walter left for Brandon, Manitoba, with four dollars in his pocket. I did not see him until the end of February after he had a ruptured appendix and he took this picture.

Taken in March 1942 I am wearing a hat and overshoes. In some parts of the country, overshoes are unheard of but they are boots made to be worn over shoes. These were trimmed with imitation fur and the rest of the boot is some type of soft velvet like material. They are not especially warm but they are convenient. It is cold and winter time and like all women we did not yet wear *trousers.* Our legs got cold. Even though I am not far from my mother's house in town, looking at the background it seems rather close to the frontier with bush and wilderness right at our doorstep. There is little buffer between civilization and the wilds.

Soon after this picture Walter and I went to Winnipeg. Walter had recovered from appendicitis. We were starting our adventures together and I was anxious to know what life would be in city. I looked forward to the trip unafraid because I was with my uniformed soldier husband. I felt ready for the future.

I am not sure how we got to Meadow Lake but we took the bus from there to Battleford and the train the rest of the way to Winnipeg. Stopping off in Regina overnight, we stayed with my cousin Kate Corney to visit. Her husband John Corny, was the son of my mother's brother by the same name. This name similarity leads to a lot of confusion. John my cousin, not my uncle, was overseas in the army.

It was largely an uneventful journey to Winnipeg, with the exception that I was unprepared to see my father. If it were my dad, then he was as emotionally confused and unsure as I was about an unplanned family encounter. Meeting my father as I left home or ever again, was never something, I considered. He seemed to have been gone from my life forever. Given another hour to sort things out, we may have spoken and had a wonderful reunion or both met a stranger rather than live to regret inaction.

In Winnipeg, we met new friends and though during a time of great tension internationally we began to enjoy life as a couple. I am pictured with our new friends. Pretending to play my accordion is Noel Boulet. His wife Phil is on the left. I am on the right. Noel was in the army but not the same branch as Walter. They came from southern Saskatchewan and lived in the same small apartment building as we did, at 57 Dagmar Street. While in Winnipeg, at Ray Hamerton Music, on Portage Avenue, I traded this accordion in for a bigger white Italian made accordion that had a nicer more mellow sound. Phil and Noel were our good friends. When David was born, Phil sent me a little carriage quilt. I still have it. We lost contact with Noel and Phil after the war.

The picture is one Walter carried in his pocket for a few years. You can see where there is some kind of burn on the bottom edge. Walter smoked. He told me the burn was from a cigarette butt in his pocket. It shows Phil Boulet and me sitting on the steps of the conservatory in Assiniboine Park, Winnipeg.

We had a good time with Phil and Noel even though we were all really short of money. Walter made slugs to look like a 25 cent coin to go in the gas meter for the cook stove. When the meter man came around I would pay him the money and he would give me back the slugs.

One night Phil and I went to buy ice cream while Noel and Walter stayed at home. We imagined someone was following us. We got spooked. We ran like mad to get home and turned into the building panting. Walter and Noel went out the back door but the fellow just continued down the street. We do not know he was up to anything sinister, and it may have been just that we were country girls not yet used to city life.

This picture of Walter wearing army shorts is in front of 57 Dagmar Street. Is he wearing stripped socks?

Before we lived at this address, we lived for a time at 390 McDermott Avenue in Winnipeg and we moved to Dagmar, as it was bigger but still not large. Dagmar was a small place. We did not have a full kitchen set up with cupboards and many dishes. We did not try to buy a lot as it was war time. We knew we might be moving around a bit. Our meals were mainly fried or boiled food.

We lived above the owner's dining room. We were a bit inconsiderate one day while I was playing the accordion. There were 4 or 5 people inside our small room dancing, laughing, and having fun. The owner sent her granddaughter up to tell us that we were making too much noise. The granddaughter delivered the message, but then also added that the noise was not the real reason for her having to deliver the message. The real reason was that the motion was causing the dust to fall off the downstairs dining room light onto the table. We quieted down but it was funny.

The rent we paid for the single room with the bathroom down the hallway was $12 a month. Walter got $76 a month but the cheque was I think made out to and mailed to me. This was because he was married, and had Walter been overseas he could not have cashed the cheque and his family would have had no money.

Then I did not eat very much and was thin. I remember we bought a pound of bacon for about 25¢. I had some and in one meal, Walter ate the rest. I remember thinking in amazement that he could eat that much.

The cook in the army camp would sometimes give Walter a slice of canned meat. It was something like Klick or Spam. It came in a long tin tube about 18 inches long and about 4 x 6 across the end. We used this to supplement our food. I would buy vegetables from a vegetable wagon, a fellow with a horse and cart that he drove up and down the streets. Some still did this with trucks in Winnipeg in the 1960's. Bread we bought unwrapped for 5¢ a loaf. If you got it wrapped it was a cent more, 6¢. While in Winnipeg, we bought a butcher knife that I still have in the kitchen drawer.

The purpose of the picture below was to show Walter laughing, sitting with Phil and I at the conservatory in Assiniboine Park. It was not until now that I see there was someone watching from left corner. He was not noticeable in the small snap and for the last 60 years we never knew he was there. He is a stranger. Can you see him?

Walter is pictured inside the conservatory in Assiniboine Park, Winnipeg, wearing his summer uniform with long pants. It is where I saw palm trees and tropical plants for the first time.

For perhaps a few weeks both Noel and Walter attended Kelvin Technical School in Winnipeg. I like the adjacent you can see Phil and I on the school steps. I do not know what Noel studied but Walter was studying something to do with engineering that the army needed him to know. With new English language skills, this would have been a challenge, but Walter did well with his training.

I guess at the time they were preparing him to transfer to the engineers but we were not told this at the time. The army never told us much about their plans. In times of war the army moves people around just as if they are machines. The troops and families are purposefully kept unaware for security reasons. We never knew what the future held. The secrecy of war keeps one on edge a lot. Many times, in Winnipeg, we thought Walter was to be sent overseas. Each time was a dreaded experience of building tension. The thoughts of the horrors of war became more real; we were more fearful and were more scared.

The first time I ever saw a retail store sale was in Eaton's in Winnipeg and it was also a scene of competition and aggression. I had been in retail stores for sure, but not one having a big sale. Until this time, I had only been in a small town where there were no crowds of customers. This sale was an amazing site. There were more customers grabbing at things here, than would fit into the small country stores that I knew. The shoppers pressed into the store in huge numbers determined to get a bargain. Walter and I watched women grabbing and yanking things back and forth. We watched, amazed as things were grabbed and tossed around in something akin to a shark feeding frenzy as seen on TV. We left walking Portage Avenue.

In Winnipeg, we spent a lot of time walking. It was our entertainment, as we could not afford to do things that cost money. On these walks, I wore my wedding dress as just a regular dress. Walter wanted to buy watercolor paints. We had no idea the cost. He looked at what was for sale and selected a set of about 18 differing colors. The woman began to wrap the set and said they were $4.00, even though it was far more than what we could afford to pay Walter was too embarrassed to say he no longer wanted the paint set. We paid the price and we had perhaps a dollar or so left in our pockets. At home Walter began to paint on paper and the backs of writing pads. One of the pictures he painted from this set Glenn has at home.

It was during this time in Winnipeg, when Walter had frequent military inspections, that I learned to rub a bar of soap down the inside seam of wool pant legs so that when pressed they would keep the seam precisely. Walter's army uniform was wool. At inspections, the crease needed to be very sharp. Brass buttons had to be polished using a special brass gadget, a metal strip with space down the middle so that it looked like tall brass letter U. This army practice of examining even small details of appearance was a method to foster military obedience so that the troops never questioned orders. It also taught military wives a few things too as we helped in uniform preparation.

While in the army Walter smoked roll your own type cigarettes. I would help to make them but still wished he would not smoke. Once, perhaps as a joke to nudge him into quitting, I took action. Trimming the sulfured ends of several match sticks I loaded them into the middle of a cigarette. and it went randomly into Walter's pocket container. When one end was lit the first puff or two would be normal, but, when more of the cigarette burned a subsequent inhaled draw of air would catch the match ends on fire resulting in a small startling explosion of fire. The plan worked out perfectly with only one small unforeseen possibility. Walter in his generosity offered a cigarette to his sergeant, who pulled the load one out of the box, lit it and it exploded in his hands. Walter was embarrassed and apologetic and I felt badly. Still Walter did not quit smoking.

studying something to do with engineering that the army needed him to know. With new English language skills, this would have been a challenge, but Walter did well with his training.
I guess at the time they were preparing him to transfer to the engineers but we were not told. The army never told us much about their plans. In times of war the army moves people around just as if they are machines. The troops and families are purposefully kept unaware for security reasons. We never knew what the future held. The secrecy of war keeps one on edge a lot

Many times, in Winnipeg, we thought Walter was to be sent overseas. Each time was a dreaded experience of building tension. The thoughts of the horrors of war became more real; we were more fearful, and were more scared.

In Winnipeg got a letter from Ruby saying Otto's brother Fred Sager, married to Nell, might be living in Winnipeg. I looked up the name in the phone book, found a number and called it.

Nell Sager answered. At that time, she called herself Alie, even Ruby later called her Alie rather than Nell. Fred was out of town working for Bird Construction. Eventually a few days later Nell showed up with her two daughters Lorraine and Eleanor, as the third daughter Cheryl was not yet born. Sometime later Nell and the 2 girls went to Pierceland to visit Ruby and Otto. During this time, Nell only visited once and we never visited their house. Later when we lived in Winnipeg after 1960, we visited back and forth a bit and I visited Eleanor's house in East Kildonan. We always enjoyed our visits and she used only the name Nell then.

Walter started in the army as a private, and took training to be a gunner. Then Walter was told he was to go overseas. I went home hoping I would not soon be a widow. In a couple of weeks after I had left for home, without telling anyone, instead of sending Walter overseas they sent him to Chilliwack. He was transferred to the engineers, A6 Camp, Sardis, BC. While in Sardis, they put him on and off overseas service. It was the same set of dreaded experiences just in a different location. Mam and I took David and went to see Walter off a few times. We always wondered how long luck would be on our side keeping Walter home. He never went overseas but he was never told he would not go overseas, and was always ready to leave. The army recognized his engineering talents. He left the army as a Corporal with two stripes. I often wondered if it was because of his Russian, German background and Romanian birth that he never went overseas. I still puzzle over this.

Leaving Winnipeg and returning to Pierceland was a big trip for me to make alone. It was less pleasant and more stressful without Walter. I was alone, pregnant, timid, not familiar with much of the outside world, and had not travelled much and had never done so alone. I travelled by bus making a few transfers and twice had to stay overnight in hotels. I was quite uneasy in the hotel rooms. The door was locked but for added safety, I put my suitcase up against the locked door. Thinking of it now, I am not sure what good that did but at least it would have made noise if moved.

The buses were not as big as they are now. The last bus I saw come into Pierceland was around the size of some vans we see today. The area population was smaller and not as many people travelled. The bus trip was a learning experience for me. I learned the bus carried an assortment of very different people with interesting backgrounds. I encountered all these strangers alone, which was new and exciting because I was still very much a sheltered small town girl without worldly experience.

Pierceland was dressed in the colors of fall when I arrived home. I now had a taste of the big city of Winnipeg. I could make comparisons of the two places. In my mind, I did just that. In Winnipeg and in Pierceland Walter and I had walked a lot, so I knew parts of the city. In Winnipeg, we walked from downtown as far as a dam near the airport that is no longer there. In Pierceland, we walked around town. Returning to Pierceland I could tell fast that I did not like the place. I had never liked it much. Now for sure with somewhere to compare it to I knew Pierceland was not a place for me.

Pierceland was probably like a lot of small towns, inhabited by many gossipy people minding everyone's business. There were few newcomers to meet and not much to do. In Winnipeg if we had money, we could go to a movie easily whereas in Pierceland there were movies only when my brother brought them to town. Walking in Winnipeg offered a lot of variety while in Pierceland it was limited. In Pierceland, we walked on soft soil but in Winnipeg, the cement made my feet hurt, but still, I preferred Winnipeg. My friends at the time must have thought the same thing of Pierceland as they all moved. In Pierceland, I was home with Mam, but I was missing Walter.

My family were interested to know what Winnipeg was like and asked me questions about Winnipeg. Mam, Willie, and Mrs Matt, asked questions. Betty Baker had lived in Edmonton so we could talk a bit about the cities. My sister Ruby was interested in Winnipeg a lot. Ruby also never liked Pierceland.

From the fall of 1942 to the spring of 1943, I was again in Pierceland. This picture of me was taken in March 1943 after David was born. We had so much snow that year that it is almost over the fence. The line of things behind me is the top of the fence and I am sitting on top of the snow.

David had been born a month earlier in Loon Lake. My mother strongly opposed me staying in Pierceland to give birth to David. I took her advice. Ruby previously had trouble giving birth to Norman and had to go into Cold Lake. Mam did not want to me to risk anything even though there was a nurse at the Pierceland hospital and a visiting doctor every few weeks for overnight and she had helped in many births. So, on around Feb 20th, I went to Loon Lake with doctor Grandy. I stayed in the hospital.

I was permitted to walk around town being careful not to fall but I was not allowed to go inside any building. That may sound odd, but in Loon Lake, there was an outbreak of measles. Avoiding possible contamination in crowds was important. I stayed, ate, and slept in the hospital. David was born on Tuesday about 4:15 to 4:30, the morning of February 23. About that time a big blizzard started. That kept me in the hospital for 17 days. I had no way to get home and nowhere else to go. There was no telephone. I had no way to let my family know that we were ready to go home. With the blizzard raging, we simply had to be patient and wait. I did not know how I was going to get home to Mam's house. The roads would be blocked and unlike today, equipment to clear the roads was not readily available.

One day I was invited to have dinner with Reverend Ashmore and his wife. I left David in the hospital care and went to their house across the street from the hospital. The minister had married Walter and me about 14 months earlier. He also later baptized David in my mother's house, in the same spot where he had married us, and then baptized Glenn 8 or 9 years later in our home in Golden Ridge at the same time Barbara McRay was baptized. Lyle was baptized in Chilliwack in St Thomas church.

On the 17th day in the Loon Lake hospital, looking out of the hospital window into the cold, I recognized a couple coming into the hospital. I knew the man and I knew the truck. He was David Pollock, a customer of Syd's from the blacksmith shop. I had not met his wife and I do not think I ever spoke to her. Realizing that Pollocks were from Beacon Hill and Pierceland was only about 6 miles further down the road. I waited until after his wife was admitted. Then I approached and asked if he could take me home. It was a trip of approximately 50 miles. He agreed. So, David and I went in a blizzard, in a truck, stopping first at Pollock's farm.

Their farm was about one or two hundred yards off the main road near Beacon Hill. When we arrived, we ate a meal prepared by his children. He asked his two sons to get a team of horses out and to go down the road. David Pollock said that there were two bad snow drifts across the highway between Beacon Hill and Pierceland. His sons and the team of horses were to wait at the first snow bank for us and help pull us through the snow. These were large snow banks, piled high by the blowing wind in the wide, flat, open prairie. The boys would then go to the second bank and pull us through that snow bank. They were to wait there for their dad on the return trip from Pierceland and pull him through that drift on the way home. I will always be thankful Mr Pollock and his family helped me get home. I spoke with Mr Pollock and I again thanked him many years later. I never saw Mrs Pollock again.

I went through the gate and up the 3 or 4 stairs to Mam's house and across the veranda. She was shocked to see me at the front door with David in my arms. Mam nearly had a fit because we travelled after such bad weather. I travelled when I could, rather than waiting longer and perhaps another storm and have no convenient ride home.

Mam was excited to see the new family member. She knew I would use the name David, Walter, because we liked the name David. Walter's mother wanted us to use the name Helen if we had a girl but we decided we would not. Mam insisted I not buy anything for the baby until the baby was born. She said buy only the absolute necessary things and to wait until the baby is home to get the rest. She had good reason to recommend this course of action. She insisted I wait because she had seen too many people buy all kinds of things for the baby only find the baby did not live. New born survival was not as assured then as it is now.

Mam would frequently travel to homes to help women deliver babies. She went to a German family and the baby was born dead. The father asked if she had baptized the baby and she had to explain she had not done so. The father was distressed. She felt badly having to say she did not baptize the dead baby.

On one occasion, I walked with Mom to take a Mrs Lapin to the Pierceland Hospital. Mrs Lapin gave birth to a son and asked me what to name the child. I said how about Leonard Glenn. So, she called her baby Leonard Glenn Lapin. Sometime around my 75th year, I heard Leonard was killed in a car accident when he was about 55.

Below is a letter my Mam wrote to me in the hospital the day before David was born. I got it a few days after David was born but before the blizzard. The handwriting may be difficult to read.

The envelope of the letter shows she posted the letter the day after she wrote it, and on David's birthday. David was by this time a few hours old. I am glad I kept this letter all these years.

Pierceland
Sask

Monday 22 Feb 1943

My Dear Sarah

Just a few lines hope you are getting along fine Mr Sherman and John are going to Good Soil this afternoon, so I am sending a few lines to Walters mother I thought maybe they would be coming that way sometime hope things are allright we shall come down if we get a chance as soon as we can I have been thinking about you ever since you went but I feel it was the best for you to be near the doctor Ruby was down this morning hope to get news soon lot of love to you I wish i was there but try and keep up see you soon from Mother

I know what you are going through but we are all thinking about you

Walter was in Chilliwack. How did he learn of David's birth? He got this telegram. It looks like it came from my Mam, Harriet Baker. She must have given the content to someone who perhaps phoned from Beaver Crossing to Bonnyville. It went to Walter's id, which was L50227, Spr W Serguis. Yes, she did not have the spelling quite right at the time.

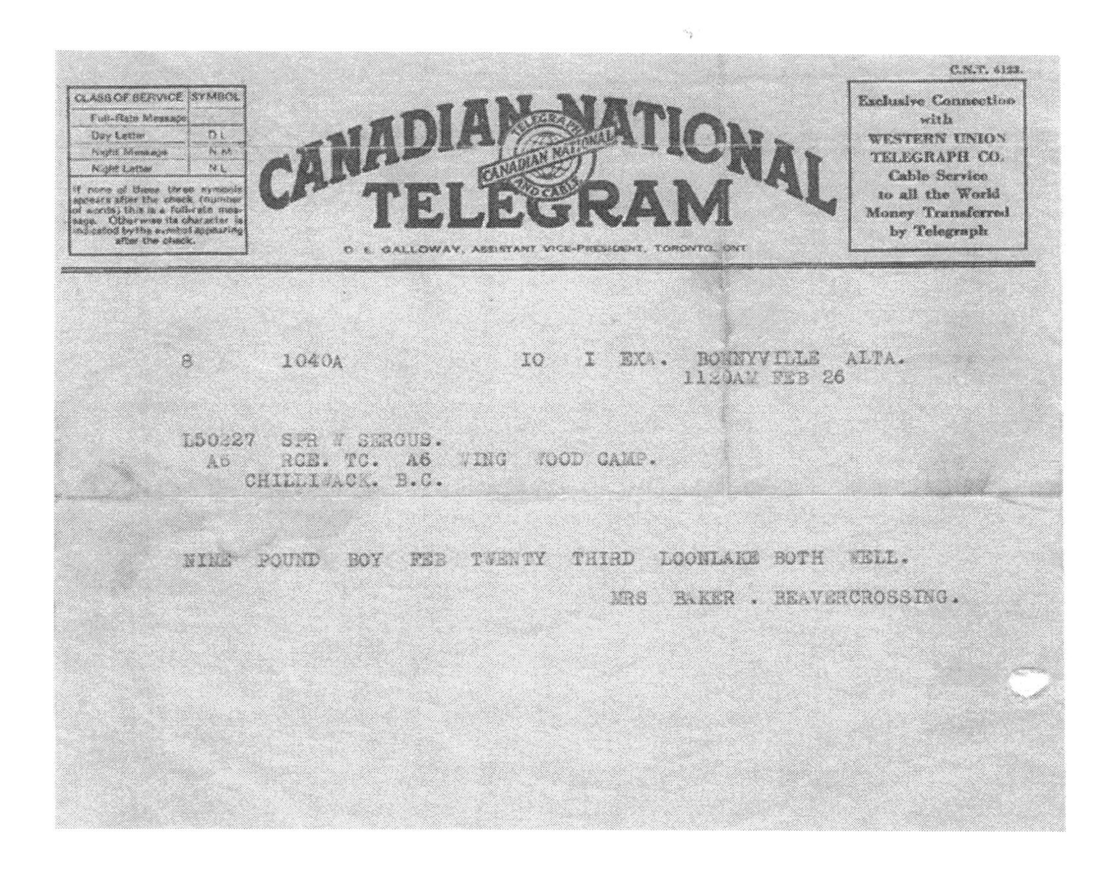

C.N.T. 6123

CLASS OF SERVICE	SYMBOL
Full-Rate Message	
Day Letter	D L
Night Message	N M
Night Letter	N L

If none of these three symbols appears after the check (number of words) this is a full-rate message. Otherwise its character is indicated by the symbol appearing after the check.

CANADIAN NATIONAL TELEGRAM

D. E. GALLOWAY, ASSISTANT VICE-PRESIDENT, TORONTO, ONT.

Exclusive Connection with WESTERN UNION TELEGRAPH CO. Cable Service to all the World Money Transferred by Telegraph

8 1040A IO I EXA. BONNYVILLE ALTA.
1120AM FEB 26

L50227 SPR W SERGUS.
A6 RCE. TC. A6 WING WOOD CAMP.
CHILLIWACK. B.C.

NINE POUND BOY FEB TWENTY THIRD LOONLAKE BOTH WELL.
MRS BAKER . BEAVERCROSSING.

They spelled the last name incorrectly, and the Spr refers Sapper, a term used to describe someone who joins the military. I am not sure why it is this way.

I do not know what it cost to send the telegram. David was a bit more than 9 pounds 3 ounces. The telegraph abbreviates the facts for simplicity. The telegram is addressed to Spr W Sergus. I am not sure why the last name has no letter 'I" but there were so many spellings of the name. When I wrote to Walter, I had to use the abbreviation for or the word "sapper", as he was a soldier, or sapper, in the engineers.

Walter wanted to come home to see David and me. He asked for leave. His request was declined the officer saying that to get travel leave, "It takes a doctor not a husband and father".

Bad weather greeted Walter the first year he was in Chilliwack. I was glad that he was only putting up with bad weather and was not in Europe being shot at and blown up. A whole troop of engineers spent some time cutting, chopping, and delivering fire wood to the Chilliwack citizens because it was so cold and there was so much snow that the town was running out of fuel. Now with global warming such weather there would be very odd. This was before the natural gas pipelines we have today. Wood was the chief heating fuel. Running out of wood to burn became a life threatening situation. The army's concentration shifted. It cut and chopped wood so the residents of Chilliwack did not freeze. So, for a time the army worked all day outside in the cold and then came back to a tent camp. I am sure the residents of Chilliwack appreciated their efforts. I know for sure that Mr and Mrs Kipp of Chilliwack, our future landlords we had not yet met, knew of the army's tent roofs. There was not much of an army camp there at that time, perhaps one or two buildings. The men were busy building bridges.

Like the other soldiers, Walter lived in one of these heated tents at the start of the bridging area camp. I had no idea what life was like in the army. Then I got this picture. My eyes were opened. It was not a nice realization, but not entirely a surprise either to see such primitive living arrangements. There were many others living like this in the northern bush. It was here that the engineers built bridges to be sent overseas. These two pictures of the tent camp each illustrate the primitive conditions for the army at the start of this wartime camp.

The camp is cut out of the trees and snow covers the area which will become muddy as the snow melts.

Below is a steel bridge. Walter's ability to weld was perhaps also a reason he was assigned to this bridge duty. Welders were needed to supply bridges in the construction part of the war effort. This bridge was built in Sardis and shipped overseas.

David had been born and Walter had not seen him. He found a place where I could live not far from the camp. Hazel Scollan, nee Laird, whose husband was overseas, came on the train with her son Garry, and Hazel went on to Vancouver when I got off in Chilliwack. Walter was there to greet us as I carried David. I handed David to Walter, of course, his dad being a stranger, David cried, but only for a few minutes, and then he was fine. We went to a small place on Keith Wilson Road and Mr and Mrs Alec Peters rented their upstairs to us. Walter would come home from the army camp on a bicycle.

Later Hazel wanted to come to Chilliwack. I do not exactly remember why. She had her husband's family in the interior and her mother went up into BC interior where she eventually moved to be with her mother. Hazel and I rented a small cabin near the railway tracks on the west side of Chilliwack. We were pleased to have the
cabin but we had to be careful because Hazel's little son Garry had to be monitored closely. David did not walk until he was a year old so I did not have to worry about him running around until the last few weeks before we moved out of the cabin. Hazel was a good friend to be with and easy to get along with, and we were happy to have the cabin together and we still send each other cards.

People in Chilliwack did not like renting to soldiers or soldier's wives because they felt the soldier would not stay too long, as they would be shipped out. The landlord would have to find new tenants soon. Some landlords also thought that there might be a lot of partying. Hazel and I were pretty pleased to get a place.

Hazel with her son, and David on the left. In the background is the cabin Hazel and I rented. All of us were across the street from the cabin in a nursery lot. I took the picture.

Out behind this cabin after a rain there was a puddle of collected water over the septic tank. I never saw such long earthworms as were on top of this water and I was afraid. I felt like they were 18 inches long. They were long, perhaps not that long, but long. I bought chloride of lime and threw all over these worms so we would not get disease. Of course, everyone laughed about it. I was being silly they thought. Now 70 years later I hear on the news that these worms are not native to the area and there is an effort to get rid of the worms. So, I was ahead of my time in my efforts to get rid of them.

While we lived in this house Walter and his army pal usually rode bicycles home from the camp. On one occasion, they thought it would be a good idea to fasten rain capes together to catch the wind while they were on their bikes. The wind could blow them home. It worked too well. They went down the road but could not control the speed and steering all that well. They ended up off the road in a vegetable field laughing at their folly.

When Hazel went north to the interior of BC, Walter and I wanted to find a new place. Taking David along with us Walter and I walked searching for a new place. Even with David along to show we were a responsible couple, people were just not too interested in renting to soldiers and their families. We did eventually find a place. For a few months, we rented the upstairs suite of a house owned by the Polychucks, a couple I knew from when we lived in the Peter's upstairs. They had sold their farm and moved to town.

Otto and Ruby came to BC. It was great to have them so close. Otto had always talked about going to BC. BC was looked upon as a desirable place to live by most people on the prairies. When they came, my Mam came with them.

Sometime earlier, perhaps 2 years earlier, Ruby and Otto had been to around Frank, BC. They returned to Pierceland with the news of the catastrophe of the Frank slide. During this time that we were apart, I found that Ruby changed in appearance quite a lot as she gained a fair amount of weight, had her haircut shorter, and wore newer clothing. It was good to see her in newer clothing and happy. Even though they had returned they still wanted to live in BC.

When they arrived in Chilliwack Otto got work as a carpenter. He was hired to build two cabins for Frank Kipp. When they were done Ruby and Otto rented one cabin and we rented the other. Granny stayed with Ruby and Otto who had a two bedroom cabin. It was a happy time even though it was war time because we were all family and together. Chilliwack was in what was called the dim out area of the country because of the war. It meant we could not have any bright lights.

The cabins Otto built were stood on a 2 x 6 base, about a foot apart, and were situated on a gentle rise in the property. On one end, there was more space than the other end. David was just learning to walk. One day he crawled under Ruby and Otto's cabin about 5 or 6 feet. He became stuck or stopped, perhaps because he could go no further. We thought we were going to have to dig under the cabin to get him out and were very worried about him, but eventually we all coaxed him out. When he started to move his legs, he realized he could back out. Stuck as he was he never cried. Later the opening was blocked so he did not get any ideas to go there again. It was an intense half hour or so.

David is sitting on a wooden horse wearing a coat someone made for him from another large worn coat, and around his neck is a wool scarf Mam knit for him. He went under to the left of the picture.

Ruby would often take David over to their cabin. She would sit David on the windowsill and teach him to say "Cheamy" as she was teaching him to talk and using what he could see for inspiration. In this case, it was Mt Cheam. Round about this time there was an airplane accident on Mt Cheam. It was a big item in the news of the day. Quite a few people were killed or survived and froze to death. It appeared that some of the victims survived the crash but froze to death as they were sitting upright against rocks.

This picture of David in the metal tub tells a lot about life at that time. He is about 18 months old and in a galvanized tub. They did not make plastic tubs at the time and this tub is quite a lot heavier than a plastic version the same size. The bathrooms were out back and outside. We did not have a bathtub. We also had to use a similar but larger tub to have a bath. To bath David we heated the water on the stove and added it to this tub. This is a lot different from bathing in a warm bathroom with bath toys.

Here Mam is holding David sometime after he was stuck under the cabin. Beside her are the owner Mrs Kipp, and a woman from Montreal whose husband was in the army.

The house is new and not painted. Paint on houses cost money and Frank Kipp and his wife Ida were an elderly couple and this building like many of the day had no paint.

When we would take David out with us when we walked around Chilliwack, he talked to everyone. Everyone got a "Hi Mr." He did not walk early but he sure talked a lot. One day after he learned to walk, he took some of Walter's hand tools to the laneway and began giving them away. I heard him talking to a person and went out to find him talking up a storm
with a stranger holding Walter's tools.

The day President Roosevelt of the US died, I was hanging clothes outside on the line. Mam had the radio on and had heard the news and asked me if I had heard the news. I had not. It was a big event because during the war he was in the news a lot and played a significant role in history.

I am wearing a flowered dress and short socks; such was the fashion at the time. Mam is wearing a nice dress and coat. We had taken Tiny with us for a walk and the picture was taken in front of City hall in Chilliwack. Ruby took the picture and wrote on the back of it "Ma & Sarah". I am in my early 20's. Perhaps some can see a mother daughter similarity.

Walter helped bring this stone from the mountains to Chilliwack where it was made into a monument.

During this time in Chilliwack Walter was notified that he would be shipped out. We usually thought this meant overseas. In Winnipeg, we did not know where he was to be sent. One day Walter came home and told me he was to be transferred or shipped out the next day. We assumed he was to go overseas.

In BC, Mam and I took David along three times to see Walter off thinking he was to go to eastern Canada before heading overseas. We stood on the side of the road and waited to see Walter march by with the other soldiers all parading off to a train. We looked at faces as the soldiers marched by in rows of two or three. We worried as the soldiers went by. No one knew from one day to the next where they would be. Everyone was kept in the dark. When Walter never passed us, we went home and waited gladly for Walter to return.

These, ship out times, rendered us emotionally drained and exhausted. Fearing the worst, expecting the worst, going to say goodbye for perhaps the last time, fearing Walter would go overseas and die life made stressful. Looking frantically from the edge of the road to see his face in the marching troops, not wanting to miss him was a horrible experience. I stood at road side searching, wanting to find his face so that I could see it one more time before he left, and hoping at the same time, that I did not see him. It was pure anguish. Even worse, I hoped that it would not be that he had walked by and I had missed his face. It was a tense time.

Each time Walter came home, we breathed a sigh of relief. We waited in fear for the next episode of men being sent overseas. We were kept wondering. How many times would he be lucky enough not to go? Walter came home each time. We never knew officially why he was not sent overseas. The army said nothing. We were left to our own conclusions.

I never liked the idea that Walter was in the army. I always feared he would die. I remain proud of him that he answered a call for his new adopted country, when so many others never tried.

There were times when Walter was on duty and could not come home each night. So, when Ruby and Otto moved to Derwent, Alberta, because Otto could find work there as a carpenter and Ruby worked as a clerk in a store, Mam stayed with me in Chilliwack until Lyle was born and about a month or 6 weeks old. Then Mam returned to live with Ruby and Otto.

I look now and see that there is far less work with kids than there was in those days. It seems to me that my sons were potty trained a lot sooner than kids these days that are wearing disposable diapers being tossed out and ruining the environment. Without disposable diapers, we had to wash diapers providing a strong motivation for quicker more efficient potty training.

Even though Walter was in the army, we did not necessarily know that the war was ending. We had no inside information. It may have been that others in the country knew the war was about to end, but we did not know that. We understood there was an easing of things and that maybe the war would soon end. We did not know it was imminent.

I was alone and the radio was on when the end of the war was announced. Walter was in camp. If there were any celebrations I never knew about them. Certainly, it was not like in the movies when people rushed into the streets to dance and sing. I was living on the edge of town with two boys and no transportation. I was very happy for sure that this horrible war was done, but still, I had no idea where we were going after the war.

Within a few days of the war's end I took a bus to Derwent staying with Ruby and Otto for a few weeks. Looking after the two boys, I had an active life. I weighed 115 pounds and had painful recurring boils on my arm. Ruby insisted I visit a doctor. The diagnosis was that I was anemic. The prescribed treatment was a bottle of stout every day. Not accustomed to alcohol, I had to drink this horrible tasting stuff in portions throughout the day to avoid being intoxicated and sleeping all day.

Walter and I wanted to settle in Vancouver where he could get work at the end of the war. We talked about it. The army wanted him to stay in the army and to send him to north of Calgary. He declined this option. In the end, we were especially glad he did not accept their request. Many of the men that accepted and went to the Calgary area died of some kind of poison.

The pressure from Walter's family to act and quickly take some desirable land was strong. Actually, his mother did the insistent talking that I heard. His father spoke little. We had to hurry and take it before someone else got it. It was a treasure, a valuable prize. Time was used as a pressure tactic. Our life change from being two single people, to being a married couple with kids made us happy. We were both thrilled to have the kids and a spouse, and to start our lives without the threat of war. With less optimism for the future and a less hurried intense family pressure, our decision would have been different.

These 640 acres with a creek running through the north portion were all very desirable virgin bush land. The family pressure won out. We went to Golden Ridge. We always regretted the decision. I wish I to hell I had never seen the place. In the end, years later, the family got the land and at a sacrifice price they demanded. We sold it to family for less than it was worth. Our feeling was that even the sale of the place was not a happy event. We regretted being manipulated, and felt that by getting rid of the place might getting rid of both a life's albatross and an avenue for more family manipulation.

Golden Ridge: A Folly

Walter was sent to Calgary for demobilization. Demobilization means in this case, discharge from the army as the army is no longer mobilized for war. We went to Derwent, Alberta, to visit Ruby and Otto. Ruby and Otto wanted us to come with them back to Chilliwack. Later we wished we had gone with them.

This picture below shows Otto and Willie clowning for the camera in Chilliwack. Unable to serve in the army, Willie went to work in a sawmill on the Sunshine Coast. He got sick. He ended up in the Chilliwack hospital. This picture was taken when he came out of the hospital and Ruby and Otto had moved to Chilliwack from Derwent Alberta. The same area now is full of buildings.

Soon, Willie left for Saskatchewan to work outside because of his lung problems. Health officials advised that outside work would not stress his lungs as much as working indoors. I am not sure it made any difference.

At the time of his discharge, Walter's family wanted us to go to Golden Ridge. We went to Golden Ridge close to Walter's family. I did not like the idea and farming as it was not what I wanted to do. I did not know where we were going to go and at the time did not speak up strongly. I probably spoke up mildly but I was not a pushy person, and I could have been more assertive. The culture of the day gave few women equal status with men and we held less sway in decision making. Walter and his family wanted us to go to this area, so we went to that small remote community for a few years. It was to be a new way of life and a time of a lot of learning for me.

Walter had applied for a farm from the veteran's department of the federal government. It was something a veteran could do. For many it was good but in our case, it did not work out. It was a disaster.

Golden Ridge was a very small place. It consisted of a single grocery store, a school on the Lang homestead, and a Roman Catholic Church surrounded by farms. We bought a small plot from Mr. Wagman for $10 and gave it back to him when we moved to our farm. On this land from Wagman, Walter, his brothers, and Dad, built a shop and our house. We moved into the house. It was mostly empty.

Our kitchen cupboards were made from wooden fruit boxes we got from the store. Walter's parents had loaned us a bed and for a very cheap price we got an older, used sofa, from Joe Holman. Holman was a good fellow that would come to visit but sometimes stay too long. I would go to bed, but Walter would yawn repeatedly before he left.

One thing I had to learn was how to drive. It was an essential skill in this remoteness. I also learned to drive because I was no longer going to push when we got stuck in the mud.
The roads were not paved and frequently just sloppy muddy ruts. Too many times David and Lyle watched me and laughed as I was covered in mud because I had to push.

Walter was the instructor. My initial driving instructions were simple. I was told here is the crank, a bent piece of metal. I had to use it to get the motor going, being careful not to get my arm broken when the engine started and kicked the crank backwards out of my hands onto my arm. I was shown the locations of the clutch and that of the brake, gas pedal, and steering wheel on Old Mary.

Old Mary was hybrid vehicle made up of an old coupe body of some car, with a truck motor under the hood. There was no trunk. A big wooden box replaced the trunk. The back window was an empty hole. We could call it an early hybrid SUV.

The wooden box was full of 5 gallon pails, some empty and some not, and some bits of junk. With that, I set off with two little boys feeling a combination of trepidation and optimism. There were no seat belts as it was long before the time of seat belts, and we bounced around a fair bit.

As a first time driver, I was concentrating quite hard on the task of going forward and staying on the road. Walter drove behind me with the Allis Chalmers tractor. We were going about two miles down an awful, dry mud, rut filled, road running from his parent's house to our farm. Keeping Old Mary on the road was a major task if you had not driven before. Somehow, you had to stay in the ruts as they wiggled down the road. Though the road went somewhat straight for a bit, but that did not straighten the ruts. One had to be careful the wheels did not jump out of the ruts and throw the vehicle off the road or into a patch of softer mud and become stuck. Down the road were two challenges, first a crude creek bridge and then a corner.

The bridge did not have a sloping grade approach. It was an abrupt change in elevation. It was just there in my path suddenly as if I had never been on the road before. I hit it without slowing down. The pails and wooden box went up and down and so did David and Lyle who were having a great time giggling at this great ride. Then the promised corner came up in front of me. My speed still did not change. I concentrated on staying in the ruts. I could not think about moving my foot off the accelerator and slowing down when I had to concentrate so much on steering. I was concentrating so much on the road ahead using my arms I sort of forgot about my feet being involved. We made it around the corner without leaving the road and I stopped and waited for Walter. I was proud of my achievement of staying on the road.

Walter soon arrived. He asked why I had not slowed for the bridge as a sort of reminder and reasonable question. I had to confess I was too busy concentrating on keeping the car on the road to think about slowing down. He asked about the corner and why had I not slowed down for it. My answer was the same. Had I been a farm girl I might have had some experience driving some kind of animal team, or farm machinery, but I was not, and had no experience driving anything. This was my first driving test and experience and I think I passed but perhaps not with stars.

On the way to Walter's parents' house were two large hills. The trip going to their place was okay, because going up the hills were not as large a climb as the returning trip, because they lived in a lower valley. Driving home required me to learn some auto mechanics. On the return drive, I always had to stop after the first hill. Turn off the engine. Pull the spark plugs out, and scrape off any carbon from their ends. Then restart the engine. Only then would Old Mary have enough power to climb the second hill.

To start farming we bought an Oliver cletrac caterpillar. Walter made a brush cutter to fit on the front of it. Working almost every day in the first year, he cut down about 40 acres of bush land. He pushed the brush into piles on the side of the clearings. He used a breaking plough to plough up the land. A breaking plough is a bit heavier type of plough used to cut into land that is not broken open, but is covered in sod. We had purchased virgin land, never before farmed, covered in trees and grass. Thus, it required preparation.

The next step was to pull out all the roots and pile them up high on the field. Then we lit fire to them and burned them. David about six and Lyle about four would help us pick the roots and pile them up. Looking back, I am amazed that they did such hard work without complaint. We would make a day camp there and stay all day. We lit a fire to boil water and ate there. Lyle would say something like "isn't it about time to have wunch".

Next Walter used a disc. This was a machine with many round circular blades similar in shape to dinner plates. It was dragged across the sod to break it into small bits. Once the soil was in smaller bits, we used the harrows.

The harrow was invented to be a troublesome annoyance to humankind. It is a large square metal frame with many metal fingers used to make the soil finer in texture. I drove the Oliver tractor many hours pulling the harrows. Every few minutes we would have to stop and lift the harrows and take out the piles of sticks that were caught. It became a tedious annoying task.

After we completed the harrowing came the seeding. We pickled the seed. This meant we put blue stone all over the grain. Blue stone was a chemical treatment, a formaldehyde solution, that prevented smut and other diseases from affecting the seeds and young plants. The stuff had a funny smell to it. Walter and I spread the blue stone all over the grain. Working with this stuff gave me an allergic reaction of itchy hives. I got them on my arms and the small of my back where my shirt had come up out of my pants. It was misery.

Walter would fill a five gallon bucket with grain. It now weighed about 35 pounds. Walter handed it up to me as I stood in the wagon box. I would lift it up and then dump it in the box. From here, we took the wagon to the field and we filled the seeder. This type of work soon built my muscles.

The first time I planted seed Walter had to show me how to do it. He showed me how to align the seeder and the tractor and to leave no space between the paths of the seeder. While I did this, Walter ploughed another field using an Allis Chalmers tractor. David would be in school most of the time and Lyle would sometimes stay with Grandma Sergius. Later when Glenn was around and a baby, David and Lyle would look after him. They had a stick or piece of wood to put up to signal us that they needed us to come, and this way we kept an eye on them. When we would get to the end of the field near them, they would tell us about whatever was the problem. They spent the day playing. We were not bothered by wild animals such as bears, coyotes, and wolves. I never saw a bear all the time I was ploughing and seeding. Perhaps the noise kept them away. When the seeding was done, my work changed. I stayed at home, tended the garden, and did farm chores.

Some months later Walter got a half ton, Dodge, truck, that he called the Cement Mixer. In the cold weather the Cement Mixer would not start. Walter would place ash and glowing embers from the kitchen stove under the engine to heat it up. He also got a used car that was a semi automatic Oldsmobile. I drove this to Golden Ridge along the main road and sometimes met the RCMP.

During the summer months, Walter would work on the farm, and if he had any spare time, he travelled to Goodsoil to work in Greshner's Garage. It was there that Walter did service work on the local RCMP patrol car. One day the police commented to Walter that he thought it would be a good idea if he quit illegally burning purple colored farm gas in his car and that his wife got a driver's license. We did neither. A few months later we moved out of the area.

We could not afford to pay the higher price of plain uncolored auto gas. It was a choice of burning colored gasoline or no gasoline. Now thinking about the situation, it was an unfair set up. With the millions of dollars, the oil companies made on gas, they could easily have sold all the gas at a farm price. The lower price for farm equipment gasoline was an obvious sign they were gouging on auto gasoline prices.

I began my closer relations with farm animals when Walter's parents gave us a cow for one summer. She was pastured in a vacant bit of grassland across the road from us. Walter's mother had taught me how to milk a cow. This was a skill all farm women needed to know. When we moved to the farm later, we gave this cow back to his parents and got another one. We called the new cow Nancy.

About the same time my mother gave me her Singer Pedal Sewing machine. It was what she used to sew my diapers. She showed me how to run the machine. When I was first using it, I put the needle through my finger. Mam and Willie pulled the needle out. The pain and shock did not deter me from sewing with this machine. I used it for years before I bought an electric version.

During this farm time, Mam sent me a parcel of something she had made for my birthday. Along with it was this note from her. She signs it "Mam". One can see from the writing that blindness was approaching because of diabetes.

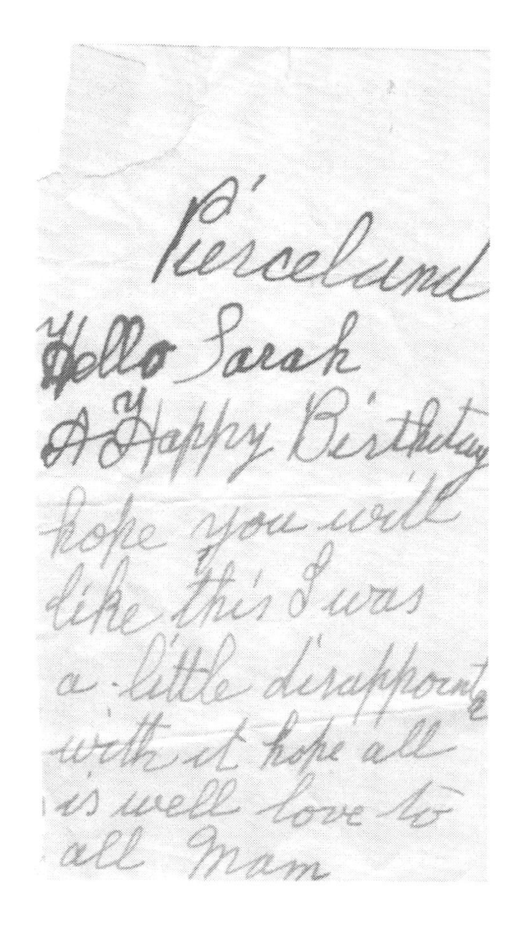

Pierceland
Hello Sarah
A Happy Birthday
hope you will
like this I was
a little disappointe
with it hope all
is well love to
all Mam

We found out Mam had diabetes in an indirect way. She went to an eye doctor in Meadow Lake who told us she needed to be taken to a family practitioner. The eye doctor told us Mam had diabetes. The family doctor sent her to a hospital for a few days to learn about diabetes.

Sometime later she fell and passed out while with Syd and Betty. I was in Lac La Ronge. Mam went to the Goodsoil hospital, a place where there were sometimes doctors but not always good ones.

Pierceland also had a hospital with questionable doctors. Two of the doctors who worked in the hospital years apart ended up being drug addicts. One was a doctor Rice. I wonder if it is a symptom of being too close to supplies, combined with being tense and depressed due to small town rural isolation.

My Mam had shown me how to knit. She never had a book to learn. She knew how to do it, but I do not know how she learned. She showed me how to knit socks. She used three needles and knit with a 4th and she showed me how to turn the heel. I was just getting the knack of this when a good hearted neighbor lady Mrs. Bunshow came and told me I had it all wrong because I needed 5 needles not 3 needles

I became confused. The sock I then made was significantly too big around. I had to undo the sock. I waited until Mam returned and again showed me how to knit.

I still have the navy blue socks I knit. They were the first and only ones I ever knit. They are pictured on my kitchen table in 2015.

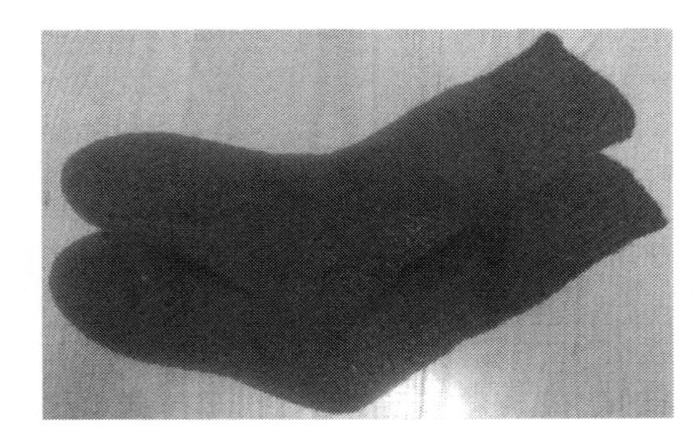

I soon got a book and knit Glenn a green Cowichan sweater with a white rabbit on the back. I knit sweaters, toques, dresses and vests later but not socks.

In a box of stuff that came up from a church in the city was a crochet hook. Granny showed me how to make a chain with the crochet hook. Using her size # 10 sewing thread, I learned how to add a border to some square doilies. I still have my first works.

I learned how to crochet baskets that were stretched out and over a jar, likely a pickling jar, and starched into standing shape with sugar starch. I sold them for about $5 a piece. It was a popular type of decoration at the time. With the basket sales I was able to help supplement our income.

Ruby showed me how to embroider when I was about 10 or 11. Before David was born I began to embroider a runner for a table in 1942. It turned out to be a long lasting project. I did more work on it when I waited for Lyle to be born, and just before Glenn was born, I finished it. I finally put the border on it when Glenn was about three. I still use it today in the dining room.

I remember Ruby came to visit one winter day around this time when there was snow on the ground. The cook stove was used to both heat the house and for cooking. The bare stove pipes went straight through the ceiling, through the attic, and then through the roof. It was a necessary and temporary situation but not a good situation. We always monitored these pipes. Still, while Ruby was there they caught fire. Busy cooking and visiting we were unaware of the fire. People in the store across the road saw the flames shooting out of the stove pipes and came to warn us.

We put out the fire in the stove. Still the pipes burned inside. I climbed into the attic to investigate. It was dangerous but I had to do it. We needed to cool the pipes down or they would set fire to the whole house. Ruby and David brought snow. Handing it to me, they waited while I pressed this to the pipes to cool them down initially. Then I helped David climb up and we both held snowballs to the pipes to cool them down. I still shudder when thinking of this situation. Later we built a brick chimney to surround the pipes but still the stove pipes needed to be cleaned to prevent fires.

We lived here in this house from the fall of 1945 to 1952 as it was later moved to the farm.

While in Golden Ridge there were few opportunities to make friends but we did make some. George and Francis Imhoff's family and store were across the street and we were friends with them. George Imhoff's father had an art studio between Meadow Lake and Saskatoon. Walter and I visited this studio later in the 1990's. The Dirks were also Roman Catholic and friends. We made it a point not talk religion because at this time it was very contentious. Walter had known these people for years but they were new to me. I had to learn their ways and they became good friends.

Lyle is about two in these pictures taken in Grandma Sergius's front garden. He had curly blonde hair. He could walk when he was not quite 8 months old. Georgette Imhoff was too young to be allowed to cross the road alone. She would stand on the other side of the road and call out, "Lalee, come over and play". I would have to go out and take Lyle across the road so they could play. They were a cute couple of young friends.

After moving from town to the farm our closest neighbors were Frank and Sis Zerr. The name Sis stood for Sarah. Their house was about ½ mile away and we visited back and forth. We were glad never to talk religion with them and they were not too bothered by the topic either. I never heard of them getting involved with either side. On one side, our neighbors were Jehovah's Witnesses and on the other side were Roman Catholics. In this time and location religion made a huge difference in society. Friendships and loyalties were frequently made and ruined along religious lines. Religion was a reason to discriminate. It is not like that now so much but in those days, it was significant. We did not go to church. There was no protestant church to attend. Perhaps we were thus looked upon as being possible converts to either side. Walter was not interested in the Roman Catholic Church. We were the dividing line and I was not going to raise my family in either camp.

When David first started school in Golden Ridge, his teacher was Evangeline La Pin. David walked across the road and down a bit to get to school. Even though he could not tell time, Lyle would somehow know that David was about to come home from school. Lyle would cross the road and sit on a fence post and wait for David to come home. I wish I had a picture of Lyle doing this.

This 1951 picture is taken in our yard at Golden Ridge. It is taken at time of a financial challenge that we were working hard to beat. Life for me was busy with three boys. The kids from the left, Lyle, Glenn on David's knee, and Gary Sager are sitting on a merry-go-round wheel that Walter had set up for the kids.

The first building is Walter's shop. The building let everyone have a good chuckle as it fell apart in the middle of the road when moved from this location to the farm. In the distance is the school with two windows. A bit behind the wheel was a fence and it is on this fence that Lyle used to sit and wait for David to come from school. In these days if I bought a chocolate bar at the store and divided it among the kids it was an expensive treat. I was only able to do it a few times.

This 1947 picture shows our house in Golden Ridge. There is no siding on the house. The boards are randomly placed to hold the tarpaper down. The windows facing are the living room windows. You can see the window frame and the good size of the window slats that were broken in the tornado a few years later. That is the back of the house. In the distance our clothesline is visible with the pegs still on the line. There is a prop holding up the line in the middle of the grass. In the back and center of the picture is a white post where Minnie used to tie up her horses when she came for a visit. It looks like the kids found the mud a great place to play. In the picture from the left is Valerain Imhoff, her sister Georgette, at the back is Jimmy Imhoff, in front of him is Lyle and David is sitting down. I took the picture when they were playing happily in the mud. Tony Wagman was a neighbor in Golden Ridge. He was about 18 or 20 years of age and brought with his guitar on visits. We would have a jam session with me playing the accordion and Walter played the harmonica. All three of us played music by ear and we had a lot of fun playing whatever song came to our mind. Tony's mother would come from the left of the picture for tea a couple of times a week. She and my mother in law both made cabbage rolls but Mrs Wagman's were large and Johanna's were small. They would tease each other about how theirs were better based upon size. These tea visits with Mrs Wagman would sadly end when we moved from town to the farm. They became remembered socializing in my times of loneliness on an isolated bush surrounded farm.

The road was in front of the house and on the other side of a ditch. The yard was a safe place for kids to play away from the road. It was the main road from Pierceland to Meadow Lake but it was nowhere near as busy as roads are today. One morning I was surprised by a knock on the door. Chuck Forbes from Pierceland was standing there holding a letter. He handed me the letter, turned, jumped over the ditch and scrambled into his waiting truck in the middle of the road, and was gone in no time. That letter is how I found out my brother Willie had died the day before. I never kept the letter. I guess Chuck knew the content of the letter and did not want to hang around for any emotional upset. I had been to visit Willie for a few days, perhaps a week or two, before he died. John, my brother in law, was going to Loon Lake and Walter asked him to take me along so I could visit Willie.

During this last visit, I noted Willie's face was white, and that his dark brown hair had a wave in it. He was sitting up in bed. I asked him how he was doing and he said that soon they would be giving him medicine made of wood. I was young and just did not believe that it would be possible, that my brother also young, would die. When I got the letter, I was shocked. I sat down and had good cry.

We arranged to go to Pierceland. We stayed in Willie's house in bunk beds. The minister from Loon Lake came and conducted the service. Willie was the first one buried in the Pierceland cemetery. He was 29 and died the last day of September, 26 days before his birthday October 25. He was buried October 3. Mam was broken, but quietly carried her sadness in her heart. She had now lost two of her children and her husband was gone.

Dorothy, Willie's wife, was upset and took a while to decide what she would do with her life. Eldon stayed with us for a month and we offered to adopt him, but Dorothy decided to take him with her when she moved to Calgary.

The receipt below shows we shopped at Imhoff's store. The spelling in the receipt is interesting. On this visit, I purchased some cookies, spelled perhaps cochies for 25¢, bars for 16¢, cigarettes spelled cigeritts for 35¢, with a 1 cent tax, and the total was 77¢.

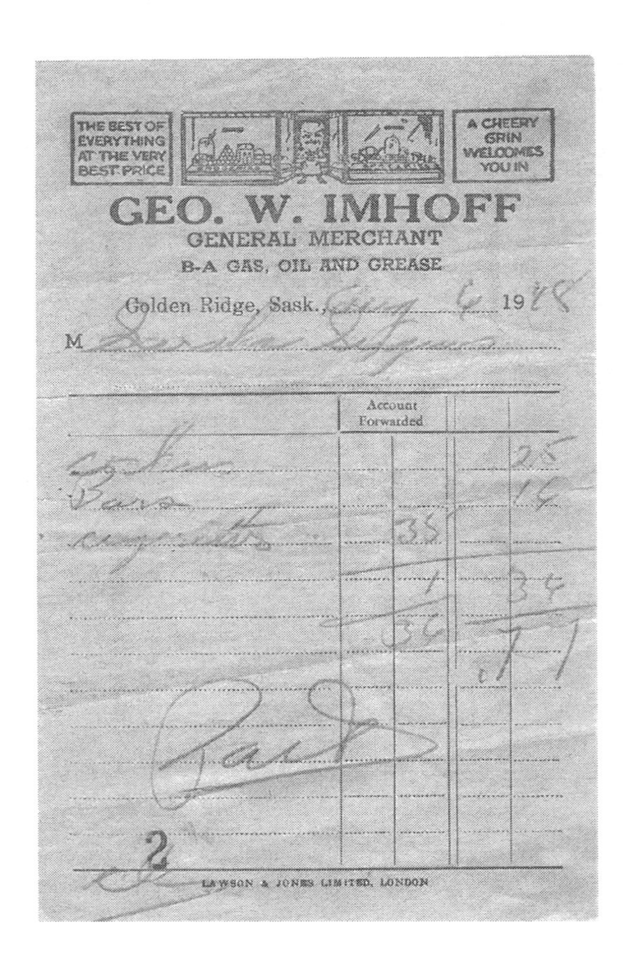
THE BEST OF EVERYTHING AT THE VERY BEST PRICE

A CHEERY GRIN WELCOMES YOU IN

GEO. W. IMHOFF
GENERAL MERCHANT
B-A GAS, OIL AND GREASE

Golden Ridge, Sask., ... 19....

M ....

Account Forwarded

Bars

Paid

2

LAWSON & JONES LIMITED, LONDON

Unlike Lyle visiting Georgette, I did not have to cross the road to visit my friend Margaret. She was about a kilometer away. The first time I went to Margaret McRae's house we decided to make rhubarb upside down cake dessert. There was a lot of fresh rhubarb looking very nice. We got it all sugared up, put in a pot, and put in the oven of her wood fired stove. Taking it out of the pan, we learned a lesson we had not known. The acid of rhubarb reacts well with aluminum. It caused the pan to go dark and we had to throw out the dessert.

Margaret McRae was a war bride and an only child. She met her husband Archie when he was in England and it was there
they got married. She had lived with her mother in England and was a bit older than I was. I remember at the time thinking that it was nice to have her around, but that I would not have made the same decision she had made to come to Canada, but that was perhaps because I saw what she could not have seen before she arrived.

She came from the urban life style of Leeds, England, to the more primitive life style of the hard working McRae family who were farmers in the remote, uncivilized bush. She came from a town with electricity and indoor toilets to outhouses and no electricity and frigid weather unknown in England. It had to be a terrific adjustment to a harder life. Four McRae brothers farmed together, Ken the youngest brother, Archie, Hugh and the oldest Orie. Ken and Walter travelled together from Regina by train that December 1941 to get married. Ken got off just before Meadow Lake because his bride lived south of Meadow Lake. Walter got off in Meadow Lake and walked to his dad's farm in Golden Ridge overnight in the cold and snow. Ken and his wife got married the day before we did.

Margaret is pictured with a full baby carriage. Her daughter Barbara is on the left, and Glenn on the right. This carriage was used for all three of my sons. Looking at the picture of the kids in the baby buggy I am reminded of an incident that happened a few years before this picture was taken.

I was pushing Lyle who was lying in the carriage and David was sitting on the front. I was in a grocery store in Chilliwack and had groceries piled around Lyle to take home. I remember a woman being very snarky and asking me if I were trying to smother that kid. I was not, but had to have a way to take the groceries home. I was more careful with what I did after that. Margaret's mother planned to come to Canada from England. She died just before she was to leave for Canada. Margaret was very upset, and very shocked. Margaret was a very gentle person. Margaret had three girls, Barbara, Cheryl, and June, and two boys Neil and one other. I never met the boys. I am the godmother to Barbara and Cheryl and Walter was their godfather. The girls were christened in their house. Margaret and Archie were Glenn's godparents when he was christened in our house. Margaret and Archie were very good friends.

Orie McRae, Margaret's brother in law, was involved in the Farmers Union, and as a result, since we were farmers, Walter joined the Farmers Union. Dorothy McRae, Orie's wife and I both took baking to a meeting. I knew Dorothy as a hard worker and a good cook and I was happy to sample her baking. Dorothy brought something with dates. I ate some of it. It was delicious, but not being used to rich foods, I was sick as a dog from it. I did not eat dates for years.

In the background of the above picture, the Studebaker truck belonged to Walter's dad. Walter's shop can be seen on the right, the building with the tall square facade. In the far distance is the Dirk's house. Walter had known the Dirks all the time he had lived in the area. Their son Jack was a friend to Walter and Jack visited our place. Jack might have been a farmer I am not sure. I remember he was tall and skinny and used to come to visit regularly. Lena Dirk, Jack's sister married and became the wife of Joe Holman. Joe was the nice fellow that was a night hawk. When Joe came to visit, I would obviously wind the clock and go to bed. Walter would be yawning but it would be midnight before Joe went home.

I remember the day Mrs Dirk died. I was so upset. I knew few people there at that time and losing Willie and Mrs Dirk was upsetting. Mrs Dirk would occasionally come in for tea. It was right at Easter. It was about seven in the evening. The sun was shining across the fields almost setting and shinning on their house. An eerie light shone on their house. She had died. I felt a bit more isolated with the death of Mrs Dirk.

David and Lyle started school while we lived in Golden Ridge. It was a trial for both the boys and us as parents. David and Lyle were the only two students in the school that were not Roman Catholic. David and Lyle had a hard time in school because of that as it proved to be a significant social handicap. The teachers and sitters were a bit mean and discriminatory. Mrs Chilliack was the sitter. She was not a proper teacher and was mean to David. She told David to loan his text book to a fellow student. The next day she gave the kids a test on the subject.

On another day, she had David and Lyle stand up in class, and told all the kids that these are the only two in the school that are not Roman Catholic. She told David not to sing because he had a voice like a horse and face like one too. I forgive her, but still after all these years I think how mean it was then, and that I would now probably react more assertively.

Lyle was a bit nervous at the start of school. One of his first days at school, Lyle drew a picture of something that was not as instructed. When she asked him, Lyle could only reply that the reason he drew it was "just because". So, he got strapped. After the second such incident, Walter went to the school and had a personal discussion and it never happened again.

About 10 years later after having moved from this area, we stopped in a restaurant in Peerless, Saskatchewan. Mrs Chilliack was running the restaurant. What a surprise! We were sitting around the horseshoe counter. She asked Glenn a question to which his response was "just because". Though we just about broke out in laughter we said nothing, and neither did she.

A few years later Chilliack and our paths crossed again. I had the three boys with me. I went into a drug store in Meadow Lake. The boys were all dressed neatly, nice, and clean. The boys went up to the counter and to their instant surprise, there she was behind the counter. David and Lyle made a special effort to say whom they were, be nice, and say hello. She looked shocked that they spoke to her and perhaps surprised that students would remember her. The boys still did not like her.

Chilliack was the reason we took the boys out of this school about the same time we moved to the farm from town. We did not think she was an appropriate influence on the boys and we wanted better. Her attitude aptly represented quite a few in the community, so she was not an isolated personality.

David and Lyle then went to Northern Beauty School. Our neighbor Sis was the schoolteacher at Northern Beauty and taught David and Lyle. Early in the morning Sis and Frank would drive Sis to work and leave their daughter Eunice at our house for an hour or so while Frank was gone driving the boys and Sis to school. Sometimes the boys rode in a wooden box attached to the back of the tractor. It was an open box and could hold a couple of kids. Many people built such attachments for tractors in those days. People would sometimes come to Golden Ridge to the store or the post office and there would be people sitting in the box. It was cheaper to use a tractor to get around because farm purple colored gasoline was cheaper for farm vehicles than regular gas for road worthy cars and trucks. In the wintertime, it might have been very cold. A normal winter temperature would be -20.

A school bus began to go past our place on the farm. The school bus stopped about a quarter of a mile from our house. The bus driver was a tall man. The kids nicknamed him Gandershanks. We thought it was a good idea that the boys went to a larger school. Thus, the boys changed schools and went to Goodsoil School. It was the last year that we were on the farm so the change did not last long. At Goodsoil School, Roman Catholic nuns were the teachers. I thought this school was a big improvement because the two boys would be exposed to more people. Lyle's teacher was Sister Henrietta but I cannot remember the name of David's teacher. I did not worry about them in this school. However, recently Lyle told me that his teacher at this school was rather mean also. I never knew at the time as the boys never complained. Now it gives me another reason to be glad we left the farm.

Here are my Mam and Ruby with David, Lyle, and Gary Sager in front of our house on the farm before we had the siding put on. It looks a mess. The picture allows you to study details of rural life at the time. On the ground under the water pail hanging on the side of the house, is a rectangular galvanized metal container with rounded ends. This is a boiler. Using a wood stove, I would heat water in this container. There were no running water taps. All the water had to be carried from the well and lifted into place and the water pails were heavy when full. Carrying water can be hard work. Many people now would not believe the amount of hard work wash days presented. Those with bigger families had more wash days. Everyone had permanent lines strung up in the back yard. Some extra lines were taken down after use.

Wash day was usually Monday and ironing day was Tuesday. Wash days were one of the hardest work days of the week. In the summer, we got water from the well and carried it about 100 feet to the stove to heat. This well water would leave a lime deposit in the water kettles. In our area, all the water was hard water with natural minerals. It was good for drinking, if you were used to it, but it was not good for washing clothing because it made the soap curdle. This reduced the efficiency of washing.

Winter made extra wash day work. We used melted snow. A washtub full of snow will melt to be only about a quarter the volume as a liquid. We would have to carry in more snow until we had enough water. The water would be heated almost to the boiling point. The house windows would steam up and then develop a thick layer of frost.

One had to be careful to sort the wash. Delicate, light colored and less soiled items were washed in different batches. These items could not be washed in the same water as other clothing. Always the least soiled items would be washed first. Sometimes sheets were the first washed, as they were not as likely to be as soiled as pants and shirts. Anything wool was separated and could not go into hot water because it would shrink.

The washtub would be placed on a couple of kitchen chairs. I would use a kitchen knife to cut bar P&G bar soap into the water. The soap bar was about 8 inches long and a bit over an inch thick. I would leave the bar on the surface of the washboard near the top because though there was soap in the water that would not be enough to do a proper wash. When the clothes went in the water I started rubbing them on the board, using the bar of soap to rub into the clothing on any obviously dirty spots. After this rubbing, I would swish them around in the water, ring them out by hand, and then put the items into a cold water rinse. I would swish them around in this rinse to get the rest of the soap out. Then I would wring them out by hand again, and put them in a pan that held them until I was ready to hang them up to dry.

Using a plunger, a stick with a metal cone on the end, I would plunge up and down in the water to move the hand towels, dish towels, face cloths, dish cloths around until one could see that they were clean. This would take approximately three to five minutes or more per item.

Then the boiler would be moved over to the edge of the stove where it was not so hot. It was called a boiler but that did not mean we boiled everything in it. It meant it was a container for hotter water than in a tub and could be boiled. Stained towels were items that were sometimes boiled with soap. Tea and towels and face cloths that needed this hot water would be put in and the water brought to boiling temperature but not left to boil. Using a 2 foot long stick, that would become bleached white from being in the hot water so many times, we fished the items out of the boiler and let them drip back into the boiler. Then the hot washed items were put into a basin and then into a washtub where they would have cold water poured on them to rinse out any soap and dirt. Clothing, and sheets made from sugar and flour bags were washed in water as hot as my hands could stand. Delicate materials got warm water hand wash and woolens a cool or lukewarm washing to prevent shrinkage. Next clothing was wrung out by hand, and hung on the line in all types of weather, warm, and in the freezing, bone chilling, hand chaffing, windblown, cold.

Some times to the last rinse, we added cubes of blueing that would dissolve in the water. Blueing helped the whitening process. Later liquid bluing arrived and one would add just a little to the water. Too much bluing would add a bluish tint to the washing. Each load of clothing was rinsed twice then hung out to freeze dry.

I used a light starch for, dresses, blouses, light shirts, ironed and folded them or hung them on hangers to be put away. Anything I thought would look better with a little starch got this treatment. The starch was added in a final dip into a light starch solution. Then each item was hand wrung very dry and given a little shake before being hung to dry

Rinso was a new soap that came out and it worked better in hard water. Tide came out around the same time but Rinso was the first soap for hard water that I used. I remember advertisements on the radio for Rinso and they were the reason I bought it. It was a great improvement.

Always, washing was hung to dry outside. The clothes line had to be strung in an out of the way location, or for sure someone would need to walk through the drying clothing. In the winter, we sometimes hung them outside to freeze on the line overnight. The next day we brought them inside to complete the drying. After being outside they dried faster than if they had not been hung outside. We hung clothing where we could; stringing lines all over the kitchen, steaming up the windows and freezing in ice sheets.

Fresh frozen clothing has a wonderful smell of cleanliness that is much like that of clothing dried on any line outside but it is more intense. It is a wonderful smell. In the winter one had to be careful bringing in frozen clothing such as long underwear, because the clothing would be frozen stiff like statues. It would be easy to break off a brittle arm or a leg.

This would take a few hours over the course of the day. This is compared to today when we throw them into a machine and do something else while the machine does the work. We used to iron the dish towels, sheets, pillow cases, and almost everything. We never ironed underwear and socks but my mother ironed her stockings. Ironing became an art. Perhaps I am now less artistic now as I see it as work. All this work sounds ridiculous, but it was mostly necessary. Materials that are more rugged were common and used to make clothing. None of the clothing materials were wrinkle free. Nearly everything washed and worn had to be ironed to remove the wrinkles and at the time I liked ironing. Ironing and I no longer have a great affinity. I do not have to do that now. It was like a gift from heaven when wash and "drip dry" items came out. The new fabrics are superb.

After washing and drying the clothes were badly wrinkled. They did not dry flat. Getting flat wearable clothing required them be ironed flat. Ironing all sorts of things is a skill where one needs to appreciate the form and function of each article and how it will look and wear best. Multiple sizes and shapes came clean but differently wrinkled from the clothes line. They need to be dampened and rolled up in a towel for a few hours and sometimes over night to make it easier to iron them flat using primitive irons.

Necessarily, one had to keep a bit of wax paper or salt close at hand to rub the irons on, removing built up starch that would make ironing difficult. The result of the process using starch and ironing was beautiful even if it was a lot of work.

Flat irons were heated on the hot stove surface. Each flat iron is like the bottom of a modern iron minus the handle. A handle was clipped onto each hot iron that was used until the iron cooled too much to be used a time span that varied from about 5 to 10 minutes. Using the handle a new hot iron would be clipped into place while the cold iron was placed on the stove to reheat.

Some things needed to be dry-cleaned only and we avoided buying these articles, as dry cleaning with chemicals was expensive and not always available. I know that some people tried to clean clothing with gasoline. Most people would hang clothing on outside lines to deodorize them especially because deodorant was expensive. This necessitated washing some clothing after each wearing.

In the summer time like everyone else, I would try to catch rain water for clothes washing and to wash our hair in. Rain water is soft water. If it was even just a little light rain, one could see people rush out to put a pot under the eaves to catch the rain water. Still we never had enough rain water.

On our hair, we used a Camay or Lifebuoy bar of hand soap. Many times, we had to brush our teeth with this soap, and sometimes we used baking soda for tooth paste. Baking soda was much better tasting than the soap. When I was in the Girl Guides in Pierceland, and went camping, we would use the soot on the bottom of the campfire kettle. It sound awful but this black soot actually really makes your teeth white rather than black.

This picture was likely taken in the spring because Gary is wearing a parka but the screen door is braced open. It must have been cool enough for the child to be dressed warmly but not in winter boots and it is not so hot as to have flies around allowing the wooden screen door to be open.

Gary Sager is playing with Walter's pipe in the picture below, but there is more to the picture that comes to my mind than that. We can see more things about life in this era. The picture indicates some elements of the everyday life of poor people and the work of a farm woman. A tough and rough life is indicated.

Just over Gary's shoulder is a spoked pulley wheel. The metal wheel is part of the mechanism that powered the washing machine that sits on the back of the platform. This is the wooden hand powered washing machine that Walter found for me to replace the scrub board. It is the round barrel like thing on the end of the porch with metal bands encircling it. Though made of wood it did not leak. The machine was like a washboard all around the inside because it had protruding vertical wooden slats. In the center were wooden agitator paddles to make clothing go back in forth inside the wooden tub brushing past the scrub board outer wall. A handle on the outside was turned to move the agitator on the inside.

Using the metal boiler seen here on the ground I heated water on the wood stove. I carried the hot water a pail at a time from inside the house to the washing machine outside. I added the soap to the machine and turned the handle. Depending upon the soiled clothing inside the machine I would turn the handle about 15 or 20 minutes. This was good muscle building exercise.

These machines came with a larger cumbersome metal wringer mechanism that can be seen in this picture. This whole apparatus was moveable but heavy and awkward. My metal pail used to transfer water from the boiler to the washing machine is hung on top. The wringer was two rubberized rollers through which one put the wet clothing to press out the water. The pressure was constant but the space between the rollers was adjusted using a large and tall butterfly shaped flat handle. In the picture looks somewhat like a weather vane. Space adjustments could be customized to best fit the clothing. Rougher garments needed more space between the rubber rollers than perhaps table cloths and sheets. The wringer mechanism swiveled allowing the user to wring clothing as it came from the machine tub and allowing the now less wet wash fall into a rinse bucket. Swiveling the wringer allowed the user to wring clothing after as it came out of the rinse bucket before it was hung to dry.

Walter modernized the washing process by installing a machine driven pulley system attaching it to the agitator gears. A long pulley belt ran from the idling caterpillar to the machine about 10 to 12 feet away. This great improvement made it easier on my arms back, and allowed me to do other work as the machine worked and made wash day move faster.

There were drawbacks associated with this system. First the caterpillar had to be moved into position, started and left to idle. It made a lot of noise and burned gas. The pulley belts were dangerous because they were not enclosed and moved fast. The belt was joined by metal teeth to make a complete circle. Anything touching the belt would be destroyed. Pulley belts were common on farm equipment in those days and were a constant danger. I had to make sure the boys did not touch the belt and stayed well away.
The fast moving belt, under tension could break and fly around in pieces hurting someone. Touching the belt could easily rip the hand open as the metal joining teeth flew past. I warned the boys all the time to stay away and not touch the belt. Still one wash night I found David's wool mittens had the palm missing as he had touched the belt but luckily not had his hand ripped open.

With the new power of the pulley system the wringers worked fast, but the new power was dangerous. The pull release that allowed the wringer to be repositioned sometimes popped out with the new power. The wringer would swing unpredictably and hit anything it its way and that hurt. The wringer would sometimes pop out while one was passing clothing through. This happened when Ruby and I were doing a load of washing. The wringer popped out of place. Ruby thinking it was going to hit me, and me trying to avoid being hit worked at cross purposes. I ended up with my finger stuck in the wringer. It hurt, but I was able to pull it back out. It is this finger that is now crooked and arthritic. Women with long hair bending over these washing machines to put things through the wringer had to be especially careful. Still one heard stories of women getting their hair caught in the ringers. I was always careful around this machine. When we moved to the farm I used tubs again for a while and had no machine.

A great day was the day Walter came home with a gas powered Thor washing machine. We had talked about getting such a machine but Walter saw it in town and bought it. It was a complete surprise when he brought it home. Washing clothes would be forever changed and easier, but still when compared to today it was a time consuming hard labor antiquated task. The new Thor machine made the washing and ringing easier, but since it was gas powered it had two problems. First, it made a lot of noise, and second it had a large exhaust pipe that had to be connected and the end placed through the door outside. You would add water to the tub of the machine along with soap, and let them wash. I would stop the wash cycle with a gearshift and put the clothes through the wringer into a metal rinse tub on a stand, and swish them around with a washing stick. Then I had to swing the ringer around on the machine and put the clothes through the wringer again and hang them on the line.

The wringer apparatus was smaller but still a dangerous apparatus. It was powerful and pulled clothing through two rollers. Subsequently Another good day after we moved to Lac La Ronge was the day Walter changed the motor on the washing machine from gas a motor to an electric motor. This meant less noise and no more exhaust pipe. I was pleased. There were no indoor sewer drain holes for the washing machine. To drain the water from the washing machine, one let the rubber drain hose down into a bucket until the bucket was full. The water was taken outside and dumped. To fill the tub with hot water I heated it in an oblong wash boiler on the wood stove and poured it into the washing machine. Still to dry the clothes, an outside line was strung across the yard, and braced up with a stick. In the summer, they dried, and in the winter, they froze and had to come into the house to thaw and finish drying. I had lines up in the kitchen and the bathroom. I would hook the lines up and take them down when not being used. Clothes dried fast after being frozen and always smelled so good. In this town, one could leave clothes on the line overnight and no one took them. So, when clothing froze on the line they were sometimes left there for a few days and they would completely dry and soften a bit. In the 60's in Winnipeg when we were a family with three boys, life was a bit different because we had a whole line of towels stolen from the wash line.

On the platform in front of the open screen door is a metal coal oil or kerosene tin with a spout. Kerosene was the fuel for the lamps that always needed careful tending. If the wick of these lamps was turned up too high, the fire burned black smoke and blackened the delicate and easily broken glass chimney. A black chimney cannot give out light. The chimney had to be cold to be cleaned. The wick had to be carefully trimmed evenly without one end or edge higher than the other edge. One had to check to make sure there was enough fuel in the lamps and that they were ready to use in the evening. Kerosene smelled as it burned. The smell filled the house.

Some lamps had thumb handles so they could be carried from room to room. Other lamps could be placed upon a metal stand attached to the wall and used to light the whole room. We never had either of these we only had the table lamp style. We did have a beautiful Aladdin kerosene mantle lamp that gave a much nicer softer light for reading. It had a tall elegant chimney about 18 inches tall.

Looking at the picture one can see that my metal wash boiler is outside the house on the ground. There was no room to store it inside and it usually sat on the platform or deck as we call it today.

One day I was with Walter's mother while she was using just such a boiler washing towels. She wrung them out and dropped them into a large pan beside a wood fuel box adjacent the cook stove. I was working in the kitchen while she did this. She left them there for a few minutes, maybe to have a rest. She returned to the basin and dumped the basin of towels into the boiler. She plunged it a few times and noticed some odd dark bits. A few more plunges and she could see that there were now the remains of a boiled mouse all through the towels. Everything was covered in bits of fur and bones and guts. It was a gruesome mess. She was some upset. She had to lug more water, heat it, and wash the bones and fur off it all. It was a lot of work. She was some ticked off at the time but later we laughed about it.
It took a fair amount of wood in the stove to heat water for laundry, heat the house, and cooking. The wood all had to be cut down, chopped, and split to the right size. We used a wood sawing machine that belonged to Walter's dad to help us prepare firewood. This machine would go to the family farms. It was a two and half foot circular saw blade. Walter and another fellow would hold one end of a log and feed it into the spinning saw blade. I was the pitcher. I stood on one side of the saw blade and held on to the wood as it was cut off. I had to be quick, grab the block of wood in a hurry, and throw it a few feet onto a pile. Both the feeder and pitcher jobs are dangerous tasks where one could easily be maimed by the blade cutting off hands and arms.

We also cut wood by hand using a Swede saw, a long cutting saw tooth blade with a handle on either end. The log would be slung in a V shaped trestle with an end sticking out, perhaps about 40 centimeters. Someone would hold the log while two people used the saw, alternately pushing and pulling it. After the logs were cut, we used an axe to split it into smaller girth pieces. Walter and I both did this work, as we needed a lot of wood. Cutting wood was a chore we did almost daily. David and Lyle learned to do some of this when they were older. I used an axe to split wood from the time I was a young girl of about 12, and I was still doing it at age 60. It was a daily job just like pulling drinking water out of the well.

At the time and in this part of the country everyone used a dipper to get water from a pail. People did not think about the germs as much, yet everyone used the same dipper and either hung it on a hook or put it on a shelf. It was washed a lot. I am not sure that we all suffered more from bouts of the flu and colds than people do now because of this practice. I would not be too keen on it now but then it was not such an issue.

I want to draw your attention to an interesting item in the adjacent picture. It is not the warmly dressed boys wearing cloth helmets. It is not Walter wearing his Veterans lapel pin. I want you to look at the brand new red Studebaker truck Walter's dad had purchased. It was his first new truck, purchased in 1947 or 1948. Look at the windows of the truck. There are frost shields on the front windshield and the side window. These plastic sheets were glued on to create an air space on the window. It prevented the warmer air inside the truck from frosting or steaming the windows in the winter. The heating system of this truck and most vehicles would not generate enough heat and air current to clear the window of frost and fog. This plastic frost shield did the trick.

My sons, Lyle standing and David pedaling the tricycle, are again wearing a helmet, and pant and shirt combination outfits that buttoned from top to bottom. This helmet was for warmth made from heavier cloth and fastened under the chin and was not designed for injury protection. I now also see the wide open space carved out of the bush, and not a hint of civilization close by. This lack of civilization was beginning to be an issue. The boys were being raised like bush kids, and we were living a hand to mouth existence.

David is holding my dog Tiny. I do not know if Tiny was a mongrel or not. It was never a concern. How I got Tiny is an interesting story.

When we were courting, and after Walter had been summoned for army duty, he bought me a cute puppy in Regina. There were no phones where we lived so he could not phone and tell me what he had done. Instead he mailed a letter telling me the dog would arrive. The puppy was shipped in a large slatted box without a return address, by train to St Walburg, then transferred to a truck and brought it to Pierceland. It was a long trip for a small solo puppy.

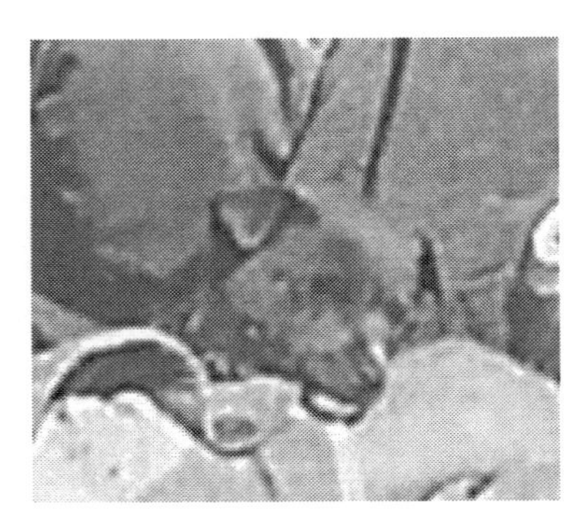

Walter and I had never talked about a dog. The only dog I ever had someone poisoned. I did not want that experience again. I could not figure out who would send me a dog. I was surprised. There were shoppers in town at the time from Moody Lake. Someone wanted it right away and so not thinking or wanting a dog, I sold it for $2.00.

The next day Walter's letter arrived. I felt so silly, embarrassed, and a bit frightened that I had messed up badly! Luckily for me, the man that purchased the dog was either still in town or had come back to town with the dog and I had to buy my present back. Everyone laughed when they heard the story and everyone knew it immediately. It went around town that Sarah had to go buy back her gift from her boyfriend.

The puppy was so small only one name seemed to fit. That is how she got the name Tiny. She was worth every penny of the money I had to give to get her back. Mam liked Tiny and I do not know that I ever met anyone that did not like her. She was a lovely small dog.

Willie use to put her in his pocket and walk to town with her. After getting married in December, I went to live with Walter in Winnipeg in March, and Mam ended up with Tiny until I came back, and then again, she had her when I left for Chilliwack. When the Sager's moved to Chilliwack Mam and Tiny came with them. Tiny travelled with us back to Saskatchewan, and then also to the farm. We had her for 11 years and she died in my arms in 1952. Walter made a nice box and lined it nicely and we took Tiny to a nice spot in some trees on the farm and laid her to rest with some tears.

In March 1950, during a short frenzy of temporary and borrowed luxury, Ruby and I took turns trying on Joan McEvoy's lovely muskrat coat. It was a beautiful coat. We could never afford such a nice coat, so it was fun to try on. Of course, today such coats are not necessary for warmth or fashion, and I would not think of wearing an animal pelt coat. At the time, it was both fashionable and warm and there were not as many good material options for coats as there are today.

Lyle is on the on the left and Gary is wearing a snow suit set I made for him. Ruby purchased the material and the fake fur trim. I measured it out and made the snow suit. We are standing out front of Ruby and Otto's restaurant where Ruby became known for beautiful pies.

Taken at the same time, perhaps by Joan McEvoy, we are inside the restaurant. I am bending over the oil cloth covered counter with the napkins and jar of suckers in front to hide that I am pregnant. I was feeling good at the time and better than the first three months of each pregnancy where I threw up every day. At the time of this picture, I was getting anxious but knew Glenn was to be born in May.

Ruby is on the left and Bessie the waitress on the right. Her real name was Elizabeth Zugelder. Her family called her Lizzie. In the restaurant, she was Bessie, and later, she was called Beth. She was a really nice person, and a hard worker, whichever of the four names she used. It is interesting to see the insides of rural restaurant and store of that age.

The huge calendar in the background shows us the date. Beside it is a poster from the federal government themed, "Education is Our Nation's Future". It was a post war time, propaganda theme, of the government. Pinned to the wall as a decoration, is a doll with a flared red crepe paper dress. On the wall are two kinds of combs, a tail comb, and regular comb, Copenhagen snuff, Gillette Blue Blades, Pall Mall cigarettes poster, and perhaps a cigarette paper packet dispenser. On the counter in a jar are cookies, candy, and an old scale on the far left. Above the cupboard are ice cream cones in boxes. There is a paper rose on top of a candy dispenser. I am not completely sure if Walter and I made the rose pictured but it is possible we did and gave it to Ruby.

Walter and I also made pink, red, and white paper roses from crepe paper and wax. I made the flower on a wire stem. Walter knew exactly how hot to get the wax enabling him to dip the flower into the wax and then take it out without excess dripping or ruining the flower. At times, I added leaves to the stem but not often because there were usually too many stems in a bunch. The flowers were wound around the wire stems with finer snare wire and the wire stems were all wrapped in green crepe paper. We made dozens and dozens of roses and gave them in bunches to everyone. They would last about a year because of the wax coating. Eventually they all had to be thrown out and we made more. We had a lot of these in our own house because we would never be able to get real ones in that location. They preceded plastic flowers.

In the picture following, Doris Rawlake and I are pictured in the snow. I am wearing my engagement ring and the watch Walter gave me for my birthday. Doris is wearing just shoes and I have on overshoes. You can see Doris's right hand. One finger is pointing down. Doris was the oldest child in her family. Her father died. On the day of his funeral, Doris was making kindling wood with a block of wood, and a knife. She cut her finger. She went to the funeral and then to the hospital. It turned out that she had cut her tendon and by the time she got to the doctor it was too late to fix the finger. So, it never bent after it healed.

When Doris's little girl was born Feb 2, 1950, a few months before Glenn was born, I was staying with Ruby and Otto. The previous summer our crop had been hailed out and Walter had to go to work elsewhere that winter. He was on Great Slave Lake in the North West Territories. He was fishing with Charlie Becker from Flat Valley, south of Goodsoil, and about 15 to 20 miles west of Golden Ridge. Walter said it was very cold at Great Slave Lake and that he and Charlie slept in tent camps on the lake. At night, they could hear the ice cracking. Charlie was selling the fish to some fish company at the time. When Walter returned, he brought some fish with him.

When we left Ruby and Otto's place and returned home, we found a mouse had got into the cook books and eaten a hole in one. The poor mouse was cold and having a rough time in life too. I still have this mouse eaten book. During this winter, we had letters from the company that had sold us a set of encyclopedia. We had regretfully purchased them in early summer and they were delivered at harvest time but our harvest was gone. We tried to send them back and they would not take them back. The company sent bills even though I wrote wanting to return them.

The company refused to heed our asking. This set of books caused us such grief. Eventually the next summer we paid for them. It was a stressful time paying for these books. At the time, these books were valuable items for education. We thought we would be helping our children when we purchased them. It was one way parents could help educate their children. However much they were valued then, they are not so valued now and a few years ago, I carted them to the side of the road, and with pleasure, left them for the recycle pick up.

I think David is planting a tree and Lyle is watching and Eldon is up a tree in the picture below. There is a winter sled on the right hand side made from some kind of wooden box to sit in and some runners cut from wood. This is on Willie's property and his house was to the left. Willie had just died and we were looking after Eldon. I had three kids to look after with one on the way and we were living in the bush. Although I took this picture to remind me of my life and the boys as they were young, it now also reminds me of the constant presence of isolation in remote farm life. I would not do it again. It shaped my perception of life. Perhaps this experience has made me more aware of and appreciative of the social benefits in urban life.

We were planting potatoes on the farm in the afternoon in May, 1950. I said to Walter that we were going to have to leave the potatoes and go to the hospital. We went home to Golden Ridge, changed clothing and washed. Walter was driving and it was supper time. He dropped me off in Goodsoil and continued towards Pierceland to get Mam. I arrived too late for supper at the hospital so I went to a restaurant and had supper and walked back to the hospital. At 11:30 at night, May, 25, Nurse Copeland helped deliver Glenn because the doctor was too late. Walter came the next morning to see us. I was there about a week and Mam stayed and looked after David and Lyle while Walter worked.

Nurse Copeland was the daughter of the school teacher who taught Walter how to speak English upon his arrival in Goodsoil. Walter would run up to the Copeland's and speak English. Copeland is the man who taught Walter to sign his name Sergius. As a new immigrant, Walter appreciated the instructions.

Walter's family came from Romania to Prelate, Saskatchewan. Walter went to a school run by the nuns. He had gone to school in Romania where he had to speak Romanian in school and German at home. He said it was not unusual to walk to school in Romania seeing dead people on the side of the road. It was a time and place of great political upheaval. There was much social unrest. It was the time of the rise of communism and social prejudices, intolerance, inequalities and violence. Walter's family fled to Canada helping several Jewish families to escape with them.

Horse and wagon took them from Prelate to the frontier area of Goodsoil. Some people in Prelate were some kind of relative of Johanna, but contact with them was lost over the years. Walter's family moved in the fall of the year. On the edge of Battleford, there was nice land available but Walter's parents were too afraid of the Communist Russians in the wide open country. They wanted to go to the bush. They wanted to hide. His paranoia of the Russians only increased as Walter's father aged. He was afraid of the Bolsheviks, communist revolutionaries, and feared being hunted even this far away and isolated. He felt he had just reason to be wary. Twice he had been part of an execution line where every second man was shot. As a train engineer he had lived through a Bolshevik attack on a train. He crouched for protection but his hand remained on the control unprotected. A bullet removed the end of one of his fingers on his right hand.

Some say Glenn still has this expression, part question, part wonder. This picture was taken in 1951 in Golden Ridge before we moved to the farm. Walter's shop is just barely in the picture on the right. I think the picture is taken in the spring. It looks like he is playing in mud but his white shoes are clean. It is possible to again see the rear tractor wheels that are not rubber.

The background of the picture following picture is the country store owned by the Imhoff family and was where we shopped in sometimes. When Lyle was about four, he was playing in the darker spot just behind him and David in this picture below. It was a ditch and it was frozen. Lyle fell onto a broken bottle frozen into the ice. He cut open his knee. It was a stressful time as we could not fix this ourselves. Walter took him to the doctor in Goodsoil to have it stitched up. Later when the stitches were ready to come out Walter took them out perhaps because the doctor was not around or because of the distance.

Preparing meals was a lot different on a 1950 rural farm than it is now in a city. I did not just drive to the market and buy a chicken for supper. One Saturday afternoon on the farm, David about 10, and I were going to kill a chicken for Sunday dinner. David was to hold the chicken's head while I was to chop off its head. Bringing the axe down on that chicken's neck was something I just could not do. It was the first and last time I tried.

David was more able. He tied a rope to the chicken's head stretched it over a log and cut off the head. The head lay on the ground and the rest of the chicken ran around the yard without its head. Probably this only happened for seconds but they were long seconds. I thought it was cruel, but I had to clean it, cook it, and eat it.

That night we drove into town with Frank and Sis Zerr. David and Lyle went to the show and I went shopping with Glenn in tow. I remember people making a fuss over the cute little boy with the curly blonde hair. I bought groceries and then we all went home with Walter driving the Dodge truck. I am not sure if Walter commented about my inability to kill a chicken.

In November, we started getting ready for Christmas. I began making shortbread. Both my mother and Walter's mother loved shortbread. We had plenty of good quality butter. I made gift boxes to mail to Mam and drove them to my mother-in-law. I added a few cookies to the boxes. It was only 22 miles to Pierceland but one did not easily travel that far. The mail truck used to make a pick-up and delivery once a week on Fridays. Later just before we left the area, the mail came twice a week. Without a phone, and no electricity to power a radio, and of course no TV or internet, twice a week mail delivery, was a big improvement that we appreciated.

In the winter of 1951, we were financially desperate. We were not making money farming. Walter had to earn money. He went to Windermere, BC, to work as a diesel mechanic. He left right after New Year. The severe cold made the winter hard. Communication with anyone was infrequent. I was lonely looking after three boys. It was like living on the moon. There were neighbors but everyone had work to do and little time to visit. We were across the road from the Imhoff store and even though they were Roman Catholic and they did not discriminate and were very nice to me, their customers did discriminate. They were either Roman Catholic or Jehovah Witnesses and they both shunned what they could not convert. The store was not a place to socialize.

Every Saturday morning, I had to climb up and clean out the soot from the stove pipes so they did not explode into flames. I was now very diligent about doing this after the previous fire. I used a steel brush Walter fastened onto a long stick. To do this I had to let the fire go out allowing the chimney to cool which also cooled the house. The soot would drop to the bottom of the chimney and then it had to be removed. The ashes from the stove had to be emptied every two days but the heater could be left for a week without emptying. We placed the ashes on the garden to help to control cut worms.

This winter was a trial. Glenn got pneumonia. I moved his crib near the tin heater. I hung blankets on three sides of the crib to keep him warm and out of the drafts. Close to spring David and Lyle got mumps. Then I got them, and then Glenn got them on one side. Then after all this, Walter finally came home. While I was sick, David had to chop wood and he and Lyle carried it in. They also had to carry in the water from the well. We had an inside toilet. Even in the winter, this pail had to be emptied, and that necessitated that the pail had to be carried out and dumped into an outdoor toilet.

Walter was home for two days. Immediately he left for the farm to work, sleeping in the granary or truck overnight. After a few weeks of this schedule, he was able to return every night. In the spring of 1952 we moved to the farm. Farm yard snow melted the usual way, melting, and freezing, making a mixture of manure slop from the animals, snow, and water. It was a dirty mess, hard to walk in, sloppy and almost impossible to avoid.

Amidst this mess David decided he should go for a ride on a heifer, a young female cow that had not had a calf. One could call it a yearling. David climbed on it and had a bit of ride. It ran around the yard and David stayed on. He was laughing and having a good time. He bounced up and down and we laughed. We were watching him with amusement when the heifer made a turn. The bouncing around stopped. David flew off. He slid across the yard splashing and ploughing through piles of cow dung, chicken droppings, slush, dirt and dog poop that sprayed up, over, and around him. It went in his hair and throughout his clothing. He was covered and wet, and completely smeared everywhere with assorted smelly manure. With clean clothing and a towel and he went down to the slough to wash himself and his clothing. On his return, he got some hugs and we laughed.

The picture of Lyle with his 6th birthday cake was taken outside because there was no flash on the camera. It is March 25, 1951. The three layered cake was most likely a Yorkshire fruit cake. It had some dried fruit in it. The icing is white and it is decorated with candied cherries. The cake is on the sewing chest that I still have in my office. Walter won this sewing chest by guessing how many marbles were in a big jar. I still have the cabinet here in my office today. It still has some of the colored threads that came with it. I look at this and think what a cute boy and a nice cake I made, and how this contrasts with how I felt about the bush behind him.

This picture was given to us. From the left, it shows Danny Sergew, Roland, Helen, and Jean standing by the chair. I think the date is about 1954 or 1955. It is in front of the house they lived in. One can see this is a squared log house, with a good joint in the corners. This building technology was now more limited mostly to rural life. It is chinked with mud plaster. This means the spaces between the logs are filled with mud plaster. The house had one door. The main floor had a big kitchen, living room and two bedrooms. The upstairs was accessed through the kitchen and there was one large bedroom. The shingles in this case are store bought. The double window is part of the kitchen. This is the third house owned by Walter's parents. When they moved to Edmonton Walter's brother August and his wife Gabby lived in it.

I was always a bit leery visiting this house because Walter's brother John had a kind of a mean dog. I was afraid of it. It would lie under the steps to the right of the picture and snap at feet going up and down the stairs. It never actually bit me but I was afraid that it might and very concerned it would bite the boys. I think John used this dog and another as sled dogs, a practice that indicates the frontier like life of the times.

John had another nicer dog called Rex. He was friendly. He always followed us home to Golden Ridge about two miles away. We did not want him as he belonged on the farm and we had Tiny. Rex was a bit too friendly. We always tried to stop him from following us and many times chased him away. One day to chase Rex away Walter put a string around a tin can and tied it to the dog's tail. Rex went home making a noise and he never came back.

Walter's father is pictured here with his horse. He was very proud of this horse called Nigger. The name is offensive now, but was a clumsy translation of the Romanian word "Negru" meaning black. Many people had black horses so named but never meant it in a derogatory way. The word did not carry connotations of racism in the community at the time. Walter's parents were not racists and would not use the term now that it is associated negatively. In those days to them, it had no negativity, as this was a prized horse. Sadly, the horse met a sad end. Nigger was found stabbed to death in the field. No one ever admitted the deed but the family suspected one of the neighbors. This may have fed the lingering paranoia of the Russian communists. The neighbors were not always the best. Sometimes the harsh economic times brought out the rough edges of people.

A neighbor Dan Heck once boasted he could steal almost anything from anyone, but could not steal the lumber from a man to build that man's coffin. We were certain he snatched, and then sold, four pigs from Walter and I just before we were to sell them. We all felt we knew what he had done. Even he knew everyone thought. There was not much we could do about the theft. No one was a witness. Though everyone assumed his guilt, and he never tried to profess his innocence. It was generally accepted that he was the thief. At the same time, if he had something you needed to use he would loan it to you.

We needed a well on the farm. Our house had been pulled to the site and positioned over the cellar hole. Until we got a well, Walter hauled water from the farm of our neighbors Frank and Sis Zerr for our use. The cattle had water from the slough.

Walter and I dug our own well. Walter started to dig the well making it about four feet by four feet. Walter threw out the dirt until he was down too deep to throw out the dirt. With the deep hole, we used a pulley and a five gallon pail to remove the dirt. Walter would dig the hole and fill the pail. I would haul up the pail of dirt and dump it about 10 feet away. Digging and the hauling up of the dirt was hard work for both of us. We made a huge hole, 28 feet deep and 4 feet across from any side.

At 28 feet, Walter noticed water slowly entering the hole. This became a good and deep well with a lot of water. Then Walter made a cribbing to go inside and line the well. The cribbing rose above the ground surface about two feet. Then he made a proper windlass, which is a pulley with a crank handle and an attached rope. At the end of the rope was a pail. We lowered the pail to the water and gave the rope a snap and the pail would tip into the water. We cranked the water up and poured it into another pail to carry it to the house.

This well also became a refrigerator. We put food such as cream and butter into another pail and lowered this pail into the well just above the water. Here the temperature was cool consistently.

Walter made a wooden trough to allow the cattle to be able to drink well water. It was located on the other side of a barbed wire fence but close enough to the well that we could easily empty the well pail into the trough. I appreciated the separation of the animals from us. We watered the cows twice a day. They would come in a group to the trough to drink. They could drink from the slough but the water was not as nice and they preferred the well water in the trough. They walked up to the trough and would stand and make braying noises, or bellers, until they got water. They were telling, and showing us what they wanted.

Bell, a roan cow had lovely horns but was at times mean and moody. She was called Bell because she wore a bell and was the boss of the herd. I was afraid to be out in the open with her unless I had a dog and a pitchfork. I felt braver and able to defend myself from the cows this way. Our dog Lulu was part Border Collie and she would wait for my command to go bring the cows to the barn. Each cow had its own stall and it knew where to go.

The cows were also fed grain. Walter's father had a grain chopping machine. We put lesser quality wheat, oats, and barley through this machine a few bushels at a time. I would place about 5 cups of chopped grains in the feed box after Lulu herded the cows to the barn.

The cows came in and concentrated on the chop while I placed the stanchion down over their necks allowing them to eat and if they wanted, to lie down, but not turn their head. This held them in place allowing them to be milked yet not be able to butt you with their horns. It would take them about five minutes to eat this much grain. I would finish milking and they would be nibbling on some hay. At the end of milking I let them out of the barn and they would wander around the field.

Bell had a daughter Daisy. The two looked similar with big horns, but Daisy had a similar but slightly more agreeable bad temper. Bell and Daisy allowed you to pat them as long as their heads were in the stanchion. Standing freely, they were less controlled and did not like being touched.

Nancy was the third cow and she was gentle and had no horns. She liked to be petted. One winter Nancy got mastitis. We got some medication for her but it did not really help a lot. I would bring hot cloths from the house but by the time I got to the barn, they were only warm. I would place these around her udder and massage it and eventually she got better. I became more attached to Nancy because I had to nurse her.

One spring the cows were in the pasture. I had cleared the cellar out of vegetables and scraps. I dumped the pail too close to the fence. The cows stuck their heads through the fence and ate the garlic scraps. For a few days, their milk smelled strongly of garlic and we had to feed it to the pigs.

One time Walter came home from working in the garage and decided to help me milk the cows. I appreciated the help and let him start. He wrongly tried to milk temperamental Bell. Bell was accustomed to me milking her. She liked the usual routine. Walter got the pail down and began to milk. As soon as Bell realized who was milking her she lifted her foot and put it right in the pail. She knew exactly what she was doing and was protesting the change. Walter had to feed the wasted milk to the pigs. He returned to milk her again and she did exactly the same thing. Walter was so annoyed that he hit her with the milking stool. He should not have done that. Bell did not like that. She lifted her leg and caught him square in the butt lifting him into the air a few feet. He landed on the barn floor embarrassed. He was not hurt but that was the end of Bell's milking for the day. Walter deserved the free air ride.

Come fall time, after the crops were cut, the fields were full of stubble. We let the cattle loose on this stubble. They loved it. They picked up ends and bits of straw with oats, barley, and wheat grains, left here and there. I had to bring them in from this feast. They were not always ready to come to the barn on my schedule. Bringing in the cows like this was a bit of a challenge for me and a bit dangerous as the cows, and, well Bell, for certain, could be moody. As a young bride, a town girl, new to farming, I was wary of most farm animals. I was afraid of some, and unfamiliar with most.

Bell was a clever cow and knew how to say what she wanted. She talked a lot. She let us know she wanted to eat, drink, or be milked. She demanded attention. She did not like situations that put her in a subservient role as was demonstrated by kicking Walter, and the day I used the tractor to insist they come in from the fields.

On the tractor, I took a three pronged pitchfork, because there were no fences to put between the cows and me. Lulu followed along. Driving this particular tractor, one sat a bit low to the ground and for sure lower than a cow's head.

I drove out to the cows. Bell felt I got a bit too close. She did not like the tractor. She was not afraid of the tractor. She would not politely move along.

She challenged. Bell turned on the tractor, she stood firm and was ready to use her horns. Had I not stopped the tractor she would have certainly put her horns through the radiator and possibly me. I stopped the tractor in a hurry and Lulu did the rest of the work of getting the cows to the barn. Bell and I both knew I was afraid of her. I wish I could have talked cow to find out what she really thought. She taught Walter a lesson when she sent him flying across the barn and she taught me one as I sat on the tractor.

I never dreamed that more than 70 years after I first drove this farm tractor, and almost as long since I had seen it the first time, that I would see it again, and be able to point to where that bellowing cantankerous roan cow Bell, had threatened to butt the tractor with her horns.

I am pleased David rented a truck, brought this Oliver cletrac track caterpillar, and donated it to the museum in Chilliwack. As a kid, he drove it a few times when he was about 12. The museum has freshly painted it to use in parades. When I visited it recently it brought back memories to me as if visiting an old acquaintance.

Daily after milking the cows, I carried the milk to the house in pails that we only used as milk pails as a precaution to help keep them clean. The milk was then poured into the cream separator. The receiving bowl is on top of the separator so it meant lifting the pail of milk up high to pour it in. Farm women develop good muscles doing all this lifting. A pail of milk can easily weigh 10 to 15 pounds if only one or two gallons are in the pail. Turning the handle of the separator made the machine mechanism go around. One had to learn the appropriate speed to turn the handle for each separator. The correct speed causes the milk and cream to separate by centrifugal force. One had to turn the handle for a few minutes to complete the job. Then the spigots would be turned open and the milk and cream would be separated and run down the spouts into waiting pails.

Separator machines would need to be very well cleaned and scalded with boiling water or they would produce milk that went bad quickly.

In the winter, we kept the cream in the cellar. In the summer the milk and cream went into the well bucket we used as a refrigerator. When there were extra dairy products we fed it to the calves or pigs.

The stable had to be kept clean. There was always straw on the floor. I cleaned it every day. Cows poop many times in one day. Our cows went into their stalls and up on to an elevated sub floor. When they pooped, it fell past to the floor, but it was clean for us to milk and walk around them. We cleaned the barn floor every day taking the straw and poop out to the manure pile about 25 yards away and later it would be taken away and spread on the fields.

When they were removed from the mother, the calves needed to be taught to drink from a pail. To do this one had to get the calves neck between your legs to hold their heads in place with a pail on the floor. Then you let the calves suck your fingers and lower your fingers into the milk.

This way they learned to drink from a pail. During the few days of time it took to teach them to drink from a pail, you would be bumped around by other calves and the one you were training. One had to learn to be strong and stand firmly in place for this job.

Many cattle were owned by one bachelor neighbor, Schneider. He let them loose to graze.
His cattle went further than he expected and they came near and surrounded our house. They came up to the house looking through the windows. The cows were only curious. Not being a farm girl, I did not know that. I was afraid of these cows and felt threatened and trapped. I felt they might try to come in or become angry and aggressive. I was a village girl and not used to farm animals.

I got Walter's 22 gage gun. I was going to shoot at them and try to scare them away. I tried and tried, but I could not make it work. This was a good thing perhaps. In desperation, I sent Lulu after the cows. There were so many cows, and they were not used to her I was a bit afraid to send her at first thinking they may turn on her. Lulu was up to the task and herded the cows away. Walter came home and I told him of my fear and the gun. He felt we would have had to pay for the cows if I had killed any. Luckily, I was a bad hunter. Odd it seems now that we would have had to pay for the threatening intrusive cows, but that we lost the money for the stolen pigs.

Pigs were kept in a pen that was made from slab wood. Slab wood is the outside edge cut off a log when lumber is made. It has all the knots and branch bumps. These planks of wood still have bark on them. People used this type of wood for pens and sometimes fences. When our pigpen was made, there was space between the slabs.

We had one older mother pig called Cyclops. She weighed well over 200 pounds. Frequently she decided she wanted out of the pen. She placed her feet between the slabs, used them as a set of stairs, and climbed out to walk around the farm yard. She would go to the straw pile and burrow under it. She liked the sun.

Poor Cyclops developed arthritis. She began to hate to move. I would have to go two or three times a day and poke her with a stick so that she would move around. She did not readily do this as she was in pain. At the time, I never thought that one day I would have it too, and that my feet too would hurt. Cyclops had several litters. In the winter, we would bring the piglets into the house, and put them on the open oven door of the cook stove to keep warm, being careful not to get roast pork. Sometimes they slept in a box beside the stove. Walter carried them back and forth.

We tried to raise a few pigs so we had something to sell a few times a year, when they were not stolen. This would give us cash income other than Walter's work at the garage. Stolen pigs meant lost income to poor people.

We kept a couple dozen white leghorn chickens for eggs. In the winter, it got too cold for them to lay eggs. Two were roosters. We called one Bing Crosby and one Bob Hope after the popular star entertainers at the time. Both roosters used to attack Lyle. He would run and they would chase after him trying to peck him. We told him to throw something at the roosters to intimidate them back. I ran out many times to chase the roosters away from Lyle. The roosters would not leave him alone. Perhaps they knew they could intimidate him, as he was young and small.

One day Walter was working on the pig fence and one of these roosters attacked him. He grabbed the rooster and rung its neck. We had a stellar supper that night. From then on, the other rooster did not seem so aggressive.

We sent away for live chicks. That means we sent a letter and payment in the mail to a company. The chicks were delivered to town by truck. To pick them up we had to go to a town, probably Meadow Lake. They came in a large square cardboard box divided into sections with a few chicks in each section. They were little yellow fluff balls. I kept them outside in the sunlight in a pen during the day. At night, they were in a part of the granary. I had the chicks just inside the door.

One morning I went to get the chicks. Instead of finding chirpy chicks ready to go outside, I found a dozen chicks piled up mostly dead. A weasel had come in and sucked the blood out of the chicks piling them up in the corner.

I thought the weasel might be in the granary. I poked my head over the edge of the partition looking for it. Two wild beady eyes were staring up at me. It jumped up at me, but not quite high enough to get my throat. It could have ripped my neck open. Luckily it hit the top of the partition and fell back. I ran out of the building. I took the live ones out to the pen. Walter came home that night, set a trap, and caught the weasel.

Wild berries were an important part of our diet. On one berry picking occasion Saskatoon berries were our target with Johanna Walter's mother, Minnie, David, Lyle, and I were going to the north side of the Waterhen River. Johanna was driving a team of horses. She had to sit in the wooden box like the rest of us, as there was no bench seat.

The horses started across the river and the water got deeper than was expected. As we got near the middle of the river, the water was really high outside on the box. The box began floating slowly detaching from the wheels. The back of the box came out of the pins holding it in place. We were in immediate danger of floating down the river in the box while the horses went straight ahead. Johanna had to act fast. Raising the reins in the air and with her arms outstretched commanding and excitedly yelling, "Giddy up giddy up" she took charge. The good training of the horses became evident as they immediately pulled harder and we made it out. Beauty and Baldy were our heroes. On the way back we seemed to have no trouble at all in a different spot.

Beauty and Baldy were the team Minnie used to drive. Once she was going down a hill quickly. The tongue of the cutter, a long wooden pole pointing forward connecting the cutter sleigh to the yolk of the horses, came loose from between the horses. It dug into the ground. Fortunately, she got the horses stopped quickly as the tongue would have jammed further into the ground and flipped the cutter forward on top of her. The good training of Beauty and Baldy saved the day again.

After we moved to the farm we had a big disaster. It was about 7pm, Wednesday, July 15, 1953. The sky was a funny color. Walter was working in town. Walter's brother August, was at our place using Walter's welding equipment. I had given him some rags made from a discarded dress. Actually, it had been the dress that I had been wearing when we played ball in our yard, and our dog Lulu's teeth cut my leg. Lulu always ran with me and carried the flare of my skirt in her mouth so the dress had been a bit extra worn.

This Wednesday day had been quiet. August came to the door. He was going home as it looked like a bad storm was coming. He put the rags in his pocket as he left.

David and Lyle were outside playing and came in as it started to rain. In the few minutes between August leaving, and Walter arriving home, the sky began to look horribly dangerous. It became a very black sky. It began to thunder. There was tremendous lightning. Then the wind started. It got stronger. It started to rain very hard. The storm came very fast.

When the hail started, it was an amazing sight. The hailstones were as big as tennis balls. They were flying through the air everywhere, and bouncing across the ground driven by terrific wind. Some were frozen together in clumps of three and four. The hail smashed everything. We sent David and Lyle to the cellar. Glenn was sitting on the chesterfield beside the accordion as the storm started. As the storm worsened, I took Glenn to the cellar with Lulu. Walter and I stayed up. We held pillows on the windows to keep the window glass from shattering into the house. The hail came with such force it shattered the window slats. The hail was being thrown around at a speed that would easily kill people and animals. Finally, Walter and I made a run for it into the cellar.

Looking south through the small cellar window we could see the storm outside blowing stuff around. We could not see much but heard a lot because the storm was fiercely loud.
Thunder, lighting, rain, wind, hail all at the same time. It was dark down under the house. We could see the window move as the storm pushed on the house. We could hear the house vibrating. We were all scared. We wondered where we should put our heads if the house lifted. This seemed to go on forever.

After about 15 minutes, the storm was gone to the northeast. We were afraid that the storm would be like many others of the day, and soon come back for a second session of hail, wind, and rain. It did not. Like an unwelcome guest, it did its damage and left.

Our house was damaged. The hail had come through the roof and melted. The roof needed repair. The ceiling paper got wet and had to be replaced. The windows in the living room were all broken but the windows in the bedrooms on a different side of the house were left untouched.

The storm flipped our binder machine upside down and destroyed two granaries. They were smashed to bits. All the grain inside was lost around the yard and into the 4 H plots David and Lyle were growing. The chickens in the granaries were killed.
A piece of sheet metal that we used in the winter to deflect heat away from the wall, and which had been placed outside, became an air borne knife. It had flown through the air, cut off willows in a swath, and landed about ½ to ¾ mile away. Our cattle had been scared and had headed into the trees down by the slough. The small barn and stable were untouched and the outdoor toilet in the trees was unaffected. Our neighbors the Zerrs not too far away were unaffected.

The newly built Catholic Church was blown away. Some of the shingles from this church were in our fields 3 miles away. Imhoff's combined store, post office and house, all in one building, was destroyed. Mail was found in our fields. I am not sure where the Imhoffs went after the storm or how we got mail after the storm.

My accordion left on the chesterfield was hit by big hailstones. The grillwork was smashed. It was wet throughout and ruined. I was sad to lose it because it was an Italian make, and had a nice soft sound. We wrote to Ray Hamerton Music Store in Winnipeg and ordered a new one. I was loyal to this company because we had purchased my first accordion from them on payments after we first married. In error, I made an extra payment of $12.95 and they refunded my money.

Such honesty by Ray Hamerton Music Store is commendable. The second accordion, the Honer, with a harsher sound, I still play today. This is the refund letter.

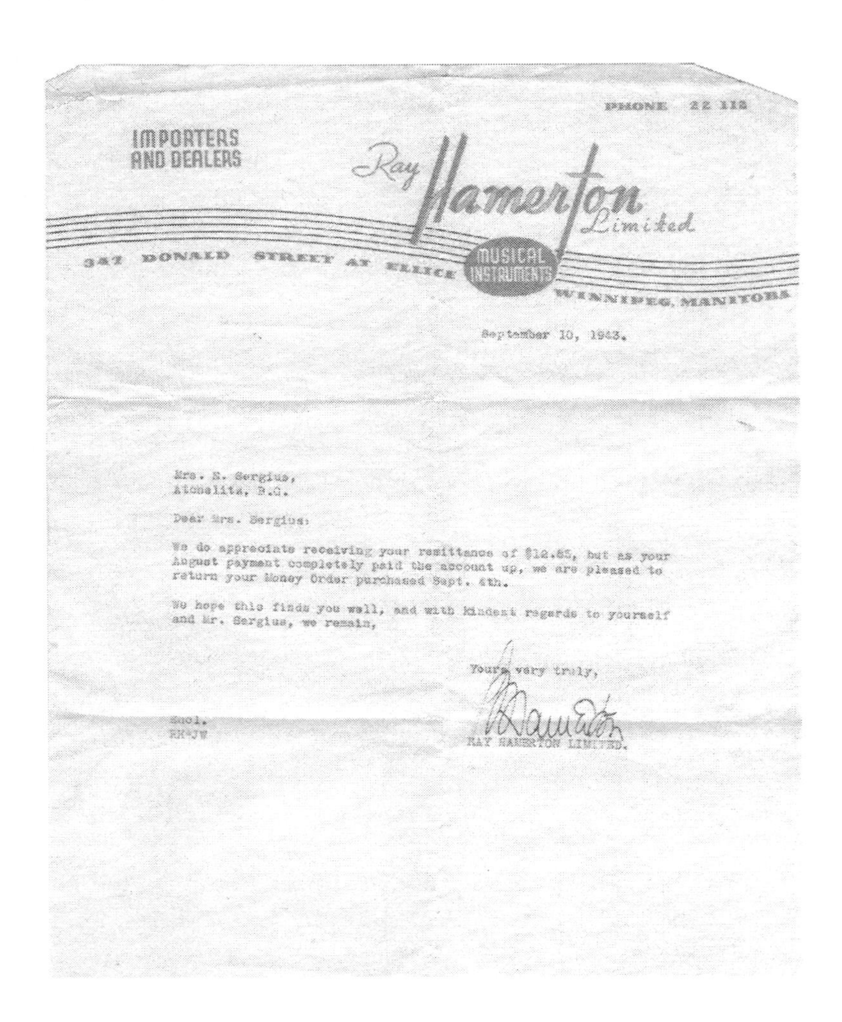

PHONE 22 112

IMPORTERS AND DEALERS

Ray Hamerton Limited

MUSICAL INSTRUMENTS

347 DONALD STREET AT ELLICE

WINNIPEG, MANITOBA

September 10, 1943.

Mrs. E. Sergius,
Atchelitz, B.C.

Dear Mrs. Sergius:

We do appreciate receiving your remittance of $12.95, but as your August payment completely paid the account up, we are pleased to return your Money Order purchased Sept. 4th.

We hope this finds you well, and with kindest regards to yourself and Mr. Sergius, we remain,

Yours very truly,

RAY HAMERTON LIMITED.

Encl.
RH:JW

Our neighbors, especially the Heck family, were not so lucky. The parents and older children were gone. Their oldest son was mentally challenged and about 17 years old. Their two daughters were younger and about 10 years old.

When the storm came, the son took the two daughters to hide under a tractor in a garage rather than stay in the house. It was a smart move. When the storm struck, it destroyed their house and spread it all around the fields. The floor of the house was left. A wall cupboard came down and sat on the floor where the bottom cupboard used to be and none of the dishes were broken. Nothing of the rest of the house remained including the rest of the cupboards. Everything else was destroyed. The garage where the three kids were hiding under the tractor was destroyed and blown away, but the tractor and kids were ok. I am not sure where they lived after that.

My brother-in-law August, almost made it home. The storm caught him about ¼ of a mile from his house.

It picked his car up from the road. He and it, were thrown across the ditch and over a wire fence where the car hit the ground. Next the storm lifted the car back over the fence and threw August out, before crossing the ditch and going over the fence again and landing in the bush. In those days, vehicles did not have seat belts. August's car was caved in and wrecked. He could not have survived had he been wearing a seatbelt. August was cut, bruised badly, but alive.

August walked through the bush to his house, about 100 yards. His wife was standing in the yard. She knew there had been a thunder storm but was surprised to see August all cut and bleeding wondering what happened to him. The storm did not affect their place. Portions of my dress rags hang from the trees. When I look at the photo of the rags in the trees, I remember that awful day. I remember how we were always aware of the power of storms on the prairie.

I also remember, as my mind and heart go back all those years, to Lulu the dog and my special friend, always holding my skirt as I ran.

The storm made life bad. It was a life changing event and it helped make our mind up about our future. Then in 1954 when I learned, I had to have my upper teeth out I felt worse. There were no dentists nearby, and they cost a lot of money and we had little of that. I am sure today that the drastic action of pulling that many teeth would not be the proper course. It was a sad, unpleasant event.

Ruby made an appointment with dentist Dr Lane in Edmonton. I took Glenn on the bus and we were met by Otto Sager at the bus station. The day after I arrived, the doctor took out a single tooth as a test. When I got back to Ruby's it bled badly. Ruby called the dentist and he gave instructions to bite down on a tea bag until the bleeding stopped. Yes, it worked, but today other things would have been done such as better stitching.

The next day I went back to him and had the rest out and then my new set of dentures put in. Dr Lane gave instructions on how to adjust the fit of the new dentures if I had problems. If the gums became sore, I was to use an indelible pencil and mark on my gums where the irritation was happening. Then I was to put my teeth back in and bite down hard. The pencil would put a mark on my dentures. I was to use fine sand paper and take a little off that spot. It happened that my new teeth did hurt. Making the pencil marks also hurt. Walter sanded my dentures and I used these dentures for many years, 20 or more.

Comparing that to what happens today makes the technology and patient care seem primitive. Of course, it was.

Walter looked after David and Lyle for the 5 to 7 days that we were gone. The three of them made butter. What happened to them happened to many people new to the butter making routine. They put too much cream into the hand turned, butter churn. It of course expanded and spilled out. The boys were excited to tell me about it when I came home. Lyle recently reminded me that Walter made stew for them to eat while I was gone.

Life on the farm in the early 1950's was not easy. It was, in truth, miserable. Walter's work in the garage brought in a meager living wage and we had so many farm expenses due to bad luck farming. It was a life hard stressed by lack of money. We were having a rough spell in farming. We had lost crops three years in a row, to hail, then frost, then wind. We had very little social life and what we had was a sporadic. I had maybe two or three dresses and women did not wear pants in those days. The dresses had to washed and lightly starched and I wore them over and over. Crazy as it seems we wore dresses in the cold weather and warm weather.

I remember I had a yellowish dress. In my mind, I can still see it hanging in the closet. I must have got it from a box of used clothing that came up from the south. My hair was brown so I could wear that color in those days. I had a function to go to and wanted to wear the dress. It required a slip and we were so poor I could not afford to buy a slip. My friend and neighbor Sis Zerr said she would lend me a slip. I was happy and wore the borrowed slip and the yellowy dress to farmer's event.

At some of these farm events, we shared recipes and techniques in preserving and farming. People relied less upon grocery stores then than we rely on them today. We could not afford new jars and equipment. Using Roger's Syrup tins, and jam tins with push in lids, we canned beef, pork, chicken, and fish. Spices and onions went in the bottom of the can, then the meat, onions and salt and pepper on top and the lid lightly pushed into place. Then the can was put into the oven for 4 hours or so. When it came out we hammered in the lid tightly and it was done. To get the meat out one had to use a can opener on both ends to push the contents out.

To have food to eat, it was necessary for Walter to illegally fish. He always had to be one step ahead of the Department of Natural Resources, DNR. They had an idea he was fishing illegally but we needed the food.

There were a lot of fish in the rivers, and the Water Hen River was close to our farm. The DNR were always trying to catch people as a large number of people fished illegally. This had been going on for a long time. When we first moved to Pierceland, I was quite young and we lived in a log house next to Ma Hasseler. She ran a sort of a restaurant and rented out an extra room.

The DNR frequently visited Ma Hassel's restaurant to eat. Ma Hasseler called Mam over and gave Mam some fish. The DRN followed her out the back door and said to Ma Hasseler something like, "ah ha I caught you red handed." Ma Hasseler's reply was something like, "just never you mind, as that is what you are getting for supper, so just go back inside." They just did as they were told and no charges were laid.

Therefore, although the DNR suspected Walter, he was never caught, and we were glad of the fish to eat. It may have been that the DNR did not try too hard to catch poor people, and most everyone was poor in the area. I made butter and sold it to add to our income but we were poor and farming was not being kind to us. Every day we worked to live. There was little if any pleasure about it.

I wish we had never gone to Golden Ridge and the farm. I have not much good to say about this time of my life. It was not an easy life. Life in Chilliwack had been better.

Without electricity, one's world shrank. In this case, it shrank to within a few miles of the isolated house, and then just to the edge of the farmyard for most of the time, and in winter storms it shrank to just the house.

We had a battery powered radio. The battery packs were large, perhaps 18 inches long and 10 wide and about 10 inches high. They were heavy and expensive. Therefore, we listened selectively and when we had time. This was in contrast to the better life in Chilliwack where we had an electric radio and could listen at will, keep up with the news and hear music.

Even as a child in Pierceland the last few years, we had electricity from a local privately owned plant. Every night in Pierceland the power would be turned off late at night, but, I remember listening to a program for younger people, and I remember Mam listening to a program she called a soap with Ma Perkins.

Any night on the farm that we listened to the radio, we had to unhook the antennae wire from the radio and hook it to a ground wire. Even prairie storms that were not tornados could be fierce and very electrical. Changing the hook up for the antennae would route any lightning strikes to the ground and prevent house fires.

Without radios, telephones, and newspapers, we were not always aware of things going on in the world. At home, Mam had subscribed to two different weekly newspapers, but on the farm, we had none. Politics, sports, fashion, national news, and international affairs, were not daily topics of interest and conversation. Conversation between Walter and I centered upon what had to be done on the farm, or in other words, we talked about more work.

Without the radio and news, much of the world goings on happened without us being at all aware. We got some news at Farmers Association meetings but not a lot, or in much detail. Most other people in the area had similar isolated lives. The Farmers Association in part succeeded because of the meetings enabled some socialization in isolated rural areas. I did not partake in the farm organization discussions but was glad to be able to talk to other women at meetings.

I did learn things in this time of my life. Mostly I learned about hard work on a farm, but, also, I learned to do needle work and be a good mother. I began to feel more self worth as a result. I began to trust that I had valuable contributions to make.

I began to learn to speak up. I learned that women needed to speak up. They needed to say when they did not want to do something and to say they had opinions. Traditionally women did not have much say in what a family or couple did. Men that made the decisions, and I had assumed that lesser role of a woman. Having to tolerate a life I did not like, helped to spur me on mentally, and I began to realize I could speak out.

I dreamed of leaving every now and then. Not to run away alone and be a movie star or anything like that. I would have liked to have taken my family and have gone where Walter was home more often. I wanted the boys to go to school close by. I wanted neighbors to talk to and see.

I was not economically independent with a career option. I thought I might like to be a hair dresser because I always did my own thick brown hair, and that type of job would be far nicer than the farm work. I did not really know all the options open for women even then, when there were far fewer to know than there are now. I think had I had the option of further schooling I would have been a good teacher. Later in life I taught Sunday school and enjoyed that a lot.

Looking back on this time it is easier to say what I would do now because I have years of experience. Certainly, I would have refused to go to that farm. I would say "no damn way". It is true I learned from it. Perhaps the intense influence of the Roman Catholic Church and Jehovah's witnesses galvanized me against religious fanatics, and perhaps that is a valuable lesson in life. These two self righteous religious groups made life awful. Sometimes life in the area was like riding a bike down a steep hill with ditches on either side. Both RC and JW were the ditches. One had to try hard to avoid the devastation of the ditches.

I think Walter found it easier. He had grown up in the area, and knew some of the people and worked in town 10 miles away. In town, he saw people. He had conversations, and his world was bigger. I think it was worse for me always being more isolated, meeting few people, and being alone a lot.

Leaving this area was like letting a bird out of a cage. The farm was an awful cage in which I just did not belong. Some people were stuck there in that remote area all their lives and they grew old there. I feel badly for them. I am glad I escaped.

So, reflecting upon this time of my life in this part of the country, I can honestly say the best thing about it was leaving it......Amen.

Lac La Ronge: A Warm Small Town

In 1955, we were stuck barely making a living on an isolated, bush surrounded, farm. We were surviving but not thriving. Walter was tired working in the Goodsoil garage commuting about 10 miles each way back and forth to the farm, and then having to work at the farm too. That drive on a bad country gravel road was equivalent to another half day of work. With successive destroyed crops, what Walter earned in the garage was our income. The farm was not making money. Our farming experience was full of financial calamity. Our crops were destroyed by hail, frost and a tornado. The first year it was frost that killed the crops, then twice they were hailed out and destroyed, and then the last was the wind of the tornado that flattened and broke everything. We were not enjoying our situation.

My cousin, Dave Corney, and his business associate, Dunc McLean, would travel through the country around us to attend anglers' meetings driving these same roads. Both knew Walter's brother, John, who fished at Primrose Lake. From time to time, they would stop at our house in Golden Ridge, have tea, and say hello on their way past.

Sometime after we moved to the farm, Dave navigated the road to our house. It is safe to say he did not like what he saw. He said something like, "Walter, I want you to take Sarah and the kids off this farm. Get you away from the garage in Goodsoil. We need a man like you in the fishing industry. You can work for Saskatchewan Fish Marketing Service doing refrigeration and diesel work in the different fish plants in the north."

When Walter answered that he knew nothing about refrigeration Dave replied, "But you will learn. You will take courses in it and at the same time you will be doing diesel work." It was a voice of confidence in Walter's ability. He had made a statement that he wanted us to leave the farm and that we could leave the farm. It shook our world. From our place, he went on to Pierceland and Meadow Lake, and said he would stop in on his way back in a few days.

Together we had to think about the idea of leaving because we had a farm. We discussed it. At this time, Walter had never seen the mechanical works of a refrigerator and neither had I. In that we were like most folks at the time. Refrigerators were new to the Canadian west. A few years later, we would buy our first refrigerator for $300.

This new opportunity did not really take too much consideration. A big decision affecting our lives was made, but not in a hasty rush. We considered our desires, our options, and our circumstances. We took advantage of the opportunity for a better life. We were much like the immigrants who left the rest of the world for the prairies and farming, only we left farming for the north. Our farming was not working. Both Walter and I were darn glad to get away from it. Walter was glad to have a steady job and would not be worrying about the bad luck of farming. I was glad to leave because all I did was work and never saw anyone, and was basically isolated with one friend I saw occasionally, Cis Zerr and occasionally Sara McRae at a farm meeting. I did not mind the hard work but really found the isolation a problem. We were living on the edge of disaster.

Our good friends the McRae brothers took over farming our land. We left many of our things in the house because we could not take everything at the time. One book I felt very sad to leave was a book about

England sent to me from my pen pal Esmie Alexander. We left a few books, dishes, and other things in the house when we left. A few years after we had left, the house was used to store grain and of course, the floor collapsed. We intended to come back and get more of our stuff from the house, but we never did. It was a stressful move. Now I question myself why I cannot remember more about the move. I think that perhaps the stress of the time has eliminated some memories. I wanted to go to a new life. Our cattle and pigs had to be sold and shipped. Everything was rushed. Just before we left, the livestock was sold and moved.

I am not sure how we got word to Dave Corney that we agreed and wanted to move, but I think he stopped in on his way back after having been gone a few days. We moved within a couple of weeks and Glenn had his 5th birthday in Lac La Ronge.

The town was strung out along the lakeshore. One entered the town from the southwest past the end of the Indian Reserve and the Anglican Church downtown. Finally, one came to the road that joined an island to the mainland. Here we lived, near the fish plant. A lot of US tourists visited the town in the summer and went fishing, or they would drive to Lac La Ronge and then fly to other lakes to fish. The fish were large and plentiful.

We had a jeep. It was loaded on to a truck and shipped to Lac La Ronge. I am not sure how it happened, but it then belonged to the Co-op fisheries and Johnny Stonehocker drove it around town for a while. Our furniture came from the farm in a truck. It was transferred from one truck to another and then when it arrived in Lac La Ronge it was stored for a while. Walter went to Prince Albert on the truck with the furniture. The three boys and I went from the farm to Prince Albert in Dave Corney's car. The five us stayed at Dave and Dorothy Corney's, in Prince Albert for a night. Walter was in Lac La Ronge before we arrived so I think he flew from PA to La Ronge.

Dorothy Corny gave me this picture and the back wrote, "This is the snap I took of Sarah Walter & boys as they left us to go to La Ronge, 8 o'clock in the morning. Send it on to Sarah." It is Dave's car. Lyle remembers Dave and me talking about the windshield of the car as he drove us to Lac La Ronge.

Dorothy stood in front of their house and took the picture. Their house is not pictured. Note the muddy road. This was Prime Minister John Diefenbaker's Federal Political riding. Dave had run against him but lost. Brenda, Dave's daughter laughs as she remembers that as a little girl ran around taking down John Diefenbaker signs so more people would vote for her daddy.

Walter's new employer was Saskatchewan Fish Marketing Service. It later changed name to Co-operative Fisheries. Walter flew into Lac La Ronge, and immediately flew out to Wollaston Lake, to fix a diesel in a fish plant. He was there in isolation for 3 weeks and did not know where we were living. Walter was in a new job, alone, without friends or family, and in a place, he had never known only accessible by air. Walter could not even locate Wollaston Lake on a map. All he knew was it was somewhere up north in the bush. Later we could all locate Wollaston Lake, and Walter was there many times.

Walter flew out of Lac La Ronge a lot and it soon became to be far too many times that he left us. He was gone between 75% and 90% of the time that we lived in La Ronge. His life was not pleasant and it was barely civilized. I was in civilization, but without Walter. At first, I was lonely. I did not know anyone and was trying to make a life with my three boys alone. It was a big responsibility. Soon I found out that everyone was friendly. Having moved from an area where religious affiliation caused many problems, we were now in an area where people were friendly without the motivation of religious conversion. Religion did not divide the community. People were friendly because it was their nature to be friendly. This a picture of it from when about 1957.

Walter finally arrived at the water base in Lac La Ronge. He was in an unfamiliar town without knowing where he was to call home. Lyle driving around on his bicycle heard the plane and went to the base, and there, Lyle saw his dad, and Walter asked where we lived. Lyle told him where we lived. It was about ½ mile from the base to Fitches Cabins. Home was not a palace. It was rustic and temporary.

We arrived in La Ronge in early May. We moved into a tiny cabin at Fitches Cabins. I took the picture of my three boys and our dog Lulu by our jeep, and the cabin that became our temporary home. I have placed an X on the picture on the one in which we lived and our jeep. All the cabins were pretty much the same. Our cabin had two bedrooms and a kitchen. I cooked in here on a propane stove. I liked Fitches cabins and Lac La Ronge right away. There were so many changes to understand immediately. The house we were to live in was not yet ready and we lived in the cabin for two or three weeks.

As soon as we arrived at Fitches cabins, I could see Ida Fitch needed help so I began working immediately. Ida was a lovely lady from Ireland. Her husband was Crawford. I helped her wash sheets and clean cabins getting them ready for the tourist season. The towels and sheets dried on an outside clothesline. There was no drier and the washing machine was electric with a ringer. The sheets all required ironing using a mangle because as they dried they wrinkled. David and Lyle explored the village on their bicycles and Glenn played near the cabin in the dirt. The kids had things to explore and I was so happy to be in civilization and have a conversation with someone.

Then we moved to Tony Woods's house closer to the school. It was a bigger house and was partly furnished and we were here again for a couple of weeks. We were waiting for the previous engineer to leave the house that was to be ours. The picture below was from June 1955 and I took it. Dave Corney stands in front of the door with a camera around his neck and Walter and the three boys along with the dog Lulu are pictured in front of Wood's house. It was just pulled into place and you can see that is standing on blocks of wood. Scraps of wood are strewn around the house and rocks. The bicycle on the ground between David and Walter is likely Lyle's, because Lyle rode his bike everywhere. On the farm, he would ride his bike to the outhouse, the door was always open, and his bike was there on the side. It was never a problem to find him. Lyle and I both do not like to have a door closed on us in strange places.

We had to live in this house because the employee Walter was replacing was still living in the house that we would get. When Walter was home, we could go for a walk and see real people, had neighbors, and were less isolated. Walter worked with this engineer fixing diesel engines and learning about refrigeration.

Electricity made studying easier and more convenient. Replacing fuel lamps of the farm with a brighter light was easier on the eyes and we did not have to spend a lot of extra time and effort cleaning lamps, fueling them and being careful where they were placed. Electricity changed our lives quite a lot. Using an electric iron, I no longer had to heat the irons on a stove and guess at their heat temperatures.

While we lived in the house above Walter began to study refrigeration but by the time he got his first certificate we had already moved into the engineer's house. The two of us worked side by side so Walter could learn refrigeration. We spent many hours reading and studying until late at night.

From the time I first met Walter, I knew English was not his first language. He spoke with an accent. As years went along his accent disappeared. Walter's written English was faulty, but he was determined to improve. I first began to help with spelling. However, with this new twist to his career my help changed. He had a textbook, a desire, and I was his learning aid. We were both determined he would be able to learn this new field of work. This was a special time and we enjoyed working on this together. I am proud of his accomplishments. It took a lot of concentration and hard work but in truth, he was capable of learning it, and seemed to have a gift to understand it. My help came in the form of understanding the written English and with study skills.

We would take a section of the textbook at a time. I would read it aloud. Then Walter read it aloud. Then he read it to himself and then I asked him questions. This way he learned the content. We went over and over the content. It became a ritual. We did this lying in bed. We spent hours doing this. I would ask a question and he would answer it. He learned the correct spelling of refrigeration and ammonia and other refrigeration terms. During March 28, 29, 30, 31, 1956, Walter did nothing but study.

Walter and I went to Prince Albert leaving the boys with Clay Cummins. David did the cooking while we were gone and he baked a layer cake. We stayed at David and Dorothy Corney's. Walter wrote his tests over two days April 2 and 3rd in the courthouse. I went downtown and met him for lunch. On the third, Walter finished his test around 10 AM, and then we went shopping and did some business. He felt he had passed the test because he knew he had the right answers. I worried about his writing and spelling. Later we had supper with David, Dorothy, and left for Lac La Ronge at 6:30 pm. It was about a four hour drive in the company truck. Walter's certificate was issued the following day, April 4, but we did not get the results until a month later. His first certificate arrived in the mail May 4 and he left the same day for Pitching Lake, on Athabaska Airways, spelled with a K, to fix a refrigeration unit. There was no time for celebration. This lack of time for celebration and relaxation was a problem with this job. He always had work to do and very little time for relaxation and mental and physical down time. In this case, yes, he was happy to get the news but was busy at work. After all this studying with Walter I think I could have written the test and got my certificate too and this later helped when Walter had his own company. This first refrigeration exam changed the whole future of Walter, of me, and of his family and descendants. I am pleased when I reflect back at my participation and how we did so much of it together.

No. 615

PROVINCE OF SASKATCHEWAN

File No. 526

DEPARTMENT OF LABOUR

Boiler, Pressure Vessel and Elevator Branch

Refrigeration Engineer's Certificate

This is to certify that Walter Sergius *having satisfactorily proved his qualifications as required by The Boiler and Pressure Vessel Act is hereby granted a Certificate of qualification as a Refrigeration Engineer and is duly recorded as the holder of such certificate.*

Dated at Regina April 4, 1956.

C. C. Williams, Minister

Walter Sergius, Signature of Engineer

Jos. Taylor, Chief Inspector

Walter's profession and his striving to learn refrigeration and get a better education, determined the future of his family, his sons, and grandchildren. He did not want to stay in the remote isolation of the farm and bush country around it. Two of his sons and grandsons studied refrigeration because of his example. If Walter had not taken and met the challenge Dave Corney dropped on him, Walter's family would not be living in southern BC and would not have had a successful company. I feel Walter started the family in refrigeration. His two sons take after their father because of his passion to do the work and succeed, just as their sons took after their fathers and their grandfather. If it were not for Walter successfully meeting and overcoming the hurdles of learning a language and a profession at the same time, his sons and grandsons would not be engineers now.

So, when I consider Polar Industries I see the fruits of Walter's hard work, I am proud of Walter and equally proud to know his sons, and grandsons have worked hard to continue in the profession. It has been far easier for them but not necessarily easy. It is easy to see the world around you, when you can stand on the shoulders of someone else and in this case, that is how it is.

Later in Winnipeg, we used the same process of reading the books to each other and me testing him using the books for questions. In 1961, Walter studied to get his fourth class Power Engineer Certification and then later again in 1968 he got his Maintenance Electrician's Licence. Both are pictured below. In each case, Walter's written English was a hurdle, but in each case, his written English had improved with practise. We worked on it together. When we moved to Winnipeg, he applied and got recognition in Manitoba.

DEPARTMENT OF LABOUR

[illegible]

June 3, 1968.

Mr. Walter [illegible],
[illegible] Cathedral Ave.,
Winnipeg [illegible], Manitoba.

Dear Sir:

Re: [illegible] Maintenance Electricians' Licence

The Board of Examiners is pleased to advise that you were successful in passing your recent examination.

Accordingly, Licence No. [illegible] and Receipt No. [illegible] are enclosed herewith.

This licence expires December 31st of each year at which time you will receive a notice to renew same.

Yours truly,

W. L. [illegible], P.Eng.,
Director,
Mechanical & Engineering Div.

[illegible]
Encls.

In his work, Walter collected many personal recommendations about the quality of his work and his character. All the time Walter worked with the first nation peoples of the north, he was appreciated, and respected. He was always trying to teach and help people to get a skill and get ahead. He was a hard worker and he expected the same amount of work from everyone else but certainly never always got it from others, which caused him have to work longer. He worked many long hours.

Walter had a hard time to get his education, get ahead, and improve his reading and writing. He respected all people. Color and creed did not matter to him. The personality is what mattered to him. This showed in his ability to make friends quickly in an environment that was at times physically challenging without the comforts of home. He wanted to do a good job and wanted others to want the same.

When we finally moved into the engineer's staff house in Lac La Ronge, it was next door to a 4-suite complex that mainly had pilots and their wives in it. I met Mrs. Hilda Brown, Sadie Horn, and Jean Barber. The male manager of the airline lived in the fourth unit. Our other neighbors were the RCMP detachment and radio operator for Northern Affairs and his wife, Jack and Mary McGunigal. Johnny and Doreen Stonehocker, I knew in Pierceland and they arrived perhaps a bit ahead of us also brought here by Dave Corney. Friesens lived not far away. We lived on an island that was joined to the mainland by a road.

In Lac La Ronge, we had a beautiful view of the lake through the kitchen window. From the living room window, we looked in a different direction to the fish plant and float plane air base. There were several floatplanes taking off and landing daily.

Lulu lays on the ground behind our house in Lac La Ronge. We had Lulu on the farm. A travelling salesman would call on the farmhouses. He sold mostly women's clothing. He drove a car with samples and pictures of dresses. A woman could order from him, he would return in a few weeks, and he would deliver them. His name was Mr. Lulu. One time he was visiting and I was talking to the dog and saying come along Lulu come here. It was embarrassing because Mr. Lulu thought I was talking to him. It took a few minutes to be sorted out appropriately. Another time I asked him if he was Jewish. I guess I thought he looked as though he could be. He was very clear that, he was not Jewish that he was Arabic. I understood, but now I more clearly understand how it can be a touchy misidentification.

Lulu was a fine dog and I still feel guilty and miss this dog. In Lac La Ronge, there was no vet and she needed to be spayed as she was constantly having pups. So, we had to have her put down in an unglamorous way. Johnny Stonehocker shot her for us and was kind enough to tell me he made it quick. I felt very badly then and still do. I wish it did not have to happen this way with this loyal dog. Could I have had any other choice I would have taken it. I still regret it.

Here I sit with Lyle and Glenn in our house in Lac La Ronge, in front of our organ. This organ was in the family from before I was born and I remember as a little girl trying to pump the bellows and pick out a tune with one hand. At the time of this picture, it was easily 50 years old. The clock on the left side and the organ were in my mother's house. Mam would point at the clock on the organ and say to me something like, "its 8 o'clock lass". Which meant it was my bedtime and I would have to go to bed.

When we moved from Lac La Ronge, I gave the organ to Mrs McKay. She hoped to have the bellows fixed and use it. Displayed on the organ is model of an armed forces boat. It came in pieces and I think David assembled it. We took special care of this boat and I gave it away when we moved. Beside it is wedding picture of Walter's brother August Gabbie, a hand grenade Walter took the insides out of when he was in the army. My crochet work is on the little stand and on the left. Walter's army picture is behind the organ on the wall. This is the picture Walter sent to me when he was in Regina before we were married. Family pictures were important to us and we displayed those we were sent.

In this house, we had our first telephone. It was a party line or communal line. Our first phone number was 54. My parents had a phone in the house in Woodrow before they moved to Pierceland years before. I remember them using it. It was a big wall mounted machine. Neither Goodsoil, nor our farm had electricity, or a phone. Moving to Lac La Ronge with electricity at a switch, and a telephone, were huge changes to our lives that made us more social and life easier and instantly more pleasant.

In this picture, you can see the wood stove we had shipped from the farm. I cooked many loaves of bread and many meals on this wood and or coal fired stove. The grate in the bottom was adjustable for either fuel. If we burned coal at night, we had to leave the lid off the stove a little so an air stream was created to pull the poison gases from the coal combustion up through the chimney. In the winter time, we had coal in this stove most nights. There is a thermometer dial on the front of the oven but it did not really work all that well. To use the oven one tested the heat with the hand. I really liked this stove. You could cook a meal on it and move the food to the side to keep it hot. I would put the bread to rise on top of the warming oven where the teapot is sitting.

From left to right are Lyle, and the Brown boys Kenny and Blake. The view through the window was of the lake and Allard's island. I think this picture is taken when I was not home. I would not have left the ash can lid open as it is in this picture and it looks like the ash bin is full of ashes as I look at the side of the stove. I think this picture was taken when the boys were alone with one of the young fellows from the fish plant who was chaperoning.

The chairs they sit on are from our dining room suite. I bought it in Winnipeg when Walter was in the army during the war. It was second hand. When Walter was to be sent overseas and ended up in Chilliwack this furniture was shipped back to Golden Ridge and stored with Walter's parents. We had it in our house in Golden Ridge and on the farm. One day I came into the house to see Walter and his brother had covered the table in newspapers and had a motor of some sort all apart all over the table. I was some ticked off at the time because I thought they could have done that somewhere else. When we left the farm, we had it shipped to Lac La Ronge. It was very much like the one we have here in the house in Surrey.

The house in Lac La Ronge was cold in the winter. One year I put all my houseplants in the middle of this dining room table and woke to find they had frozen overnight. It was 58 degrees below zero for two weeks. We had two heaters one oil and one wood, in the living room and the kitchen stove to heat the house. The fuel oil line jelled from the cold. Thus, the heater quit. I had to get up every few hours to add wood to the heater and stove. You can see the floor is linoleum and it goes all the way through bedrooms, living room, and kitchen. House proud, I used to keep this floor waxed with paste wax. In addition to good housekeeping concerns, I also wanted to be sure it was evident we looked after the house because it belonged to government. I wanted to make sure we were worthy of the house. The boys would put on wool socks and slide all over the floor to polish it.

We started to go to the Anglican Church. I had gone to church in Pierceland and occasionally in Chilliwack. There was no formal church in Pierceland, as we did not have an Anglican Church minister. Student ministers would come in the summer time and then we used my mother's living room or the schoolhouse. After a while, there was a United Church built in Pierceland and we would go to the United Church. Mr. Wright became the minister for the United Church and he and his wife lived in town. While his wife was there, I joined Girl Guides. The leaders of the Guides were Opal and Nellie Stonehocker.

For the years on the farm, we had not gone to church at all because there was no Protestant church around. Walter would not attend a Roman Catholic Church and I would not either. So, to find an Anglican Church in Lac La Ronge was special. All Saints Anglican Church in Lac La Ronge was the first real church with a dedicated building that I belonged to as a member of a congregation. Later I began teaching Sunday school and I belonged to the Anglican Women Auxiliary. Being able to socialize with other women was a delight. This had not been possible much since we moved from Chilliwack to the farm, because we had no money and there were no people around to permit social visits.

In Lac La Ronge, I remember on one day Reverend Doctor Stan Cuthand came to the door. I felt very happy and honored that he came around, still I made him take his shoes off and wait a few minutes until the wax was dry. It was a new and unusual privilege, to have a minister make a home visit. The boys had not finished polishing it. Stan was such a gentleman he just did as asked and then we visited. Stan Cuthand was the younger brother of Adam Cuthand and both were ministers. Adam was the minister in Montreal Lake and Stan in Lac La Ronge. Stan became very well known for his work in the Anglican Church and for the Saskatchewan government.

Walter was in Wollaston Lake when we had a medical problem with Glenn and having a helpful community around helped. At school, Glenn had gone to eat his lunch in David's classroom and sat in David's desk. Lifting his leg up underneath himself to sit down, a thumb tack meant for David went into Glenn's foot and caused a rare infection. I had Glenn bath his leg in Epson Salts but the infection spread quickly. I took him to Enid Broom the public health nurse who said we should take Glenn to the Prince Albert hospital. Enid drove us to see the doctor. He could not be admitted to the hospital because it was full. In my mind, I worried whether either the infection would kill him or he would lose a leg.

We stayed for a few days at the Corney house and I had Glenn soak his foot in a bucket of Epsom Salts water. From there he went into the isolation ward at the hospital. I was grateful to be able to stay at the Corney house during this episode. When Glenn went into the hospital for two weeks, I think I took the bus back to Lac La Ronge. I had to return to look after the other two boys. It was hard to leave the youngest in a strange place far from me. Dave and Dorothy Corney were in touch with the doctor regularly and reported Glenn's condition through radiograms to the DNR. It was a stressful time. My motherly attentions were divided between two older boys needing care and Glenn in a hospital. He improved and after 10 days or so in isolation, he was allowed to come home and Walter and I went to get him. While we were gone, David decided to make Seven Minute icing using a double boiler. What he was going to put the icing on I do not know. Having watched me make it, he knew he had to stand and whip it while it was cooking. The water boiled and blew the top pan off the bottom. Icing and water went all over the stove and made a bunch of burnt sugar and steam, but he did a good job of cleaning up the mess.

The wall behind the stove backed onto the bathroom that was entered through a door just to the left of the meter on the wall. Here we had an indoor chemical toilet that had a bucket that had to be emptied daily.

My electric ringer washing machine was stored inside to the left of the meter. It was my first electric washer and what an improvement it was. The machine had been shipped from the farm. Wash day life improved when Walter changed the gas motor to an electric motor. Gone were the horrible exhaust and is pipe. The cold air no longer rushed in and it was quieter.

On the farm and in Lac La Ronge there was no such thing as a sewer line. The lack of this convenience makes for a different life style. Sewer lines make life easier for most people. Without sewer lines, it means that any water, any fluid had to be carried into the house for use and after use, someone had to carry it out of the house. The human body of course took some out to the outhouse but not always. The water and peelings from vegetables and hand washing water had to be collected in pails and carried outside and dumped. On the farm, in the winter, I would leave a 5 gallon pail of peelings and water on the edge of the stove to heat up overnight and then carry this heavy pail out to feed the pigs in the morning. In Lac La Ronge peelings and assorted kitchen water or slop, was carried outside and dumped in a pile but not too close to the house, and the inside chemical toilet full of human waste also had to be carried outside and dumped into the pit of an outside toilet.

We once had three visitors from Asia. One fellow was from Burma and two were from Indonesia. These were exotic visitors to us and to our neighbors. We had seen a few Chinese people but never anyone from anywhere else in the world. To have visitors from the other side of the world in a small place like

Lac La Ronge was exciting, interesting, and enjoyable. We felt privileged to meet them. They had come up to investigate the fish business and automatically came to our house, as Walter was the engineer. They came, played their ukulele and guitar, sang, and spoke in broken English. I am sure I would have played music for them on the accordion. They showed us dances from Indonesia using a scarf. Plastic curtains flank the men, and my accordion case is on the left. On the wall between the two visitors is a mirrored bird picture we had for years. Certainly, we did not have expensive furnishings.

The Asians missed this winter transport of the fish business. This a picture of a Beaver airplane, call number HQG, outfitted with skis instead of pontoons. In the Winter Walter flew in these planes that took off from the frozen lake and on this occasion, was flying off to Pinehouse Lake, April 7, 1956. On a subsequent day, I had the opportunity to have a plane ride to Pinehouse Lake as the pilot was just dropping something off and returning. It was a memorable trip. Returning to Lac La Ronge a thunderstorm was raging. Not having been in many small planes the lighting was scary and the thunder loud. We landed in winds and rain and I had a better appreciation for the danger Walter was in flying around all the time.

The fish company did not own the planes but had an agreement with the airline to fly Walter around. The Beaver was a work horse of an airplane. It was utilized a lot because it was reliable. It was a noisy airplane. One could hear a Beaver coming from a long way off, and of course, it had a lot of engine noise on the inside. Many times, our family flew in a Beaver. Every day the Beaver or a smaller Cessna went somewhere. The planes flew on a schedule visiting different communities. For Walter and fish company employees the planes operated like a taxi taking them to the seven fish plants: Lac La Ronge, Pinehouse sometimes called Snake Lake, Pelican Narrows, Deschambault Lake, Wollaston Lake, Reindeer Lake, and Beaver Lake now known as Amisk Lake. These were the main places and every now and then, he went to small packing plants located elsewhere.

In July 1955, Walter is pictured again leaving. He is reaching for his sleeping bag. When he arrived, he slept in a bunk house and ate in the camp kitchen. Seeing my husband leave again, I felt a feeling of loss. I began to wonder if the kids would ever grow up to have a father. I got involved in everything I could and it was easy because in a small town every organization needs members. As I said earlier it was a change for me to be able to socialize, but Walter could not.

I worked for the public health nurse when she needed help. I had no experience working and this was my first real job other than helping at Fitch's Cabins. Enid was a very patient woman. I would sharpen vaccination needles using a type of sandpaper. She sterilized the needles in a solution. I would go with her to the Indian Reserve to vaccinate people. The first time we visited a woman who had had a miscarriage. The woman was lying on a bed in a cabin with a dirt floor. The legs of the bed had sunk into the dirt floor and she was barely off the ground. I was shocked to see the poverty while Enid talked to the woman.

When Enid had clinics, people from the reserve would come to see her and I would file patient record cards for her. She was a very nice lady and everyone liked her. Enid's husband was Eddy Broom the manager of the Government Trading Store. Lyle and her daughter Joanne Broom were good chums. Joanne Broom was a real nice girl. Lyle was about 15 years old. He bought her a jewel box. Lyle changed his mind and bought her a nice record because they liked dancing. He was then stuck with the jewel box because he could not return it. To help him forget about it I traded him and gave him a small pink box to store his cuff links and tie clips. The plan worked and that is how I got the jewel box I still use, not that I have expensive jewels because I do not. Situations like this come up when you raise boys.

In the winter of 1956, shows Lyle pulling Glenn on a toboggan in front of the house. The snow covers the ground and you can see that although Lac La Ronge was a town, it was a northern frontier town, and the wilds of the bush were at our doorsteps. There are no street lights, traffic lights, signs, and little traffic.

Walter took the picture below. It shows the native workers of the fish plant in the winter in Pinehouse north west of Lac La Ronge. Walter had travelled to this outpost type location to repair machines during the cold of the winter. Fish boxes are piled on the right side of the picture. These boxes may have been made by David and Lyle.

David and Lyle made fish boxes from supplied material. The pieces were all precut and nails were supplied. The boys had to hammer them together. Lyle remembers getting paid 7¢ for a box large enough to pack 100 pounds of fish and 5¢ a box for the 50 pound size. In a day, they could make $5.00. They earned money to buy their bicycles this way.

Lyle is the closest holding a hammer and David a bit further away. In the background to the right of David is an outdoor biffy. The house with the two windows on the end belongs to the McGunigal family. Further, behind that the building might be on the other side of the road and be part of the RCMP detachment.

On the dock in the picture below, you can see a couple of fish boxes with lids nailed down. These are the same as what David and Lyle had made. On the rollers, leaving the airplane is a tub of fish. Not all fish were flown in boxes. The fish arrived by plane in boxes and tubs, was unloaded and taken up this dock straight into the fish plant where they were filleted and frozen in the Lac La Ronge plant. Having jobs for the boys kept them busy and for the most part out of trouble and taught them the work ethic.

In 1956 August and July, we were in Beaver Lake as Walter was working on the diesel engines. Walter is blowing bubbles from Glenn's bubble jar. You can see the bubbles along the side of the building. We drove in almost a complete circle from Lac La Ronge south through PA east through Nipawin into Manitoba to Cranberry Portage, Flin Flon and on to Beaver Lake.

April 4, 1956, I took this picture from side an airplane showing the open water of Reindeer River flowing from the south into

On a hazardous rough northern road, we drove to Beaver Lake from Lac La Ronge in the summer of 1956. We stayed in the trailer pictured below. The trailer was a good place to stay. It was clean, had a stove and a good place to sleep, and was in a nice northern location. It is our car pictured. David and Lyle would go to the fish plant with Walter and he would give them things to do. Glenn used to sit in the tall grass in front of the trailer and play with a little girl that lived close by. I was happy. I knew where the boys were, and we were together as a family.

In the summer of 1959, as a family we flew on a small float plane to Deschambault Lake. We were there three weeks. Walter was working on the diesel engines and the refrigeration in the plant. It was maybe an hour flight. We just got off the plane and settled for the first night Walter was called away to Wollaston Lake. He was gone for a few days and we were alone in an unfamiliar place it is true, but safe and it would be somewhat like camping today.

The first night we experienced a very wild thunderstorm with heavy rain and hail. The uninsulated corrugated tin roof made a terrible noise. It was like being inside a snare drum. We were all kind of nervous sleeping in this big one room building perched on the side of the lake, with only a stove and table. David got sick and had to go to the bathroom. The river was flowing fast and the sky was dark. We had a flashlight and I went out with David to make sure he was safe and did not fall in the water. Inside, the rest of night the rain made a deafening and terrifying noise on the roof.

Perhaps the next day we walked up from the fish plant to a small store a few hundred yards from the house. We met the local store owner and as a way to be nice to strangers in the area, he later took the boys and me on a boat ride. We were thrilled to get the ride. Some of the local natives decided they were going to make home brew. Alongside the path, they had an oval metal wash boiler pan about 12 inches deep and 2 feet long, the same thing in which many people boiled laundry. When we got to the store, we found out that the fellows had bought raisins and other things. They thought they were going to make home brew. As we passed them, they were laughing and having a great time. I do not know how their home brew turned out. They may have had other things with them as they were sure laughing. It is unlikely they had been able to assemble the necessary ingredients, as they were not likely sold in the store. They may have had bottled alcohol from another source. However, it was a sign of alcohol abuse on the lakeside frontier.

The huge stones along the Nelson River gave me a good place to wash clothing. I rubbed P&G soap into the clothes on a large flat stone rinsing them out in the flowing water. I wrung the laundry by hand and hung the clothing on the trees to dry. I cooked on the stove in the shack. We had brought our bed clothing with us. We had a few wiener roasts and for the boys it was a fun time. Walter felt he was losing tools. He had locals helping and tools would be difficult to come by in that location. To stop it Walter had a plan. He identified who he thought was taking the tools. He asked this fellow to keep an eye on things and make sure no one took anything. From that time on, he never lost tools and earned a loyal worker.

Walter went to Reindeer Lake in the winter of 1958 and 1959. It was a typical sunny and frigid winter with continued temperatures far into freezing. Most days were colder than 25 below zero. This kind of weather is nice if one is dressed warmly. The ice on the lake would easily be much more than a foot thick.

On this trip, Walter had a few helpers. One was Klouse, from Germany. The banter of the camp ended up with someone daring Klouse to go into the lake in the middle of winter for $10.00. Klouse took up the offer and the pictures below document the experience. The first shows Klouse in the water up to his neck. The water was much warmer than the air outside. You can see the water intake hose for the fish

plant at the edge of the hole. In the second, you can see him accepting two five dollar bills from the fellow who dared him to do it. In the north and isolation people had to create fun like this or have none.

We are having a group Saskatchewan Fish Marketing Service dinner in a restaurant in Prince Albert. Walter and I are on the end of the table facing to the left. This type of corporate function was nothing like farm union meetings because there was no complaining. In the blue sleeveless dress, Dorothy Corney my cousin is talking to a man. Dave took this picture. We were glad to be able to attend this social event. This is a significant picture to me because it shows us being social again. Escaping the farm, we were glad to be able to socialize again.

I became active socially in Lac La Ronge. I helped to organize the first Girl Guides in town. This was at the time, the furthest north group of Girl Guides in Saskatchewan. I enjoyed the kids and we tried hard to enrich their lives socially and practically. The girls were not allowed to wear red nail polish and if they showed up with nail polish, they had to make sure the next time they did not have the nails painted. We were trying to teach them self discipline. We went on hikes for a couple of miles around the edges of town. We taught them how to make a bonfire with sticks, how to make beds, and how to brush their teeth if they were camping using the soot under the campfire kettle or Lifebuoy soap, and follow the Girl Guide rules. We stayed pretty close to town on hikes and never encountered any bears or threatening wildlife. The bears and wild life were there but stayed away from us. When I left, the guides gave me a Lac La Ronge plate, cup, and saucer. Looking at the girls faces, I still recognize them but have forgotten most of their names.

These girls were a happy group. I look at this picture where I stand in the middle at the back, and I can hear their laughter and feel their enthusiasm for life.

The newspaper clipping came from the Prince Albert Herald. It talks about our Guide group and has my name in it. It was very unusual to have one's name in the paper and I felt honored. I was glad to be part

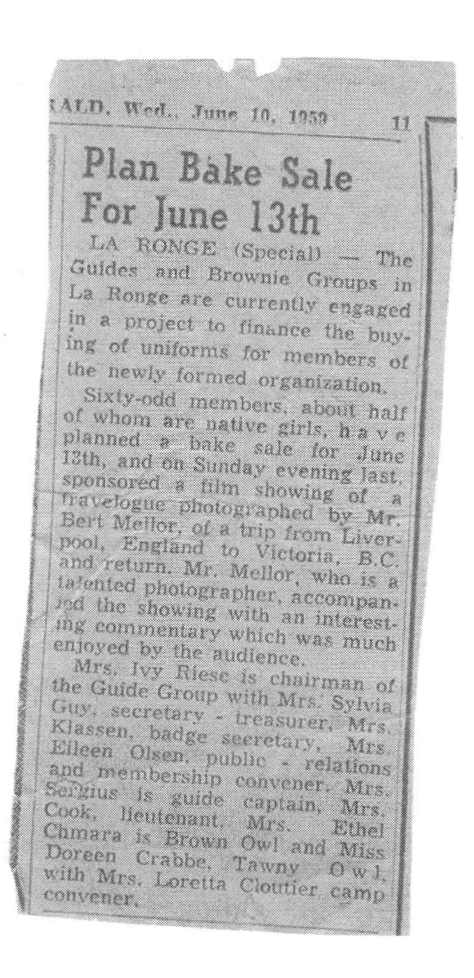

ALD, Wed., June 10, 1959 11

Plan Bake Sale For June 13th

LA RONGE (Special) — The Guides and Brownie Groups in La Ronge are currently engaged in a project to finance the buying of uniforms for members of the newly formed organization.

Sixty-odd members, about half of whom are native girls, have planned a bake sale for June 13th, and on Sunday evening last, sponsored a film showing of a travelogue photographed by Mr. Bert Mellor, of a trip from Liverpool, England to Victoria, B.C. and return. Mr. Mellor, who is a talented photographer, accompanied the showing with an interesting commentary which was much enjoyed by the audience.

Mrs. Ivy Riese is chairman of the Guide Group with Mrs. Sylvia Guy, secretary - treasurer, Mrs. Klassen, badge secretary, Mrs. Eileen Olsen, public - relations and membership convener. Mrs. Sergius is guide captain, Mrs. Cook, lieutenant. Mrs. Ethel Chmara is Brown Owl and Miss Doreen Crabbe, Tawny Owl, with Mrs. Loretta Cloutier camp convener.

of an organization making a positive contribution to the community. I got a nice card with all the names of the Guide committee on it when I left. was also on the Boy Scout Council and here is my membership card:

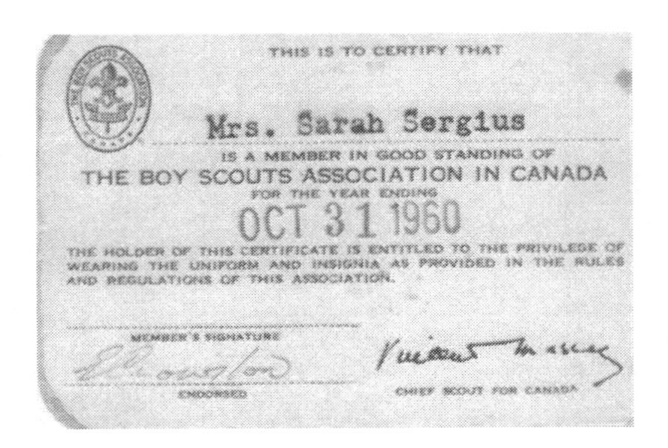
THIS IS TO CERTIFY THAT

Mrs. Sarah Sergius

IS A MEMBER IN GOOD STANDING OF

THE BOY SCOUTS ASSOCIATION IN CANADA

FOR THE YEAR ENDING

OCT 31 1960

THE HOLDER OF THIS CERTIFICATE IS ENTITLED TO THE PRIVILEGE OF WEARING THE UNIFORM AND INSIGNIA AS PROVIDED IN THE RULES AND REGULATIONS OF THIS ASSOCIATION.

MEMBER'S SIGNATURE

ENDORSED

CHIEF SCOUT FOR CANADA

In Lac La Ronge, I was busy all the time going to meetings and helping in the community. Perhaps I was making up for lost time after having lived on the farm. I had gone from a small town where everyone knew everyone's business. Most of the time if they did not know, or were not sure of the details, they just added a little to the story. I moved from the isolation on a farm back to a larger small town. I certainly learned more social skills of living in a community. Walter was gone all the time and the small community always needed volunteers. I was involved with All Saints Anglican Women's Auxiliary, as president and secretary of this group, the Home and School Group, Lac La Ronge Ladies Club, Scout Council, Girl Guides, worked part time for the Health Department, took a course in first aid, and taught Sunday School.

Many groups like the Women's Auxiliary for the church and the Ladies club had meetings in our house. This group of women is a meeting of the Ladies Club in our house. Hilda Brown is on the far right wearing glasses and leaning over, the second person to the left partly hidden is Doreen Stonehocker. I am sitting and of course have my mouth open; the woman beside me is Mrs Ida Fitch. I remember their names because we had great fun together.

I always seemed to be baking buns and cookies that the sales the groups would have. There was always some organization needing baking. I did this on the wood stove in the earlier picture. I look back on my time in Lac La Ronge with fondness for the place, the people, and the memories of friends. I look now and wonder about such an active schedule.

I earned a certificate for taking a Home Nursing Course. Living in the north one never knew what kind of medical situation might arise. Many times, there would not be anyone around to help. Travelling to remote places with Walter and the boys gave me ample reason to want to be able to do first aid. In such situations, immediate medical help was not available. One had to know some basic skills. There is now a hospital in Lac La Ronge but it was built, as we were to move out of town. I worked in it for a brief time. The doctor was Dr Cook who had his office in the hospital. The certificate has the official signature of the Governor General who was Vincent Massey acting as President of the Canadian Red Cross Society.

The attendance card is copied front and back. It is interesting because it illustrates that the course was taken seriously, and shows the method of record keeping in a small town. I am not sure how I ended up with the card.

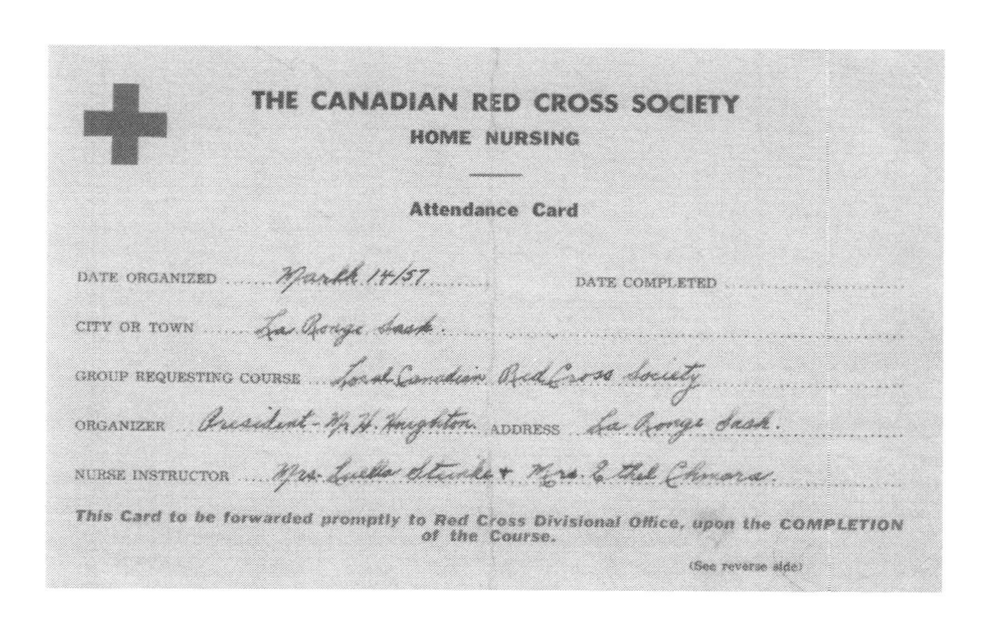
THE CANADIAN RED CROSS SOCIETY

HOME NURSING

Attendance Card

DATE ORGANIZED March 14/57 DATE COMPLETED

CITY OR TOWN La Ronge Sask.

GROUP REQUESTING COURSE Local Canadian Red Cross Society

ORGANIZER President - Mr H. Haughton ADDRESS La Ronge Sask.

NURSE INSTRUCTOR Mrs Luella Steinke + Mrs. Ethel Chmara

This Card to be forwarded promptly to Red Cross Divisional Office, upon the COMPLETION of the Course.

(See reverse side)

The course had two instructors Mrs Luella Steinke was a friend of our family friends the Stonehockers and they all went to their Evangelical Church. The other instructor was Mrs Ethel Chamara a nurse whose husband was the policeman. Glenn played with their kids. Thirty one years later Walter and I went to Vancouver Island to visit Ethel and Nick Chamara. It was the last time we saw them.

The Canadian Red Cross Society

\- Home Nursing -

It is acknowledged that

Mrs. Sarah Sergius

has attended a course in Red Cross Home Nursing.

Date May 16, 1957

Vincent Massey
President Canadian Red Cross Society

Interestingly the names use the prefix "Mrs." for the women. Today we might easily drop

	NAME	ADDRESS	Attendance
	Mrs. Hittie Mac Auley		
1.	Mrs. Sarah Sergius	La Ronge	
2.	Mrs. Hilda Brown	" "	
3.	Mrs. Loretta Clouthier	" "	
4.	Mrs. Lorraine McRae	" "	
5.	Mrs. Eileen Mullock	" "	
6.	Mrs. John Thompson	" "	
7.	Mrs. Peggy McKnight	" "	
8.	Mrs. Ethel Reimer	" "	
9.	Mrs. Elaine Shafer	" "	
10.	Mrs. Mary McGunigal	" "	
11.	Mrs. Roberta [illegible]	" "	
12.	Mrs. Laura [illegible]	" "	
13.	Mrs. Reta Woods	" "	
14.	Mrs. Genevieve Folkwood	" "	
15.	~~Mrs. Cummins~~	" "	
16.	Mrs. Eva [illegible]	" "	
17.	~~Mrs. Eileen Mullock~~		
18.	Mrs. Eileen Olson		
19.	Mrs. Ida Fitch		
20.	Mrs. Elsie Callbeck		
	~~[illegible]~~		

this reference to the not present male. Today there is a more solid recognition of women as individuals and not just husband appendages. Gone is the pointless built in need to recognize the marital status of a woman.

The back of the card lists the people that attended the class. I remember them all as friends. Hettie MacAuley was a neighbor when we first moved to town. She became a close friend. We always shared good times together. Hettie died, before the year 2000. Her husband Norman lived in Kelowna for a long time. Hettie came from England and she married Norman who was a first nation soldier in the Canadian army. I wonder if she was prepared for life in the Canadian north after life in England. They had two boys, Angus was one, but I have forgotten the other one's name.

Hilda Brown lived next door to us upstairs in the government duplex. We went back and forth for tea. Her husband was an engineer at SGA, Saskatchewan Government Airways. She was about ten years older than I was and has been dead for a while now. Her two sons Blake and Kenny were similar in ages to David and Lyle and the boys chummed together so we had that in common as well. Loretta Clouthier had a husband in the Department of Nature Resources, DNR. He is the one that caught the group of boys, David, Lyle, Blake and Kenny Brown, Jack Broom, Ray McKay, and maybe Jimmy McKnight after they had shot up the DNR signs on the side of the road with a gun. The boys were reprimanded and sentenced to do labor leveling the ground for a skating rink and paint more signs.

I do not remember too much about Lorraine McRae, as I did not get to know her. I think Eileen Mullock was the wife of a pilot. Mrs John Thompson was known as Freddy Thompson. I am not sure how we abbreviated it to Freddy.

Peggy McKnight was the wife of pilot Sam McKnight and they had two boys one was Jim. Bernice Reimir, Elaine Shafer I do not remember her personally as well as I did not know her as well. Mary McGunigal was a neighbor and Glenn played with Lilian and Sharon her daughters. Roberta Qwant was the wife of a government worker. Laura Renniberg and her husband owned a garage I think. Rita Woods and her husband Tony rented us their house when we first came to town. Tony worked for the Government Trading Store. Genevieve Folkvord was wife of the Evangelical Church minister. Dolly Cummins' husband worked for the fish company with Walter for a while and stayed with David and Lyle when I had to take Glenn to the hospital in Prince Albert. Eva Friesen also went to the Evangelical Church and lived by Stonehockers. She had several children. Eileen Olson, I have also forgotten. Ida Fitch owned the cabins where we stayed and I worked. Elsie Callbeck and Jean Austin I have also forgotten.

I had a lot of friends in Lac La Ronge. I was honored that when I left they gave me a farewell party. When I look back now at the time in Lac La Ronge it seems that a different part of my life started and that the time on the farm was laborious, and life stunting and that I began to enjoy life again after we moved to Lac La Ronge.

Ruby and I are pictured sitting on the grass in front of the Jasper Park Lodge in, 1956. Note we are not wearing slacks. I do not think we had any at the time. The three boys and I went by car to Prince Albert and from there caught a train to Edmonton, but sadly without Walter who was away working. The 4 of us and we all managed to cram into a small sleeper car. David and Lyle in the upper bunk, and Glenn and I had the bottom. We enjoyed this trip. Ruby, Otto and Gary took us to see Jasper, and Jasper Park Lodge where Otto had been doing some work. We stayed in tents in the park on one night only. There was a bear not too far away at the garbage cans. I took Glenn to sleep in the car and I sat in the car keeping an eye on the tent all night in case the bear came around.

I am standing on the steps of the TV Station CFRN in 1956. Walter carried this picture of me around in his wallet for 20 years or more.

Ruby talked to someone at the station. The next thing I knew I was invited to the station. They interviewed me live on TV about Lac La Ronge. Being involved in so many things, I could tell them a lot.

The experience was kind of like being foreign reporter. Glenn watched me on TV in Ruby's house. The dress looks white in this picture but it was a type of yellow.

Once again back in Lac La Ronge I did other things than just attend meetings. Music could again be a pastime. Doreen Stonehocker played the banjo and I played the accordion, together we had fun making music. We played together at some of the dances in town in a
community hall that doubled as a movie theatre. Doreen's real name was Doris. When she worked in a grocery store in Pierceland, there were two people with the name Doris. So, this Doris took the name Doreen.

For the fun of it, Doris and I entered an amateur show. We practised a bit before we went to Prince Albert for the monthly amateur show. We played the Helena Polka and maybe some old time waltzes. We won first prize, and perhaps $25. She belonged to an Evangelical church and she just slowly stopped playing. I felt it may have been her church that stopped her playing, because we were playing dance music and not spiritual music. I was saddened but had to accept her absence though I did not agree with her church. She certainly had a good time playing but our musical career ended.

Betty played the piano for us in 1956 when we travelled from Lac La Ronge to visit the Baker family on their farm outside Pierceland. This picture was taken of most of the "R" named kids. From the right counter, clockwise are Roseanne, Rita, Robert, Ronnie, and Raymond. Above their heads on the wall are two instruments. The guitar is Betty's and the mandolin is Syd's. I remember Syd playing the mandolin when we lived in Woodrow. I never heard Syd and Betty play together. I remember singing with Betty as she played the guitar. Betty had a nice voice and her mother taught piano and taught Betty how to play.

You can see the house is not yet finished but it was a nice house that years later met its demise on the front end of a bulldozer as it was bulldozed down into the basement.

This picture was taken around the same time. Walter and I and Glenn drove from Pierceland to visit Walter's two brothers. It was nice to be able to visit them and we felt happy as we left. John was in the process of building a house living in the basement at the time. This picture of Jean, Helen, and Glenn sharing a chair in August and Gabby's house that had previously been the house of Walter's parents. On

the wall behind them, are a picture of the queen, and pictures of Minnie and a young Glenn on the chest of drawers. He was very shy as a child. Lyle was a bit shy and David was not shy at all. I raised three boys all different as children.

April 21st, 1957. I took this picture from just outside our house. Spring can be a dangerous time because the firmness of the ice is unsure. The pilot is walking away from the plane that has wheels and is sitting on the ice. He is carefully walking towards the fish plant and the SGA site, Saskatchewan

Government Airlines. In the foreground, it looks like the snow had been cleaned away for a skating rink but only part of the outline of the snow edge of the ring is left visible. The snow has begun to leave. The ice where the pilot is walking near where the plane sits, will in a few days, be too soft to walk on. In this strip of water a lot of airplanes coming and going save for this time between seasons as the ice melted.

Allard's Island is in the background. In the summer time, the natives left their dogs on the island. The dogs would howl, perhaps to be fed, and get attention. In the winter, the dogs were used in sled teams but were lean because they had not been fed well during the summer months.

One year I took Glenn and we went to Rita Baker's wedding. I think it was 1957. Aunt Lottie and Uncle Charlie were visiting us at the time in Lac La Ronge. We drove with them to Pierceland. I was driving and Aunt Lottie was in the front seat and Glenn and Uncle Charlie were in the back seat. Lottie kept telling me to drive faster and would not stop harping. She was known for wanting her own way and harping to get it. I drove the speed limit even if the roads were not full of traffic. Eventually I had enough of her constant harping. I spied a bus stop along the way and I stopped the car. I told her she had to shut up and get in the back seat or Glenn and I were getting out and waiting at the bus stop to take the bus home. She did get out and got in the back and Uncle Charlie got in the front with a big grin saying it was the first time anyone stood up to her. Further, down the road we stopped in Shellbrook so Aunt Lottie could post some cards. She and I got along just fine after that adjustment. We continued on to Pierceland and spent the night. The next day I took Glenn and we went with Johnny McEvoy to the wedding. It was a hell of a scary ride. I would never want to repeat it. He drove like a maniac all the way there. It was a dusty dirty road and he kicked up quite a lot of dust having a good time passing and swerving back and forth across the road.

I made Glenn sit on the floor of the back seat. There were no seat belts in cars at that time. We stayed with Rita's in laws. I refused to ride back with Johnny McEvoy and I cannot remember how we travelled back to Pierceland, and how we got back to Prince Albert I cannot remember. Maybe the ride scared all those memories away.

On one trip when we very nearly ended up in the ditch and stranded in the cold. Christmas 1958, we borrowed Dunc McLean's car and drove from Lac La Ronge to Edmonton. Winter driving was rough. On one occasion, the car jumped out of the ruts made a complete circle in the road and back into the ruts facing the right way. I was in the back seat with Mam and Glenn. Walter was driving and David and Lyle were up front. We were all jaw dropping amazed at what had just happened. We could have ended up in the ditch in the cold weather. We always drove with garlic sausage and food with us in the car and blankets in the back and were prepared for bad weather. We drove along ruts of snow in the road. We were taking Mam to Pierceland. How she got to Edmonton, I do not know. It may be that she took the bus as she had taken the bus to Edmonton a few times.

Here everyone is gathered around the dinner table at Christmas in Minnie's basement. It was a good time and a good dinner. Sergei played truck and car with the chicken bones on the kitchen table.

Walter's father could understand more English than he let on. Both the boy's grandmothers are in the picture. Starting at the bottom left of the picture those present were: Glenn Mam, Otto, Ruby, Johanna Walter's mother, Walter, Me, David, Lyle, Gary, and in the back Minnie and Sergei Walter's father.

The management and structure of the Co-op Fish changed and so we left. We moved to

Winnipeg in 1960. Walter had a job with Pete Lazarenko of Northland Fisheries. Dave Corney was already working for Northland. I think Walter took the bus to Winnipeg and was already up North working at Island Lake when we left Lac La Ronge.

I had taught David to drive in Lac La Ronge. David could drive a tractor a little bit, but not a car. Two or three times we went to the airport about 3 miles away and practised stopping, starting, driving and using signal lights. There was only one stop sign in town so he practised stopping at it and looking around.

We left Lac La Ronge after school was out the end of June. David was driving our Buick and it broke down as we were approaching Prince Albert. Just like in a movie, a bus came along. I got in with Glenn leaving David and Lyle back in the car. My intent was to get a tow truck to go back and get David and Lyle in the car. Luckily, Leo Gorscht, a worker of Co-op Fisheries, came along the road and found David and Lyle on the road. David just had the car started when Leo arrived. David drove the car into Prince Albert with Leo Gorscht following. I was at the garage and car lot. I was arranging for a truck to go get them when David and Lyle drove up. What a wonderful sight that was!

The car was in Walter's name. I needed permission from him to sell it. I had to get him by telephone and radio so the owners of the car lot could speak with him to allow the car to be traded. We had to call Winnipeg and the phone company used a two way radio to Island Lake. To converse one had to say what was needed, and end the sentence by saying "over". This way we got Walter to talk to the garage owner. We had bought the car we were selling at that lot so with Walter's approval we sold the car. The inequality of men and women was apparent to me at the time. I did think about it. I did what I had to do. Since I had to 3 little boys to look after it was not an issue to deal with at the time. In 1960, it was customary for things to be only in the husband's name. About 50 years later, when I was 88 I bought a car myself, and decided to buy it on time, making a monthly payment. Things have changed as I needed no one else's permission and my age was not an issue either.

Back in Prince Albert, in the car lot, we bought a Buick and it was a nice and good car. David and Lyle liked it and the power it had. The next day we left the hotel and headed to Pierceland to visit Mam. I sat in the front seat between David and Lyle so I could keep my eye on the speedometer. Driving down the highway at this speed was new to David. I wanted to be sure that I was watching 17 year old David as he was driving. Highway driving to larger centers and traffic were new to David. Both David and Lyle were thrilled at the speed this car could go. Thus, a few times the speedometer did go up over the speed limit. Glenn sat in the back.

In Pierceland, we spent time with Syd and Betty Ruby and Otto, and Granny. We were there for a few days. Syd thought it was a bad idea for us to be moving to the big city with three boys. He thought the city would be a bad influence and that it would be better that we found a place like Pierceland to live. This type of life was not an option in my mind. I wanted my family to have a choice of friends that were available in a city and it was a choice they would not have in a small town. I told Syd that, but we did not agree. I could see his point. He was concerned but we did not argue about it. Ruby and Otto never expressed an opinion but they also lived in Edmonton at the time.

In the picture below, Mam stands in front of her three remaining children, Syd, Sarah, and Ruby on the right. Rick Sager her great grandson is with Ruby. Glenn is partly visible on the left. The blue and white car we bought in Prince Albert is behind.

Mam, at 80, was moving this weekend from living in Pierceland with Syd and Betty, to live with Ruby and Otto in Edmonton. She would be much happier in Edmonton because she was getting older and the hospitals and doctors were close. She had been a diabetic for 15 years. Living with Ruby was also better because she was not on her own. Ruby was to give her a needle everyday but Ruby could not stick her mother with a needle, so Otto gave her the needle just above her knee. She was at the time losing her eye site. Later she was able to take diabetic pills. She was never a complainer. Even though she was in pain near the end, she did not complain.

On that day pictured in 1960, we left Pierceland for Winnipeg, and Mam moved to Edmonton. We stopped in Indian Head to see Aunt Gladys. Her husband Bert May was out on the fields that day. They had farm fields on both sides of the highway. We stayed for only a few minutes to talk. Later Bert was killed on the highway driving a tractor.

Heavy rain rushed in a big storm as we were on the highway. We went into the town of McGregor because it was raining so hard. We saw all the ditches full of water. When we left McGregor, David did not completely stop at the stop sign pulling onto the highway. A half mile down the road a policeman watched David pull on to the road and quickly stopped us.

The policeman said, "Do you realize you have to come a full stop when you pull onto a grand trunk highway". David did not get a ticket, we continued our way, and we all learned a valuable lesson.

Our trunk was full of stuff but the furniture was shipped by truck. The rest of the trip to Winnipeg passed without much excitement other than that inside ourselves at what it would be like to see Winnipeg. Dave Corney had found a duplex for us to live in when we first arrived in Winnipeg.

I cannot imagine what our sons would have chosen for their life's work if we had stayed on that isolated farm and not moved Lac La Ronge. When we moved to Lac La Ronge, they had many friends to play with, and a school close enough that they could walk to school. No longer did they have to ride a bus and be the only ones not RC or JW. We lived close to the lake where they could swim. It was a good move, but so too was the move leaving it.

When we left Lac La Ronge, it enabled our sons to access more opportunities for education and friendship. We wanted our sons to grow up to be good citizens of our country, and be happy and healthy. It seemed moving to Winnipeg was a good option.

Winnipeg: In A City My Family Grows Up

Late on a warm sunny day in early July, filled with excitement we arrived on the west outskirts of Winnipeg. The city rose up out of the flat prairie like a forest. No longer were we in the land of rolling hills, rock, scrub brush, lakes, swamps, and wild life. We had arrived at a noisy, almost flat land without a hill. Similarity could be found in the hordes of mosquitos. In Winnipeg, the summers would be hotter, and the winters a bit milder than the far north.

On the edge of the city, and from a phone booth, I called Dave Corney. Using his instructions and a map, the boys and I got to their place in St James with David driving.

Dave had rented us a half a duplex for about three weeks. He immediately led us to the new place which came completely furnished including bedding, which was good because our furniture and belongings arrived later. All we had to buy was groceries after we found the place.

As we got back into the car Dave gave our son David a good tip on driving knowing David was not accustomed to driving in the city. Dave said always make sure you shoulder check both sides before you change lanes and or turn, because there is a lot of traffic in the city. David was glad of the tip and seeing the volume of traffic realized it was a good idea.

We stayed in this rented house 792 Bannerman, close to a busy railway track for a month. That proved to be a new noisy experience because the train went by a few times a day going to Winnipeg Beach and returning home as many times. The second day of our stay I started to find us a permanent home, partly because it was a noisy location, partly because it was an expensive place to rent, and partly because it was only available for a short time.

Walter arrived for 2 days and left again for Island Lake in Northern Manitoba. It was a too short a stay with his family in civilization. David took Lyle and Glenn to the pet store and came home with a creamy white colored dog with flop ears. Walter suggested Glenn call him Pal and that is how he got the name Pal. Pal became such an intricate part of our family some of his characteristics are worthy of mention here.

Pal acted as a loyal guard dog. All I needed to do was loop my fingers through his collar and he became a guard dog for strangers at the door. Reversely his bravado disappeared quickly and Pal would hide under the bed if he heard the word "bath". On Bannerman, we did not have a fence and Pal had to be tied up on a long rope. On one occasion, the rope was just a bit too long. David advertised an old car for sale in the paper. When the salesman came around to collect the money for the ad Pal objected to him. We had to buy the salesman a new pair of overshoes.

Pal was playful too. He used to jump onto the bed when I would make beds. When flipping the sheets and blankets across the beds he would get under them to play. We taught him to play a kind of game

where we would hide something, and he would wait for us to hide it and they he would go retrieve it.

When we lived on Cathedral Avenue, we had a fenced yard and Pal would have the yard. In the winter, we dug a place for him through the snow to have to walk around. Walter made a snow sided run for him on Smithfield. He lost a lot of long white hair but looked so beautiful when he was freshly bathed. Pal lived to be 17 and disappeared one night when Glenn let him out the back door and he never returned. He was just gone. Perhaps he went some place and died. He just did not come back in. Pal was not a purebred, and what breed he was I do not know but he was a good dog. Perhaps Pal had some influence on my youngest son Glenn being a successful dog breeder.

On a day when I washed clothes, I took them off the line folding and leaving them in a pile on the kitchen table. I went out to do a few errands. I was not gone long. When I came back, Pal had clearly not been too pleased that I left. He had gone through the pile of laundry taking an assortment of only my clothing. He laid them all over the floor in the kitchen. Resourcefully he had used the chair to climb up onto the table and make his selections. Climbing on the table was not something he did, but on this occasion, he showed he could if he wanted to.

Now with 3 boys and a dog, and Walter gone again after a few days' visit, I had to find a house for us fairly soon. Luckily, using the newspaper I found a pink house two blocks away on the same street, 689 Bannerman. The style was what was called at that time, a war time house, because many homes of this style were built especially for veterans returning home from the war overseas. The veterans all needed homes and many of the same style were built in a short time frame. They all had one bedroom on the main floor, along with the bathroom, kitchen, and living room, and upstairs were two bedrooms with slanted ceilings. The picture below shows that it has storm windows on the front windows in the summer time. The zinnia flowers I grew from seed.

We met the neighbors and we were so pleased to meet such good people. Ina Longmuir had lived in the house before we did and had downsized to a smaller house just down the street a few houses. She became a good friend for many years. She also moved to BC in later years. Across the years, we would always talk and visit. The neighbors I have now in Surrey I hardly know.

The neighbors beside us were also friends. Marian and Bill Prokopenko had three boys all younger than mine. Marian was a friendly happy person who liked a good joke and to tease. She knew and liked the boys and one day Lyle, about 16 or 17 years old, was upstairs secretly smoking. From her kitchen window, Marian could see Lyle bent over blowing smoke out the storm window holes. He was not allowed to smoke but kept up the habit. The houses were close together and Marian could easily see Lyle when she looked up. Marian telephoned over and asked to speak to Lyle. I answered the phone and called out to Lyle to tell him the call was for him. Poor Lyle, right in the middle of a good smoke a phone call comes and it is for him. There were no extension phones in most homes in those days so Lyle had to come downstairs to answer the phone. He quickly had to throw his partially smoked cigarette out the air hole in the window frame and come downstairs. Marian watched him do this. When he got to the phone, Marian just asked him "having a good smoke?" and laughed. She later told me about it and we both laughed, since then the story has been told a lot and Lyle laughs too.

When the Prokopenko neighbors moved to Vancouver, they asked us to rent their house so they would be more content it was being looked after. So, we moved next door to 685 Bannerman, also a wartime house but with one great attraction, a garage.

The summer before we moved from 689 Bannerman, while Norman was up north working at Lynn Lake, his wife Joan, and sons Rick and Brad stayed with us. It was during this time that Merilee was born. When Joan came out of the hospital, she came to our house. Brad was cute and so excited to see his baby sister he jumped on the bed and Merilee bounced up and down a bit. Soon he calmed right down and contained his excitement. The boys seemed happy to have a younger sister.

While living on Bannerman I got a job working at Miracle Bakery. It may have been located on Main near Bannerman and Atlantic. I liked the work and we needed the money, but I was not too happy with the boss's wife. She paid me 85¢ an hour and I was not to tell the other women what I was being paid. She never explained why I was not to tell. A young boy would come in on the weekend and assemble boxes for 40¢ an hour. I am not sure about her motivation for keeping the pay a secret and I could have been paid more, or less, or the same as my fellow workers. She seemed to want to create mystery. It was not much of a wage but we needed the money.

Had the wife of the owner stayed away things would have been a lot better in the bakery. To clean the show case, she used to take food from the display cases and pile it all over the floor where we were walking behind the counter and in a busy store. We had to step over and around fresh iced cakes, cookies, fruit cups, slices and other sugary treats while we were working. The fresh product was exposed to muck from our shoes and the air born dust floating near the floor. It was a disgusting habit and the health department would not have approved. She refused to move it so I quit. When I quit, she told me I could not quit. I gave her my apron and left. I thought I might not be paid for the week when I went to get my cheque.

I was paid, and also surprised. I was asked to come back to work by the boss. He explained his wife's nerves were bad and he was sending her on a trip to Israel. Still, I felt I had enough of that experience and decided to find work elsewhere.

I was not out of work long. I got a job almost immediately working at the local small corner J&W store. I wanted to work to add income to the $300 a month Walter was earning. I wanted work close to the house so that I could look after my family. Luckily, this store was just around the corner. The owner Bill Skakum had two such stores. This small crowded store, about the size of a small house, was busy all week long in a time when there were many corner stores in Winnipeg. I worked almost every day some weeks, and other weeks only 2 or 3 days. I got paid less money, only 76¢ an hour but it was a job close to home. I could walk to work in 10 minutes.

In the store, I was packing groceries and working the cash register. I would help Bill make his own sausages sometimes working late till about 9 pm. When I got home, Walter did not like the idea that I had to work so late and come home in the dark. I did not like it either but we needed the money.

At J&W, I learned some of the ways to keep a store profitable. Bone in hams, were sold but sometimes not as quickly, as was hoped. We had to examine them every so often. If there was a spot that did not look especially good and fresh, we wiped the area with vinegar to make it look better. I also worked the meat slicer slicing cooked meats weighing them for sale much like a deli counter in Safeway. At closing time, we had to wash up the meat slicer taking it apart and then sweep the floors.

At the cash register, some people were allowed to run an interest free bill. Providing credit was one way Bill retained customers. Certainly, it helped people in a time before credit cards were common. When people shopped, and wanted to pay by adding it to their bill we had to search through the book pages of bills with names at the top and update their tab with new totals. I got to know many people this way.

Keeping the shelves stocked was a continual job. There was little storage. All stock had to go on the shelves as best we could get it there. That meant sometimes cans and bottles were on the floor in the small aisles making walking a careful exercise. On busy Saturdays, people would place orders over the phone. The store was even more crowded with boxes of delivery orders stacked on top of one another, on top of the groceries, and in the aisles. Every place that could hold an order was piled high. Bill's brother Paul did the Saturday deliveries in a station wagon. Boxes and boxes of deliveries in several station wagon loads would go out of the store that day. Both Bill and Paul treated me very nicely with respect.

I was the only one that never smoked in the store. Mae the other clerk smoked, and Bill and Paul my two bosses smoked. Many more people smoked in the 1960's than smoke today. Clerks could smoke right in the store where they worked, at the till, in the deli area, etc. I would clean a lot, but I would not empty an ashtray. I never worked in the store at late at night alone but I did sometimes stay until 9pm. Nothing even hinted at being a robbery. The walk home was short and safe.

Bill would bring in pre-ordered cheese cakes from home. His wife was a good cook. They sold well in the store but they were not secured in plastic wrap and not put in plastic bags. Wrapping paper was on a roll at the end of the counter. Things were wrapped in paper, tied or taped together and put into paper bags. It is likely the cheese cakes were wrapped in paper a lot of time. We wrapped meat, cheese, and glass, to give some protection.

The customer was always the boss and they would have some rather strange requests regarding the product sold such as fresh sour cream, and sliced meat. Some customers would ask for fresh sour cream, as it had to last all week. Some wanted the deli meat cut paper thin and others wanted thick cuts. Annoyingly a few waited till just before closing time to rush in for sliced meat, by which time the slicer was already washed and put away for the night and it meant cleaning it again after their small two or three slice order. Nothing was pre sliced. However, we always obliged and got the customer what they wanted.

I had forgotten about the one older, stout man, in his 60's, until Glenn reminded me of him. Glenn was visiting at the store and I told him to listen as he came in as he always said the same thing. He would slowly climb the stairs to the store. Reaching the landing and the door he paused and would always loudly say, "Whaaaaat the? Oh, Hello".

All in all, the customers were nice people and liked to come in to talk as they shopped and traded neighborhood and personal stories. The good thing about working in the store was that I was able to meet and to know everyone in the neighborhood and people were friendly. I remember loaning my good steak knives out to a customer. The knives came in a satin lined box, but unfortunately, she lost the box and returned them in a cloth. I was disappointed but it was not the end of the world. I still have the cloth, and the knives, and the satisfaction that I loaned them to someone who appreciated having them.

In the end the cloth is likely an easier way to save the knives. Many customers would come to shop and to chat and my boys could come if they needed me.

One day Lyle came galloping into the store out of breath saying, "David's after me, David's after me." Of course, David, heavier set, could not run as fast as the slim erect Lyle could.
After a few quick steps, David soon turned back. Whatever the little spat was about, it was over when Lyle went home.

It seemed Bill had owned the store long enough to even know what some customers liked to drink. Bill had a steady business selling home brew. I do not know how or where he had it made. I never saw it being delivered to the store. I always saw the bottles rolled up in a brown paper bags. Many times, Bill would be at the counter serving a customer taking money for a bottle of home brew while I was right beside him serving a policeman. I knew what was going on and felt guilty about it. Alcohol caused enough problems in society without stores having to sell it illegally. I did not have anything to do with selling the brew. Just knowing what was in the packages worried me. I am not sure if the policeman knew what was going on or if he even wondered what was in the wrapped parcel. The policeman and the customer were regulars. Perhaps the policeman was also a steady home brew customer. No questions were asked.

I quit this job on a Wednesday night. Bill wanted me to go get a bottle of home brew for a customer. That was crossing a line. I did not want to be involved. I quit that night and never went back. It was a nice job while it lasted. The store ran for a few more years, but the customer base slowly dwindled as large branded stores such as Loblaw's opened and took customers.

In a couple of days, I had a job working for Home Furnishings. This company sold household linens such as bed sheets, pot holders, tea towels, blankets, little side tables, bedroom furniture, other small furnishings, pedestal ashtrays, beds, some toys, mirrors, and dressers. The owner was Mr Stibbard, a man in his 80's, and his salesman was Jerry Ottenbright. Stibbard was good to me because he taught me how to do his books and in general other things about business. They were skills that were to come in handy a few years later. Stibbard made it easy to learn.

Salesman Ottenbright went door to door selling furnishings. He got steady customers this way. The customers would ask him to come or they would phone in with an order. This kind of business is not around anymore, and even then, it was slowly disappearing.

People got to know and like Stibbard and Ottenbright. They had some long term customers. I would take telephone orders and sell things in the store. Sometimes people would run a bill. Ottenbright would later go collecting and sometimes people would come in to the store to pay their bill. I updated the records.

The store was heavily crowded with product and was in a little strip mall along with a liquor store, a bank, a frozen meat pie shop, and a Woolworths store. One day a man outside asked me for money. I refused to give him money because I thought he would buy booze. He looked like he might sometimes drink too much. I went with him to the Woolworth food counter and bought him food.

I thought I was doing a good deed, but the woman at the counter looked impatient as if she wanted to say something like, "Oh not again this guy is getting another free meal". Perhaps he had a successful

record getting food this way, but it was my first time to do such a thing. The waitress made me feel like I had been taken in by a scoundrel but I was not so sure. One way or the other this man needed to eat. I made sure he had a lot to eat.
I bought him a lot of food and coffee. I had coffee with him for a bit and then went on my way.

One October while I worked for Home Furnishings, Lyle was going camping with the boy scouts. I made him egg sandwiches. There was a bit of filling left over and I ate it. I promptly got painfully sick with a gall bladder attack. I had these same attacks years earlier on the farm and spent some time bent over a dining room chair. This time however it was worse. I ended up in the hospital. I think David phoned an ambulance. I was in for X-rays first. I had another attack that night and the next day I had surgery. Doctor Cook said to me at the time, "if anyone ever says you have appendicitis you can be assured you don't as they were in the way and I took them out too."

More than 40 years later, this comment became the crucial factor in getting a different doctor when one in Surrey actually suggested that I did have appendicitis. Clearly, the doctor was not as diligent reading the charts as necessary and I asked for a different doctor.

Our neighbor Ina Longmuir came to visit me while I was home recuperating. Ina was a good soul, perhaps a little too tolerant of some kids. She brought Ricky Zimmerman a little neighborhood brat she used to look after in the afternoons. Ricky used to hit Ina, bite her, and generally abuse her as he wished. He was a boy that would not listen to words. Ina would always have stories of the bratty things Ricky would do and say while she had him. He was a willful, abusive, little boy.

While visiting me, Ricky climbed up on something, grabbed our cuckoo clock, and broke it. I grabbed the little brat turned him over my knee and spanked him. I did not really hurt him, but I guess maybe his feelings were hurt and he was shocked. Ina was afraid his parents would be upset, and indeed, they were angry. I was not too upset, because Ricky was not going to treat me the way he treated Ina and his parents. After that, Ricky was never a problem when he was around me, and was then always a well behaved child; however, with Ina he remained abusive. Years later Ricky with some of his friends came to see me and say hello. Ricky was all friendly and happy to see me and I am sure the spanking did him good.

In 1963, Walter's parents came by train to spend Christmas with us at 689 Bannerman Avenue, Winnipeg. They said the train ride was cold. At times, the heating system in trains would freeze up because of the low temperatures, so passengers were glad to get into warmth. I am not sure if trains still have this winter problem or not but it was once common. The visit of my in-laws was a big and much anticipated event. Walter's parents had not been to our house for Christmas. This made for a lot of excitement. We did not really have a lot of room. Sleeping and eating were to be crammed experiences during the visit.

Norman Sager took this picture. We had moved tables into the living room to be able to eat together. You can see in the picture from the left a smiling happy Joan Sager, that something one did not see often as she had a stressful life as a girl growing up. Next, Sergei, Walter's dad, then Walter and I are standing, Johanna is sitting, and Glenn is on the corner, then Rick, Brad, Lyle, David.

We took Walter's parents to a Roman Catholic Church in the morning and then to St John's Cathedral later. We felt honored that they came to our church because they were very strong Roman Catholic and did not visit other churches. Remembering the earlier years of religious struggles made these visits even more impactful. We felt pleased Walter's parents came to our house for Christmas as we had for most years missed being able to have them with our family on this great day and we were glad religion was not a problem.

Our family was growing up in Winnipeg. David was the first to leave the nest. David was in high school but not liking it too much. David left St John's High school to attend training in refrigeration. He graduated and got a job In Winnipeg. When David became engaged, I got my friends to help me organize a wedding for them. Chris Langevin offered her basement to use for the reception so that is where we had it. We attended St. John's Cathedral for a few years after we moved to Winnipeg. It just so happened that the assistant minister there was George Morrison the brother of my good friend Ina. I contacted Rev Morrison who agreed to officiate at David and Sharon's wedding. Lyle was Best Man at their wedding May 2nd, 1964.

Ina's husband, Bill Longmuir was a bartender. He volunteered to make the punch for the celebration from his recipe. I bought the ingredients and delivered them to their house where Bill did as he said and made the punch. Ina did a lot of testing of the punch. This made her happy and a bit late getting to church. She said she ate some of the fruit that had sat overnight in the punch, which of course contained alcohol. She ended up getting a bit drunk but remained charming.

We had records for music and people were dancing. Ina, dancing with a dress without pockets, took her earrings off and put them in the pockets of her son-in-law Doug. She had a great time dancing but the next day thought she had lost the earrings, as we could not find them anywhere. About 3 weeks later Ina's daughter Beth phoned Ina all upset. Beth said she had found another woman's earrings in Doug's pockets. It was then that Ina remembered where her earrings were and the episode ended happily and she laughed when she told the story.

Ina was a very good friend and I could always talk to her. She was not a gossip. Her house was spotless and even though her brother was a minister at the church we went to, Ina refused to go to church at all. David's wedding was an exception. She arrived late and sat at the back. Her husband Bill worked late and we were both alone a lot, so Ina and I spent time together in the evenings going for walks, or having tea if I did not have to work in the store.

David getting married changed our family. New ways of doing things had to be established so we could be a family unit. Walter told David and Sharon pictured above, that when they were getting married that they were to keep their spats to their own house and not bring them to our place. He also told them they had to have their own home immediately even if it were just a tent. We stressed that if there were serious problems like illness and emergencies they could call us but they were starting their life together. They had to be a couple.

It was not easy for David and Sharon starting out married we were all poor. For the first few months, they did not have a lid for their agitator washing machine and I did their laundry at my place. Later they got a lid and this made it easier for all of us. They lived only several blocks away and would visit in the evenings.

Thursday, January 28th, 1965, a phone call from David about 5 in the morning woke us up.
David was asking if we could get our car started because he could not get his started. Sharon needed to go to the hospital because Darcy was about to arrive. They wanted me to come with them. It was a

horrible -48 F or -49 F below 0. I had answered the phone and Walter felt certain we would not be able to get our car started either because of the intense cold. We agreed I should get a cab and go to David's and then go with them to the hospital. It seemed like the best solution.

I had to hurry and get ready, as the cab would arrive soon. I was in a rush. In the hurrying trying to get my winter boots on to be ready for the taxi, I slipped on the top step leading from the kitchen to the back door and basement. I landed on my butt breaking my tailbone. Pain made it impossible to sit for months. The bones pinched my flesh. I could only sit on one side or the other. I was in agony.

The taxi came and we picked David and Sharon up and went to the hospital. After a couple of hours at the hospital, I came home in a cab. I was in too much pain to stay all day and not really needed. David stayed at the hospital and Darcy was born sometime before noon.
In pain, I went to the doctor in a few days. I needed to know what was causing the pain, but the doctor said X-rays were not possible because my tailbone was too swollen. It does not seem reasonable now as I look back at the process because broken arms could be x-rayed. Every few weeks I would go back and the swelling had not changed. It was not until 9 months later that I had my tail bone removed and the pain left. I disappointingly missed a trip to Edmonton with Walter.

Sharon's Mom and Dad decided to pay her a surprise visit and surprise her when she came home with Darcy. I was not too sure a new mother needed to have anyone jumping out of the closet yelling surprise as planned, especially because she had not seen her parents since before the wedding. In talking with David, he decided to tell Sharon her parents were there so she could be ready for them. They stayed with David and Sharon for about a month, and I was able to get to know them.

It was a bitterly cold, snowy winter. Before Darcy was born, Sharon had asked me to come show her how to look after her baby. With her parents visiting, she still wanted my help, so for the first month I walked from our house to David and Sharon's house. It was about a half hour walk, which was not all that easy with a broken painful tail bone, but the excitement of helping with my grandson was a countering force.

About 4 months later David left for Vancouver to find better work. Sharon and Darcy stayed with us for a month. David quickly got work and found a place to live. Sharon had her first airplane ride with Darcy in her arms.

The picture below shows me holding Darcy my first grandchild when he was about 2 months old. It is in the living room of our house 666 Cathedral Avenue. It is a small room. Most of the rooms in this house were small and the closets equally small and shallow. It was a house built for a different life style from an earlier age. It was not for people who watched television, or had more than one or two items of clothing. The closets were always jammed.

With the long cold winters, I tried to have some living green around the house by growing indoor plants. I sometimes had success with growing vine like plants that wrapped around the kitchen or other rooms. Sometimes I was teased about the plants. I think I got this love of house plants from my mother's influence. When I grew up my mother had many house plants. The bay window was full of them and she had them where she could. My house too had a lot more than this picture indicates.

One day Norman came over to the house. Looking around at all my house plants in amazement, because I had, ivy, geranium, baby tears, begonias, mother-in-law's tongue, wandering Jew etc, he teasingly said you know Sarah all you need in here with all these plants is a snake. One day a long plastic snake did appear amongst my plants courtesy of Norman. Plastic props and toys were not all that common then, certainly much less common than they are now. Everyone had a good laugh because he found such an item and because of how he teased.

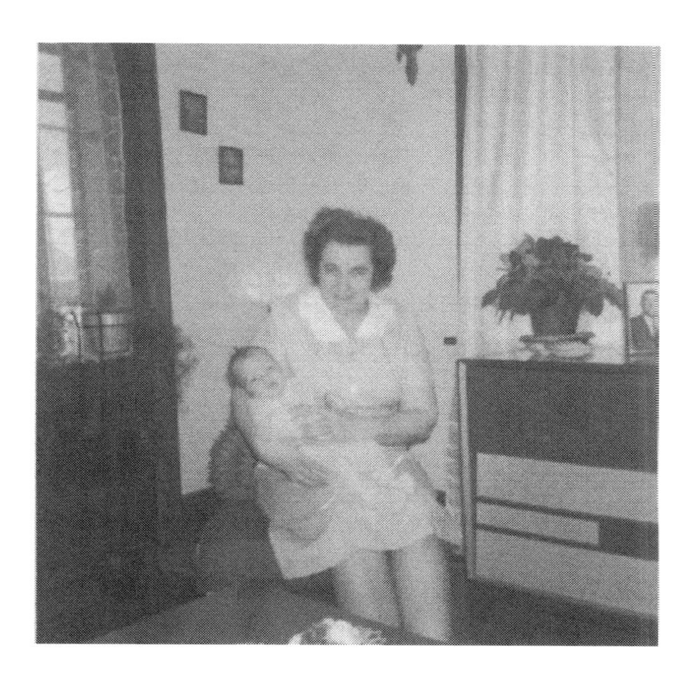

You can see some of the plants I grew. A gloxinia stands on the Fleetwood combination radio and record player, beside the picture of Walter's father, which is part of their Golden Wedding Anniversary picture. It would have been a new picture at the time. I had ferns and other greenery. I have a plant stand in front of the front door. We never used the front door in this house. It would open directly into the small living room and let all the cold air in as well as track in snow. The side door was used all the time, as it opened to a stairwell that could be closed.

The radio and record player combination was bought in Winnipeg when we lived on Bannerman Avenue. The glass of the radio dial was broken. I now have learned it happened when Glenn threw a shoe at Lyle. In Vancouver, I gave this old technology away to a neighbor who took it to his basement.

The summer of 1964, I went to Edmonton on the train taking Glenn with me to visit Mam, while she was living with Ruby. They asked me to take along my accordion and play. They all liked the music that I played and I enjoyed playing for them. The picture below shows me with the accordion and Ruby talking to Glenn. On the picture back Ruby playfully wrote: "Glenn's Gracious aunt and Beautiful Mother".

You can see Ruby has her right arm wound with a tensor bandage. This is because she had breast cancer and the missing lymph nodes caused her arm to swell. The bandage helped to control the swelling. She wrapped and then unwrapped and rewrapped the arm a few times a day. She never complained about having to do this and always tried to have a cheerful attitude towards life.

I was glad to be back when I returned home to Winnipeg. I frequently would be after Lyle to stop smoking. I always seemed to be catching him. One day Lyle came home wearing a short sleeved shirt. He was always so fastidious about what he wore. Clothing had to be ironed, clean, and neat. He had been out somewhere, and forgotten to take his blue package of Belvedere cigarettes out of his front pocket. So, he was caught again, and I gave him a lecture.

Another time Lyle came home late and shined the lights of the car right into my bedroom window. It woke me up. He was drunk. He did not want me to smell his breath so was bending his head down trying to tell me there was something wrong with the car, slurring his words. I gave him hell. I sent him to bed. I would not let Lyle drive the car for about a week. Lyle always listened to me at the time but I never really succeeded at stopping him from smoking. It was a struggle raising boys alone.

Gary Sager came to live with us for a summer and this is when this picture below of Gary, Lyle, and I, was taken. We were going to church and it is in front of 685 Bannerman. They were both sneaking cigarettes and were not supposed to be smoking. I do not think going to church changed that at all.

Gary usually came down and sat on the back steps coughing in the late evenings. He tried to convince me he had not been smoking. I did not believe him. He was not at all believable hacking away as if he were choking. I gave him a good big spoonful of cough medicine that did not taste all that great to cure the cough somewhat, but mostly he got the foul tasting medicine to try to convince him it was not worth his effort to smoke. It did not work. He was determined to smoke. The issue of his smoking and me wanting him to quit is a discussion that is still going on some 40 years later.

During the Christmas season, our house was usually full of people. Family and the boy's friends, neighbors, everyone would come over. We played games and ate, laughed and talked. The meals were huge. I did lots of cooking as well as lots of baking and we had a lot of company. Walter wanted bowls of fruit in the house at Christmas. He would polish apples and have bowls of fruit around the house.

Every December 23, Walter bought me Maraschino Chocolates in honor of our Wedding Anniversary. The boys always liked to eat them and looked forward to them. It became a tradition. The boys, the neighbors, all our friends all enjoyed these chocolates. When once he bought something else, the boys noticed and asked, "Where are the Maraschinos?" There always seemed to be young people around at the time laughing and talking. The friends of the boys were always welcome in our house and they all ate well and had a good time playing games. The sound of happy people was great to hear.

Our first TV was a small black and white TV. Walter rescued it from the garbage at the airport of Netly Air Field. He used a light bulb and wire coat hangers as antennae to get reception. It did not work well but it worked. We could not afford to buy a TV at the time. It was a few years later that we were finally able to buy the new TV pictured herewith Walter and the 3 boys.

On the TV is a cat ornament. That ornament is a bit of a mystery. It is not something I would buy. It was perhaps a gift. Perhaps people gave ornaments as gifts more then, than they gift ornaments today. This gift was likely from someone that did not know I was never a big cat fan, though I had a cat when I was about 10 or 11 living in Pierceland. Our log house was close to the blacksmith's shop. Up the street was Grandma Orcott's restaurant and her son would later be pictured in Ruby's and Otto's, wedding picture as a witness. Beyond Grandma Orcott's place, there stood a recently new pool hall. One day the pool hall caught fire and burned down flat. I was terrified my cat would be burned in the fire. I think my fear came perhaps because it was an unusual, terrible, scary, event in a docile small town where there was little such excitement. I can think of no other explanation that would generate the fear that my cat would go to a pool hall during a fire. I found the cat and held it while the fire burned. That was the only cat I ever had. I never wanted another. Even having a cat figurine ornament is odd for me.

At the time of the fire, we also had a black and white, medium sized dog, about the size of a Sheltie, called Mickey. Unfortunately, he was poisoned. I am not sure why anyone would do that, but in those days as now, some strange people do such sick things as poison pets.

Next to the pile of ashes that had been the pool hall was a grocery store owned by Dan Flagel. His daughter and I tried to make cigarettes. We were not very good at it. She got the makings of the cigarettes from her father's supply. She brought them to our back yard where we climbed into an old truck cab. Our intent was to act grown up rolling some cigarettes. During our efforts, Willie caught us. He threatened and teased saying "I am going to tell". Willie never did tell though, and we quit playing with matches, we caused no fires, and that was a good result of being caught.

In the 2 pictures above, a portrait of my dad hangs in a nice wide metal frame. That picture is part of a pair I now have. The matching portrait is of my mother. Both pictures were taken at the time of their marriage. There is also a small and stylish pose of Ruby on the other wall. In the foreground, Walter and the boys are playing Crokinole. Behind David to the left is a thread cabinet that Walter had won in Goodsoil. The new TV was nice to have even though it did not have a remote. Viewers had to get up walk to the set and push a button to turn the set on, or turn the channel dial, an actual knob, located right on the TV.

In 1964, Eldon Baker the adopted son of my brother Willie came back into our lives as pictured below. Eldon and his wife Marg and family came to stay with us for a few weeks as they tried to get a new start in a new place. They were headed to Ontario. They hit bad weather east of Winnipeg and had to turn around. At the time of the picture below, they had two kids and Marg was pregnant with a third. Eldon tried to find work but failed. The family later returned to Calgary.

We were glad to see Eldon again after so long. Eldon and Lyle have birthdays close together. I made two birthday cakes. Eldon´s cake is hard to see and on the table. Lyle is posing cutting his cake that is sitting on top of a bowl of a set Lyle had given me. There is another piece to the set on the end of the table. I still have this set and use them. I also still use the Corning Ware casserole dish in the picture and the white measuring cup. This was Lyle's 19th birthday and Eldon's 20th. Around the table starting on the left are Eldon, Sharon, David, Glenn, Carla a girl friend of Lyle's, and Lyle.

We had a full house for a while. Walter was away up north at the time of this birthday party. The stresses, emotional, psychological, and physical were hard on him. The physical stress built up due to Walter working long hours 10 to 14 hours a day, day after day, 7 days a week, for weeks and years. The psychological stress came from him being isolated from his civilization and his family, yet responsible for a lot of equipment and the jobs and safety of many people. The emotional stress of being away from his family and being unable to interact with them daily, and only being able to see them grow and change in bits and pieces depressed Walter. He is pictured going away again. Walter is just through the door and Norman is beside him. They are in an amphibian airplane that could also be used as a water bomber and it is the late 1960's. They are all smoking. Can you imagine all that smoke in a confined area?

No one is wearing seat belts and they are just sitting around amongst the freight. That is how we all travelled to these remote outposts. Considering the stresses, that people would feel in these outposts it is understandable that they smoked and drank to escape. This working in the north caused a lot of alcohol problems because the workers spent a lot of time in heavy isolation in cultural deprivation, away from things to do other than drink. Drink snuck into my life, and snuck into my family like a virus and would not willingly leave.

When Norman and I talked alone together, he never called me Aunt Sarah, but if he introduced me to someone, he would always say that I was his aunt. If there were other people around and we were talking, he would then also call me Aunt Sarah. Norman was a kind hearted man that loved to laugh and have fun. He would tell me a few times over the years, "you know Aunt Sarah you are too strict with your boys". I did not necessarily say anything because it was nothing serious, but I disagreed with him, and thought he should be stricter with his own kids.

In this above picture, Norman is back to being his old self. He had some problems with alcohol and I had dragged him in to an alcohol treatment location. One cold early spring evening I went to the back of Pete Lazarenko's office when Norman was working with Northland Fisheries. Norman was sitting outside the office. He had called to tell me he was there. I told Walter that I would go get him myself. I did not want anyone else around. I felt hate for alcohol at that moment. Norman and I had always been close. He was like a little brother to me. I wanted to help him look after himself and get his life back together. He related to me as an older sister. He knew I meant the best for him. Of course, he put up a fuss and resisted. Even though I was a lot stronger, then than I am now, and he could see I seriously was serious, he could still have run away had he really wanted to bolt. The truth we both knew was that he really wanted the help he was getting, so I could strong arm him into treatment.

A few weeks later, he was back to his normal neatly dressed self. The next day the four of us Norman, Glenn, Walter, and I drove to Duluth, Minnesota and stayed the night in a hotel. We ate in a revolving restaurant on top of the hotel. The next day Norman and Glenn drove home to Winnipeg, and Walter and I flew to Seattle to start our time in Alaska.

Norman died July 10, 1980, a date before both his parents, and on his daughter Merilee's 17th birthday. He had bought Merilee a birthday present, and was going to finish up a project and drive to give her the present. He was driving a commercial truck moving a camp kitchen near Rocky Mountain House. The new assistant driver was beside him. The camp cook was behind in a seat or a sleeper. He said he did not feel good. The cook told him to open the window and put his arm out. Then Norman slumped over the steering wheel.

The assistant panicked and could not move, but the cook jumped forward and took the wheel as Norman lay over the steering wheel and died. He is buried in a grave in Edmonton. Joan died a few years later and is buried in the same cemetery, but they are not side by side.

At the funeral, the first of 5 funerals in Edmonton for our family in 3 years, David and Lyle drove from Vancouver and were pallbearers. Norman was much loved and everyone was upset. Minnie was certainly upset with Norman for dying. We had lunch together. She was so angry Norman died. I understood why.

When Ruby and Otto's restaurant burned down Norman stayed with us. Minnie and Norman went to Jack Pine View School together. Minnie and Norman had known each other a long time and were in love. Although Ruby and Otto would allow the marriage, it did not happen because Walter's mother, Johanna, would not approve of the marriage. Minnie was not allowed to marry Norman because he was not Roman Catholic, and truthfully, Norman was not much interested in church. Johanna was a strong controlling influence and Minnie was her only daughter. Johanna had no say in Walter marrying outside the church but she did have influence with Minnie.

Though Walter married outside the family church, I must say Johanna never tried to convert me or directly control me and we never argued. When David was young, Walter refused to consider the idea of allowing David to spend overnight with his parents away from us. The reason may have been that Walter did not want David to be taught the Roman Catholic religion as Walter remembered his own hard up brining and the church, but I am not sure. I did not consider the idea simply because David was our responsibility, and their religion was not a consideration. We had left David with a sitter once and the results were bad. I did not want that to happen again. With Walter and his own parents, I cannot think of another reason other than religion for him to have his mind so firmly set. Certainly, his parents knew how to look after a baby. Walter realized religion was a strong factor with his mother.

Norman and Minnie had an enduring love that never stopped. They loved each other until they died. It was not much of a secret. Most people knew as they were seen together quite often. For their own happiness, I wished they had been allowed to marry.

One winter Otto came to Winnipeg to visit on his own and I think he was to visit his brother Fred. He visited us when we lived in 666 Cathedral Avenue. The family of Lyle's girlfriend Carla owned this house, and we rented from them. We had space in the basement to have dinner in an area that had a patterned, tin, ceiling, something uncommon today.

In this picture from the left are Otto Sager, my daughter in law Gwen's mother Marian Arkison and her brother Wilf Edwards, Joan Baker, Bob Baker and Lena Korbet who later became Lena Dean and is the sister of my daughter in law Sharon.

Bob Baker sitting at the end of the table is the oldest son of my brother Syd. Joan, his wife sits beside him. By this time, they were living in Winnipeg, we saw a lot of them and we became close. They had lived in England and the US and were now home in Canada. We would drive back and forth for dinners. Bob worked at the university and showed me an early computer with a small screen. Joan began to sew all kinds of things. She still sews and is very good at it. We went on picnics and country drives together.

When I look at the table, I see more than people and dinnerware. I see stories of events and people. I recognize the plates as those we bought for David and Sharon's wedding. We kept them separate and did not use them much so that we had something to use when a crowd was around. I have only a few platters left but still use them in the kitchen. I see a cut glass bowl with a metal rim Glenn gave me, and there are pickles in glass bowls that I have had for years and still use. A rectangular casserole dish between Marion and Lena is one I still use and got in Lac La Ronge as a gift from Dr Cooks wife for baby-sitting their little boy. The map went to the kitchen wall when we moved to Smithfield Avenue, and is still here in my office cupboard. We had maps up in the house so the boys would get help with geography education. I like maps and have a collection of them from my travels.

Walter and I were in the inter lake area of Manitoba on a job when Otto died in 1981. He had been breathing oxygen but living at home for a year. Otto died when Ruby had gone grocery shopping with Laura. It was an expected event. On a visit to Edmonton, Ruby and I both thumped his upper back to help make his breathing easier. This helped temporarily. Walter and I left our job site and drove straight to Edmonton for the funeral. We were gone about a week.

My sister Ruby died in 1982, in the Royal Alex Hospital, August 6, in Edmonton. When she died Gary, Laura, Dorothy and I were all with her. She had lung cancer, and a few years earlier survived the breast cancer operation that left her with the fluid enlarged arm. She did not smoke until she was in her early 30s. A nurse told her to learn to smoke to relax. I think this was what caused the cancer. The picture below shows Ruby in the hospital bed and her grandson Brad Sager and I visiting her.

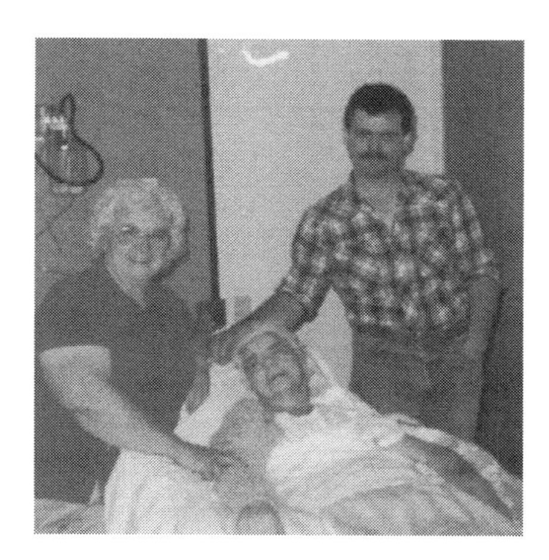

Ruby and Otto were cremated. Gary and Laura brought their ashes to BC. Gary scattered them on the side of the mountain around Bridal Falls east of Chilliwack. Ruby's wedding ring had come from France. Otto found the 22-carat gold ring on the sidewalk in Paris and brought it back and had it resized for Ruby. This lovely ring was special to Ruby and when she died, she wanted Annette to have it. Annette did have it for a while but, sadly, it disappeared when a friend who was staying with Annette moved out. I wonder where it is now.

When we lived on Cathedral Avenue Walter made a Christmas decoration for the front door using a frame of copper pipe. It was a star shape. At the time, almost no one decorated the outsides of their homes. There were lights on a few houses but a decoration like this was unusual. He had it wired for sound so that we played a tape of Christmas songs inside and they could be heard outside. It made coming home feel good in the cold Winnipeg winter. We had good comments that people really liked it and we could see people looking at it. The little twin girls two doors down, Janet and Janice Klaus, said prayers outside in the snow in front of the star. It looked good and was something we were proud to have on the house. I think it was part of Walter´s creative spirit emerging again as it had when we were first married, and then did later in his paintings. I wish he had more opportunities to be artistic in his life.

There was a lot of action when we lived at this address. The neighbors were friendly and we visited back and forth. The few stories I recount here are funny and just made the neighborhood interesting.

A neighbor lived beside with two little girls. Marlene always had problems with her husband, Jerry. He came home drunk and miserable a lot. One time Jerry became the usual drunk and went to sleep on the couch. She was annoyed. She unfolded the ironing board lowered it to the couch height. Then she took a rifle, a 22 or a shotgun, some kind of rifle Jerry had in the house for some reason I am not sure why, but it was not out in the open, but in a closet somewhere and not loaded. There was no ammunition for it and Marlene did not know how to use it. Marlene lined up the rifle even with Jerry's face and gave it a little nudge on his head. When Jerry finally awoke in a drunken stupor, he was looking down the barrel of the gun. Marlene was waiting and watching for his reaction. I guess he was mighty frightened and knew Marlene was annoyed with his drinking. She laughed when she told me the story and laughed harder when she got to the part about him being so scared. Another time she hit him with a cast iron frying pan. He called the police. When the police arrived, they could not find Marlene because she was hiding in the broom closet. Nothing seemed to interfere with Jerry's drinking.

Marlene was a hairdresser. She kept her scissors and clippers at home. One day her oldest daughter gave one of the neighbor twins, Janet or Janice, a close haircut. Perhaps she had seen her mom do the same for people. Then new haircut was a silly mess of a lopsided haircut, long hair on one side, and irregular tufts on the other side. Perhaps a stylish cut today for some but not at all for any at the time. The mothers met on the street in front of our house and had a big argument about whose kid was at fault and if they were at fault. Marlene offered to fix the hair cut so that it did not look too bad. The twins' mother Mary refused the assistance until a time when the hair had grown out a bit more. The kid had to go around with a bad haircut for a while. The mothers then realized the silliness of the situation and remained friends. A few days later, one of these mothers dropped in and told me that one of their daughters found a pair of scissors and went through the laundry sitting on the floor and cut the toes off all their socks.

Marlene's youngest little girl spent a lot of time on my lap. She always needed attention and I enjoyed the child. Then they moved from our relatively quiet street, to Mountain Avenue a busy street about 15 minutes away. The two little girls aged about 7 and 4 went to the store and had to cross Mountain Avenue. On the way home, the youngest ran ahead of the oldest one. She ran onto the road and was hit by a car and flung through the air landing on a metal road grate.

After the death, the mother was distraught when she came for a visit and tea. She was not really feeling right yet and when she left, I too was upset. She told me, it was my fault that the little girl was hit by a car. It was my fault, she said, because the child always sat on my lap and always wanted to come to our house. Of course, it was not true that it was my fault. I did not believe it then or now, but it was sure upsetting at the time. I do not hold it against the mother and understand how upset she would be. I am sure I would have been equally distraught. I liked the mother and forgave her. I knew she was a nice person just horribly distraught.

Mary, the mother of the twins one day went to the doctor. She had an innocent crush on this doctor. She usually made herself look as nice and as fashionable as possible when she went out. Mary especially made sure her hair was nice when she went to see this doctor. She would elaborately put her hair up in a beehive of coils. She was a smart looking woman when all dressed up. On this occasion, she did not have her hair done and was nearly late for her appointment. To avoid having a bad hair day she wore a tall crowned hat and stuffed a dishtowel in the hat to keep it filled out nicely. She marched into the doctor's office looking good. He said to her something like, "well where is all that beautiful hair of yours?" and reached over and pulled off her hat. Her uncombed hair fell down and the dish towel flew out. She laughed in embarrassment when she told me the story. Together we laughed a few times over this story.

My clotheslines in the back yard were sometimes borrowed by the neighbors when they had big washing days. They used them, but not when I used them. I always washed clothes on Monday and hung them out on the line. The other women were not as regular about washing clothes as I was because they had a lot of other things to get done as well. That meant clothes their washing was postponed for a few days or longer. That meant there were even more clothes they had to wash and needed to use my lines as well as their own.

I am still particular about how clothes are hung out on the line. It probably comes from having to use clothes lines a lot and knowing how to do it properly to make life easier, a notion that is missing or forgotten when clothes dryers are always ready at hand. Sloppy eyesores of badly hung clothes thrown on a line unsorted without a pattern seem to indicate at least carelessness and washing all types of things together. This seems common lately.

One Monday Mary came over and we were having tea and chatting. I had washed clothes and hung them on the line. I knew everything that was on the line. I looked out and made comment that it was odd that one of Glenn's T-shirts was missing from the line. I knew what should be hanging on the blank spot of the line. You could see there was a spot missing. Just then, Mary's teenage son Sonny came to the door to tell Mary she was wanted on the phone at home. He was wearing Glenn's T-shirt, the one missing from the line. I guess he thought he needed to wear a shirt to knock on the door and thought his Mom was hanging their clothes on our lines and just took what he thought might have been his, even if he could not recognize it as his own. We laughed both at him grabbing the t-shirt from the line, and the idea that he thought he needed to have a t-shirt on to knock on the door.

Another day I went to Mary's to have tea. The twin girls about 6 or 7 years old came over to get me as they often did. I was happy to go over. Mary proudly showed me her new, large, and expensive ring that her husband had bought it for her for some reason. It was very nice. Her twin girls were always around when we had tea, on and off my lap, sometimes one on each leg. We were all oowing and awing over this new beautiful ring when one of the twins asked me to show them my rings. I proudly held out my finger with the simple and very inexpensive ring Walter had bought for me on his soldier's salary. When the twins looked at it in comparison to what their mother was now wearing it was clear there was a significant size difference. One of the twins said, "Uncle Walter sure did not think much of you when he bought you that ring did he". I laughed aloud and I wished Mary had, but poor Mary was so embarrassed. She later laughed too. Kids say some amazing things.

Ray and Lena got married July 28th, 1966, but I was up north with Walter and Glenn at Warren's Landing when they were married. The fruit cake in this picture is one I made using the same pans that had been Mam's. Mam had used them to bake our wedding cake in 1941. These same pans were also used for wedding cakes for David and Sharon, and Lyle and Gwen and their 25th anniversary, and our 50th wedding anniversary. Here they have had the cake beautifully decorated. Lena is Sharon's older sister. Ray is Gwen's cousin. They are a very nice couple.

Lena had stayed at our house for a while before she was married. When we all moved to BC, having Ray and Lena over for family events was always nice. Our family had grown and they were part of it. On cold winter weekend nights, they would visit, talk, and play games.

Winters in Winnipeg were dark, long, and cold. The nights were the longest and coldest parts. The wind roared in over the flat prairies making already cold days feel colder. The snow piled up on the sides of the road where street ploughs went and you had to dig a pathway through the snow banks to get to your car on the roadside. Sometimes snow ploughs covered your vehicle in more snow. High piles of snow mixed with gravel and salt along the street edges and at intersections, made driving dangerous and life generally uncomfortable. When after months the cold left and the weather warmed, the snow mounds melted, and the city endured a few weeks of the filthy site of brown wet snow and dirty puddles. Finally, with the snow gone there was the mess of tons of salty gravel on the streets and plenty of potholes and cracked roads. The cold finally relieved by such a mess made a lot of people wish for something different.

Lyle investigated the warmer climate of Vancouver. It was not too much of a surprise when Lyle said he was sick and tired of pumping gas at a gas station in the freezing cold winter of 1966. It was a cold job for low pay.

Lyle had been to Manitoba Institute of Technology, and acquired an apprentice license as a diesel mechanic. Lyle was 21, talented, ambitious, and anxious to see the world. He wanted to get a job doing what he had been trained to do. Mid winter, the desire to leave town built up and he had the chance to leave. He took it. Lyle and his friend Les Leibrecht left to find work in BC. Yes, I was worried about his future but felt confident he would survive and do well.

The picture shows Lyle and Walter at Walter's parents 50th Anniversary in Minnie's house, February 15th, 1966 in Edmonton. Walter and Lyle are standing behind Johanna and Sergei seated in Minnie's living room. Lyle was there because he was on his way to BC. He and Les Leibrecht went north to Edmonton to take in the celebrations. Walter flew from Winnipeg. I was not there because I could not sit long enough to attend. Earlier, January 28th, 1966 to be exact I broke my tailbone the morning Darcy was born.

Les's car broke down in Calgary. They got it going enough to get it to Edmonton where Peter Ternowski got one of his contacts to do some economical repairs. With the repairs, the car made it all the way to Vancouver. Les and Lyle were grateful for his Uncle Peter's contacts getting the repairs done.

Lyle came home to visit when Glenn was in his last years at St John's High. Lyle drove a sports car, a Barracuda, a high powered convertible. I think this picture was taken in the morning when Lyle was to return to Vancouver and Glenn was off to school as the light comes from the east. The picture was

perhaps taken by Les Leibrecht. Our dog Pal is on the ground looking the other way. Our house looked similar to the ones in the background, and white.

A few years later, on a visit home Lyle met Gwen at a house party and a few years after that they became engaged. For a few months, they were engaged. Then the engagement was ended. Lyle came home and gave me the ring to look after for him. Happily, a few months later, he wanted it back and the engagement was back on.

Gwen's mother Marion and I were good friends. We knew each other before Lyle and Gwen knew each other. So, we were happy the wedding was back on.

Lyle and Gwen were also married in St John's Cathedral and Dean Harrison married the couple. They had a reception in East Kildonan and Glenn was best man. I baked the wedding cake and someone else decorated it.

While Walter flew around the north, I worried about him in airplanes a lot because they flew in some dangerous weather. Flying in the winter on these small planes was cold. There were heaters sometimes but these were not nice passenger planes with soft warm seats. Even in the summer time, these planes were noisy, cramped, cold, and sometimes quite old. The plane bodies were frequently made from a combination of wood and metal, and so unlike the new lightweight materials used today.

Walter had flown many times and hundreds of hours without incident. Walter's flying luck dramatically ended. The planes were never brand new airplanes but they were well looked after. The picture above is certainly no evidence of that, but maintenance was not an issue in this crash. In March 1968, Walter was in a crash in a plane loaded with a cargo of frozen, boxed, fish. There were only two people on board, the pilot and Walter. Nearing the south end of Lake Winnipeg, they flew into a snow storm and were in a white out, a time where there was no way to tell up from down as below and above is all the white of snow blowing around. The pilot pushed down on the control to descend and they crashed. Walter perhaps more experienced as a passenger in his multiple times flying in all types of weather had told him not to descend but he did not listen. Perhaps the white out conditions confused the pilot's brain a bit.

It was early afternoon. The lake was frozen. The thick ice was covered in deep, hard, snowdrifts. It was about 20 below zero. As the plane hit the snow, Walter's seatbelt snapped in two and he flew through the window unconscious. Pictured below is this mangled airplane after the crash. Unbelievably, Walter managed to walk away to get help.

Somehow, in the conflicting forces and speed of the crash, Walter's leg managed to be squeezed between wooden fish box crates full of frozen fish. The heavy boxes came down on top of him and spread across the snow. His metal suitcase was beside him in the snow.

In the hospital, Walter told us how when he became conscious and thus avoiding being frozen to death in the intense cold. He wondered where he was. Seeing the plane scattered around in pieces here and there, it took him a few minutes to understand what had happened. His situation was life threatening. I was very cold and he was injured and disoriented. It was getting dark.

He spied his suitcase and limped to the broken body of the plane. Inside the mangled airplane, he found the pilot alive, and bleeding. He looked for his polar sleeping bag because he knew he had sheets inside it. Using his strong arms and hands, developed through years of hard work turning pipes, and welding, he ripped the sheets into strips. He ignored the biting cold of the -40 temperature and his own pain and bleeding while he made bandages. Walter wrapped the bandages around the pilot's head, and then under his jaw and back over his head. He put his sleeping bag over and around the pilot and left.

He told the pilot that if he stayed still he would live until Walter found help. The pilot was in no condition to move on his own. Walter found broken wood from the airplane body to use as canes. What he found were really just broken jagged sticks. With these, he started limping in the wrong direction and towards a mirage of buildings east towards the middle of the lake. He struggled this direction up and down and across high the piles of hard blown snow for a few hundred yards. Pausing to rest and consider his situation, he stood still in the cold and wind. It was then he realized that he was headed in the wrong direction. Turning around he saw faint lights from the shore in the opposite direction to that he was going. How had he missed these earlier? In the late, afternoon, sunlight they were not visible. As night came and light faded, they could be seen.

Falling, and getting up again, repeatedly, he struggled in the freezing cold, towards the lights of a lakeside lodge. Luckily, a group of professionals were having a weekend party, and there were kids playing outside. Normally no one was much there in the winter. Walter got to the door, and he fell into the building.

This was a time before cell phones. Luckily, there was a telephone line. The group could call for help. A plane or helicopter arrived to take Walter and the pilot to the hospital. The pilot was loaded on to the plane but Walter refused to get in it. He was taken to Winnipeg General Hospital by car. I suppose after just crashing in an airplane it might be natural to refuse to get on another right away.

In the lodge, he was taken care of, I think by doctors in the group. They called me to tell me he was being taken by car to the hospital. I did not get to talk to him then. I talked to him later at the hospital. I timed it and went to the hospital with Glenn to wait for him. We arrived first. We waited around the emergency waiting room and when he arrived, he could talk and was on a stretcher. To kill the pain at the lodge they gave him alcohol. His head and shoulders were cut. His leg was mashed and cut. He was alive and one of the luckiest people on earth.

Downstairs, I still have the broken strips of splintered wood Walter used as canes to help him walk. Though not broken, his leg was painfully and severely, bruised. It looked a horrible color. The 1.5 to 2 miles walk to the lodge over the ice and frozen snow drifts in such freezing temperature and wind made the injury worse. His face and arms were also cut and bruised. The doctors said a break would have healed faster than this mashed type of bruise.

The pilot was in and out of the hospital in 4 days. Walter was in the hospital for a month. The doctors feared that the leg was so badly squashed that gangrene would set in, and he would lose his leg. He walked with a cane and limped for another month. It is hard to believe he actually survived the crash.

After this crash, Walter did ride in airplanes but always insisted he wanted to sit over the wing. The pilot whose first name was Clause came to visit Walter in the hospital and they discussed the crash. A few years later Clause died in another plane crash.

The picture above is another view of the wooden body airplane and destroyed nose area of the plane. The snow ski attached to the wheel is sticking up and the contents of the plane around it. The picture was taken the next day when people went out to the site. On the left of the picture is a Bombadier. It is a type of snow bus used in the north. The front has skis and the power comes from the cletrac around and over the wheels.

That Walter looked after the pilot to save his life, and then went for help is commendable. It is amazing that he could have the presence of mind to do so after the bashing around he took in the accident. Having to work in the intense cold made his injuries worse. He rose to meet the challenge presented as he did many times in life. Walter sacrificed a lot of his life for his family as he rose to meet the challenges thrown at him. In this case, he nearly sacrificed his life for his family. I still shudder when I think of this accident, and in reflection, I have even more love and respect for him.

After the crash and with David and Lyle gone that left only Glenn at home with us. We reflected on the accident quite a lot but we were not in a financial situation that would allow Walter to immediately quit and look for work that did not involve flying to the north. We could make no immediate change to our lives. It may have started Walter thinking about having his own business again.

Walter and I, and Glenn spent the most of one summer, 1969, I think, on Warren's Landing on the north end of Lake Winnipeg where the Nelson River begins to drain the lake into Hudson's Bay. Walter was establishing a fish processing plant for Northland Fish on an isolated, remote, sandy, edge of the lake. It was a convenient shipping location between, fishermen on other lakes and close to lake freighters. As much as it was convenient for shipping, it was impractical for any type of settlement, but that is where we stayed.

Further along the lake shore, about 2 miles by boat, was a small, and poor, Cree settlement, in a slightly more livable site. The plant location was really, little more than a sand pile surrounded by bogs, swamp, small lakes, and scrub brush, on one side. The other side was large Lake Winnipeg. To get to this almost uninhabitable place one did not travel overland. There were no roads. The visible land was wet, soft and barely supported the plants growing on it. Access was either by boat or by plane. In such remote areas, the beauty can be truly romantic, if you have ready ability to leave.

We were isolated to the plant area near the sandy shore of the lake. The rest of the area was bog and not walkable. Float planes would come by frequently and occasionally a large freight boat would unload dry goods and equipment to be flown to more remote areas.

Approaching by air made for an unusual greeting. One could easily see the large orange roofs of the buildings identifying Northland Fish. They stood out in a sea of green land and helped pilots as a land mark being visible from afar. The bright orange could be a friendly greeting for a lost pilot. Looking down from high up in an airplane, there was something more interesting, and not nearly as friendly as these roof tops. Around the lake shore edge, and for a hundred feet or so up into the air was a thick, smog like border, of allied bugs, mainly nasty, blood thirsty mosquitoes, annoying moths, and large biting black flies. This army of gazillions of insects worked in shifts, dividing the 24-hour clock into equal hunting hours. The mosquitoes were at their biting worst at night. The black flies bit and drew blood during the daytime. The moths were always everywhere, and into everything, inside closed books, drawers, down inside bedding, and clothing. The fine sand of the location worked its way into everything just like the moths. Sand was found in the beds, always found on the floors, and months later, we still found it and dead moths inside suitcases.

Glenn and I arrived by plane and we could see this dark threatening ring around the shore. Walter stood on the shore waiting for our small two seated plane to arrive from the south. He watched helplessly as a frighteningly horrible wind and electrical storm came up, and a scene worthy of a movie unfolded in front of him. It was horrible to see it from land. It was worse to imagine what it would be like to be up in it and for sure, that was not pleasant. The pilot and Glenn were in the front seats and belted down. I crouched behind them on the cargo area floor with Pal, holding on to his collar and the legs of their seats.

We had boarded the airplane where the Red river flows into Lake Winnipeg, 358 miles south and flew to Warren's landing where the Nelson River flows out of Lake Winnipeg to the Hudson Bay. We had a view of the lake shore and lake the whole flight. It was a dramatic site below us. The storm certainly spiced up the ending.

A strong wind began to blow the clouds around, and more importantly blew the shallow lake into huge waves that were a few feet taller than the height of the tiny airplane called a Found. The Found was a small float plane of which only a few were made. To get three adults, a dog and two suitcases into it took effort. It very nearly became our tight fitting coffin. The shoulders of Glenn and the pilot were against the doors as the plane body quickly narrowed to the tail. They both had seat belts on and Glenn had to hold the passenger door tightly shut as it was a bit loose.

The pilot descended to a few feet above the lake looking for places to land between the nasty waves but without success. The wind confused the pilot. He tried to land the plane going away from the fish plant and the plane was hammered by the wind as he did so. The whole plane shook violently. For us passengers, every time the plane slammed into a wave it shook our bones.

On the first two attempts, as we descended to land, the waves hit the airplane pontoons with such immense force that the airplane was hurled back into the air with a jolting ferocity. Glenn and the pilot had the seat belts to hold them into their seats. Pal and I bounced up and down and back and forth getting to know the ceiling and the walls. Every time the plane hit the water, the passenger door opened a little.

Walter stood on the dock. Not too long after his own crash, he watched the plane with his family aboard be thrown high into the air like a yoyo on a string. There was the strong possibility that the airplane would be driven nose first into the water by the wind or catch a wave crest and have the same result. He would have a front row seat to view the accident. He had no boat to rescue us if there was a need for rescue.

The first two landing attempts produced a scary bouncy ride like a stone skipping across the waves. Had the pilot landed between the waves the plane would likely have sank. The strong wind made the 6 to 10 foot waves dangerous. The waves would have caught the wings, and driven them down into the water and sunk the plane. Even if I had known how to swim, it would have been almost impossible to get out of the plane from the cargo area.

On the third attempt, the pilot found a wave wide enough. The waves need to be at least 10 to 15 feet wide at the crest to be wide enough for the plane. He followed the wave crest as he bounced the plane to a landing. The plane however was going in the wrong direction. It was going away from where Walter waited and away from the safety of the pier. It was going towards an unknown shore and hidden rocks. With patience, and a lot of luck, the waves took us closer to shore where smaller sized waves permitted the pilot to maneuver the small plane around to head in the proper direction. We made it to the pier lucky not to be sunk by the waves as we bobbed along. We came to a stop at the pier in the bouncing waves the plane was tied up and later moved to an on shore mooring with the pontoons out of the water. Glenn discovered his seat belt had broken, and as he let go of the door handle the door beside him fell off into the lake. I was glad to climb out of that sardine can, and be done with that awful ride.

We had planned to be there for a week. We brought clothing for only a week. We stayed for the summer. Glenn had a job, and he was earning money and we three were together. We ran out of clothing. I mended, and then again mended, the same clothing that later we threw out when home. All three of us worked. Glenn still remembers this summer. Walter worked long hours installing machines, overseeing the building construction, and the building of a filtration well, which was in this case unique in that it was a well in the lake. The well casing was to protect the water intake system from sand and floating lake debris.

I cooked and baked for a varying number of employees and pilots ranging from 5 to 10. I do not remember being paid for my work. Pilots and others always seemed to be arriving hungry at differing hours. I found I had to be ready to feed someone all the time. I washed a lot of clothing for us frequently as we had so few, and for some of the workers. I also helped doing different things such as painting. Walter found things for Glenn to do including gassing and loading planes with freight, and selling supplies to the temporary local unskilled workers.

Two workers came up from the south. One was a toothless fat man by the name of Johnson. The other was a carpenter that had the nickname of Sweet Pea. Sweet Pea had the name before he arrived at Warren's Landing. It seemed appropriate. It was a reference to his smell. He was a nice fellow, just a bit uncivilized and could have bathed more often.

A few months after that summer, I again met Sweet Pea in Winnipeg. It was a bit funny and a bit embarrassing. I boarded a crowded bus. Sweet Pea was on one of the seats across the aisle. He was happy and excited to see me and in a loud surprised voice he said something like "Ah Sarah, I see you dyed your hair Sarah". Well, now the whole bus knew, and looked to see my hair. I was embarrassed even though it was not a secret. Sweet Pea was a good natured man and I could not be miffed with him for telling the truth. We had a nice chat.

A freight boat travelled the length of the lake and to Warren's Landing every week or two, unloading groceries and hardware to be transported by plane to other lakes and more remote destinations. Almost daily fishermen brought loads of fish in smaller boats. Sometimes planes also brought in loads of fish. Warren's Landing was but a temporary stop as the fish were flown elsewhere for processing.

The engine room, freezer, warehouse, and pier were connected to the bunk house by an 18 inch wide elevated, wooden plank, walk way, a foot or so above the sand resting upon poles hammered through the sand. This made walking easier. The beach sand was fine, loose, and lightly colored. On this sand, one would sink a few inches with the slightest movement of walking. Only with great effort could one walk any distance. Still, even with a walkway, the sand managed to come into the bunk house and kitchen, and settle everywhere. This indoor collection of sand meant frequent sweeping of the unpainted plywood floors.

A two way radio sat in the corner of the kitchen. It was on all day long, either crackling, or, with shouting voices trying to connect. I heard about all the planes landing and of where they were going within the few hundred mile range of the radio reception. St Therese, Pelican Narrows, Deschambault Lake, Savage Island, Garden Hill, and Gods Lake were other names on the air a lot. I heard who was piloting which airplane and who was going where. It was not that interesting, but it became our equivalent of local news. For the most part the radio was just a constant noise.

At night, the bugs came in thick immense waves, hunting for some warm blooded creature to bite. An unprotected human would be a buffet. The insects could easily kill an unprotected human. The lake areas of Manitoba can be bad for bugs. I have seen cattle standing in water up to their necks to avoid bites, and heard them complaining in the fields because the bugs were so bad. The bathroom was an outhouse. It was inland across the sand from our elevated cook shack and bunk house combination. To use the toilet at night we had to run out to the outhouse and spray Raid insecticide inside and down the

hole. We ran back to the bunk house waiting for the bugs to die and the raid to dissipate just enough so that we could breathe when we ran back to the outhouse. Still we would be bitten.
At Warren's Landing, I had the pleasure of introducing Glenn to berry picking. He was a city kid and never had picked wild berries, and never learned the peace and quiet, the chances to experience nature, and the chances to talk associated with berry picking. These new pleasures he learned but his older brothers never enjoyed it as much, even though they too picked berries. I am not sure he wanted to learn it but he did. Behind the cook shack in the tall grass between the bog and the lake were patches of the most delicious succulent wild strawberries. Daily, or almost daily, for part of our stay we would pick berries for dessert. They were so small that it took quite a few to make even a cup full. They were intensely flavored. Perhaps the mosquitoes thought the same of us, as we had to pick in the heat of the summer sun and silence of the area, disturbing the insects hiding in the tall grass with the berries, we were home delivery of takeout food for them. The insects became airborne in squadrons to feast on us as we picked berries for our dessert. Still, if you ask either of us, we would say it was well worth the effort, and I know Glenn is glad he learned the joys of picking berries.

Our dog Pal spent his time chasing and playing with the killdeer birds. The birds swooped over him and dived at him. They teased him with their noise and broken wing acts, pretending to be injured, and chirp at him until he ran after them. Then they flew into the air. Once he caught and killed one. Glenn and I had a short funeral for the bird and buried it, as Pal looked on rather sadly after having killed the bird. We thought he felt badly and had not meant to catch it.

I awoke late at night during a storm. I told Walter it sounded like there was water hitting the floor underneath our bed. It was an unusual thought. The pile of sand we were on was a good three to four feet above lake level and then the building was about 18 inches above that. The next morning, we saw the storm evidence. We could see where the wind had blown the water up over the beach area. Our living quarters stood on poles that had kept us dry, but indeed, I had heard the water hit the bottom of the floor boards on its way over the top of the sand pile. Then the water ran to the dip in the ground behind the camp, and flooded some of our berry patch.

Walter was working for Pete Lazarenko. Pete came up for a visit. Walter and Pete had a tiff. They both spoke their mind on some issues. They were not talking to each other. Around noon, they came into the kitchen and tried to avoid each other. They were both just sulking with each other and it was clear they both liked each other because they did not want to disagree. At coffee time, Walter came in for coffee, and Pete waited until Walter had his coffee and had left the room, then Pete came in. Eventually they worked things out before Pete left the same day.

Pete and Walter had more than a few squabbles over the years but they respected each other. That they lasted so long as a team is a sign of their respect for each other. Pete was sometimes tight with his money and that may have been the cause of the Warren's
Landing tiff. Pete may have wanted the work done faster but helpers were hard to find even if he would hire them to help Walter to finish the project.

Even I once had a tough discussion with Pete. At some earlier time, in Winnipeg, Walter was spending a lot of time working at the Netly Airport where Pete had his Northland Airways and Northland Wild Rice. Walter was owed holiday pay but did not like to ask for it. Pete never paid it. Walter never took holidays and worked through every holiday. He had earned more pay, but he would not ask for it. He might have been shy to ask for the money, or perhaps felt Pete would eventually give it to him without asking. I am not sure if Pete was trying to avoid paying, or just kept forgetting. Finally, my mind was made up. Pete was going to pay. I called. Pete and I talked, and Walter came home with the cheque. So, Pete and I were familiar with each other at Warren's landing. We liked each other and talked in a friendly way. Pete had an interesting personality. He was a schemer.

Pete had a contract to harvest and buy wild rice from a certain area of Manitoba. Walter invented a wild rice drying machine that would dry hundreds of pounds of wild rice efficiently. It was a new type of machine for the company and it gave Northland Wild Rice a good advantage because no one else had such a machine. Pete was always trying to get an advantage to make more money. He was involved in some perhaps illegal wild rice purchasing as well. He knew he was being watched and monitored. He devised an unusual way to avoid being detected in his water runs to get wild rice. His boat would head out in one direction and the authorities would watch him from afar. They always saw his boat leave but never saw it return. Cleverly, he had the boat painted one color on one side and a different color on the other side.

After Pete left, having had enough of trying to get around walking in the sand, the summer past with the long days. When the time came close to September and we were still working at Warren's Landing, Glenn and I had a choice to make. We could wait a week or two and come home with Walter or leave immediately. I explained our options to Glenn that if we stayed the weather might turn suddenly and we would be stuck for a longer time. We decided to leave. Glenn did not want to miss any school. He wanted to be ready for his final year of high school to qualify for university. We did not like the idea of leaving Walter but it was hopefully only a couple of weeks at most.

We flew out but not on the Found. We took a larger airplane back. Walter stayed back to close up the plant, drain machines and put things in order for the winter. We realized as we left that the adventure was indeed a different part of our lives as we were isolated and together for a long time when the days blended and the rest of the world was a long way away. City life would be a big change.
The weather indeed did turn bad. For two weeks Walter was ready to leave. For two weeks, they waited for the arrival of favorable weather. As it grew colder, Walter feared he would need to wait months until the ice froze solidly enough to hold a ski plane. There was a short brief break in the weather and a plane flew in and took them out.

During this period of two weeks, Walter had a worker with him who was perhaps, not shall I say, the most polite, person. Walter did the cooking. He laughed later when he returned home and told us that he had made a meal of something for the two of them. Wondering if the food was ok Walter asked if it was good enough. He did get an answer. The fellow looked up from his plate and said, "well I am eating it ain't I".

Then in this same time, Walter got a bad toothache. With no dentist around, and no way to get to one, Walter pulled his own tooth with his own pliers! Well, that takes guts and resolve.

We were all glad to leave Warren's Landing and the bugs, and sand, and the long hours of work. It was not a nice place for me to live even for a short time. I saw no other women to talk to and I had to do a lot of work. It was not fun, but it was a time we could be together as a family while Walter worked and Glenn had a summer job, and I know it influenced Glenn's thinking in various ways as he has told me so.

After that summer, in the winter of 1969, Walter, Glenn, and I flew to Edmonton for Christmas. The picture below taken in the kitchen of Walter's parent, shows card players from the left clockwise: Jean, Glenn, Peter, and Gary. Grandma usually had a tablecloth on the table.

You can see the importance of religion to Walter's parents as Grandma's rosary is hanging on the wall around a religious picture and above it is a depiction of the Last Supper. They were Roman Catholic but before arriving in Canada they were married and Sergei changed from Greek Orthodox and became Roman Catholic. Peter Ternowski was also Greek Orthodox and had to become Roman Catholic to marry Minnie.

Sometime around 1969 Glenn no longer had confidence in me cutting his hair. I had cut all my boys hair. Lyle and Glenn were fussier about the results than David. This picture below testifies to this change, as well as some interesting fashion. His hair is, well, at least longer....

Some short time after David started working for Polar Refrigeration in Vancouver the owner wanted to get out of the business and sell the name. Walter and I purchased the name of the business. We made a Special trip from Winnipeg to bring money for the purchase. The used truck, a few customers, and few parts were of little value.

The partnership document above shows that our intent was to have Polar as a family business owned by Walter and his three sons. This document was signed by, Walter, David, and Lyle, in 1971. Walter retained 50% of the business, David got 30%, Lyle got 20%, and if Glenn were to join the business, he would get 15%. In the end, this is not how the company was registered, and David got all Polar, and later Lyle got a percentage. Unknowing, we returned to Winnipeg.

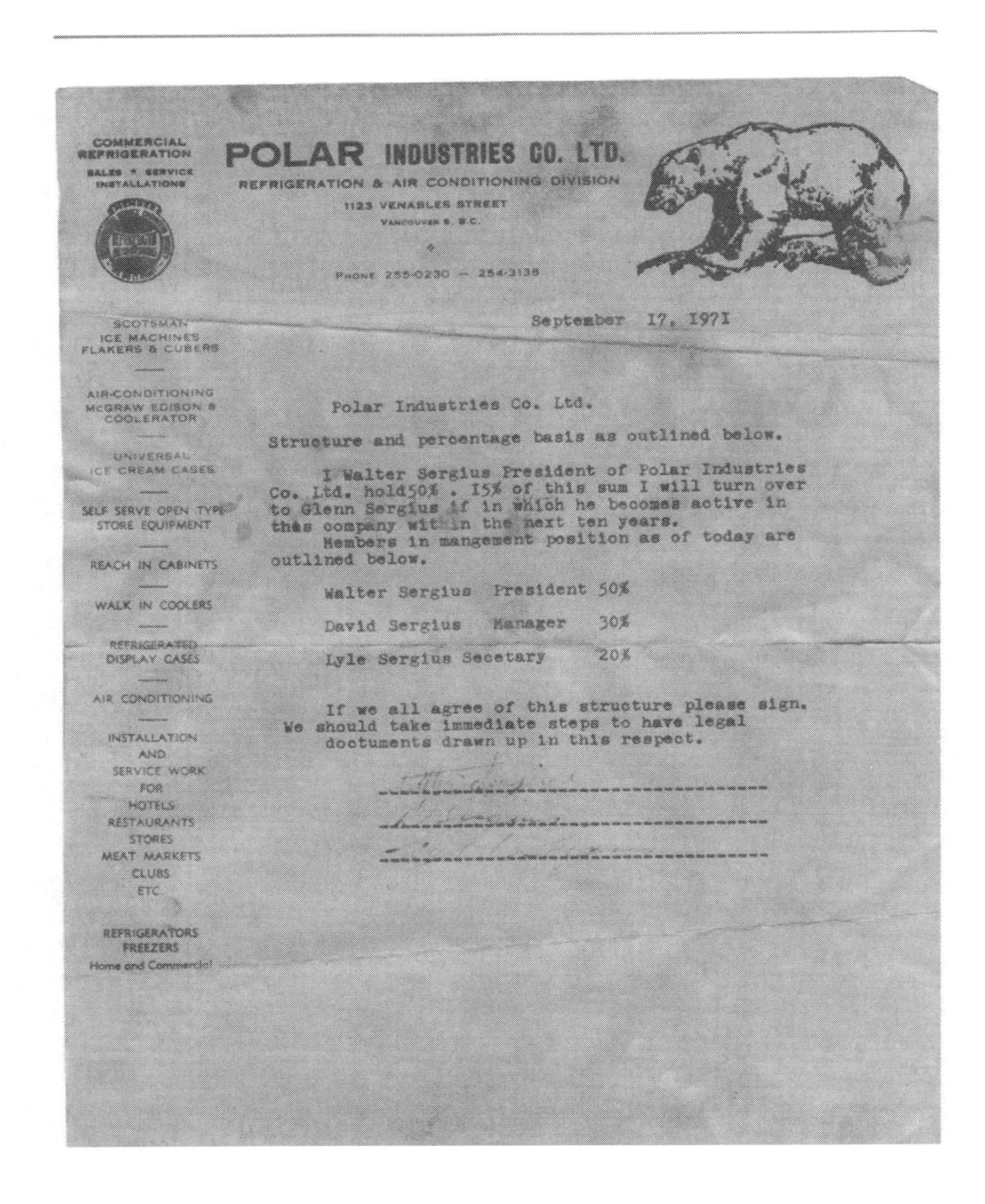

COMMERCIAL REFRIGERATION
SALES * SERVICE
INSTALLATIONS

POLAR INDUSTRIES CO. LTD.
REFRIGERATION & AIR CONDITIONING DIVISION
1123 VENABLES STREET
VANCOUVER 6, B.C.
PHONE 255-0230 — 254-3138

SCOTSMAN ICE MACHINES FLAKERS & CUBERS
AIR-CONDITIONING McGRAW EDISON & COOLERATOR
UNIVERSAL ICE CREAM CASES
SELF SERVE OPEN TYPE STORE EQUIPMENT
REACH IN CABINETS
WALK IN COOLERS
REFRIGERATED DISPLAY CASES
AIR CONDITIONING
INSTALLATION AND SERVICE WORK FOR HOTELS RESTAURANTS STORES MEAT MARKETS CLUBS ETC.
REFRIGERATORS FREEZERS Home and Commercial

September 17, 1971

Polar Industries Co. Ltd.

Structure and percentage basis as outlined below.

I Walter Sergius President of Polar Industries Co. Ltd. hold50% . 15% of this sum I will turn over to Glenn Sergius if in which he becomes active in thäs company with in the next ten years.
Members in mangement position as of today are outlined below.

Walter Sergius	President	50%
David Sergius	Manager	30%
Lyle Sergius	Secetary	20%

If we all agree of this structure please sign.
We should take immediate steps to have legal doctuments drawn up in this respect.

Walter and I worked on Bison Refrigeration while David and Lyle worked at Polar. Glenn went a different direction. For a time, there was a cold wind through the family. Walter never got to own a business with his sons, but when we moved to Surrey he did get to work with David and Lyle a short time.

About 1972, I was working part time at a corner store, not far from home, for owner Leona Slotec. The Slotec's lived in the back of the store. Leona's husband Nick was away working in Thunder Bay on an engineering project.

Tragedy struck. Leona's sister living in BC accidentally drove over the side of a bridge and died. Leona was in a bad spot because she wanted to go to the funeral. Leona wanted someone to work in the store so I did that for a couple of weeks. Her youngest son Jimmy worked in the store when he was not in school. Jimmy and I made a good team and I am pleased to know that now Jimmy lives in Toronto and is a journalist. Helping in the store lead to Leona and me becoming good friends and she years later visited me in Vancouver.

I worked there more regularly after those first few weeks and enjoyed it. I was always able to get a job quickly, and was glad to earn the money. A few jobs I enjoyed. I worked over the Christmas rush at Eaton's one year. Twice over the Christmas rush, I worked for Canada Post. At the start of working at Canada Post, I was standing up sorting letters. Then was sent to work in the dead letter office, which was better because I could to sit on a stool and complete addresses on letters. Working at Canada Post I did not meet as many people as I did working in the grocery stores or for Home Furnishing.

Working in the stores, I found if customers were treated with respect, they gave respect back. Bill Skakum's J & W Store was far busier than Slotec's store and had many school kids spending a few cents on candy. The one place I was glad to leave was Miracle Bakery because the owner's wife seemed unstable and odd.

The winter working with Leona was hard financially. I bought Bingo tickets and won $700. This was a windfall for us that winter. Bison was new and generating small jobs around Winnipeg. Business was slowly growing as people got to know Walter. Walter really did not like driving around Winnipeg. He had spent so many years in the north away from the multitudes of the city that the city traffic and commotion bothered him. I began to go with him driving, and sometimes I would be helping using a map and telling him where to drive.

One of Bison's early calls was to an Indian spice store. Indians were just beginning to emigrate to Canada from India. I was not familiar with people from India. I did not know their culture at all. I carried some of Walter's tools into the store and had a new experience. I had not been into a store that had so many spice smells so it was a bit of a surprise for me. I was not so sure I liked it. It is less of a surprise to me now that I have had more experience with Indians and spices. In my own cooking now use more spices now than I had previously used.

The customers made me some masala tea in a small kitchen in the back of the store. The tea had a lot of sugar and spices in it and as I never had strong tea, or tea with sugar, this masala was not my favorite, but I was glad of the experience. Since the space was small, and without enough room for me to stand around and help, I left.

I sat in the van with the door open. I was reading or doing crochet work. A cute, talkative, little girl from the store came out and started to talk. She asked me if I wore lipstick. I said perhaps, "yes sometimes". She then asked when I wore lipstick. I told her something like when I go visiting. She said to me, "Well you're visiting now why don't you have it on now?" I laughed and said something like because I had to work carrying tools in and out.

Walter did some work in Thunder Bay for George Humby in the fall of 1972. Humby had some kind of fish business and Walter was doing some refrigeration work for him. Walter drove to Thunder Bay in The Beast. Glenn and I took the dog Pal and drove to Thunder Bay for the weekend. We stopped to see the great divide where water either flowed south to the Mississippi or north to Hudson's Bay. We were in Thunder Bay for 2 or 3 days and then drove home. Walter was there a couple more weeks after that. This work for Humby became known to Louis Kemp, because Humby and Kemp were friends and business contacts.

In the following cold January of 1973, I answered the phone and the voice on the phone identified himself as Louis Kemp from Duluth, Minnesota, and he wanted to talk to Walter. He explained to Walter that he had a barge on a river in Alaska, and that he needed a man with ammonia Refrigeration qualifications to do the refrigeration. Walter of course had these qualifications.

Walter said he no longer went anywhere without his wife. Louis said it should not be a problem, as they needed a cook. Walter said we would think it over and we would call him back. We discussed it for about 10 minutes. Walter called him back and agreed.

Previously through the years Walter and I had many times talked about how great it would be to be able to see Alaska and drive the new road. We talked about how we would enjoy it. It was a frequent talking point about this dreamed of adventure. So, when Louis Kemp called we were all ready to go, and the pump was primed so to speak. It did not take too much time to decide. We did not have any concerns to hold us back. Glenn was in school and able to look after himself. David and Lyle were in BC. We were glad to go. It seemed like a golden opportunity for adventure.

Walter was to be paid for the work both of us did because they could easily have found someone local to do the cooks work and therefore had no need to hire a foreign worker, but finding Walter's qualifications was not easy. We insisted to be paid in Canadian funds because our dollar was worth more than the US dollar at the time.

There were many phone calls back and forth and we made lists of things that would be needed. I made a list of things that were needed for the kitchen as I was told I would be cooking for maybe three maybe four others. Walter and Louis talked a lot, but still this was insufficient because Louis did not know the barge, or about machinery in general.

We were ready to see a new environment together, we were ready to do new work, and meet new friends. We excitedly looked forward to this great adventure in a new country.

Alaska Adventure: A Great Experience, With Great People

Our Alaska adventure started on a very cold winter evening, after supper, in 1973, Walter was sitting on a kitchen chair. The phone hanging on the wall rang. It was a long distance phone call from Minnesota. He was becoming accustomed to getting calls, but not calls from the US. Over a few phone calls, we agreed to work for Kemp Palucci Seafood. Walter's combined expertise in ammonia refrigeration and the fish industry made him the perfect choice for the assignment. We put Bison Refrigeration on hold and agreed to a great adventure.

Looking back, it seems it was a stroke of good luck for us and Kemp Palucci Seafood to get both of us. We had the combined experience needed to make the system work. We met our employer in Duluth and started our jobs by shopping for supplies. The first night we stayed in a nice hotel and dined with Norman and Glenn in the revolving restaurant. The next morning, Norman and Glenn pictured here, drove back to Winnipeg. Norman stayed with Glenn for about a month before leaving for Vancouver to work with Polar.

The backdrop of the picture is an industrial building in Duluth, Minnesota. It was owned by Kemp and maybe Palucci. Louis Kemp had taken over the fish processing business started by his father. The building had once been a horse meat processing plant. We learned the Palucci portion of Kemp Palucci Seafood was the frozen Palucci Pizza distributed in the US. Through conversations, we learned Louis Kemp was a friend of the singer Bob Dylan.

In this picture from Duluth April 25, 1973, I am wearing a dress. Women rarely wore slacks. It was just as fashion designs were about to change for women's fashion. I wore a dress until we reached Bethel. Proper dress for women travelling meant a dress. I soon left the dress behind to be used for other occasions and wore pants at work. We had our first experience of the luxury of first class seating on a flight to Minneapolis.

In Seattle, we stayed at the Edgewater Hotel, a place the Beatles had stayed in a few years earlier, a fact that made the trip even more exciting. We ate in a tall building in a revolving restaurant and looked across at the Space Needle. It was quite exciting for us to travel first class in an airplane rather than on the top of frozen fish cartons, stay in a famous hotel rather than a rustic cabin, and use a luxurious bathroom rather than an insecticide sprayed outhouse. Seeing the ocean was a big event for prairie people. A post card I sent Glenn at the time, shows where we stayed and indicates my reactions at the time.

Fish from
Edgewater Inn, Seattle

After getting assorted machine parts, we left two days later. The Seattle airport felt huge and we certainly had to keep our wits about us to get to the right flights. We flew direct to In Anchorage, we stayed in the Captain Cook Hotel. Excitedly, we immediately hired a taxi for a city tour. Damage from the earthquake a few years before was still visible. It appeared as if a giant plough had been dragged through the city. It cut a deep path through the roads and buildings. Despite the damage, we could see that we were in a beautiful urban setting but that would soon change.

Two days later, we took a smaller airplane of Wein's Airlines to the remote gravel runway of Bethel. Getting on this plane in Anchorage was our first experience of being searched prior to boarding an airplane. They found some old tin foil in our pockets, perhaps from gum, and that was the end of the search. It was unusual to be searched and the searchers did more talking than searching.

To get to Bethel we flew over mountains and saw the opening of the Kuskokwim River to the Bering Sea. The airplane was loaded with freight isolating us from the pilot. We were in a cargo hold and a familiar location for air travel. We had just travelled first class in a foreign country and a few days later were in a freight airplane. We were aware of the differences. It made the trip all that more special.

A map of Alaska shows where Bethel is located. Look towards the south west of the state along the coast to find Bethel. To get an idea of where we were going the map shows Anchorage, and Bethel. This map does not show where the Johnson River flows into the Kuskokwim River and the location we were anchored in with the YutBiat.

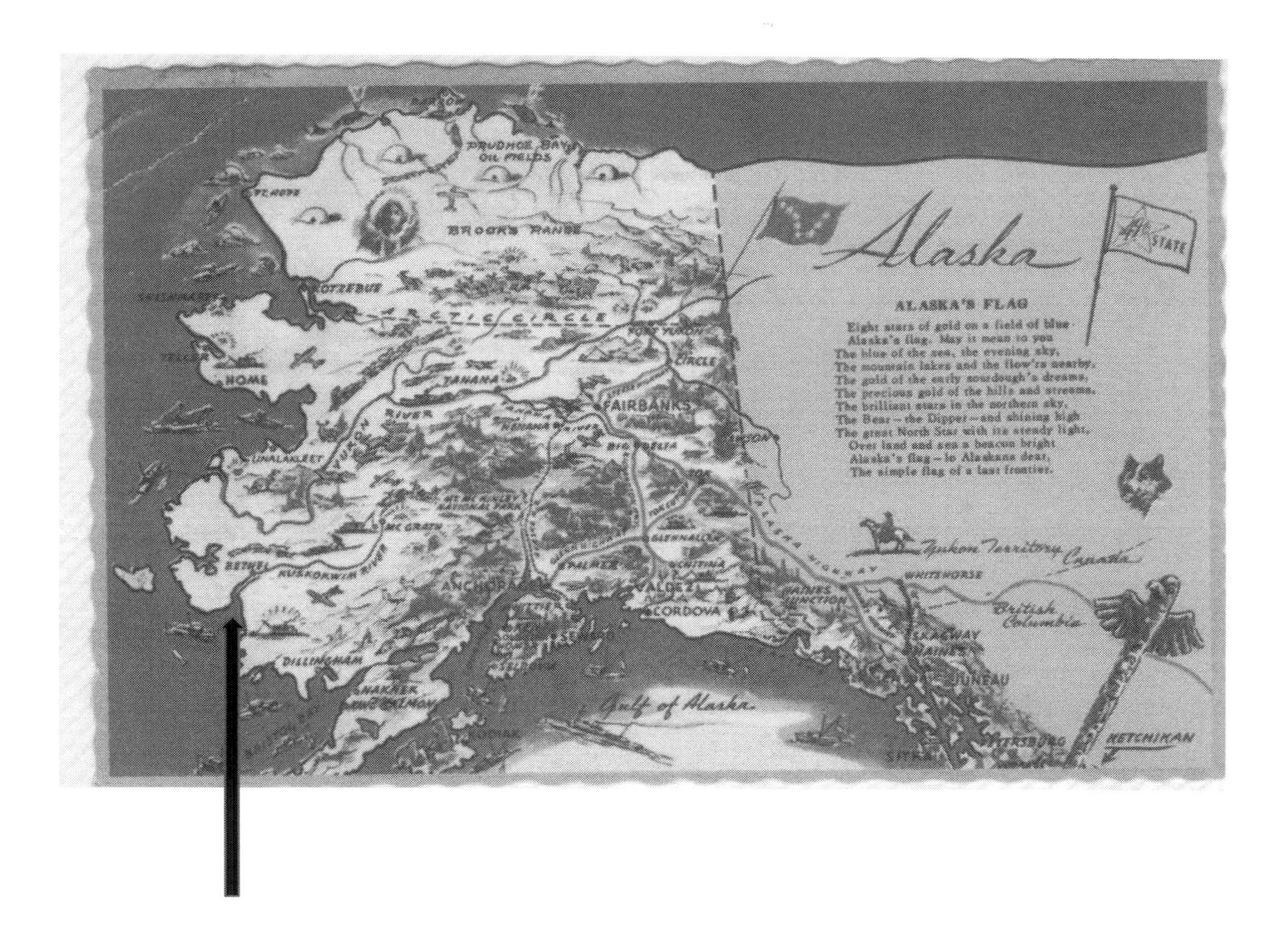

What did Bethel look like from the air?

Bethel is not what one might call picturesque. Built in a flat treeless tundra area, affected by climate changes, and water, Bethel has challenges in the beauty department.

We were not expecting a resort, and looks can be deceiving, but in this instance, they were not deceiving. For some it would be foreboding, perhaps disappointing. Our experience with the impoverished north gave us an idea of what to expect. It looks like many northern settlements. A high tide and a storm would put a lot of this town under water. The picture below shows a town built on flat tundra along the Kuskokwim River in between spots of water. YutBiat, a barge, is shown before our living quarters were built on top. It sits in the river on the upper right, a white bit in the river, but is a bit small to see easily in this shot.

The homes in the upper left are called Bethel Heights. Louse town is the part of the community along the river where YutBiat is anchored in the river. On the lower left are the Standard Oil buildings and above it center left is the hospital complex. The airport is not in the picture as it was 2 miles from town off the picture to the bottom left. The house rented for us for a few weeks would be off to the bottom left.

In the airport, I first saw real Alaskan natives dressed in flounced dresses. They wore layers of clothing under these dresses. I was excited and so happy to be able to see and hopefully meet real Alaskans, the Yupik. I had read and heard about these people and now, I was with them. I was happy. I looked forward to being able to meet some as friends.

Galen Steinbeck met us as we got off with the rest of the freight and took us to the Kuskokwim Inn in Bethel. It was a full hotel. Full in this case does not mean a full service inn with spa, gym, and other amenities. There were no such amenities. It means no empty beds. The room was tiny and miserable. Our personal luggage was all around us sort of like a continuation of the freight ride we just left. We were squeezed into the room. I am sure now, that had we known how rustic it would be we might not have come so enthusiastically or charged more. Yes, we would have still taken the Alaska contract because this was too good an adventure to miss.

In the cubicle like hotel room, the curtain rod fell off by itself and it was hard to put back up, and on the other side of the glass it was miserable and cold outside. The room could have been cleaner and could have smelled better. It was depressing. It was not so depressing as to change our minds. We viewed our situation as something to experience and savor.

Galen Steinbeck took us to lunch in the area known as uptown Bethel, at the Elegant Moose. Building materials are scarce here so this establishment looked like the inside of an old granary. Once inside the porch, the first entrance, you push aside an old curtain to enter the restaurant. It was nice and clean and a nice Eskimo girl asked what we wanted. I asked for a cup of tea and she said I do not think we have any and they did not, so we each had coffee and I think a burger.

I remember thinking of the contrast of the name to its surroundings, and compared with the limited food choices and printed menus as being somewhat like wearing an evening gown and tuxedo and stepping into a trapper's tent. It was a little joke of a name, because a moose is not considered elegant, and neither was this restaurant. I giggled to myself at the northern style joke. I understood the people were trying to provide a nice service and had little supplies to build with, and a lot of the environment to contend with, and so with my northern isolated life experience I could easily understand their situation.

The next day we went to visit the house we were to occupy for a short time, owned by Mr Crow. On the way to the Crow house Galen gave us a small tour of town. He pointed out the bank, hospital, and school that were all a fair distance from the store that we visited, and we were instructed to make sure we walked on the walkway to the store. The store was huge. It carried everything from groceries to hardware and clothes. I found the town disturbing because it was messy, and dirty. The snow was almost all gone revealing months of garbage. Mud and muck everywhere made the place most uninviting.

The government built about 200 houses in Bethel. Nicely built they stand up on piles without foundations. The houses are all up in the air in the summer time. There is garbage all over the place frozen to the ground. Bethel was in need of a good clean up. It was not pristine clean northern territory. Humans had made a mess of it and they needed to clean up the less pleasant effects of civilization.

The Crow house was located between the main part of the town and the airport. It was far enough from everything to discourage me walking to town. The airport is on the west side of Bethel. The hotel where we first stayed was in the mid town area. Louse town is on the east end. Louse Town got its name because of the frequency of head lice in the area. The Crow house was not in Louse town but on the western portion of the town, about 2 miles out from the town center and up kind of high. I could see river in the distance.

There are 2 roads in Bethel. Still one cannot get to Bethel by road. One gets to Bethel by water or by air. Bethel is situated on a curve of the Kuskokwim River and is surrounded by low watery country. In some places the river bank is very steep. The river bank is eroding badly as there is little if any rock on the banks. This erosion had destroyed many homes long before we got there in 1973.

We arrived in the spring of the year and global warming was starting even then, though I am not sure we knew it as such then. Finding firm land to build or walk upon is a difficult task. The town sits on permafrost and many of the buildings are on stilts. The permafrost is thawing. The roads were safe to be on, but stepping off the few wooden plank sidewalks meant meeting the possibility of sinking at least to one's knees in the soft soil above the permafrost. As the temperature rises the ground thaws and it becomes mud. The plank sidewalks were elevated above the tundra.

A paved road ran through town but the sidewalks did not. To leave the road and get into a store one needed rubbers even if there were a sidewalk because the road and sidewalk did not abut. There was a span of mud between the road and the sidewalk, and between the sidewalk and the store. The snow melt causes the river to flood every year and the ground water level to rise. In some places because of the spring flooding, it was hard to distinguish between river, and what should have been land.

Bethel had at least one doctor and a hospital. This was a significant and needed profession and facility. There were a few churches in town. The main ones were Moravian and Greek
Orthodox, left over from when this was Russian territory. I attended one service in the Moravian church. The resident church goers are Yupik Eskimos. The language of the service was Yupik and the minister spoke only a few words in English. The service featured a lot of singing. There were different services in English but I never made it to such a service.

I saved the order of service. You can see that the order is written in Yupik and English so that everyone could follow, but most of the language of the service was Yupik.

THE BETHEL MORAVIAN CHURCH
Bethel, Alaska
Jacob Nelson, Sr., Pastor
Larry D. Wetzel, Associate Pastor

MORNING WORSHIP - 11:00 A.M.

(Yupik)

Prelude
Agaiyutlrim
Yuarun # 53 "Anegtogyserka Agaiyutim"
Atorerkat
Kaniryarak — James 1: 16 - 21; John 16: 4 - 15
Atortit
Kanrutkumarkat
Yuarun # 69 "Kuyogtukut Agaiyutvut"
Kanirvarak
Yuarun # 86 "Nunanerkilra tang'gaka"
Postlude

(English)

Prelude
Hymn "O Worship The King" — # 158
The Liturgy of Confessions — Page 9
Special Music
The Holy Scriptures — James 1: 16 - 21; John 16: 4 - 15
Children's Sermon
Concerns
The Presentation of our gifts
The Offertory
The Doxology and Prayer
Hymn "Fairest Lord Jesus" — # 214
Sermon
The Pastoral Prayer
Hymn "My Faith Looks Up To Thee" — # 332
The Benediction
Postlude

****

ORGANISTS: Mrs. Leta Brown, Mrs. Paul Gregory

THE VESPER SERVICE - 7:30 P.M.

The Organ Prelude
The Call To Worship
The Opening Hymn "Tell It To Jesus" — # 191
The Pastoral Prayer
The Special Music
The Holy Scriptures — Revelation 3: 7 - 13; Matthew 5: 1 - 12
The Choir Anthem
The Concerns
The Presentation of our gifts
The Offertory
The Choral REsponse and Prayer
The Hymn "Since I Have Been Redeemed" — # 232
The SErmon
The Closing Hymn "Softly and Tenderly" — # 294
The Benediction
The Organ Postlude

****

CONCERNS

MONDAY	Youth Fellowships	3-6	4:30 p.m.
		7 - 12	7:30 p.m.
TUESDAY	Women's Fellowship		7:30 p.m.
WEDNESDAY	Bible Study and Prayer		7:30 p.m.

VACATION BIBLE SCHOOL MAY 27 - 31

****

HAPPY MOTHER'S DAY..

Many of the Yupik youth are sent south for schooling in the winter. The Yupik in this area work in the summer time to fill their larder with as much food as they can find. The larder is full of dried berries and dried fish. Each family tries to save enough fish for their dog teams and for each family member. When this task is complete, they will then take a job where they are paid a wage. The people that I worked with told me this was their order of priorities. This dependence on traditional food guaranteed their survival. Thus, there would be fisherman catching fish but not bringing it to the barge for sale. They would first take it home to preserve it for winter supplies.

Into this community and into the Crow house we moved and began our work. Mr Crow rented his Bethel house to Kemp Palucci Seafoods and we were glad to stay there. The house came furnished with some dishes and pans. Although it had been somewhat cleaned I knew I had to clean before we moved in because it seemed to have sat unused. The window ledges were full of dead flies. There were dishes on the table and bits of food here and there so I began immediately to clean. On the main floor was a washing machine and I was glad to use it while we were there. In the basement was a large freezer and I wondered if it could be used. I lifted the lid and closed it in a hurry. The top layer was dead ducks complete with feathers. I had never seen ducks frozen this way, and I was certain I did not want to see it again.

Mrs Crow was a nice person. She came back to get something she needed and we chatted a bit. She said, "Oh my I would not recognize this as the same house it is so clean". I did not know what exactly to say and said something like I am glad you approve.

I include the first page of introduction I wrote when I put my album together:

1973

Adventures of Walter & Sarah Sergius.

Our life on Yut Boat (Peoples Boat) in Upik.

Located on the Johnson & Kuskokwim Rivers near Bethel Alaska. The Kuskokwim river begins its journey in the Mount McKinley area between Anchorage & Fairbanks, then makes its way south west to the Bering Sea. The Johnson river joins the Kuskokwim fourty miles before it runs into the sea.

We were located at the mouth of the Johnson river. This area provides some of the finest salmon fishing in Alaska.

We arrived in Anchorage the last part of April to see buds on the trees.

One day the Bethel community flew in a live cow. The schools all took the kids to the airport to see the cow because the kids had never seen a cow. This gave them first hand experience with something most kids in the other states would see easily. Years before the community had farm animals, but I am not sure where they would have found solid footing. This temporary fly in cow was a way to educate the youth and allow them to see a real cow up close.

Honey Bucket service was available. This sweet, pleasant, sounding service is not part of gourmet cooking. It is a highly valued service though. This involves a removable inside toilet pail. There was a separate room for the honey bucket. The service would come every so many days to pick up and empty the pail. As they entered the house, they would just walk in yelling "Honey Bucket" and walk straight into the room, take it outside, walk up a few stairs to dump the honey bucket into the container and throw the empty container on the ground for you to retrieve, clean, and put back. Yes, this is not as easy as a flush toilet, but it is an improvement over a fly infested smelly outhouse. Honey bucket delivery is not a job I would want to have and I hope they were well paid.

Our work had started. I was cooking in the Crow house. Already this number was more than the three or four I had been told to expect. There were already at least four or five men for supper. I note in one of my letters I wrote to Ruby at the time I was cooking for one woman and seven men. The woman was particularly lazy, getting up late around ten in the morning, and doing nothing, but later was the first to eat, perhaps because eating was something for her to do. She was bored and unhappy. Her husband was to help but was not too talented around the engine room. After two weeks of doing mostly nothing, they left. Cooking for two less people, not having to move around them and their draining negative energy as we started out, was an improvement.

I spent most of my time in this house cooking and baking but I never froze any batches, as I did not want to get near the ducks. Many people came into the house regarding the fish business. Louis Kemp had business meetings there. I always had to bake bread, cookies, and other sweets for these meetings. I was never back down town. The men did all the shopping on their way home from work using a list I gave them. I just cleaned the place to my standards. I baked buns, cake, pie, and cookies and cleaned. Soon there were never less than 8 or 9 people and more eating. I loved to cook and they loved to eat. I was sort of mom to a lot.

Walter would look after morning coffee and brought me coffee in bed at six AM. This was something Walter did almost all the time. I would be up to have breakfast ready for seven and work until ten most nights but not always. I did not leave the house very much at all for these four weeks. There was a lot of work to do cooking, and cleaning. Walter would insist I lay down for an hour every afternoon after the dishes were done.

Walter was busy getting the barge ready. To get to the barge they took a small truck from the house using dangerous seek and find, trial and error, drives along the ice of the river, until the ice became too soft to support the truck. Then they came back on to the land not far from Louse Town and close to a swamp where the barge was located. Getting onto the barge for a while was difficult because of the water, mud, and soft dangerous permafrost. I worried about this daily drive but they seemed confident in what they were doing.

Walter oversaw building the living quarters and getting all the refrigeration and diesel engines ready and working. He had to install and repair equipment and order parts to be flown to Bethel. On the barge, Walter built our living quarters with a bedroom, bathroom, and shower down a hallway off the kitchen. The rest of the crew had communal living arrangements, with four per room, and separate rooms for men and women. All sleeping areas were upstairs. The crew had separate showers and bathrooms downstairs near the working area. There was usually only one crew woman and she had a room across from ours. If an extra woman was employed the two shared the room.

When the ice on the river left, it was dramatic. The river was at least a mile wide at this point. River ice would flip, and the bottom would become the top. The bottom was full of large icicles at least four to six feet in length. The ice breakup noise lasted several days and was akin to hundreds of crystal bells being rung at the same time. A marker of some sort was placed in the middle of the river. The time when this marker disappeared marked the official ice breakup time. Breakup was a much discussed and anticipated event. People were excited. There was organized betting on the date and time that this would happen.

Breakup meant that it was just days before our departure from Mr Crow's house to the barge. Still there was cooking and feeding to do right to the very last minute. The day we relocated to the barge and it was pulled from the slough to the river side was a big event in Bethel. It was like the opening of a residence and dining hall all at once.

All the beds bed clothing mattresses, sheets, pillows, pillow cases, towels, soaps, dishes, fresh food, cases of canned food, cooking equipment were all loaded on to the barge before I arrived. This all sat in piles to be sorted. I was one of the last to get on the barge and had to climb up a rope ladder to board. It made me feel like a real sailor. Soon after I boarded, tugboats started to push the barge down the river. The barge had no engine. That would become an interesting attribute.

Below you can see the YutBiat. The name means peoples boat in Yupik. It is 50 feet wide and 150ft long. Empty, it was about 28 feet out of the water and loaded about 24 feet out of the water. The living quarters that are clad in corrugated metal, sit on the top deck. The freezer and fish gutting areas were on the main deck and the freezer holds were underneath our sleeping area. It was an industrialized floating fish processing station. There was no smell of fish upstairs partly because the processing and freezing was clean and fast, but perhaps too because there was a breeze on the water.

The first night approached chaos. In the kitchen there were boxes of food, equipment, cooking utensils, dishes, sheets, blankets, and other things all over the floor. It was a big surprise that there were about 50+ people for supper there that night. I had a lot of busy fast work cooking for so many.

Six or seven Japanese workers who were to collect salmon roe also had all their cooking equipment loaded onboard. They were certainly assertive. Perhaps pushy is a better word. I guess they were not accustomed to working with a large group of people and just did not comprehend what others had to do. The Japanese workers of course were hungry too and were camped everywhere, sitting everywhere, and were on top of the freezer and sat on the floor to peal oranges and were generally messy with their peelings and in the way. They wanted to eat their own kind of food. They appeared to have an entitled attitude and we were to be honored with their presence. Later this attitude changed. They did not understand English and they could not communicate and did not try to communicate, and I could not make them understand they had to get out of the way and get their stuff off the freezer and move so we could work. They did not understand they had to move and could not see that they were in the way. I am not sure how they could not see they were in the way, but I could not get them to get out of the way. They did not seem to care they were impeding our work. They were perhaps unfamiliar with how we would cook in the kitchen, but did not go to their rooms. They were not northerners and did not pitch in to help.

Eventually I had to send someone to go ask Walter to come up from down stairs immediately. I do not know who went to get Walter, but there were people everywhere. I just grabbed someone and asked. Walter succeeded where I had failed. Later they knew to listen to my authority in the kitchen. We ended up being friends and they understood they had to be more respectful to others, perhaps women in general, and that I ran the kitchen.

I was not prepared to have so many people on board wanting to eat. Two or three Yupik women saw I could not keep up so they took dishes out of boxes washed them and put them away. They were on board to work in the fish processing. Some could understand English and some could not. There was mess everywhere. The beds and mattresses all had to be unwrapped, the bunks put together. The sheets and blankets were all plastic wrapped, pillow cases were in bags etc. There was an entire mess in the barge as things were opened there was packaging to be dealt with. We all worked until about one in the morning.

I was cooking hamburgers and wieners all night, they ate that and cookies and bread. This was fast food, not great food. Everyone got enough to eat eventually. I did the cooking and the helpers did clean up. The water had to be heated on the stove to wash dishes. This cooking and cleaning for 50 visitors was all on one stove.

The next day there were still a lot of people around and the Yupik workers helped peel vegetables and get things ready for me to cook. For the first few days, Louis had not hired anyone to help so I asked the young Yupik boys 16 – 18 years old to help. The boys all spoke English from school as well as Yupik. I would get them to bring things for me. The girls would help me get the food ready. After the first 3 days, things began to settle down a bit. It was obvious I would be cooking for a lot more than four people. Louis needed to hire kitchen help. The number of people that I cooked for would never be less than ten and many times, it would be more than twenty-five people three times a day at least. Many times, the fishermen who had just delivered fish would come up to eat. When out on a cold sea, a warm meal you do not have to cook, in a nice warm kitchen, is more than a nice thing to have. I would prepare something for them to eat at whatever hour it happened that they came upstairs.

The first girl Louis hired was such a nice girl. One weekend she went to Bethel and came back drunk. She could not work and I had to let her go. This first year, alcohol was a big problem for their society. It ruined many people's lives and sometimes, unexpectedly, it would raise its ugly head. The next year alcohol was not allowed in town as the town had a plebiscite and voted not to have alcohol in town.

Louis hired Bessie Charles pictured later, and Grace Nichols to share the job on different days. When they had a day off another girl would work. Bessie pictured below, had two sisters Rachel and Edith, and they sometimes filled in. Rachel was 19 in this picture and is Bessie's older sister. Rachel was a good worker with a friendly nice personality. The picture shows the messy shoreline of Bethel in the background.

Below is a picture of 15 year old Edith Charles on the upper deck of YutBiat. Behind her is the wide expansive view of the wide river. In this picture, it seems flat. However, the river was not always calm, and there were swells and the river current was affected by the ocean tide.

Bessie,came from Kasigluk. She would go home every now and then. She talked about her grandparents and older people in her village eating rotted fish heads. The fish heads were buried in the ground. When they had rotted to be something like cheese, they were ready to eat. Her parents used to make this but I do not remember her saying she ate it. I imagine she did. Certainly, I never had the pleasure.

One time Bessie brought me Eskimo ice cream from home. I could not eat it but I had to taste it. It was awful. I appreciated the kind gesture, and now understand it must be an acquired taste. It is made of whipped fat with added berries and sugar. I think it would need a lot more sugar. Perhaps in a culture where sugar was less evident in cooking, the sweetness was more profound and my tastes were contaminated by plentiful sugar.

One of the first girls Louis hired was Margaret Tinker. She was such a nice girl and came from Kasigluk. I sent her a Christmas gift from Winnipeg along with other girls. She sent me a picture of herself and a

little brother. Her father was a Moravian minister. I wonder where Margaret is. Below are two pictures, one of Margaret and one of Margaret and her little brother.

Walter would send boys up from the engine room to help whenever we got excessively busy They did not come up all greasy and always washed up before they came to the kitchen. One of the boys came from Nelson Island in the Bering Sea. The boys would help wash dishes, prepare vegetables, and set tables. All the helpers learned how to set a table. I would hear from them all until the time I moved to Vancouver.

Breakfast usually meant I prepared bacon, eggs, regular toast, French toast, porridge, pancakes, fruit, coffee, and tea. Around 10 in the morning the workers would stop for coffee and cookies. Sometimes I made cookies and there were usually store bought cookies that came in large boxes. I made peanut butter, sugar, and chocolate chip cookies and a variety of others.
At lunch left overs were served. If twenty guys came in for lunch and there were only five left over pork chops the first five to get there would get the pork chops. I made soups made from scratch such as chicken and oxtail soups and puddings for desert. I would as per Walter's direction, rest for a bit but mostly for 30 minutes only, right after lunch. As soon as I was ready to work, again I would be back getting ready for the next wave of workers. I made about six pies a few times a week, and cakes, cookies, cinnamon buns, and fresh buns. Frequently I had to prop up the cake pans in the oven to keep them level because YutBiat would be heavily loaded to one side and slanting. YutBiat's loading also meant the kitchen floor was sometimes slanted requiring a bit of learning time to know how to walk around and develop the skills and sea legs to be able to cook.

Lately I have wondered what it was that I was thinking about as I worked. I do not remember, but I do know that I was enjoying the constant change. YutBiat was constantly moving from side to side. I would be working at the sink and look out the window and notice the scenery had changed. A boat would be out the window one moment and a bit later, it would be gone. A ship or a barge would be seen coming up the river, and in a few minutes, it would be docked, or gone by, or the window would be facing the shore and I never knew what had happened to it. There was a lot of action and that made the time enjoyable and challenging.

There were some characteristics associated with life afloat that were not necessarily similar to land life. The barge always seemed tilted one way or the other. We had a terrible time trying to sleep because of the tilting and noise from the processing below. Frequently we would have to move from one end of the bed to the other and slept with one end tilted most of the time. On the water, there was always a breeze, and it never warmed up as much as it did ashore. I remember thinking how nice it would be to see a flower and not have to wear a sweater all the time even in the summertime. There were no flowers on the edge of the river and the breezes could be cool. The river was so wide it was like living in the middle of the ocean.

There were some bugs but not a lot. Had we been on the land we would have been bothered by bugs, but because of the breeze on the water, the mosquitoes did not bother us too much. There were only a few odd mosquitoes. The doors were always opening and shutting, and were more often open rather than closed. Flies were not around even though fish was processed below.

The picture below was taken just before we left in 1973. We just installed the second stove and it made things a lot easier. I could look out the windows and see a changing scene from the water.

There was an afternoon coffee break about three in the afternoon. I would bake and serve fresh cookies and sweets as before along with fresh buns with jam and jelly. Supper was always the biggest meal of the day. We would have roast beef, or roast pork, beef, or pork ribs, stews, roast and fried chicken, liver and onions, and only once seal liver. Surrounded by fish as we were, we did not eat it that often. We had fish only once in a couple of weeks because the fish was for selling. Dessert was pies, puddings, and ice cream. Everything was eaten. There were many good appetites and there was little if any waste. The girls I had helping used to love baking cookies. Every day we made something.

Sometimes events would make the kitchen very busy. Even in the busy times all those eating at the table had to remove their hats. This custom was an attempt to assert that civilized manners were valued even in the remote wilderness. People seemed to appreciate the effort everyone made to comply. The men were all appreciative of the friendliness around the table. It was like a big family. Everyone was friendly and all were willing to help at any time. At the table over coffee and meals there was always a lot of talk. People would eat ten at a time. This necessitated people leaving, to permit others to sit down. Between fishing seasons there would be ten to eighteen workers.

In this picture is the boat pilot for LCM, the call letters of his boat. He was a nice fellow and he always liked to clean the icing bowl. I knew when he was coming sometimes because he would bring the barge in and bang the anchor cable holding YutBiat firm and that made YutBiat shake.

Susie Charlie was a fish dresser from Tuntutuliak, Alaska. A fish dresser used a knife, gutted, and beheaded the fish. She worked on Shank's Ark a smaller barge attached to YutBiat, and is pictured below having coffee. She came up to talk to me on this day all happy and told me she had just returned from vacation in Waikiki, Hawaii, and had a nice tan. It was hard for me to tell the difference so I just believed her and took this picture. In the picture, I can see she is tanned, but at the time it was hard to tell because I had not known her before. Tan or no tan she was a good person to have as a friend. I wondered why she went in the summer rather than the winter. She is sitting at the mess table in the kitchen at coffee break.

Natashia Hoffman worked counting fish when the boats were unloading. Here she is seen walking from the night workers lunch room, to the kitchen.

On the table, you see hot sauce, jam and cigarette ashtrays. It was acceptable then to smoke at the table but is not now. Walter is on the left side of the picture and Tim Schwanke a regular worker, is beside him. The fellow in the blue shirt was a local, and may have been there at the time of lunch and just ate with everyone. At the table, the mix of people eating included men, women, race, age, religion, and nationality. Floating in the middle of the river, we worked together as a team oblivious to differences. As the men finished their meals and left the table the kitchen helpers would remove their plates and set a clean plate for the next person. Even though people had to wait to eat the atmosphere was always up tempo and happy. They all loved to eat and I loved cooking for them.

Tim Bee is lighting a cigarette after the meal. In those days, smoking at the table was allowed at the end of the meal. They must have been the last group to eat.

Three young men came up to work on YutBiat from the south or lower states. The three below are from the left are Doug Pattison, Mike, and Rick Amys. They had a good experience for the summer and earned some money doing so. In the background, you can see the flatness of the land that was barely above the level of the sea. I wonder how long until global warming submerges this area.

The flat river delta is also obvious in the picture below of Andrew David, Jim Henkelmen, and Walter on the top deck. Here the land rises from the river a little but this is tidal water and the tide may be out. In this shot, one can see a closer view of the flat river delta and that it has vegetation but I never saw any animals on it. It is permafrost and the surface is soft and unsafe. I never walked along the shore. To do this one had to shinny along the steel cable from YutBiat to the shore. Some of the men did. They told me they were growing a garden there and I believed them not knowing it was marijuana. They had a good laugh at my expense and over their little secret. In the land of the midnight sun's long hours of sunshine, and good earth if it were not flooded out, their garden would grow very well.

Niles Alexis was one of the several fishermen that ate with the crew when he unloaded fish. I had to be prepared for extra drop in people to feed without a schedule. He was a fine level headed, responsible man, and a good person. He can be seen on the end of the table in blue, to the left of the refrigerator and yellow flowers.

After lunches and supers, talking around the table Niles told us some of the history and stories of the area. One story in particular, stands out. He told us how his parents were told one day to keep their children away from the river. Warning had spread quickly along the coast. The reason seems hard to believe but it was certainly taken seriously. Some kind of monster had been spotted in the river. Niles Alexis said there was oral history of such warnings and monsters coming from the sea. This community would have seen all sorts of whales, sharks, seals and other recognized sea life. They saw something that they did not recognize and that made them afraid. I cannot say what the monster was but the warning was definitely taken seriously.

One day a Yupik worker spotted a seal on the Kuskokwim River. The seal had come up the river chasing salmon. Word spread so fast that soon everyone knew the seal was there. Four workers, including Mr Nichols, stopped what they were doing and immediately left in boats carrying guns. They circled the seal and shot it. It sank. They waited and it soon floated. They were all happy to be able to eat seal.

The Japanese roe workers initially they tried to cook their own food with all the equipment they brought, but soon gave up trying to do that. They were far too tired and disorganized at the end of the day to be able to work and cook. The decided to blend in rather than remain apart and they were happier for it. I cannot identify the man in the green raincoat, but the one in the middle we called Moo Juice, and the man in the sweater on the right is Tamara. Moo Juice was worker named. He called all liquid juice. When he wanted milk, perhaps for his coffee, he would say moo juice. He was learning English this way. He was a well liked fellow. On the wall behind is the map of Alaska. I still have it.

When I cooked the seal liver from the hunt mentioned above, not everyone knew it was seal liver. Tamara from the island of Hokkaido, Japan, the gentleman on the right of the above picture, did not know it was seal liver but he ate it and liked it to start.

Later, when he looked over my shoulder and asked what I was cooking and I said I would cook him more seal liver and asked if he wanted it, he waved his hand and said "no,no, no,no".

The seal liver seemed rather large, about 10 inches long and 4 inches deep. I ate only a little of it. It was tender. In my imagination, I could see the eyes of the seal looking at me and I could not eat any more. I think Tamara felt the same way.

Air pilot Charles Pike is eating late. He may have brought a passenger or the mail, or maybe he came to take someone out. He was not an overnight guest and lived in Bethel but frequently ate in the kitchen. The door in the background to the left, opened to the hall, and a few steps later a stairway led to the main processing deck. Our room was on the opposite side of this room. The walls are unpainted plywood.

This is the hallway facing the door above on the opposite side of the room. If one came in the door behind Charles Pike the hallway was visible. Our room is the second door and is marked with an X.

The first door to the right was the bathroom for the kitchen staff and Walter and me. The Japanese workers were permitted to use this shower only after we had used it as they were supposed to go downstairs. Other than one error they were pretty good about making sure I did not have to have a cold shower.

Here you can see the metal shower. The toilet is special. It was one of those special, and prized facilities, one only gets to use in remote areas. It was both a great invention and a real pain in the well..., a real pain in the butt. All the toilets on YutBiat were this model of propane toilet. The great advantage of a propane toilet is that a flame burns the contents. The flame comes on when the lid of the toilet is put down after use.

There were several of these toilets down stairs for the workers to use. Burning the contents heats up the seat and it is soon too hot to sit on. It could be called an environmental hot seat. Thus, people would always be saying leave the lid up. If the lid were left up the toilet would get too full for when the lid was to be put down. This caused these propane toilets to burn out. There always seemed to be toilets burning out.

Across the hall from us was the room shared by my helpers, Bessie Charles or Grace Nichols. The children's pictures on the wall of the kitchen are from Annette and Tina Sager my nieces. My sister Ruby would send me their art work. You can also see the two fire extinguishers and door to an eating room that a night crew would use to eat their lunches. Near the end of the hall, the Japanese workers shared a room. Bessie or I would walk down and knock on their door to alert them that supper was ready. When their mail was delivered from Bethel, Bessie would say the workers were laughing and giggling and it smelled funny. I assume they were smoking grass.

One day Walter said that perhaps the next day we were going on a trip, meaning we would go when he could get time to leave. It was an announcement that was more like a surprise present and certainly, it was a relief from the daily routine. He had to go look at two barges that had been marooned high and dry on tundra during a bad windstorm. They were about one quarter of a mile inland from the river near Quinhagak and the Nushagak River. These tents are part of Qunhagak. We left the Bethel airport in a small plane that you can see is equipped with both wheels and skis.

We landed on a small airstrip at Quinhagak near the Nushagak River. The pilot was Charles Pike just previously pictured eating. This small airplane pictured above carried four of us: the pilot Charles Pike, Galen Steinback, Walter, and I. It was on this trip that Charles Pike started to call us Crazy Canucks. The nickname stuck. We landed on a narrow strip beside the Kanektok River.

We climbed into a heavy wooden framed Eskimo fisherman's boat and we went to the village of Quinhagak where the barges were grounded. Walter and I sat in the very middle of the boat. We looked up and over the edges of the boat and could see the river ahead of us. The ice still clung to the dirt river edges. The ice stuck out over the waters edges like tent canopies, and we could see under the ice to the banks. When we slowed, and stopped the tinkle of the melting ice could be heard.

Pictures of the two barges the Elook, and the smaller Christmat, show them sitting on tundra. Stepping across the grass hummocks our feet sank into water. The soil was soft, wet, and almost at water level.

Walter used water to get these two battered looking rigs moved. Using water pumps, the areas under and surrounding the units were flooded. Two tugboats and long cables were used to pull the units out. Only one tugboat was necessary after the units started to move. I was not there to see it happen.

The barges look neglected, weathered, and battered up. I only remember one of them being used, the Elook. The pictures show close up what the tundra looked like in much of the area. It is easy to imagine how a storm could easily push a large floating vessel inland and that as the storm eased the vessel would be marooned. We took note of this thought.

Below, on the left of the picture, Walter is waving from the deck of the floating Christmat after successfully getting the two vessels off the tundra. I see it has a different name on the back but I cannot figure out what it says.

In late June or early July, I woke in the middle of the night. Our bedroom was over the freezer. Sometimes the crew worked 24 hours, banging shut the freezer doors loading fish to freeze. We had to get used to that constant noise if we wanted to sleep. On this night, I awoke because the noise was different. No processing and freezing were taking place. It was a period of a few days down time between fishing seasons. The sound of metal banging had awakened me. The tide was on the way in and a wind storm had arisen. What I heard was metal siding blowing around. I woke Walter immediately. In a hurry, he was dressed and downstairs. Waking the two men left on board the boat, Walter led them out in a hurry. They all scrambled around to secure everything. The wind was blowing hard and making a terrific noise. Metal siding was being ripped off the barge. Things were flying around the deck. You could feel the YutBiat pulling at its moorings hitting the end of the mooring cable again, and again, as the wind pushed the barge back and forth and the cable stretched. It was as if the barge was a wild animal trying to escape capture.

We watched the wind blown water rise along the river. Normally even in areas where the land could hold a tent or a building, the water was not too far below the land surface. The river rose more than three feet in a few hours. It was getting closer and closer to a small group of temporary residences. In a few minutes, it would easily flood the land.

As the water rose and the wind howled, I could see the homes of some people I knew beginning to flood. Grandma Nichols, who had begun to come and have tea with me, had a tent shack home exactly in the path of the rising water. The storm was getting worse. The residents abandoned their homes and boarded YutBiat for safety.

On board Grandma Nichols watched as her tent went down in the water. She forgot her wallet in her tent and cried. Her mattress was also in the tent. There were about 20 people from the village. Then our power quit, and for several hours, we had no lights or heat and a barge full of wet worried passengers.

Grandma Nichols was dripping wet. She was in her 70's. I knew she had to get dry or she would get pneumonia. I took Grandma Nichols and her daughter in law into our room where we could find clothing and use towels to dry her off. We were doing fine, we were stressed, but we knew what we had to do.

Grandma Nichols was modest but realized she had needed to be dry clothes. She had long johns on made from flour bags. I recognized the bags and I remembered making use of flour bags in the depression. She most likely made them herself. I remembered that it took five flour bags to make sheets for a bed and no one wanted to sleep near the seam where the fifth bag was cut and sewn to the others for length, and I remembered making aprons and tea towels from them. I imagine they were used for underwear too.

I found some of my underwear and offered them to Grandma Nichols. Store bought underwear were an unfamiliar concept to her. She held them up in the air in outstretched arms and looked at them in puzzlement, and then broke into loud laughter. All three of us laughed and laughed. Eventually Grandma Nichols put them on and we found a housecoat and a sweater for her to wear. When the heat came on and we were afloat we hung her things up inside to dry. The others just wore their wet clothing until they dried. We all needed to eat and have hot drinks so we made tea.

The picture shows the disaster on shore just outside YutBiat and the submerged Nichols Fish camp. The Nichols stayed in this tent shack and this was their fish camp. The river has risen and a boat is about to go into the Nichols front door. The water has flooded up over the banks about three feet and is going beyond the shack tent. The storm came as a fast surprise sweeping in from the ocean. There are still clothes on the wash line someone had no time to remove. People are already aboard the boat ready to come to YutBiat.

In only a few minutes, we drifted past the settlement dragging the anchor with us as we were blown up the Johnson River against the current. This middle picture is normal high tide. You can see that the river is quite close to the top of its banks at high tide. The Nichols camp is then normally not too far out of the water. It did not matter how far away from the river they went they would be at no higher an elevation. They were inches above the water. The land was flat and much of it under water or soaked all the time. Their camp was in the best place it could be as there were no better places.

Here is about the same area in low tide. In both pictures following, one can see the dead man buried in

the land and the cable from the YutBiat to the dead man. Low tide shows the difference between high and low tide of about 3 feet and the black rich soil.

The wind noise was loud and threatening. There was nothing to break the wind it swept in over treeless land and across the sea and hit YutBiat full force. YutBiat the biggest obstacle the wind met was also pushed and bounced by the wind and waves. Then the cable to the dead man snapped. It whipped around and could have whipped back over the deck like a cutting blade killing people but it did not. With this securing cable missing, YutBiat was freely pushed by the tide and the strong winds. YutBiat dragged the anchor and cable down the river. We went up the Johnson River about half a mile and not in a straight line. YutBiat hit ground first on the left side in the shallow but fast water. Then YutBiat hit the bottom of the river a few times before we came to a final rest. Here the wind blew strongly and held us in place, partly on the water covered land and partly in the river.

There was danger. If the wind broke, and the tide changed at the same time, we would be in a precarious position. YutBiat would tip because the shore side was marooned on the bottom and the river facing side would sink with the water. YutBiat had no engine and could not move itself. The danger was more than sinking in a few feet of water. The horrible danger was that the tipping might cause a leak in the ammonia pipes used in the refrigeration. Escaping gas would poison everyone. This was a real danger if there was a lot of banging about. Walter had to act fast and close the refrigeration during the storm. That was immediately accomplished.

Using a two-way radio, Tammy the Tug, was summoned from Bethel. The tug arrived 4 hours later, a wait longer than normal due to the high winds of the storm. The wait seemed longer than 4 hours because we were wet, cold, and afraid. It was a tense time.

Tammy held YutBiat in place until the wind and tide subsided. This kept us from breaking free and floating elsewhere. Tammy sat holding the barge in place for several hours. You can see the water boiling out behind Tammy in her effort to keep YutBiat in place. Eventually Tammy the tug was able to move YutBiat safely into water.

We were hung up on the river bank for more than twelve hours and the storm was a good twenty-four hours in length. When all was settled we again anchored in the river, but now the goal was to anchor in the slower Johnson River but not far from the Kuskokwim River that was too swift. It took several attempts to reposition the anchors in the river bottom where they would hold, even though they weighed 500 pounds each. The river is fast and about 17 feet deep and the bottom is soft. The first attempt failed.

We were very nearly beached again as YutBiat dragged the anchors and drifted. Eventually the anchor held, a dead man was secured, and YutBiat was held securely in place.

The second year again while anchored in the flooding and fast Johnson River, YutBiat dragged the anchor. This time we were in no trouble but ended up in the middle of the river near the Kuskokwim. The Kuskokwim was the bigger and faster river, and we wanted to stay away from there as it led directly to the Bering Sea. Again, a tug had to come and relocate us.

During the first storm, the villagers were on board for a day and a night. People just slept anywhere but it was such a tense time there was not much sleeping. The women all helped cook for everyone when they were on the barge, just as they had the first night we moved onto the barge.

In a letter to my son Glenn on July 26, 1974, I wrote this about the flood:

Tammy stayed with us all day while the water was still high then at low tide we were to try to get down to an inlet to the Johnson where we would be more sheltered anyway after investigation spots in mind that were not deep enough as we would have pump trouble in low tide.
As I write this Tammy is pulled up right at the Kuskokwim around the point of the Johnson. The Kuskokwim looks mighty wide. It is nearly 2 miles where I see. As were up high I could see for miles on the tundra. As far as the eye could see it was just raised up into a lake with odd willow clumps sticking out.

This morning it is all gone back to tundra and willows. As we came along at low tide now we can see a couple of fish nets washed up and strung out almost like they were put there on purpose. They were hooked on willows with fish hanging on them as the water had gone. There the fish hang like apples.

Oh Glenn I wish you would have seen and we will be able to tell you in person and describe all the details that will make much more sense than I can write. So, as I write now Tammy is trying to locate us and Dad is trying to get the anchors to hold. They are real heavy but they are having a hard time to find a sand bottom in the Johnson. The anchors pull out. The Kuskokwim has more sand but is very fast and not sheltered. We were 18 nervous people for the past two nights and one day. The Eskimos went back as soon as the water went down and cleaned up the mess. The one tent we saw go down was that of the 73 year old mother of the man whose family was in the house. The poor old soul felt awful and I felt sorry for her."

When Grandma Nichols returned to the campsite, her tent was still there but under the water. Eventually she even found her wallet under the tent. Her son's the tent shack, with its lumber sides and possible lumber bottom, was intact. I am not sure what kind of floor it had. The shack tent was intact but wet throughout.

On a subsequent visit, I took this picture of Grandma Nichols and Bessie Charles. They were not related. They have known each other all Bessie's life. Bessie was working with me at the time. Grandma Nichols would talk and drink tea. Bessie translated, and I listened. Then I would talk and Bessie would translate again.

You can see the washing machine and a stack of Styrofoam cups. These environmentally unfriendly cups were such a nuisance. Walter tried to get people to put them into a garbage container but people would take them and throw them overboard where they would get stuck in the water intakes for the fish processing. He never really succeeded. Frequently he had to get someone to go down and unplug them. I do not know where exactly they went, just that it was somewhere below the water line.

On the wall behind the coffee pot I had to put a sign up to keep people out of the kitchen as they would congregate and get in the way of the staff. The sign says, "If you have nothing to do Please don't do it here." It was a humorous way to remind people and it worked. I just could not keep moving and working around people and I could not always ask them to move. I can understand they wanted to be where it was warm and friendly and be in a place like at home in a kitchen but it just could not always be this way.

When Grandma Nichols came for a visit and tea, she found it easier to drink tea from a saucer or bowl and always poured her tea into one or the other. We would chat while I worked. Bessie would translate for us. When Grandma Nichols left, I would always give her a gift of tea bags, cookies and buns. She was always very gracious accepting my small gifts.

Grandma Nichols did ink drawings on wood blocks and containers made from grass.

Bessie Charles translated this for me July 20, 1974:

Prayer Song

"Jesus hear us your children, watch us when we sleep. Be with us.
Take our sins away in our minds and Bless us."

Grandma Nichols was born on a rat trap line. She was the youngest of a family of thirteen and the only one left alive. For many years, she tended her own trap line alone. That meant travelling alone in the forest in the snow and cold, to harvest the traps and reset them, make camp, cook and sleep in the wilderness and be self sufficient. It is a tough hard life. She lost two sons to the Kuskokwim River. Still she would paddle her own kayak even at her advanced age. In Yupik, she was called Nayagak. She remembered having to hide in dirt caves as a child. She also said there used to be conflict or wars between the different tribes. Yupik was spoken around the Kuskokwim River area, but a few miles away on the Yukon River, they spoke a different dialect and the two groups did not always understand each other. There are Yupik in Alaska and Siberia and several varieties of this language. During the Easter season Yupik from Siberia and Alaska, meet on Little Diomede Island in the middle of the Bering Sea and exchange gifts. It was a tradition and perhaps coordinated with radio communication or announcements.

On YutBiat we had a short wave radio and listened to the Bethel radio station. Sometimes we could listen to Russian radio stations but could not understand the language. We sometimes also heard stations from Germany and Holland. We could not get Canadian radio, and we did not have TV. We saw no newspapers. We had no Canadian news unless someone sent a letter. We felt starved for Canadian news.

The Bethel radio station was full of local events. Maggie Lind was a frequent personality on the Bethel station. She was always interesting. She spoke about life as she knew it, and spoke English very well. She was always interested in the local kids and their welfare. Maggie Lind would encourage parental responsibility. She would ask on her radio interviews something like "Where are your kids tonight? Do you know what they are doing?"

Alcohol was a problem in this remote location. Alcohol seems to be a problem in many remote locations. Alcohol would cause a reduction in parental guidance of children. The community would suffer. Maggie Lind did her part to improve things. There were so many drunks that the Bethel hospital needed a guard at the doors to deal with drunks. Some people had to be kept out, and some let in, to allow the nurses to deal with the medical problems.

Even the Honey Bucket service had to deal with alcohol. If the honey bucket fees were not paid on time the house number would be recorded and no one in that house would be allowed to buy alcohol until the fees were paid. Alcohol caused wild behavior and lawlessness. From January, to May 1973, alcohol figured in the shooting death of one policeman and 7 civilians in Bethel with a population of less than 3500.

Maggie Lind was a sweet woman, aged somewhere over 80. She was known as The Needle Doctor of the Fur Trade because she was an expert seamstress. She knew what threads to use and how to sew the multiple different skins and hides the locals used. Her husband was the son of a fur trader and a friend of the Moravian Missionaries of 1885. Maggie was raised in a Moravian Children's' Home.

When we first arrived, and were staying in Mr Crowe's house, we could watch Bethel TV and saw Maggie Lind on the Bethel station. One day she came on the radio and thanked some of the men for bringing her some seal meat. It was a local station talking about very local issues. Discussing the event when they brought a cow by plane for the students to look at and see a real cow Maggie Lind went on to say:

"Before this place got so civilized we had horses, cows, chickens, pigs, and goats up here." At the time, I was not so convinced of the advanced civilization status of Bethel at any time. I had just come from the pleasantries of the south. Bethel was a pretty rough frontier location, with more people than the average northern settlement, but with much the same attitudes. For the North, it was civilized. I spent a lot of time in such civilized surroundings. Northern people are wonderful and you learn to accommodate to the lack of city services and ease of life style. Some places were rougher than other places.

Bethel, in the spring was not pretty. The mud and alcohol problems were different kinds of problems but both were serious and both were unpleasant. The radio announcers tackled the alcohol problem with their social reminders. The mud was a different problem and I do not remember it being talked about on the radio. The locale was primarily desolate looking, with lumpy grasses, uneven prairie tundra, and small willows. There were no tall trees and no forests. The settlement clung to the edge of the river as if human habitation really did not belong there. Certainly, the modern style of buildings, were for the most part precariously situated and foreign to the environment. We had stayed in opulent hotels on our way from Winnipeg. When we arrived in Bethel these memories made the life styles we were now experiencing look even more deprived and primitive.

The Bethel radio announcers had little formal training and perhaps, or most likely, no formal training. That made listening to the radio at times quite funny. The announcers would read out the punctuation marks and instructions. For example:

"1/4 horsepower motor for sale exclamation mark, good condition exclamation mark."
And,
"one bed box, spring and mattress for sale"
instead of saying
"one bed, box spring, and mattress for sale."
The announcers were amateur, and folksy, with enthusiasm, and that made them funny.
For example:
"This is Toooosday April 30. Oh no. I made a mistake its May first, guess I talk to much eh" And then to the music of "Home On The Range" they sang these different words:
"Oh give me a home between Anchorage and Nome
Where the bear and the musk ox play"

The Yupik radio talked about White people taking too much of their land, about musk ox and court trials. It was hard to want to know about Canada and never hear anything except what we got in letters. We used a CB radio to send messages and call a tug or airplane or talk to the fish boats. The CB radio was busy. Women would talk to each other from one camp to the next just as they might now use a cell phone. The lack of news of Canada was put to the side by all the new and unusual things we saw and heard about talking with the people.
Fishermen that came up for meals and coffee or tea could almost always speak English though not always did they speak it well. I would always say hello and they would respond and be glad to sit and have a warm drink but they did not bring any news. They liked to have cookies so in addition to the ones we made we bought cookies by the case.

One or two of the fishermen wore fish skin raincoats. Here is an enlarged portion of the larger picture further below. You can see the joins of the fish skins and their translucence.

The picture below shows three garments in the museum with an X on the fish skin raincoat. We were not there in the winter so we never saw people wearing these garments. Many times, I saw women wearing dresses with flounce or trimming around the bottom. These garments were in the museum but a short time after we visited the museum it burned down. There is a fish skin raincoat in the UBC Museum of Anthropology.

One day I left the kitchen for a few minutes to look out across the water or something. I returned to find two or three men sitting at the table and they had guns in holsters on the table. This was offensive for Canadians but apparently not Americans. I told them they had to get their guns off the table immediately and they complied. It was later that I found out that they were river policemen. Their guns were still offensive.

Alcohol was not allowed in the kitchen at all. One day I came into the kitchen to find two white men from the lower states sitting at a kitchen table drinking whiskey. The table was a public place and it was the kitchen. The Yupik were not allowed to have alcohol and the Yupik were coming and going. These two guys knew they were not to be drinking. I told them they had to get the whiskey out of the kitchen and to take it away. They thought they were entitled to be obnoxious and grumbled.

One fellow wondered around the kitchen before deciding to hide it in a little cupboard that had coffee machines on a top shelf and on the floor, were large bags of sugar and flour. Bessie and I watched where he put it. He angrily left the kitchen and I took the bottle of whiskey and threw it into to the Kuskokwim River. It could have floated to Japan or Russia by now it is hard to say. I did not feel at all bad. I was angry and viewed their actions as an attack on our happy community. For several days, he came into the kitchen and looked all around the floor for his bottle of whiskey. He never mentioned it, but he looked in the cupboards. His actions were examples of alcohol stunting reason. It is what happens when there is a dehumanizing effect of alcohol and isolation.

To help maintain a civilized attitude and to help keep the place clean I did weekly laundry. Once a week I made sure that everyone staying in a bunk had their sheets and pillowcases off the beds and in the hallway by a certain time in the morning. This washing amounted to about six sets of sheets, five single bed sized, and our double bed size, plus all the pillowcases each week.

We used an electric washing machine with a ringer on it. To dry them I hung them on a cable around the top floor of the barge. In all that time, not a single article of clothing was lost to the river.

When the washing was dry, I folded it and left it in the hallway ready to pick up. I do not know how the workers got their own clothing clean. I did washing for a couple of fishermen, and Andrew David who picked up fish operating Barge One. I would wash a lot of his clothing mainly jeans and t-shirts and give them back to him.

Andrew David learned I had hair clippers and cut Walter's hair. He would borrow the clippers and cut all his own hair off. He usually wore a hard hat and something soft over his head. However, when he came to the table to eat he had to remove both. Every time he had his haircut short, he would try to sneak into the table to eat with his hats on. I would catch him and of course, he always took them off. We would laugh in a good natured way. Here Andrew David is working and showing his big smile that won him many friends.

When Andrew David delivered a load of fish, and he was staying overnight, he would tie his boat to the side of YutBiat, eat with us, and sleep in the tin roofed boat cabin. He had no alarm clock. Walter was his alarm clock. Walter would be up start making coffee and walk around the barge looking down into Andrew's barge to see if he was walking around. If he were not walking around Walter would throw a block of wood down onto the tin roof. This made such a loud clamor that Andrew would be up in a shot and out of the cabin. Later he would throw the block of wood up to the top of YutBiat so it could be used the next time. Here Andrew David is working in a fish boat that is tied to his boat, Barge One. The roof of Andrew David's boat was Walter's target and you can see an alarm clock piece of wood and other junk on top of it.

Andrew David was a popular fellow and had the nickname Shoot-em For Eat-em. He wanted to take Walter hunting for weasels, rats, and small game, but when he found out Walter was in his 50's he said "No no too old too old".

When someone asked why Andrew David went hunting for these things, he answered: "shoot-em For Eat-em"

Boats, like the ones pictured, would arrive laden with fish to YutBiat, or were delivered to Andrew David's pick up boat out on the river. Above Andrew David in his yellow hard hat is standing in a small boat as below.

Since the Kuskokwim River is wide and in some spots the bottom is very shallow, ocean going boats unfamiliar with the area were required to have pilot boats with local river expertise to bring them in to Bethel. This picture below shows a pilot boat the Husky 11, guiding a fish boat towards YutBiat.

The Western Pioneer and the Dolphin are larger refrigerated boats that sail from Seattle to haul fish south. Even though they were regular visitors, each time they still needed a pilot boat as a guide. The crew of these boats would all come over for coffee. Some crews stayed for lunch or dinner. I cannot remember the names of the people but they were all pleasant. The crews of Japanese boats were more interested to come aboard to have coffee and eat than the Western Pioneer and others like her from the US. It was a pleasure to have different people to meet and talk with in our watery isolation. Perhaps they had come further and it was a chance to see a new culture for them, as it was a similar opportunity for us to meet them.

Shallow water prevented The Western Pioneer from getting too close to YutBiat to load fish. In these circumstances Shoot Em for Eat em, Andrew David, would have to load his smaller Barge 1, with boxes of fish and take the fish to them as pictured.

The fish roe was collected by the Japanese workers. Several times various Japanese ships would stop to collect it. The last shipment of the year left the barge in Bethel and went by air to Anchorage. Below you can see a pallet load of white five gallon containers being transferred from YutBiat. Next, they would be

put into shipping containers called igloos. There are two colors of shipping igloos in this picture, white and yellow, but the shape is the same as they are designed to fit into cargo airplanes easier. These igloo shipping containers were on the airplane that we were crammed into on our flight from Anchorage to Bethel.

A similar type lift and a conveyor belt were used to help load the fish onto and from YutBiat because the fish were large. A power lift was required because a few fish would weigh several hundred pounds. A single fish would weigh between 30 and 80 pounds.

Here Louis Kemp stands amongst the catch holding a salmon but he would not be doing so long as it likely weighed more than 50 pounds. Louis always wore sunglasses and a cap and he was the only one at the table that would wear a cap. People thought that he wore the cap because he was going bald and having

hair transplants. He was the boss so I did not think I could make him take off his hat and knew it was a sensitive subject for him. Still knowing the situation, everyone still felt he was being rude but on the whole, he was well liked and a nice fellow.

Louie was a businessman and friend of Bob Dylan since childhood and would attend his concerts. He managed Dylan's 1975 Rolling Thunder tour and has written a book about Dylan.

Fishing season for different species was a timed event. Some seasons were a few hours long such as 36 or 48 hours. It was not always known until the very last minute how long the season would last. Everyone would get excited about the opening season for a specific species. It would be on everyone's mind. It is comparable to a big hockey playoff game in excitement.

Sometimes entire families would show up with the loads of fish. Parents and children would all be involved in the fishing. In the picture below from 1973 shows a family with four kids as they arrive with a load of fish. The family looks neat, clean, and not grubby. The fish are just lying in the bottom of the boat. The family would have just pulled their nets and come straight to YutBiat to get rid of the fish. You can see the four kids and the mother on one end of the boat. The father is at the end of the boat wearing a rubber over all suit and is close to the right edge of the picture. Children were taught at a young age how to fish. Grandma Nichols son Mr Nichols said he took his son fishing when he was ten years old. I have tapes of this man singing and playing his guitar. Natashia Hoffman with the long hair tied back, pictured earlier, a fish counter, has her back towards the camera.

The large fish are very big. A cross section steak does not fit in a cast iron fry pan. Walter taught himself taxidermy and mounted one that was about 64 pounds. It hangs downstairs and it is huge it is about a meter long.

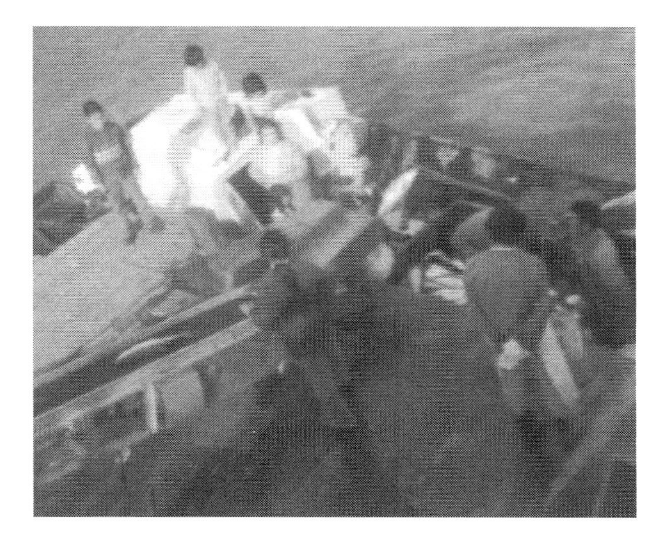

Below Silver Salmon are lying on the deck of Barge 1 or LCM, and in the bottom of the boats. Immediately they would be transferred to the freezing rooms.

The ship the Takashiro Maru came from Kotzebue Alaska, north of Bethel. It was partly loaded and could only take 500,000 pounds of fish from YutBiat. It looks a little rough for wear in this picture below. I was fortunate enough to be able to get a tour of the boat. They had come on board YutBiat and wanted to see all over. They had coffee and dessert with everyone.

They did not invite us to see their boat but I asked to see it. The captain and some of his crew had a little conference. They decided I could see it but I had to wait ½ hour. I imagined they had to clean something up. I am not sure if they had any superstitions about women on boats and never thought about it at the time. I could not be away from my work too long, and thus could not have toured the other boats that visited. This boat was tied to YutBiat and I had the time so I took advantage of the opportunity.

Walter made sure that I was safely down the ladder to their boat that was lower than YutBiat and off I went to have a look. Inside the boat was very clean. The captain guided me through the boat. I saw the radio room that had bamboo on the floor and offered to take my shoes off but they said I did not have to do that. The kitchen was tidy and spotlessly clean and on the center of the table was a container of chopsticks. The captain gave me souvenir some chopsticks. Now I see them all the time but that was not the case then because now our culture has a lot more international flavor. In Winnipeg at this time chopsticks were a rare and unusual site, so to get some from a Japanese boat and from people who used them daily, was a nice cultural experience.

On a little corner shelf in the kitchen I saw an ornament. I asked if it was coral. I did not know what it was, as I had never seen such a thing. The captain said it was and he gave it to me to hold. I asked if it came from Australia and he nodded his head. I am not sure he understood what I had asked. I gave it back to him but he refused to take it and said it was a gift. I still have the coral and now hope it was not a piece of the Great Coral Reef. It survived a suitcase ride home to Winnipeg, and then to Vancouver when we moved.

I sat in the pilot's seat, the one who steers the boat, and when we walked past the hole in the floor, the entrance to the lower level and to the engine room he shook his head and said "no no no". I agreed with him that I knew what an engine room looked like and sounded like, and right then you could hear the engines as they were running. There were about six sailors that all shook my hand and bowed their head to me as I left the boat. I never saw a bedroom or a bathroom and never asked. They were only with us a short time, about two days.

In September of both years, we were pushed into Bethel by a tugboat. It might have been Tammy the tug. As we went down the river, I snapped this picture from the front of the deck of YutBiat. In this picture is behind the fish boat, across the river, looks like a string of tents in the tundra. It is a village and it is on the map of Alaska as the village of Napaskiak, close to Bethel.

As we came into Bethel this is what we saw pictured below. Bethel nestled against the river, on tundra. There were no trees, and the view is mostly river and sky. There were no tall buildings, no neon signs, and no smell of pollution.

It is a bleak sight because it is not painted nice colors, and is not neatly ordered with buildings in rows, and trees and flowers, as we are accustomed. However, to those who have been afloat for a few months it looked good. One has to remember, in Bethel buildings are put where permafrost allows near the river's edge.

high with supplies. In this industrial picture, you can see a vehicle on the fourth level up, along with pipes and goods of all kinds in the containers. This is how supplies and vehicles came to Bethel.

Leaning over the edge of YutBiat I took the two pictures below as we neared the pier to be tied up. We had bounced around and now the underfoot sensation was steadied by the pier. After three and a half months, at sea our time was ending. Tied up in Bethel we worked for 3 or 4 days putting things away on YutBiat. All the rooms were cleaned, and the bedding was all washed and put away and the kitchen closed. We never left the boat until we left the barge on the last day, and then we left Bethel and the barge at once.

Leaving the airport on the way to Bethel from the airport as far as the eye can see, there are no trees. Along the Johnson River, there were many short willow trees in the wet river delta. Big trees would disappear into the tundra.

Then you come across a sign that says "Welcome To Bethel National Forest" and in the distance, stands one lonely spruce.

As we left YutBiat on our ride to the airport, we stepped onto solid ground for the first time in a long time. We then immediately left ground as we took off, and flew to Anchorage to stay in the Captain Cook Hotel, and that night there was an earthquake.

On YutBiat, we grew accustomed to the bed moving due to the wave actions and winds. The bed sometimes moved across the floor and the room tilted. This was not the same type of movement. I did not think about an earthquake in the middle of the night but the next morning I realized that is what it had to be. As it happened, I just thought it was odd.

Earthquake

PALMER (AP) — A moderate earthquake was felt in Valdez and Anchorage early Thursday but no damage was reported.

A spokesman at the Palmer Observatory said the quake registered 5.5 on the Richter Scale and was felt very strongly in Valdez. The quake occurred at 1:59 a.m.

The quake's epicenter was in Prince William Sound, 35 miles southwest of Valdez and 100 miles southeast of Anchorage.

At breakfast in the hotel, the next morning Walter and Galen Steinbeck said that my notion of an earthquake was because of the nice drink I had had with our fine meal in the hotel and the first night on dry land. For me the one fancy drink was special, and unusual, as I rarely drink alcohol but this drink was a celebration. They teased me because they felt nothing.

It was not until we were on a tour bus that people in front of us talked about the earthquake. Sitting on the window side of a tour bus, I leaned forward to talk to the woman by the window in the row ahead. They showed us the paper and I took the clipping below. Indeed, it had been an interesting few hours that included the movement of YutBiat, the plane, and the earth.

This shot of Anchorage shows how beautifully it is situated. It is a clean city. Everything is neat. The damage from the earthquake was still visible even though it had been ten years prior. The post card below shows how beautifully the city sits in front of the mountains up against the inlet.

In the center near the bottom is a larger brown colored building that is the Captain Cook Hotel. My faded ink X marks the building we were in during the earthquake. We only stayed in Anchorage the one night. I remember the airport as having more airplanes than I had ever seen in one place at that time. The Winnipeg airport was not so busy. Seeing so many airplanes in one place was impressive.

Late morning, September 8, we left on a tour bus going to Fairbanks stopping overnight at Mt McKinley and arriving about noon. We did not know it would be as unusual and stressful as it turned out to be. The scene below shows the early fall colors yellow leaves in Mt McKinley Park. We thought how good it was to see color and real trees and just sit and go with the flow with someone else responsible for the driving. Our minds could relax.

A few miles down the road, we came to Hurricane Gulch Bridge. This bridge was built by a Korean work crew at a cost of 1.2 million. At Hurricane Gulch is the location where two crews one heading south and one heading north met and joined the new road, The Alaska Highway. Besides the deepness of the gulch

and the grace of the bridge, you can see the wonderful colors of the countryside when you look at the top of the pictures below.

On the way to Fairbanks not too far north east of Anchorage we passed through the Matanuska Valley and passed this farm. Matanuska Valley is a very fertile valley noted for growing some rather terrific exhibition size vegetables. Cabbages over 40 pounds are pictured on post cards. The weight of this enormous cabbage from the Matanuska Valley is 44 pounds. It makes a lot of sauerkraut and cabbage rolls. We did not see similar cabbages.

The beauty of the park colors and the mountains were certainly spectacular. Perhaps we appreciated them even more after several months of being a sea. McKinnley is 20,300 feet high the second highest peak in the world and apparently, it is still growing, as Pacific and North American continental plates collide. So perhaps what I felt during our first night ashore was burst of growth.

Mt McKinnley is about twice as tall as Mt Baker just to the south of my home in Surrey; a mountain that I am teasingly sure, is named after someone in my family. Mt McKinnley is about 4 to 5 times as tall as the mountains I see from the living room window, Mt Seymour, and Grouse Mountain. Our bus tour went winding up the mountain and the scenery was spectacular. A few weeks later other tourists were not so lucky. Their bus went over the side of the road.

At Mt McKinley, we stayed a night in a rail car hotel. The rail car room was cramped. Like bumpkins, we sat on the bed with our legs crossed counting money. Walter had cashed the last cheque from Louis Kemp. We had what we wanted, to be paid in Canadian funds because the Cdn $ was worth more than the US $. We folded the money lengthwise and stuffed it into the waist and belt lining of Walter's pants. We sat giggling doing this trying not to be too loud so that people in the next room would wonder what we were doing. The money all went into the one pair of pants Walter was wearing.

Why did we not just use a bank machine and deposit the money?

Well there were no bank machines. Such microchip cards were not being used. We were travelling.

We were taking a bus trip to Fairbanks. Leaving our luggage outside our room in the rail car hotel just as instructed, we were happy it was to be picked up and taken aboard the train for us and we did not have to oversee this detail. When we got to Fairbanks and the next hotel, we learned our suitcases had not arrived and we had to go buy clothing, and toiletries. Of course, we had all the money in the pants Walter was wearing. The bus tour staff made phone calls searching, but no one could locate the luggage.

In Fairbanks, we toured ourselves around. We met a couple who had a greenhouse and sold bedding plants. We had our picture taken in their garden. They had beautiful flowers in their garden that were so nice to see so far north and after being on YutBiat for so long. We were please they took this picture of us.

We returned to Anchorage by train stopping in Mt McKinley. There on the platform was our luggage. The coachmen picked it up for us. Relieved of the stress of not having luggage we carried on much happier.

So exactly how big is Mt McKinley? It looms over everything a giant among giant mountains. As you drive down the road the snowy upper levels dominate the sky. In Fairbanks, we could see it easily even though it was 200 miles away.

Our train travelled along a high ridge and we were up among the mountain tops. It was as if we could reach out and touch them. It was a beautiful ride. Sunlight was still around for a long time.

We saw several severed moose heads along the tracks. These were hunter's trophies complete with antlers. Where was the rest of the moose? I do not know. It seemed like a waste of nature. However, the rest of the animal may have been given to guides to take home. Still, trophy hunters wanting only heads, seems like a horrible waste of life and an unbalanced way of looking at the world.

The train would slow down and stop for people standing along the tracks waiting for a ride. The people seemed to come out of the woods. There were no buildings. Suddenly just some person would be standing along the tracks waiting for a ride. Stopping to pick people up prevents people being stranded in the wilderness.

On the way, up Mt McKinnley and then again on the way down we saw caribou eating. The post card below is a good example of the plant color and the caribou. We saw a mother grizzly bear with three cubs. Three cubs are a rare event as they usually just have two cubs. The bus slowed down so everyone could have a good look but I did not get a picture. This is how the countryside appeared as we were on the train. The Caribou Bull is shedding antler velvet.

Returning to Alaska for a second time in 1974, Walter, and I left Glenn outside the Radisson Hotel in Duluth, Minnesota, and he drove home. Unlike what most people feel today, we still felt we had to get dressed up to be able to fly on the plane. We were in a Seattle hotel overnight. Lyle and Gwen drove down to see us in the hotel. Lyle had been to the airport once before we landed. As the traffic was bad, we took a cab to the hotel. Seeing such heavy traffic was a new experience Winnipeg certainly had nothing similar. Even in our excitement and anticipation to see Lyle and family and our trip, we knew that this intenseness was in sharp contrast to life in the remote area where we were going. It was ample reason to anticipate the north.

This year another barge, Shank's Ark, was attached to YutBiat. Walter designed a pulley and winch system to attach the two barges. Fish were received and gutted on Shank's Ark and sent via conveyor belt onto YutBiat for freezing and storage. All that summer I never had time to go on board and look around Shank's Ark.

We were also joined by a Cessna airplane that paid us frequent visits taking people in and out, making deliveries etc. To accommodate the plane a small floating dock was attached to Shank's Ark. From a distance, our barge community looked like a floating island. YutBiat measured 50 x 150 feet, and Shank's Ark was 35 feet by 110 feet. This added to the ability of YutBiat to process fish. It was a large operation.

Fully loaded YutBiat could carry 2 million pounds of fish. On one occasion, we had about 1.5 million pounds. Powered by two Frick ammonia compressors, YutBiat could freeze 50,000 pounds in 24 hours. The doors of the freezer immediately below our bedroom were sometimes banging 24 hours a day.

What the freezers looked like inside may be of interest to some. First, off, there were two doors, a front, and back door, each door was thick and heavy and had to be slammed shut. The picture below shows the inside of the freezers empty after opening the front door.

The top red line shows the back wall and the lower redline the door in the wall. On either side of the room are refrigerated shelves. Here fish could be spread out on trays and frozen quickly.

Once frozen the fish would be moved into another freezer and were kept frozen. I saw these before and after they were used, but I never went inside when they were in use because they would be too cold and had been in others. Frozen fish, ready for shipment, were stored in a large freezer compartment. The picture below shows compartment # 1. It has wooden floors and plywood wainscoting made from sheets of plywood 4 ft by 8 ft. Across the ceiling are the refrigerant coils containing ammonia. Empty it is somewhat like an old dance hall.

These huge fish were shipped out in cardboard boxes stored onboard. They are seen below in piles as identified by the red line on the right. In front are flattened not assemble boxes. Sometimes if they would fit, fish were placed on a rolling shelf as identified here with the red line on the right. This would be used for smaller and processed fish. Large King Salmon would probably not fit on these shelves because the space between the shelves is too narrow for these big fish. These fish could easily be 10 inches' side to side.

Walter was responsible for all machines on board, including ice makers, plumbing, freezers and the water purification system. The ammonia for the freezing system was stored in a large tank. The top red line points out the large condenser for the refrigeration process, and below it the other red line identifies the ammonia storage tank on the bow of the barge.

The panel of controls works the freezers and controls the refrigerant. These controls look complicated. They are. Know what they do is complicated. They are things and details of which I have no idea. To a mechanic, it means science and a process but it means something different and more than that to me. When I look at this picture, I see many things.

I look at these controls and I remember how Walter was determined to learn three and four things at the same time. He learned the social customs of a new society, plus he learned written English, and spoken English, the duties of new husband and father, and then refrigeration at the same time and not in a classroom either. He taught himself. Yes, I helped him, but he learned at home when he was tired, after a long day of work, and straining his eyes in a place where the lighting was bad. It would have been great if he would have had a lot less things to worry about when he studied. He did not have the luxury of a warm classroom with good lighting, and an expert teacher. He had no teacher at all, just me as a study assistant.

I do not now remember the details of what we went over, but Walter had a mechanical gift and learned his trade quickly. I was proud of him. After the war on the farm, when the weather ruined our crops, I remember that he was determined he would learn. In this dingy picture of controls, I see how a man strived and studied, directed, channeled, and controlled his determination to succeed. In Alaska, I was glad he was in control because I knew that he knew what he was doing. I am still proud of Walter, and I know his sons are too.

I took this picture of Walter in the YutBiat engine room. He worked 18 and 20-hour days for long periods. What a man! I am sure the loud noises of the engine rooms and the gun shot noises of the army may have contributed to his hearing problems as he aged.

David, Sharon, and Darcy came to visit us in the summer of 1974. David and Sharon arrived and they had just got off a float plane and boarded YutBiat. Darcy had arrived on a second airplane that had hit a rock upon landing and was slowly sinking near the shore. David immediately sprang to action and used Walter's come along cable pulleys to pull it out of the water. Had it gone down Darcy and all the still unloaded mail would have been lost to the river.

David, Sharon, and Darcy stayed with us a couple days. It was a special pleasure to have our family come to see Alaska. Glenn also came to visit and stayed for more than a week and Walter found him some work to do.

The wide flat river looks still but it is not. It is a fast river. This is a picture of kitchen helper and fish floor worker, Julius Henry from Quinhagak standing on the edge of YutBiat's upper deck. Beyond him is the flat featureless tundra stretching to meet the sky. It may be that the horizon and shown here in these two pictures say there was not much to look at on YutBiat.

The water and the skies constantly changed. It was like an on-going movie. Is suppose it is like that everywhere but up there the absence of other things to look at one appreciated its beauty and mystery a lot more than other places. This group of clouds were out over the tundra and water towards Siberia. A white cloud in amongst dark clouds above the dark river seemed to stand out. Both the Johnson and Kuskokwim rivers were very wide and shallow and more than a mile across. The surrounding land was like a fully wet sponge, low, and flooded easily.

Near the end of the fishing season in September 1974, we had an opportunity to see the bare rock of the mountains up close from the air in this small plane. Here you see it on the shores of the Kuskokwim River. In this instance, it is a tall sandy river bank but these were not the norm.

The rocks were multiple colors and shapes and just beautiful. The mountain tops were amazing sights to see so close from above and were also right beside us. We were very high up and yet very close to the mountain tops. We felt we could almost touch the crags and tops now not covered in snow this late in the summer. Being in a small plane, we could experience the sudden rise and fall of the mountains as we passed between them. This was very exciting trip. I knew at the time I would never see such spectacular sights again. The plane could twist, and turn, and get close to some peaks. Such a ride is not possible in a larger plane.

In this short trip, we went to Dillingham where Walter was to look at a building and some equipment. I remember the land here too being unusual in that it was soft. If one stepped onto the tundra, it moved like a water bed.

Below using two pictures spliced together, one can see Walter standing on the steps of the building on Nushagak Bay, near Nushagak River.

While Walter was busy doing his engineering evaluation, I stayed outside and talked to some local people. For the first time, I saw Norwegian Elk Hounds. They were lovely, unusual dogs, and a breed I did not know.

Walter finished his building evaluation and we flew by more direct, slightly different route, to avoid an intense storm. We were pleased to fly over Tikchik Lake. This is the area Shoot-Em-For Eatem, Andrew David, talked about so lovingly and wanted to take Walter hunting and fishing, but changed his mind when he found out Walter's age thinking that Walter was too old in his estimation to make the trip. We chuckled as we flew over the lake. The water of the lakes seemed crystal clear from the air, though this is not apparent from the pictures below. The lakes were not all that deep and it was as if we could see to the bottom. They were still untouched by pollution. When we returned, we were pleased to be able to Andrew David that we had seen his special place from the air.

The ground is a most unusual and beautiful gold color. I do not know the source of the color or if it were plant or mineral in nature but thought perhaps gold lichens.

This flat rutted landscape is the top of a high mountainous plateau. In the distance, on the left, is a Pingo, an awesome looking land formation. I have since learned that a Pingo is a dirt crusted mound of ice. Pingos have been used by the locals to spot herds of caribou and whales in the water because they give a good view from a high elevation. Pingo grow only a few centimeters a year in a process perhaps similar to frost heaving. Some Pingo are 70 meters tall.

This is a closer picture of the above pingo.

The scene below us changed and soon we were back into the forested peaks. I commented to the pilot that I could see a waterfall off to the right. He said he would give us a closer look. He dramatically banked the airplane. The mountains peaks just below us swung past.

We swooped around and down for a closer look. We were not too far above the waterfall when I took this picture below.

At the end of the season, we returned to Bethel, YutBiat was unloaded, the window boarded up, and Shanks Ark was unhitched and taken for winter storage in a shallow slough. I stood on the upper deck to take this picture below as the boats maneuver Shanks Ark in the powerful force of the fast, muddy waters.

Control of the operation was difficult because of a strong wind. Combined with the fast river current the tugboats had a hard job.

Twice the tugs lost control of Shanks Ark and it drifted away and up against the sea wall pushed by the current. Luckily did not go down the river. Shank's Ark was not a small unit and it took skill and time to get it in place.

This picture is not all that interesting except for one thing. It provides a scale reference. Shank's Ark in the foreground, can be contrasted in size with the seaplane, on pontoons, in the background. Maneuvering this barge on the water is a dangerous job.

On the left hand side of picture, Walter on the front deck of Elook and Dale Henkleman is on the top deck. Dale Henkleman was a very nice fellow. The picture on the right shows three vessels: Elook, the red cabin of Barge One, and a blue fish pick up boat.

A few months later, at night, in a storm, Dale Henkleman was operating a blue pickup boat similar to the one pictured in the bottom right hand corner of the right hand picture. Three people were on the boat. Two women were inside the covered bow, but Dale was driving standing at the back. He may have hit a sandbar. He was thrown overboard and drown.

When we bid our friends goodbye one by one, as they left YutBiat we did not know whether there would be a third year in Alaska.

Bison Trips to the North: Work and Fun in the North

Walter had started his own refrigeration repair company, Bison Refrigeration, in 1972. He did the mechanical work. I did the bookkeeping. The great Alaska adventure interrupted Bison's growth. After the second year, our Alaska adventure ended. We never went back. We felt badly about not returning. Our concern was operational safety on the water. We could not get Louis Kemp to make required purchases to improve safety. Louis may soon have changed his mind had he been on the barge and scared when it broke loose, and had he gone drifting uncontrolled up the river, onto, and off the river bank. Perhaps he had other reasons to end the adventure.

We stayed in Winnipeg and started a new chapter of our lives. There were only two people in Winnipeg that could work on ammonia refrigerant, and Walter was one of them. Walter started more earnestly to establish Bison as a business. The name Bison was chosen because it was close to the front of the alphabet because Walter and I liked the name. We did not have a long list of names. We could have called it Walter's Refrigeration, but the letter W was too far from the start of the listings in the Yellow Pages.

Bison succeeded. Walter had all the work he could handle in and around Winnipeg. He travelled south of Winnipeg to Vita and worked with small business clients. He was getting calls from Saskatchewan, Western, and North Western Ontario. On one trip over a single weekend we drove about 1500 miles and fixed two machines. We drove to and from Vermillion Bay, Ontario, fixed a machine, and climbed into The Beast and drove to Denbeigh Point, on Lake Winnipegossis, and then back home.
I did most of the driving. Walter would sit beside me and nod off to sleep exhausted from his work.

We still thought of our friends in Alaska. We got quite a lot of mail from there, and were always glad to hear about what they were doing. I certainly missed working with the Yupik girls. I missed the visits and the company of Grandma Nichols. She and I both a made a great effort to communicate and perhaps that is what made it so special. Their company had made my work enjoyable and I often did think about them as we were now entering a new phase of our lives. I still think of the people of Alaska with fondness, wondering what they are doing.

In all the time, we had Bison we had only one call where the customer threatened not to pay. That is unusual and it happened on a remarkable day. It was the very day the space shuttle exploded in the air, and the customer was a small grocery store in Transcona. The owner refused to pay and Walter walked out. I asked Walter what the bill was and Walter said the guy would not pay. Walter, felt we should just cross this guy off and never help him again. I thought differently. I made the bill up, went in, and collected. Where Walter would not argue, I was prepared to argue. Actually, all I did was present the bill and ask for payment and waited for it.

The business listing in the Yellow Pages helped get local businesses, but I think it was word of mouth, that spread Walter's name and Bison Refrigeration outside the city. A fish plant would check to see if he was available and then share the information with other plants. Walter was well liked and well known for his work and people shared their satisfaction with his work.

At the start of the business, Walter used our car to do service calls in the city. He was slowly becoming comfortable with city driving. If it was a location, he was not sure of then we would go together first to identify the location. Then he would drop me off and he would go on his own. He was not fond of doing work for city customers. He had a few regular city customers such as Neptune Fisheries where he did a lot of work.

At the wholesale refrigeration, supply companies other people just starting in the business all drove new vans nicely painted and would laugh at Walter for using his older Oldsmobile car. He told them they were getting into debt before they had a thriving business. A few years later, when we bought The Beast, a new 1974 Dodge van for the business these competitors were all broke and gone.

Walter and I never wanted to go into debt and always wanted to make sure we had money to pay for parts from the wholesalers. Before a purchase, Walter would phone to make sure we had enough money in the bank to cover what he was going to buy. We did not owe suppliers money. Sometimes before he left the house, I would tell him how much money there was in the account. Bison had its own bank account. We did not mix the accounts.

Slowly our financial situation got better, but Walter was always careful regarding buying parts. I looked after the finances. Walter once took someone out for coffee. When it came time to pay, he had no money to pay. He was embarrassed and from then on, I made a special effort to make sure he carried enough money with him for coffee.

In June 1975, we went to Lac La Ronge in the van. Walter named it The Beast. I am not sure why, perhaps because it was fairly large. It was a good vehicle to drive and we both drove it many miles together and alone. It lasted a long time.

Travelling north, we saw many swamps, as they seemed to be everywhere. Be certain knowing there were hordes of mosquitoes. We saw quite a lot of wildlife caribou, moose, bear, deer, and skunk. Spotting wild life from a country drive in a van is a pleasure I miss now that I am living in urban Surrey. Here seeing any kind of wildlife, even a skunk, is an event.

Roadside trees were a mixture of pine, tamarack, poplar, and others, many stunted and scruffy looking. Trees in the far north a very old, or much younger, may look the same. The picture below shows quite old trees. The picture may have been taken on the way to Lac La Ronge or many other places in the North, as it is typical countryside. Some trees are dead. Some may have been killed in a fire, or just died. Top soil on the Precambrian Shield is a thin layer and thus plant life is not as lush as elsewhere. Plant life has developed a life cycle that does not produce large growth.

In Lac La Ronge for a few days, we were glad to be back to visit and see places of our past, but we had no desire to return permanently. We never regretted moving. We drove past our old house as pictured below.

When we lived here, the small added storage or tool shed was not there somewhat blocking the south, kitchen window view of the lake. The other small kitchen window is to the right of the front door that opened immediately into the living room. In this cold winter area, a porch on the front would be a definite improvement for keeping cold air out. I wish we had had a porch. As it was, every time that door opened cold air rushed in.

The larger window on the other side of the door is the living room window and the last smaller window on this side was the bedroom window for Walter and me. On the opposite side of the building to this window was the bedroom the three boys shared. As we drove past, we looked in detached wonder akin to the emotion of looking at pictures in a magazine. It was a life but not now our life.

It was a cold house. To keep it warm we had oil burning heater, a wood burning heater, and coal in the kitchen stove and we used all three. One winter when Walter was at Wollaston Lake this house got so cold that the oil line to the oil heater jelled and the fire went out. I had to get up every few hours to put wood in the heater, and add coal to the kitchen stove. I took plants off this living room window and put them on the dining room table about 6 feet from the stove. The plants froze. The water pail on the kitchen counter froze with the dipper in it. I left coal in the wood stove and left the lid slightly off the fire pit to keep a draft of air moving the poisonous gas up the stove pipe. I was not afraid we would freeze to death because we had a wood stove, but certainly, it was not comfortable. As we drove by I remembered those times when it would be minus 60 for weeks at a time. I was glad they were long ago, and that I was in a moving vehicle.

A few days later in that July Walter flew to Reindeer Lake where he worked until September. I went home on the bus perhaps. I am not too sure how. We were not too pleased that Walter went into isolation to work. It was not something we wanted to repeat. In late August, I went back to Lac La Ronge, but how I got there, I do not know. We were making so many trips we were like yoyos. When I examine the bill books for Bison for this time, and yes, I still have them some 40+ years later, I see a combination of Walter's handwriting and my handwriting, yet we were miles apart. Most times I would write everything up to the amount charged, and Walter would add the amount charged and present the bill. My handwriting is in place for the whole bill August 25, 1975, so that means I was in Lac La Ronge on that date.

We spent Christmas in Winnipeg. Walter returned to Lac La Ronge in February of 1976, and I followed in April of 1976. We did have short family visits during this time but they were never long enough.

At the end of May Lyle, Gwen, and Lara came to Lac La Ronge for a visit. Walter posed with Lyle, Gwen, and Lara beside The Beast near Shellbrook. Lyle's truck is in the background. As they went home, Walter and I went to Dore Lake. A month later, at the end of June, David, Sharon, Darcy, and Glenn arrived. We took them all to Nemeiben Lake. Walter and Lyle had moustaches popular with men at the time, while David and Glenn did not.

David, Sharon, and Darcy stayed in the Riverside Motel owned by the Louis family, in Lac La Ronge. In this picture, you can see that Darcy is nearly the same height as his mother.

July 5th, we all left Lac La Ronge like a bad storm. Walter flew to Reindeer Lake. I did not like Walter going alone but it could not be helped. David and Sharon went to Vancouver, while Darcy, Glenn, and I drove to Winnipeg in our car.

Part of the way across Saskatchewan we drove into a sand storm. We had to drive slowly, but keep moving so as not to plug the vents of the car. By the time, we made it to Mooseman, further south in Saskatchewan, we made a necessary stop close beside a garage to take shelter from a wind and hail storm. The wind was shaking the car on the road and we needed to get off and to find some kind of protection immediately. We stayed near a small old wooden shed or car garage for about 15 minutes. I do not remember how big the hail was, but there was the potential for the pieces of ice to get bigger, and come through the windshield. I remembered the hail and wind from the tornado while on the farm, and I remembered the storm when my father stopped on the side of the road. I insisted we stop in shelter.

In Lac La Ronge, I would drive from the motel through the reserve to where Walter was working at the fish plant, about a 15 minute drive. On the reserve was a log home I passed daily. The owner was away trapping. The neighbors slowly dismantled and burned the pieces of his house starting with the steps, and then the roof. Every day something else was taken and gone. We were never around to find out what happened when the owner returned.

The motel was out near the Montreal River not far from the airport and before the town proper started. Even in the really, cold, weather there is a part of this river that does not freeze over because it is flowing so fast. The picture series below was taken in December, 1975, a cold time of year. In the coldest winters this section is smaller, but still always open.

On one visit to Lac La Ronge, I flew out on a scheduled route that came from Uranium City and went on to Regina or Saskatoon. The pilot was Blake Brown, who I had known as a boy living next door and a friend of David and Lyle's. Now a grown man he came back to talk to me for a few minutes in the passenger section. From Regina, I caught another plane to Winnipeg.

The Lac La Ronge Cemetery is typical of others in the north. Frequently the graves are marked with fences. In the lower picture, an old bed frame is used for a fence. Finding an area in and around Lac La Ronge that has dirt deep enough for a graveyard is not such an easy task. Most of the area is the bare rock of the Canadian Shield.

The entrance to the Lac La Ronge cemetery sign reads:

La Ronge cemetery
If we did not as
brothers live
Let us as brothers lie

In these fall pictures, you can see this graveyard is cut out of a stunted forest of small trees. There are few head stones. Sometimes people would write memorials on paper or a piece of wood. In the above picture, there are two modern head stones on the stony ground. Below a bed frame has been used to mark off a grave rather than small picket fence as in two others.

The rock and stone are big reasons why the northern roads were not frequently paved. Most of the roads were gravel with boulders pushed to the sides, as in the pictures below taken in 1975. The stones of these gravel roads were very hard on tires. We were careful and had only a few flats. Bigger trucks with tougher tires drove on the roads a lot more than smaller personal vehicles like The Beast.

On one occasion on the way to Big River a big truck took an inside corner too fast and too wide. Our only choice to stay alive was to take to the ditch. We made it off the road in time and luckily remained upright. Had we gone a little bit further, off the road we would have tipped over. Walter's fast reaction kept us alive. This passing truck saw that we had to hit the ditch but just kept right on going and did not stop to help. The Beast stopped precariously balanced ready to tip.

Behind us came a fish transport truck and it was very nearly side swiped. Luckily, the fish truck had 3 or 4 men inside. They held the vehicle upright and pushed from the side to stop the van from tipping as Walter backed up. After much thanks, we got back on the road.

These roads in the winter were uninviting. Most are not too high above the surrounding areas, and when covered with snow the roads become very difficult to identify because everything is the same color, white. One does not easily know where the road edges start and stop. With snow, it may appear as if there is no road at all. Winter can be a bad time to travel.

In the picture an oil truck is at the end of the road waiting for a barge to come. The truck is on the way to the village of Wollaston on Wollaston Lake. You can see there is a sign on the road. In the second picture, you can read the sign. In the summer the road ends where the truck is waiting.

When the lake freezes in the winter, the road continues across the frozen lake ice to the village of Wollaston Lake. Sometimes the ice would break and whatever was on it sank. We watched the truck load on to the barge and sail away. Then we took a float plane to the village. You can see the makeup of the road was a pile of gravel and stones but at this point is nicely a few feet higher than the surroundings.

The small plane we flew in is just visible in the previous picture but in the shots below, you can see Walter on the left, and the pilot loading Walter's tools onto the floatplane. The tool boxes were heavily filled with tools. Walter had strong hands from using these tools and carting about the tool boxes, in and out of the van, onto boats and barges, and into airplanes.

About an hour, after we took off we were landed in the village, and about 4 hours later, the barge arrived. Today there is a road and the barge and ice road are not required.

The plane is right close to the rocky shore and that the toolbox is so heavy it takes two men to lift it. First, it is lifted onto the hollow pontoon, then into the small airplane. Just the three of us were on the plane with the tools. We were only in Wollaston this time for a few hours and flew out and the pilot waited for us. This remote location was one of a few that also had a helicopter pad. It was an unusual and certain advantage. It was little more than a small flat square pier on the lake shore. The helicopter has pontoons enabling water landings.

Wollaston is located right on the lake, in an area of sparse soil with plenty of rock and gravel. The few trees near the buildings are tall, slim and not thick trunked. Scrub brush is a term that best describes most of these slow growing low trees. The bit of soil is sand and rock. The houses are all the same style because they were built by the government department of Indian Affairs. These homes came up in parcels of just enough precut lumber, easy to assemble and ready to build each house.

The people at Wollaston speak Chipewyan, which means people of the barrens, and is actually, a type of Dene. They are a bit shorter than the Cree that are not too many miles away.

Wollaston Lake is unusual in that it is the world's largest lake that drains naturally in two directions and into two oceans. Scientifically this is termed a bifurcation lake. The Cochran River flows out of the northeastern side of the lake into Reindeer Lake, which then drains into the Churchill River emptying into Hudson Bay part of the Atlantic Ocean. The Fond du Lac River flows from the northwest of Wollaston Lake into Lake Athabasca and then through the Mackenzie River to the Arctic Ocean. I was only at Wollaston Lake this one time but from the time we moved to Lac La Ronge Walter was there many times. I was glad to see a place where Walter had spent so much time in away from his family. I am sure he was glad to have me with him when he was there this time and that we could leave easily.

From the air the country side around Wollaston Lake is spotted full of lakes and ponds. Maps of the area used to show roads with notations that the road was closed in the summer time because it went over swamp. In cold weather, swamps freeze making the roads through them drivable. In the warm weather the swamp is soft and vehicles would disappear sinking into the swamp just as did at least one early train engine as the first rail line was being built across Canada.

In 1976, Walter and I drove The Beast to Dore Lake, in Western Saskatchewan. It is not as far north as Wollaston and we were glad we could drive in and out. On this trip, I picked cotton. It grows in the acidic soil of the bogs. Walter went into the woods and got Glenn two nice pieces of birch bark. I bought a small ornamental birch bark canoe for Glenn. It is down stairs in the basement today. I am not sure but Glenn may have wanted it for teaching history and social studies. Many have looked at this model and appreciated the ingenuity it took to develop the real thing.

Michel Point on Dore Lake is a beautiful location in a wide and wild area that is all beautiful. On this time we stayed in cabins at Dore Lake across the bay from the fish plant, work site. We were there about a week. Walter was putting an ice machine on the top floor of a fish shed. It weighed about ¾ of a ton. There were quite a few First Nation and Metis visiting from Beauval, and Green Lake, because it was fishing season. That did not matter. Almost no one could be hired. No one would work. Walter had only the help of 17 year old, Richard Gautchier. He is pictured here polishing his shoes.

You might wonder why it was like that. How did they get the money to buy alcohol to start with?

It is many times a sad repetitive situation. The week before fishing all the fishermen got drunk. Then they fished for a week and made good money, not thousands but a few hundred dollars. During the next two weeks, they bought alcohol and drank away all the money they had earned fishing. Periodically the men look at what was happening and leave to go drink more. They were intent on finishing all their booze, and then their plan was that they were going to, as they called it, “shack up” with a woman, and then live on welfare after their money was gone. Sadly, that circumstance happens far too often in the north.

These men could have earned money for helping Walter. Had they helped our bill to their band would have been less. Getting the ice machine to the second floor was a job where they could have helped. Walter and Richard got the machine up by themselves.

Selecting four spruce logs Walter cut a V shape into one end of the logs. This V cut away was wedged into the floorboards 15 feet up on the second floor. This shape jammed into the floorboards and stopped the logs from moving around with the added weight of the ice machine. Using a come-along pulley hoist, Walter and Richard pulled the ice machine up the logs to the second floor.

Daily Walter drove from the cabin down the road about 1.5 miles onto a u shaped point where the fish shed was located. On one of these trips, The Beast broke down and had to be towed into Prince Albert for repairs. It took the best part of the day. The owner of the lodge Alex Shukin owned the tow truck. We followed behind the tow truck in his car.

We stayed in this cabin and since The Beast is at the cabin, I know Walter was back at the cabin. Entering through the door one was greeted with linoleum flooring, a kitchen table, and wood cook stove on the left. I do not now remember the use of the thing out front that looks like a mailbox or barbeque. Our cabin had two bedrooms and single pane, glass windows. The cabin was built to use in the summer and was not insulated for winter.

You can see the cabins spaced out in the woods. Look at the size of the trees. They are tall but remain very skinny with little girth. This is typical of the north and you can see it in other pictures I took.

The distance from the cabin to the ice shed was a bit too far away for me to help Walter. He had Richard Gautchier but needed strong men to help. My daily routine was then different. I took this picture of the pile of wood and it is my shadow in the bottom of the frame on the far left.

I chopped this pile of wood to keep in shape. It is about 5 foot high and I used it in the cook stove. I would cook, and crochet to pass the time. I washed clothes and hung them on coat hangers in the trees. All Walter's tools were in The Beast and he needed them so I was stranded. If cell phones were common at the time we would have been glad to use them to coordinate our efforts.

One day a weasel came into the cabin and ran straight under the bed. I left the door open so it could run out. I did not trust these wild, potentially vicious, biting, little, critters. For sure it is not my hand in the picture below. One of the people living in one of the other cabins came out to put coffee grounds into the garbage and I took this picture of the weasel being coaxed with a morsel of food. I certainly would not get this close to a weasel as I remember clearly the one that jumped at me in the granary on the farm.

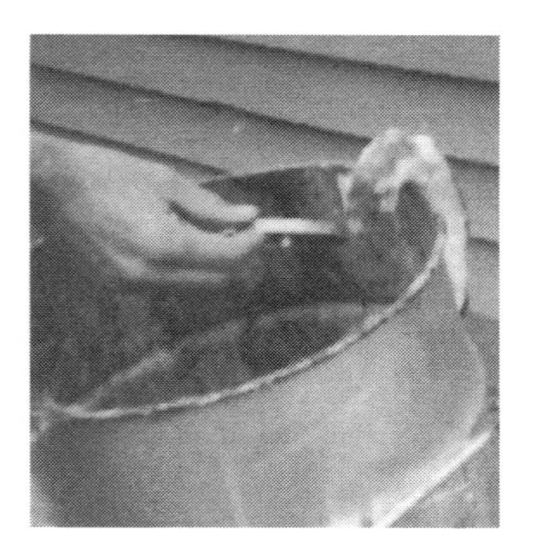

Though I did not trust the weasel, squirrels were different and I trusted them a bit. The one pictured below was a friendly squirrel. I took several pictures of it. This rodent was not afraid of me at all, and would almost eat out of my hand. This fellow came to the cabin. It would run in and out on its own. In this picture, he is sitting on a piece of wood in my wood pile. He is a smart looking fellow.

On one trip leaving Dore Lake, Walter was driving and I was on the passenger side. We spotted a caribou along the side of the road. Quickly I got the camera and took the two shots below. Walter drove and clocked it. The caribou ran 40 mph in the ditch alongside The Beast and then ran off into the bush. It was exciting to see this animal run this fast. It is a blur in the pictures because it was moving so fast.

The picture below shows a new road through the muskeg. For the most part this is a better quality remote road situated in a wide area of bad roads or trails called roads. The road is much higher than the surrounding land. It has been built of rocks, gravel, and sand hauled onto the site and dumped. The rocks sink, and over time stop sinking. On top of the rock pile a road is built.

Being a new road, perhaps 2 to 4 years old, it is not yet full of pot holes, but like death and taxes, unrepaired pot holes on northern roads are inevitable. These road surfaces are generally left unfinished sand, gravel, and rocks. This road, and most others, are left unpaved, sometimes oiled. This lack of finish invites pot holes and decay. In dry conditions like in this picture the roads were terribly dusty. Every vehicle created a dust storm at least a half mile long. The blowing dust covered the vehicles and surrounding trees. This September 1986 road section of road is south of Beauval west of Lac La Ronge and North West of Prince Albert.

When it rained, the roads could look like the picture below which is taken of the road just north of Green Lake.

Truly, these were frontier roads, on the edge of civilization connecting pockets of humanity. The picture above and the picture below are on the same length of road just a few miles apart. Below it is a mud road after a rain. We charged more mileage when we had to travel on gravel roads because the roads were hard on The Beast. A bad road in the north is a great improvement over no road at all. People in the cities do not always appreciate what the rest of the country endures to snatch civilized life from the arms of the frontier. It might do urbanized people substantial good and help them to appreciate the ease with which they travel, to experience some remote hardship every now and then.

We took these roads to Isle La Cross and Buffalo Narrows. Beauval is on highway #155 that heads roughly in a north to south direction. This was not a busy gravel road. It sits high above much of the surroundings. This elevation would be of some help in determining the road location in the snow of winter. Still, this road is really just a long pile of gravel. It is tidied up with a grader now and then. By this, I mean the grader infrequently comes down the road to flatten out and fill in some of the potholes by scraping the

gravel around. Still it was surprising to see this boat in the middle of the road. We drove around it. Further up the road a mile we met people coming back to pick it up.

We arrived at Isle La Cross about mid day. No one was around. We could see a couple of little shacks. The place looked desolate and deserted. We drove further down the road to Buffalo Narrows to see if there was a place to stay. We were familiar with the name Buffalo Narrows because, Walter's brother John fished in the area in the 1950's when the fish was primarily exported to the Eastern United States.

The road went along the side of Isle La Cross Lake, which we could see from time to time. The road follows the lake making a hairpin turn back as the land comes to a long point in the lake. At the end of the point is Buffalo Narrows. We hoped for a hotel. Things may have changed a lot over the years, but driving around we found it quite a rough town. Buildings had plywood over the windows. The Co-op store seen here was open, but the glass windows were no longer there. Anything that would normally have been glass was now wood. Even the windows in the doors were not glass. We assumed that the glass had been broken by drunks too many times to be replaced.

A cement sidewalk is alongside the post office ends dangerously because the dirt along the side of it has washed away. This leaves the sidewalk exposed like a hat on a post. Sadly, no one seems to have enough interest to correct this mess. The road is dirt. The post office window is boarded up. We never got out of the van. We drove slowly around town and left without stopping at the one hotel we saw.
We drove back to the Isle La Cross, fish plant location. The fish plant was across the lake 10 minutes by boat and about the same by land. We drove in to this site about 6:30 on a Sunday evening. We parked the van in the center of the yard. Walter walked down to the fish plant a few yards away. It was a large, long, old, wooden building. From here, Walter ran a long electric extension cord to the back of The Beast. Using the electric frying pan, and a tea kettle, I made our supper outside. We ate sitting on wooden fish boxes. A romantic description might describe this meal as picnic style or a riparian repast. It was actually

pleasant in the clean air of the north, in nature, and in the sun. It was enjoyable. That was about to change.

Walter was checking the location to see where the ice machine was to be installed. I was beside the van cleaning up after supper getting stuff out of the van so that we could sleep in the van that night. I was arranging the bedding including a pair of air mattresses we had bought in Prince Albert that would help make sleeping in the van more comfortable.

In the picture above, you can see the community across the lake. From there came two or three boatloads of people. Among these were some drunken men. The drunks moved
from the lake to a cabin not too far away and read the Bison Refrigeration sign on the side of the van. As soon as they saw white people, they began to holler obscene words in our direction.

One of the fellows wanted a gun. "Where is my f'ing rifle? I want f'ing rifle." he bellered. They were talking about how they were going to shoot the sign on the van. I did not exactly know what to do so I just kept on working and listening. I refused to let them see that I was uncomfortable. I was not going to run away.

Soon, a pretty, young woman with a child came up to me and told me the men were all drunk. She apologized for the language and drunken behavior. She said she had a terrible time with all the drinking in the community. I told her to tell the men that they better put the guns away and that if they did not do that we would leave that night and they could wait until hell froze over before they got their ice machine. I added, that we did not care if they got all the ice they needed by chopping it by hand, which is an arduous cold winter job and something the men might be able to remember doing. I must have been feeling a little brave. I told her to tell the drunks that if they did not settle down my husband would give them each a good licking and pile them up like cord wood. I added that he had to do that before elsewhere and would do it again.

She said she would tell her husband even though he was also drunk. It seemed to have worked. In a few minutes, they were all quiet. We hoped the quiet would last.

I went down and talked to Walter in the fish plant to tell him of the situation. He had heard none of this commotion. He went out and directly talked to the men and told them that we were going to sleep in the van that night and that we wanted absolutely no noise at all.

Walter went back to work and I lay on an air mattress in the shade to read. My attention for some reason went under the van. It was full of black creepy crawly caterpillars. It was then that I noticed these caterpillars were now everywhere. So, during the night, time, and time again, I would awaken dreaming these crawly things were on me. Every time it turned out to be just the flannel sheet.

The drunks seemed to all listen and cooperate. We slept without their interruption. The next day Walter fixed the ice machine and we left.

Many times, parts for the diesel engines, and fish plant machines were not always readily available. Walter had to be ingenious in fixing things. Sometimes Walter made the parts. Other times he

scrounged parts and assembled bits and pieces to get what he needed. While at Isle La Cross, he needed something and we made a trip to the garbage dump. He was taking some kind of part from this old car. There seems to be many similar garbage dumps across the north and it certainly does not speak well of the residents' concern for the environment. There is little if any recycling, and usually no concern for recycling. There are, and were, so many locations of northern garbage dumps, that they represent environmental abuse. These prolific sites show no reasonable concern for nature.

This picture shows a fuel tank beside an ice house, a building used to store ice gathered from the lake in the winter time. Ice is cut into chunks and put into a building like this and sprinkled with sawdust. The buildings are insulated with more sawdust as it is a readily available from lumber mills. The ice will usually last longer than a year. Without refrigeration, these ice houses were important as the ice can be used to preserve fresh caught fish. With all the saw dust the buildings are flammable.

Walter is pictured near the entry to the packing shed at Isle La Cross. It is not a new building and the roof has been repaired a few times. A lot of buildings in the fish industry were aging like this one. The boardwalk is elevated above the low, sandy ground at lakeside, and around the building. This low mosquito ridden area was once the bottom of Lake Agassiz, and thus the sand is almost as plentiful as the mosquitos. Walter put the ice machine in this building.

The village of Isle La Cross is pretty much the same as Buffalo Narrows. It is rough. The building pictured below looks like storage shed because it has no windows, but that is not what it is. It actually is the brightly painted Co-op store. Sadly, it was a retail store with no windows to display goods because the glass of the windows could easily be broken.

It is a rustic setting even for 1976. The roads are just dirt, and not maintained. There is a little patch of cement on the end of the building and no windows to be seen. The picture of the Hudson Bay store below is similar though there is glass in the door. Both villages are frontier civilizations, and still it is common for some of the residents to use these towns as jumping off places as they go to the bush to hunt, trap, and fish. These people are not necessarily interested in fancy retail stores but this typical setting is a function of poverty, bad leadership, a lack of caring, isolation, and alcohol that allows drunks to ruin property and destroy windows and inducing lethargy.

Both the hotel and cafe actually did have glass windows, but they were very small and high up and out of reach. The post office also had small glass windows but they were well covered with bars to prevent

theft, break and entry, and damage. It is likely they were repaired a lot. It describes a sad situation common to many a place in the north.

It would be strange to come across a building in this area with any glass windows. It seemed even stranger, and a real anomaly, when I saw this house on the edge of Isle La Cross. It had many windows and all intact, or at least were intact at the time. It had not been lived in for some time. The locals told me it had been owned by a doctor by the name of Hoffman, and that a woman had been found dead in the house. Locals had looked inside and found the furniture still there including a piano. Still an abandoned house, or even a lived in house, this big, with this many intact windows, was odd for the area.

If you look carefully, you can see an empty glass bottle lying in the grass not far from the house. Amazingly, this bottle had not gone through one of the main floor windows.

The drive through Buffalo Narrows and the gun incident at Isle La Cross showed some of the social dangers we occasionally had to deal with. We were afraid to stay in Buffalo Narrows because it looked like there were too many rough drunks, and then a few hours later we ran into them face to face at Isle La Cross. Alcohol and race were factors in both circumstances. We were isolated, not native, and therefore targets for drunken natives. We were glad to leave. Alcohol does not usually bring out the best in drunks and I am sure at a different time when these people were not drunk we would have had mutual respect.

Not far from Isle La Cross and from the van window I took this picture of a root cellar. Most people now would not have used a root cellar. There was a time when root cellars were a common sight in the rural and northern areas of Canada. Root cellars were used to keep vegetables and other food at a more constant temperature year round. It is like a large walk in cooler in the ground without refrigeration. The soil covering stops the sun from heating the inside space.

Along highway # 155, the Beaver River runs close to the road. You can see the river from the road. It is wider here than it is about 100 miles further west, where just about 10 miles south of Pierceland there was a ferry crossing. This river makes a pretty and peaceful setting. I thought about how this river had come from along the area of my past, my Mam and my dad, and family. How they would marvel at my roaming life.

As we came down the dirt that is the lonely isolated Hansen Lake Road, near Deschambault Lake, we came across a big moose in the middle of the road. It was exciting to see this huge, big boned, animal of around 1000 pounds and at the same time it was dangerous. Luckily this one took to the bush ad I could not get a good picture of it. Animals generally avoid people. We were glad it chose to run into the bush rather than to challenge the van. Such challenges do happen. An animal that big and that fast with such large antlers can do some big damage to a vehicle. Had this animal charged and disabled the van on this road would be in a bad spot. It is just a dirt trail through bush. There are no services. It is not a well travelled road. There is no shelters, thus we would have had to sit in the damaged van and wait. Although it quite far away in the picture below because of its large size, it still shows up as a dark blob on the edge of the road.

Along the roadside, we frequently came across areas that had been burned, usually good for berries. These miles of destruction were not nice areas that hold your gaze with beauty. Acres of burned out bush give you a sense of loss. Sadly, too many of these fires were a result of humans and their carelessness. The moose pictured above is disappearing into an area of regrowth from a fire. We would pass miles and miles of burned out forest. It was ugly. It was sometimes hard to tell if the area was burned out or had died from other causes and was awaiting a fire. Below the tall scrub trees are dead and the undergrowth is lush, a sign of a fire.

Looking ahead down the hill gave us a good view of the destruction of a forest fire. As far as the eye could see in every direction, everything had been burned and the animals had to flee. We had already been travelling for a few miles in this re growth area when we took this picture. The new trees are short and coming into fall color.

Several miles down the road between Flin Flon and Deschambault Lake, we stopped and took this picture below. It is an area not recently touched by forest fire. The forest is tall and the trees are a mix of types.

On the dirty, dusty, Hanson Lake road, is the Three Lakes Camp. Here we unexpectedly came upon a pleasant meeting. We met our neighbors and friends of 16 years previous in Lac La Ronge. George and Sadie Horn were operating the Three Lakes Camp. George was a pilot, and Walter and I had been on many flights with George as the pilot. Glenn had played with their son Russell as boy. We chatted over tea, caught up on many things, and were on our way.

It turns out Sadie has a famous relative. Bobby Clark the famous hockey player and Sadie are cousins. Sadie also told a funny story I still remember. A couple of her relatives travelling by train had sleeping berths for the night. In the middle of the night, the wife had to get up and use the bathroom at the end of the sleeping car. When she came back and climbed into bed saying something like "move over Jim", but to her surprise found herself in the wrong berth with a stranger.

On this same dirt road, a few weeks later we had another lucky meeting. We stopped at The Half Way House and were happy to meet our friends Hettie and Norman McAuley whom we had also known in Lac La Ronge. Norman a First Nation soldier met Hettie while in England. They married and she came to Canada. They had two sons. Hettie died recently but last I heard Norman was living in the Okanogan. I took this picture of them with Walter.

In the summer of 1977, we spent the first few weeks at Denare Beach, on Beaver Lake. The proper name for Beaver Lake on maps is Amisk Lake and it is 14 miles west into Saskatchewan from Flin Flon, Manitoba. I have heard it said that the pickerel fish from Amisk Lake is the best tasting pickerel that can be found.

34202
REPAIR ORDER

NAME Co-Op Fisheries Ltd DATE 19

ADDRESS 28-15 St West Prince Albert

ARTICLE Re-Beaver Lake

May

DATE WANTED			DELIVER
Mon 9	15 hrs @ 14 p.h.		210.00
Tue 10	15 " "		210.00
Wed 11	15 " "		210.00
Thus 12	15 " "		210.00
Fri 13	15 " "		210.00
Sat 14	15 " "		210.00
Sun 15	15 " "		210.00
			1,470.00
Milage (picking up) 290 mi			58.00
			1,528.00

Norman Sager

ESTIMATES ARE FOR LABOUR ONLY. MATERIAL ADDITIONAL. WE WILL NOT BE RESPONSIBLE FOR LOSS OR DAMAGE CAUSED BY FIRE, THEFT, TESTING OR ANY OTHER CAUSES BEYOND OUR CONTROL.

TERMS - NET CASH

AMOUNT / TAX / TOTAL 1,528.00 / DEPOSIT / BALANCE

CLAIM CHECK 34202

REC'D BY / READY

TERMS: NET CASH NO GOODS HELD OVER 30 DAYS

My sister Ruby's eldest son Norman Sager worked in administration in the fish business and visited us at Co-op Point not far from Flin Flon. This invoice he signed for on a bill we gave for work at Beaver Lake. His neatly written, back hand style signature is on the bottom of the bill.

Flin Flon is an interesting mining town. The ore the mine produces is full of copper, gold, and silver. The homes are built on the high rocks of the exposed Precambrian shield. The rock is uneven and buildings are stuck on rock next to cliff edges. Some of the cliffs are sharp, and some are rounded and all are treacherous. At the bottom of the cliffs might be more rocks, and maybe, or maybe not, a path or a road depending upon the space available. The cliff or top of the rock where the building is located maybe be only 10 feet high or it may be 40 feet high. There are many guard and handrails leading from place to place going down the street. Wooden stairs are everywhere up and down to get from one place to another. Flin Flon is an interesting and unusual sight to see and a movie set of a small town could not be more wondrous.

One of the bleaest sites that we saw as we entered Flin Flon was this mining smoke stack. Here it pictured through the windshield of the car so you can see how industrial and environmentally unfriendly it looked as you drove up. This stack has now been dismantled but it was a much identified and talked about feature.

In 1774 Flin Flon was the location for the first fort of the Northwest Company, the fur trading rival of the Hudson Bay Company. Of course, later the two rivals become one larger company under the name The Hudson Bay Company. This northern site would have been home to a lot of fur trade traffic before it became a mining town.

In July, we visited Kinoosao, also known as Co-op Point, and as Reindeer Lake. Yes, three names, one place. It is on Reindeer Lake in Saskatchewan, the village is Kinoosao and the plant is on a portion of land named after it Co-op Point. So, the name used was somewhat determined by the conversation and the people having it. There are many instances in the north where this type of situation might happen. For example, people, may have talked about Island Lake and really have meant Savage Island on Island Lake, or spoken of Island Lake and really meant St Therese on Island Lake. There are really no rules to determine which name is used and you know by the conversation the exact location for that conversation.

Reindeer Lake has portion that is rumored to be so deep that the bottom has not been found. I actually think the bottom has been found but the story persists, perhaps because it is more romantic to think of it this way.

We contracted the fish business for a season at Co-op Point on Reindeer Lake. That means we bought the fish from the fishermen and sold it to Co-op Fisheries. This part of our work was a paper work job, Walter still had machines to fix and tend to at the same time. When fishing started, we made out cheques from the Co-op, and kept track of production for a commission based upon what was produced. Co-op Point is some 70 miles north of Lynn Lake, Manitoba, the most northerly point that can be accessed by road in that province. From there one heads northwest to Co-op Point into Saskatchewan. This stretch of road is the narrowest, bumpiest, curviest, stretch of track ever to be called a road. A creek ran right beside the road inches from the tires of The Beast. In the picture below the water is rushing along the roadside and then crosses the road on a few feet of relatively straight road. We stopped and spoke to a fellow washing a fish in the water running across the road. He had
caught it in a nearby ditch.

In July, of 1977, we brought groceries in from Lynn Lake. Necessary things that were needed for the kitchen were also purchased. When we left, we left the kitchen supplies there to be used in the kitchen. From experience, I knew there might be a table or counter, likely well worn and well soiled, too difficult to clean and needing an oilcloth cover. The invoice attached shows we purchased cake tins, fly swatter, bread tins, cake tins, electrical tape and assorted tools. I made bread and cakes almost every day and whomever was cook after me would need to do this also or go without. Walter bought additional parts in Winnipeg, as the parts on this bill are only a few of the many needed ones. The list of parts would have been extensive.

Beson Refrigeration
161 Smithfield Ave Winnipeg
Man

DATE July 11/77

SOLD TO Co-Op Fisheries Ltd
ADDRESS 27-15th St W Prince Albert

SHIP TO
ADDRESS

To - Co-Op Point Reindeer Lake

Qty	Description	Amount
2	plastic basins 680	13 60
1	recep plug	1 10
1	[illegible]	1 16
[illegible]	window pane glass	40 04
1	fly swatter	54
4	bread pans 200	8 00
1	can opener 505	5 05
3 yd	table oil cloth	9 00
1	sauce pan	18 00
1	" "	19 00
2	electrical tape 99	[illegible] 98
1	cake tin 1.29	1 29
1	" " 189	1 89
4	files	4 32
2	hammers @ 10.19	20 38
2	" 622	12 44
2	friction tape 266	5 32
4	6789 WH whitehead valves 6.02	24 16
8	6 x 4 fitting for same 75	6 00
300 ft	#12 TW black wire 17¢	51 00
300 ft	#12 TW white	51 00
300 ft	#12 TW red wire	51 00
100 ft	#6 TW black 48¢	48 00
		379 41
	Prov tax	18 97

37178 SIGNATURE TOTAL 398 38

One trip was memorable. We left Lynn Lake at about 6pm. We had another 5 hours of daylight because in the summer days are longer up north. Walter drove a rented truck, and I followed in The Beast. The road was so bad we wanted to limit the number of times the loyal Beast went over it and thus rented a truck. It was a terrible road. At times, we went two and 3 miles an hour, and sometimes as fast as 17 and 18 miles an hour. Faster was not possible because the road was just too bad. It would take us more than 3 hours to do the 70 miles.

A portion of this bad road travels along the top of an esker. An esker is a sand ridge left by glaciers. Below you can see the view, and see how the esker is above the surrounding areas.

This long, winding, narrow, peak of sand and gravel, carried the road along its spine because it made for easier road construction. From here one could see for miles to the left, and right and forward. After leaving the esker, we were back to the narrow road full of holes, weaving between, and around rocks, and passing white foam water at the roads edge, with bordering swamps, and green lumpy moss at the road's edge.

Just twenty miles from our destination, we met two fellows in a truck telling us we could not get through to Co-op Point that night because a large truck was jack knifed at a bridge. With a heavy sigh and at 9pm after miles of tortuous driving we had to turn around and go back to Lynn Lake. Turning around was not an easy task. We had to jog the trucks forward and backward in the road to turn around. Driving on this type of road for about 100 miles is tough on the arms, back, and neck, and an active, and stressful, job, to stay on the road, and yet be able to miss potholes and rocks. We were back at Lynn Lake at 11:30 just lucky enough to get a room but no tea or coffee.

The next day we started in the morning to make the same trip. Walter remembered that at Wolverine River a fellow had started a water wheel. It is a very fast river. So, we stopped along the road to walk in to see it. It was a great big rusty spool circling at a fast speed as water foamed before it. It became a regular stop for us to get a break from driving on this road. There is a story that a daring young native boy went under this water wheel and came out unharmed. He said his boat and motor were wrecked. Is it any wonder?

Soon after this break, our legs stretched and back to driving, we arrived at the bridge blocked with the truck and trailer. They were jack knifed blocking the road. It was at a small bridge. The truck was on one side of the bridge and the trailer on another. The cook that was travelling with the trailer had tried to sleep the night inside it but could not as he was afraid the trailer would fall into the river. For 17 hours, the trailer was held out of the water by a large boulder. We waited. Soon a large, road building, front end, loader with a large bucket, and a lot of power, arrived. In two hours as we watched the trailer was rescued.

The airplane had made a tricky landing in the widened Wolverine River. I think the plane was carrying some official perhaps to do with the trailer, who had come to see the trailer rescue. It was there when we arrived so we never saw the skillful landing.

We went on our way immediately after all the action was settled. In a short distance, we were in muddy road conditions as the sandy road ended. Lucky us! It had rained the night before. It would be difficult to imagine this road any worse than it was before, but the rain did not leave anything to be imagined. The road was horrible because of the slippery mud and water adding to the bends, pot holes, rocks, gravel, boulders, hills, soft shoulders, no shoulders, crossing streams and ruts.

Over this treacherous bumpy road, we transported supplies including glass. Forty panes of glass were wrapped securely and placed inside the wrapper of a new bed mattress we were transporting in the van. They arrived safely. They were to be for the windows in a trailer where we were to stay. The locals had broken every pane of glass and even the toilet in the trailer. To discourage future drunken window breaking we boarded up the windows of the trailer before we left. The area carved out of the forest was not scenic even though the surroundings were beautiful. The plant location was a dull looking mess of sand and gravel more an industrial storage lot than a place to live.

Pictured is the yellow truck we rented to save The Beast from the horrible road, and the picture shows the trailer the day we left. The trailer is not luxurious accommodation but it was dry and close to the fish plant. The dogs in the picture below were nice friendly dogs. I fed them scraps of food and they always came around to get a pet. They had fun grabbing my washing from the clothes line almost as if I put it for them to play with as a toy.

The kids also had fun. An official from the Health Department came and complained there was no toilet paper in the outdoor toilets. The kids got the toilet paper and unrolled it all over the trees, going from tree to tree, decorating each one. The kids did not appreciate toilet paper. The Health Department was out of touch with life in the north where toilet paper is frequently an unknown luxury.

When we first arrived, we stayed in the frog path kitchen, a tin trailer parked behind the boarded up one closer to the truck. Both are up off the ground. One day Walter and I were standing in this rickety old tin building and looked on the floor. It was covered in frogs less than 2 inches in size. There were hundreds maybe thousands of them. They were all going in the same direction, which was a good thing. It was a kind of migration. They did not make a lot of noise, and within 15 minutes or so, they were all gone. The tin shack was in their path and they just hopped through the building. How they got in and out I do not know. It was not a tight fitting building. I know they came from the right of the picture above and went in a line through the tin shack across the sand and through the grass. It is hard to believe perhaps, but true.

We lived in this frog path shack while the trailer was being repaired. It had once been a very nice trailer but was a mess when we arrived. So, when we got the trailer with the windows we were glad to get a bit better place to stay and were glad to put up the boards to protect the glass as we left.

Walter installed a flush toilet and ran water from the fish plant to the trailer. We had three local natives working with us cleaning up the trailer and other things before the fishing season began.

Walter worked long hours up north. Rarely did he take time off. There was not much of anything to do if Walter had taken time off. On one trip to Lynn Lake, we stopped along the road at a bridge over the Wolverine River where just upstream from the metal spinning wheel; Walter wanted to try to catch a fish. He succeeded and caught one. The setting of this picture shows the rich greens and dark blues of the north, and importantly the edge of the road dropping immediately into the lake without warning, and no real road shoulder, and that is why one had to be alert when driving. It also shows Walter's thick strong hands that he got from pulling wrenches and doing hard work.

We were stopped there along the road enjoying the silence and loneliness of the highway. We felt we were alone in the quiet of the wilderness. Just us and nature. Suddenly, we were surprised when a man and a woman came out of the bush. Without warning, they were just suddenly there. They headed down the road walking towards their vehicle somewhere on the road ahead of us. They said they had been rabbit hunting in the bush. I do not remember seeing a rabbit. Whether they were or not we did not know but this made a good picture showing the nature of the northern bush and the roads through it.

In the northern bush at night the stars are bright and the evenings peaceful. One sees far more stars in the north than in the cities of the south. There is no ambient noise of traffic, and no heavy trucks of the city, no horns, no sirens, just quiet. One night we heard a loud air chopping noise and an engine. It was getting mighty loud and mighty close. A helicopter was landing behind our shack on a very small airstrip. Having an airstrip there was unusual. It would have required a lot of work to find an area they could easily make flat for that distance. Still there were no landing lights on the landing strip and the pilot only saw the strip by moonlight and starlight. So, this was quite a surprise. It made a lot of noise and caused excitement in the quiet of the night. The pilot was looking for assistance. He wanted to land on an island in the lake where there was a tourist camp. We could not help him. It was dark and he was a bit lost. As day light came like a dragonfly he was gone.

The coffee room in the fish plant was the scene of more than one birthday celebration. If I learned someone was having a birthday, I would make a cake and cookies. We needed reasons to celebrate and be happy in this atmosphere of hard, long hours, of work without distractions. In this picture, the fellow holding the green cup is having a birthday. He worked in the fish plant. He was from Brochet and therefore not a local but he came to work at the right time. He was a good soul but prone to drinking and wanting to visit and talk at odd hours. He liked to socialize but would forget
the time and not want to leave.

Walter rigged a copper pipe at nose level through the wall with a hose attached to an ammonia cylinder. A slight turn of the tap and the porch would be filled with the rotten egg smell. We would watch him through the window trying to find and plug the hole with his finger. Always too drunk to succeed and he would go away. Nothing was ever said about this and during the daytime, as he was sober. There seemed no point to bring it up or reveal our method of getting him to go home.

Annie Razor Neck was one of the interesting people in the area. No one could pronounce Annie Razor neck's real last name, but it sounded a bit like Razor Neck and the nickname stuck. She did not seem to mind and was a pleasant person. She ran a fishing camp on one of the islands in the lake. It was perhaps her camp the helicopter was trying to find. I never went to her camp. In the off season she had no tourist customers so she moved over to Co-op point. She had a box car trailer pictured below. Had it been painted bright orange, it would stand out better from the air.

Annie Razor neck drove the red truck. It was practical and useful, style was not the first consideration in its purchase. Here you see it atop the esker and one can see how it wiggles through the bush and the narrow road at the top. The steep dropoff either side makes this stretch of road dangerous any time of year.

Annie used this boxcar as a house and as a take-out restaurant, of a sort that can be found in the north and isolation, where conventions of style as found in the south and cities do not apply. Here it sits in front of a sand cliff near the fish plant. Various bits of lumber and assorted other trash lay around it. She is in the doorway. The windows of course are boarded up.

To the left of Annie's establishment, perhaps a quarter of a mile distant was the Saskatchewan and Manitoba Provincial boundary. The road was so terrible people did not want to drive back and forth on it unless it was really necessary. Caucasian bootleggers from southern Manitoba motivated by big profits would make the trip to bring up alcohol to sell to the First Nations people. These bootleggers would hide the alcohol in the bush close to the border. It was illegal to sell First Nations people alcohol, and socially unacceptable. I do not know how the money exchange occurred but I know that they hid the booze in the bush.

Annie Razor Neck did a lot of selling but I do not think she was a bootlegger. The call of the peace and quiet of the north must have been strong for her. I know for sure she sold hot dogs, and her customers were mostly the kids. She was good with the kids. She and the kids came to the door late one night to borrow mustard. The kids have their faces all painted with food coloring and she and the kids were having a good time clowning around.

Walter pulled this fish boat out of the water. We never saw it used. It sat on the shore all summer near the metal fish plant building. Did the owner know or care that it was out of the water? We never found out. Perhaps they knew. News that it was out of the water would travel fairly quickly in the north by word of mouth to the owner. It is most likely the owner did not care, as they would get a new one with a government loan.

The scene of fishermen loading gas drums and other supplies into their boats on a messy pier is too common in the north. This tendency for messiness causes problems. A lot of garbage is generated from a lack of respect for the environment. Broken bottles, packaging, tin cans, all kinds of mess can easily be found anywhere. Old oil drums in the bush, in the lake, plastic oil containers, and cigarette packages can be found everywhere both in the water and on land. Little if any attempt to clean this up is being made. It does not show traditional or contemporary environmental concern.

Oil drums were usually a mess and not neatly stacked. The contents were used and the drums just thrown around or rolled into a lake. Disposable baby diapers were in piles of garbage. The diapers prevent infections but increase the garbage. The messes on the pier, in the bush, and in the lake occurred in many places where humans gathered.

Environmentally friendly ways had nothing to do with ethnicity and race. The north was cleanest where there were no people. We found youths, using 22 caliber rifles indiscriminately shooting birds on the lake. It was another disturbing example of lack of respect for the environment.

At times, the kids would ride their bikes down the pier and right out into the lake. Then they would fish out their bikes and do the whole thing over again having a lot of fun. Though they never were hurt, I was always ready for one to be injured.

We were sometimes the first aid station. We always took a good supply of Epsom Salts with us when we travelled to the north. As a medical aid, Epsom Salts came in handy many times. One day in the kitchen at Co-op Point, we had three generations of one family receiving first aid around the plywood tables. A grandfather was soaking his infected hand
in a bowl of Epson Salts. He had cut his hand while cutting fish. His son had a human bite on his shoulder from some kind of fight with another man. After bathing it and cleaning it, I made a poultice of Epsom salts and applied that holding it place with tape. Earlier his wife had been in with a black eye and had to be taken out to a hospital for treatment. When I asked the man, what had happened to his wife. He held up his outstretched arm and pointed his finger telling me his wife had run into his finger. I did not believe him but did not know what to think.

With these two men being nursed, Walter was working on the third generation, a grandson of the one man and son of the second. The child had been running barefoot and stepped on a discarded lamp glass, thanks to the terrible abuse to the environment. Shards of glass were all in the sole of his foot. Walter had the kid on the table and using tweezers picked glass from the cut foot. Later he soaked the foot in Epsom Salts and we bandaged it.

The boats on the trailer in front of the Co-op store on Reindeer Lake, Saskatchewan, had to be brought here over that horrible twisty road. The truck and boats are covered in dirt. Such a long trailer on the back of truck would have had some trouble to snake along and make the delivery. Their destination was further north east on the lake to Brochet, Manitoba, but there was no road to get there. The boats were government purchases and they were going to native fishermen as an economic action plan to help the local economy. It is one that is repeated time and again. The local fishermen at Co-op Point were also waiting for boats. They had ordered 35 hp motors and larger boats. The equipment was purchased and the fishermen were all loaned $4000 to pay for the boats. Government delay caused the fishermen to be a bit disappointed when these smaller boats showed up and they found out they were not theirs.

This is the last day at Co-op Point, or Kinoosao, on Reindeer Lake. Walter has The Beast backed up to load his tools. The red van color stands out. When Walter first went to register the van the person behind the counter called it an orange colored van. Walter was upset and made the fellow change the color to red. He did not want to drive an orange colored truck. Of course, The Beast was red. The door to the plant engine room is open. It is inside this engine room that I washed and hung sheets to dry in the heat of the engines and the air currents of their fans. The sheets and other clothing dried fast in the engine room. Well that is, they all did dry nicely except for the two sheets that were sucked into the radiator of the diesel engines. I never was able to get the grease marks out of those sheets.

When we left Co-op Point, we drove to Lynn Lake. On one of our trips to Co-Op Point, Norman Sager and I went to the location of a burned down fish plant. Though I had never seen the plant before, Norman had worked as an administrator in the fish plant a few years previously when the plant was in operation. The plant burned down a few years after Norman had worked there. On this trip, we stopped to look at the ruins.

Norman stands in the uncleaned mess from the fire from at least six years previous. People had just left the debris site untouched to blow around and disintegrate. No one took responsibility to clean up the mess. The place burned down and people just left when the flames died. This environmental eyesore lay untouched, as a statement for not only what once was and could be, but as a testimony to the lack of environmental concern by some northerners and governments. It is abuse and is far too common.

Norman noticed a bundle of papers that had managed to survive the fire, and then survive being outside in the rain and snow. He picked up the bundle of papers and found his own signature on the papers from

his time as manager. He put them on this burned ice machine or some other machine and I took this picture.

Why has no attempt to clean up the mess or even rescue records been made? It is an irresponsible, lazy, lack of concern for nature, record keeping, privacy, and mother earth. It shows no understanding of the link between our actions and inactions and our future environmental wellbeing. How disgusting!

We travelled the roads of Manitoba and saw some interesting sights. On number 6 highway going north from Winnipeg to the inter lake region we came to Lundar just east of Lake Manitoba. On the edge of the town, they have this gigantic Canada Goose to attract attention to the town. Canada geese are a common site but this large bird was the biggest of them all. Were it real, for some, it would have made a fine roast, but for me I could skip it. I do not like the taste of Canada Goose.

The big prairie chicken is outside Ashern, Manitoba. I do not like the taste of prairie chicken either, and I have had to eat a lot of it in years past. I do not know the prairie chicken dance either but still I like to dance. I do see the similarity between the prairie chicken and myself. Both the bird and I were native to the western prairie and bush and we have both have left.

The big man with tire legs is also outside Ashern. These sights were looked for as familiar settings as we travelled around. They helped make the travelling more interesting.

After passing through Ashern, perhaps to Denbeigh Point on Lake Winnipegosis, we came to the Fairford River and this dam. The road goes across the top of the dam. I am not sure why the dam is located in this spot.

Through the railings on top of the dam, we could see the level of the water on the other side of the dam. It is barely visible in this picture. The difference is about 20 to 30 feet. In an area without great elevation changes and enormous hills, this is a big difference Walter is riverside fishing for our lunch. He caught nothing this day and later we moved on up # 6 Hwy and ate elsewhere perhaps a small pull out camping area.

Our travels sometimes took us to the same familiar places. Travelling on highway six, north or south we stopped at a small roadside pull out on the edge of Devils Lake. A telephone box was there but it had been vandalized. It could have been done by anyone but we thought most likely drunks. All the time we travelled past this park we never saw the telephone repaired and almost never saw anyone else in the park. Cell phones were not used then and the help line that could have been extremely valuable was destroyed. This beautiful wild rose bush survived and was always a pleasure to see in the park.

At this turn out we would have a rest and a lunch, perhaps a wiener roast, and maybe with roast marshmallows on a stick, and always at the same fire box. From there we could watch the action on the lake. There were always birds like ducks and loons on the lake.

Our trips were especially beautiful in the fall even when a storm was soon possible. The trees changed colors and the roads were for the most part used sparingly. Roads like this one pictured, that had open areas along side before the thick trees allowed us to see a lot of wildlife, mostly deer. This is a section of Highway 6 just north of Devils Lake, Manitoba. On one trip, the leaves were all gone. Everything was brown and dry. We were all alone on the road. We had seen no one in a while. Everything seemed dead and dying. It felt like everyone else had gone. We were like the last ones alive on earth or the last ones to leave the area. It was a lonely drive but we had gas and a good working vehicle and enjoyed our own company stress free going home.

All of a sudden, it started to snow. It quickly snowed much heavier. The visibility went from clear to almost zero in minutes. I got worried. A stress free drive changed immediately to one of danger. I suggested to Walter that he drive. I thought he was more experienced in the snow. Walter wanted me to continue because I was doing fine he thought, although I was not so sure I was doing fine, or that I wanted to drive. Walter seemed to have equal confidence in me doing the job as in himself doing it. Soon it was snowing so heavily I could not tell the difference between the ditch and the road. Afraid, poking along slowly, and checking the rear view mirror, I discovered a truck approaching. At first, this made me even more nervous. I felt the pressure of the truck behind me. Walter encouraged me to continue and keep going slowly.

Soon the truck passed us on the road. That was a fortunate break. I do not know how the truck could see any better but I followed his tracks. Perhaps he was higher up and was it was easier for the driver to identify the road as he looked down on it in a sharper angle. The truck seemed to be going towards The Pas. I followed it until we made it to the road to turn off to Bilenduke's. The Bilenduke's location was 5 miles off the main road. Those five miles of road were not very good. The snow made them worse.

Truthfully, what we called the Bilenduke Road, was only a very ill defined sort of a road, running downhill, winding through a swamp. It was more of a trail than it was a road. It had been made by fishermen years previously. It went over stumps around rocks and wound back and forth. In the storm, everything was all white. Road and swamp blended. No one had been on this road for a few days. I drove slowly and we both searched for the road. We made it to the Bilendukes' place where we happily spent the night safe from the snow storm and off the highway.

Bill and Milda Bilenduke were very good people widely liked and respected. In 1982, we were working at Denbeigh Point at the top of Lake Winnipegosis. Here Bill and Milda, and Bill's brother Harvey, owned a store and fish plant. In the picture below, Milda and Bill are standing next to our car. For part of every year they lived to the left in the trailer with the wooden roof and blue trim. Just inside the door of the building in front of the car, and behind Bill and Milda, was the kitchen and is where the pumps were located. These pumps made noise 24 hours a day bringing up water from many feet below. The water was used in the fish plant and in the kitchen. We slept not far from these pumps and got to know their noise quite well.

The two noisy 24 hour water pumps made sleeping difficult. The owners and even Brownie their dog slept nowhere near the kitchen. We sort of got used to the noise but never missed it later.

The kitchen is where Milda prepared meals for the workers in the fish plant. Sometimes a store customer would come around noon and be invited to come to eat too. It could be a busy place with lots of great food smells wafting out the doors.

Bill and Milda had Brownie, a large short haired but not heavy dog and he patrolled the yard. I was always glad when Brownie around at night because we stayed in the kitchen. Bears would find the scent of the kitchen food attractive. The flimsy doors would be no challenge for a bear wanting in to get at the food. Brownie would bark if something unusual like a bear wandered near. His warning made us feel safer.

Regularly wild life officials in the area would bait bear traps with fish and catch bears for relocation. Bears were always around. We could not and did not always see the bears. Brownie's alerting bark when wild life was near was a welcome.

Usually Brownie's barking would keep the bears away from the buildings. One night after Brownie had barked quite a lot, I took the picture below of a bear track near the fish plant. Walter worked in and around the plant, and past the location of the track daily. Bears were certainly not afraid of people.

In the kitchen stood an old wood and coal fired cook stove. Its smoke pipe went straight out the roof. In the summer when an electric stove was used the wood stove became extra cluttered counter space.

There were mice in the building so there were traps set around. We called it Milda's trap line. This was just a fun, northern, way to tease and recognize the problem. A real trap line is of course miles of traps set to snare or catch fur bearing animals. This is a common way to earn money in the north but mainly in the winter time. Every morning Milda would check the traps. She would just look at them. She would never touch the traps. If mice were caught, she would go outside and with a desperate pleading tone to her voice, she would holler, "Harvie, Harvie, trapline". Her brother-in-law Harvie would empty the traps she could not touch.

Bill and Milda became good friends and they came to Surrey to visit us. Bill did not look well. He wanted to see things but was tired easily. I took him to a doctor. The doctor was concerned. As soon as they got home, it was learned Bill had cancer and he soon died. Milda had heart trouble and her death followed Bill's in a couple of years.

Bill had some business deal with Indian Affairs. He was going to run the fish packing plant Easterville about 20 miles away on Cedar Lake. Walter was fixing the ice machine, diesels, and other equipment to make the plant operational. Every day we drove to Cedar Lake and then back to sleep at Bill and Milda's. As usual, we had picked up new parts in Winnipeg so the red van was loaded with tools and parts, camping equipment etc. I cooked breakfast, lunch, and dinner outside on a gas stove by the van and fish plant. This fish plant was a huge building. Part of the building was used as an ice house. The ice was packed in layered sawdust to retard melting. The ice house was open so that anyone could easily get inside, and they did. People needing to get in would help themselves to ice.

We spent quite a lot of time going to Easterville. We would drive there and sleep at Denbeigh Point. Bilenduke's Easterville fish plant had a lot of old equipment, diesels, ice machines, pumps etc.

One fall Walter was putting in a power line and the adjacent picture shows him dressed in winter clothing making a cement hole for the pole beside him. The rocks would go in the hole with the pole and more cement.

I am pictured wearing a Polar hat and cooking outside at Easterville. I no longer have that particular portable gas stove as it was soon replaced, but I still have the hat and use the cast iron frying pan all the time. If I needed to cook outdoors I could. I keep the watch even now that it does not work.

Hot running water is not always available in the North. Hot running water is something we all take for granted in cities and small towns, even on farms, wherever there is electricity. The picture below shows how it was valued in about 1986 in an area where no one had hot running water. The picture shows the fish shed in Easterville. The refrigeration condenser for the walk in freezer drained alongside the building from a hose high up on the outside wall. The water was a nice warm temperature so the local men and women came to wash their hair in the free running warm water. This is what the plant looked like, and it was soon to be different completely.

Disaster struck May 23, 1983. Fire!

The Easterville fish plant burned to the ground. At one in the morning, the police came to Bill and Milda trailer. Then they came next door and woke us up. Our stress levels sky rocketed immediately. At first it appeared that, it may have been my fault. I was responsible for locking the padlock on the door when we left. I took the responsibility. Had someone gone in an open door I had not locked? I had a horrible, sickening, and sinking feeling. It was horrible being awakened in the middle of the night while staying at someone else's place.

The police came to us for an explanation. Perhaps they were thinking we had done something to start the fire. Had Walter's work caused the fire? Had we left a door open? It is logical. The RCMP wanted to know about details such as when we left, what work was done, and had I locked the door and other details.

We gave the time when we left, and I said I had locked the door. With all the tools, parts, and other things we had inside, I had to be careful to lock it up overnight. I locked the door whenever we had to leave for a while. Had we not locked everything up each time we were gone for a few minutes, the tools and supplies would most likely have been stolen. We had some experiences that motivated our attention to this detail. On one occasion, I was unloading buns and other groceries and putting them in the filleting room with our camping stuff. I was gone for maybe two minutes and came back to find a group of kids throwing the buns all over the place. As I entered and complained they scattered. The buns all went into the garbage. I knew to lock the door even if I went to the bathroom.

In the process of the investigation, the locked padlock was found. It was determined that the fire had started in the ice house, not an area we had been working in. We were glad to have the locked padlock as evidence and know where it had started. A few months later teenage girls one of whom was the chief's daughter admitted they had been in the ice house.

They climbed in through an opening used to put ice in or take ice out of the ice house. They sat in the ice house smoking. One of the girls had dropped a cigarette or a match. The group fled as the fire started. Luckily, they got out.

We lost about $4,000 in parts, tools, ladders, food and camping equipment, welding equipment, pans dishes etc. We never were adequately compensated for anything other than the parts we had left in the plant, as we had no evidence to prove we had them with us on location. The implication even for a short while that we had done something wrong bothered us for a long time. We loved our work and the people we worked with and felt really badly. Vindication in such an event is good, but does not fix all the emotions.

In the ash and destroyed equipment and machinery, one can see the square lines and shape of Walter's vice close to the center right of the picture. The vice is a rust reddish color. The steel vice was soon stolen along with the toilet from inside the plant. Walter made a fuss about losing the vice because it is a good heavy vice. A week later, it was returned. It is now in the garage waiting for Glenn to take it home.

The picture below shows the icehouse and that the metal siding has peeled away with the heat of the fire and lays curled in a mess to the right of the building. The wooden walls of the ice house are burned down to the ice level. The ice is still covered in darkened sawdust. After the fire the ice continued to melt away in the summer heat. The ice is exposed and it is the white color in a few spots on the end of the building.

This fire came at a really, bad, time. It was at the start of the fishing season. The refrigeration was needed for the fish. Fortunately, there were no fish yet stored in ice in the building. The hundreds of pounds of fish were yet to come. The filleting tables are the white metal tables in the pictures. No jobs would be available for fish processing this season. There are no remains of wooden fish boxes or melted plastic ones near the rollers or anywhere to be seen. Luckily, the fire did not catch the forest on fire or burn down the yellow and blue green building behind the ash. That building that shows in the background I had not seen until after the fire as I never walked around the building. It might have been a house or a shed. Perhaps the sandy ground without much fuel to catch fire helped to contain the fire. Some arrangement had to be made in a hurry to provide storage for the soon to be arriving fishermen with loads of fresh caught fish. Economic disaster loomed big. Luckily, another ice machine was found in a nearby shed. Walter made the necessary connections to make this ice machine functional.

The fishermen were about to bring in their catch of assorted fish in boxes and red containers. Still there was no building to store the fish. A semi trailer truck with a refrigeration unit solved the problem. Eugene the semi driver, whose last name I have forgotten, is shown in the picture with his back to the picture wearing a blue t-shirt. This arrangement did not perfectly solve the problem, as the fish could not be processed and frozen. The fish were iced and loaded directly onto the semi trailer. We left feeling upset after Walter connected the ice machine and I never found out if they rebuilt the building or cleaned up the mess.

Before enlarging the picture below, I never saw Walter half under the back of the semi. I was happily surprised to see him there and wonder what he was fixing.

Immediately after the fire, we had to leave for a short trip of one or two days, to Winnipeg to do the taxes. On this trek we bought new cooking equipment. The stove pictured below was purchased on this trip. When we returned, Walter connected the ice machine. We camped beside the remains of the plant and the ash. The camp stove is now in the garage and I use the frying pan lid to this day, September 23, 2014. Today it jammed my stove drawer. I guess I will have to keep it elsewhere. Funny it would happen on the same day we write about it. It was from an old saucepan I think I had when we lived on the farm in Goodsoil. The kettle all shiny and new is now in the basement, and it is the same frying pan as in the previous picture, that I still use. Cooking by the remains of the fire, even with a new stove was stressful. It was the end of this job and any in this location.

Kid starting fires in Easterville is not common but it certainly happens. Here is a helicopter picking up water from the lake in a bag to airlift to a location and dump on a fire at the garbage dump.

The day before the fire some form of government official came up to visit the natives. I rushed to finish a letter to Lyle and Gwen or Glenn. She kindly agreed to mail the letter for me. In the letter, I described how the kids were playing around running back and forth in the rafters of the building in the ice house. They could travel back and forth across the entire length of the buildings. They were unsupervised and did as they pleased. I wondered if they might fall and get hurt, or one day and do something worse like catch the building on fire.

The First Nations communities in the north area still hunted. Here a bear skin is stretched between trees. Perhaps it was to be a mat for a floor. You cannot trust a live bear. Maybe this one came too close to the community and they killed it to be safe.

For the most part these houses below were not lived in when we were at Denbeigh Point. I think they had been there for years, and had been used when a sawmill operated on the location. When we were there they looked like this run down and deteriorated and just shacks waiting to fall over. I was invited into a house, similar to the white one, with the red triangle and just behind it a few steps. A man and woman with a little boy lived in it. They were camped here while the fish plant was working. The husband worked in the plant. The lady invited me in for tea. It was not a fancy tea and we drank out of mugs. It was a pleasant and happy visit. The little boy sat on my knee and we colored. The little guy was frequently following me around when I was cooking or when I was working and when he saw me in the yard. On this day, we had a good time coloring and talking and I enjoyed making a fuss over him.

On my 60th birthday, September 14, I had to go into Winnipeg from Denbeigh Point. The distance was about 300 miles. We had been at Denbeigh Point since before Walter's 65 birthday on August 18. The next day, the tax forms had to be filled out. These forms needed to be in the mail before a certain date and if the date was missed, the tax department became quite disagreeable.

The fish truck was going into Transcona, to the Freshwater Fish Marketing Plant. I caught a ride with it. Eugene was the husky young truck driver with arms like stove pipes. We left Denbeigh Point around 8 or 9 pm and Eugene said we could stop and get a Buffalo Burger on the way at a lonely little stop. I looked forward to that. Unfortunately, we arrived in the middle of the night and the stand was closed. Eugene said he needed to have a rest and that I should wake him up in ½ hour. He put his big arms on the steering wheel and slept. For Eugene it was comfortable. Being the driver, he had a special cushion. I did not have such a nice seat. I had an ordinary not so soft transport passenger seat without springs and little padding. It made for an uncomfortable ride, and sleep was not possible. In 30 minutes or so, we were on our bumpy way again.

We arrived in Winnipeg in the early morning. I was dropped off at an intersection. I caught a cab the rest of the way home. I filed the forms and posted them. I got a cab back to meet Eugene at the same intersection a few hours later. Eugene slept while the truck was being unloaded. We were back on our way to Denbeigh Point by mid afternoon. That was a 600 mile trip in just over 24 hours, but in that seat, it seemed quite a lot longer.

While I was gone, the mother with whom I had tea, left the little boy sleeping in the cabin and drove off to Winnipegosis. The little boy woke up and went to play in the sawdust pile pictured. The sawdust pile is remnant of the wood mill that had once been on the location and quite large even though it had not been used in years. You can see the old decaying logs and the pile is rounded and flattened with age. The houses are just to the right of the road in the lower part of the picture.

Walter used the radio telephone to call me in Winnipeg and caught me while I was filling out forms. He had very sad news. Playing with a stick in the sawdust pile the little boy encountered a bear. It killed and ate part of him.

When they tracked the incident, the conclusion was that the little boy had seen the bear and was following him and carrying a stick. The bear went into the woods, came around behind the boy, and caught him from behind. They found the bear in the woods near a tree; it was guarding what was left of the child and covering it with leaves. The bear was shot immediately.

I am sure had I not left to do taxes the child would have got up and come to hang around me. I would have seen the bear. I would have been able to save the boy, but that is not how it happened. I felt sick to hear the news. It was a horrible event.

Denbeigh Point on Lake Winnipegosis was 27 miles south east from Easterville on Cedar Lake. The two locations are close and this bear incident happened in the area. Sometime after Easterville, we were again working for Bill and Milda Bilenduke at Denbeigh Point. We worked at Denbeigh Point quite a few times at least twice a year and sometimes more. Walter worked on the machines and I would help him as I could, and would do most of the driving. When I was able, I also helped Milda preparing food for a constant stream of people. I certainly never lacked for work.

Milda would take a break once a summer and if I were around, I would take her place as cook. She would go to the town of Winnipegosis where they had a lovely home. They did not live in Denbeigh Point year round. Milda always cooked good meals for the workers. They always had meat, vegetables, and dessert. Once a week perhaps we ate fish, unlike in Alaska where we almost never ate fish. The workers would often have hearty sandwiches and bowls of soup and dessert for lunch. The workers always enjoyed the plentiful good food, talk, and socializing.

In the middle of each table in the dining room sat the sugar, catsup, salt and pepper, and canned milk in Northern work camp style. Around these items, the meal would be served on long wooden plywood tables covered in a flower patterned, oilcloth. The diners sat on square, metal and wooden stacking chairs. Food was put into bowls on the table and passed around. The atmosphere was camp like and congenial. The walls were of pressed board, wood paneling, and Milda had made curtains for the windows. You can see her handy work over the window in the back of Walter in the pictures above and below. A poster of types of fish found in northern waters is on the wall.

Milda had a nice flowered set of dishes, but frequently these were too few, and regular camp style cups and bowels supplemented her nice service. In the pictures, you can see these mixed in with the nicer good set Milda used.

On Walter's 65th birthday, Milda made Walter a birthday cake and decorated it. She did a pretty good job. I do not know the identity of the man on the left of the picture as Walter is ready to cut his cake. It is Bill Bilenduke eating on the right side of the picture. I think we had fried chicken, cabbage rolls, and mashed potatoes. It was a few minutes after this evening meal I caught a ride with the truck driver, Eugene, hauling the fish to Winnipeg.

The kitchen was interesting. It was small and full of stuff. A pot that would hold about two gallons of water sat on the electric stove. A dipper hung over the edge of it. This was the only available hot water. Anytime you took water out of this pot, you immediately replaced it with cold water from the only one water tap in the kitchen.

Dishes were washed by hand in a big dishpan. They were leaned over in another pan to drain off. A dipper of hot water was used to rinse them off with before they were dried. Wet T-towels were hung on a rope cord line above the sink in front of the window. The kitchen was clean, small and cramped. There never seemed to be enough room for anything. Any flat surface had something piled on it. Items were store on top of the fridge and on top of the cupboards.

I never saw the wood stove below when it was used as I was always there in the summer. It most likely would have been used in the winter. I only saw it looking like this, like a crowded counter top, with stuff

piled all over it. A pass through window was never used as a pass through either. More kitchen related stuff was piled there. Considering how much room she had to work in, Milda turned out good food and much appreciated meals. She was a good northern camp cook.

Our bed was on the other side of the wall not far from the droning water pumps, that I have to repeat make an irritable noise 24 hours a day Though I was afraid of bears because they could easily have bashed in the doors looking for food it may been the pump noise that kept the bears away with the help of Browne's barking. Bears could easily find food away from noisy machines.

Milda and I were in the kitchen one day when there started a lot of noise and rattling coming from the wood stove. This stove top was full of stuff as usual. We thought, maybe a bird had fallen down the stove pipe. I got the stuff off the top of the stove and opened with the metal handle. Immediately, out flew a soot covered squirrel. I jumped back. Milda was yelling. I was yelling. The squirrel darted around. I guess our noise was scaring it more than it was already scared with the fall into the cold stove. It jumped to the top of the warming oven of the stove, and from there to a few places, and through the curtain acting as our bedroom door, that I note was not much of a bear impediment had one come into the kitchen through the flimsy outer doors. Leaving a trail of soot the squirrel jumped around and onto my cotton dressing gown hung on a nail. Any nail in the wall had something hanging from it. The poor creature had to be frightened with all the noise we were making. I opened a window but had to struggle to get the screen off and stepped back.

The squirrel jumped a few times and then through the opening and was gone.
Had it been a bear that had come into the kitchen, the curtain door would not have helped protect us, and we would have been in trouble. There were two doors to the building but both were on the other side of the kitchen full of food and we had to go through the kitchen to get out.

One end of the dining room had a low cupboard without doors. The shelves were concealed by a pleated curtain stapled to the top edge and reaching almost to the floor. What might be behind the curtain on the northern camp cook's shelves? Jars, dishes, cooking pots, and assorted junk and nothing of great importance were hidden. On the counter top was a small old television. When Milda had a few moments, she would watch TV and crochet. Milda did lovely crocheting. She crocheted large bedspreads and tablecloths using fine # 20 or #30 crochet threads. Threads this size could be used for table centers,

dresser scarves, and doilies. She worked fast. On the end of the table below I see boxed Betty Croker cake mix. I wonder if this is what she used to make Walter's birthday cake.

It was for Bill and Milda that Walter and I built a power house in 1983. Making the floor was a job for two people. Walter and I worked on this building together. I worked with Walter following his instructions. I mean to say I did not just stand around and watch. I actively helped with hard labor and sometimes learning the process as we went along. We had a good system worked out and could talk to each other as we worked. This was a pleasure we loved. For too many years Walter had worked away and we had been apart and we truly loved being able to be together working. I wish more couples had the same opportunity.

The cement floor was a job that took several days. We worked from dawn to dark almost every day. That means after supper we went out and worked until the sun went away. At 65, Walter was working as hard as a much younger man works, and enjoying his work.

There were two large and heavy diesel engines in the old decaying power house. One at a time, these were moved out on an earlier visit. Using a pry bar and rolling logs they were moved. Eugene the truck driver, helped with the bigger of the two engines. With the engines moved Walter tore this building down. This being the most level and best location for the building it was here we made the new floor.

I loaded the electric cement mixer and used the lever to dump the cement into the wheelbarrow. There was a formula of so many shovels of cement to so many shovels of gravel plus water. When the mixer had finished, mixing Walter had the wheelbarrow in place so I could fill it up with the wet mixture. Walter wheeled the barrow full of heavy wet cement to the right spot and dumped it out. Then he smoothed the cement to make a nice flat floor using a trowel. Nearing the end of the cement work to speed things along a bit I doubled the amount of cement per load without telling Walter, and it seems absent mindedly, without realizing I had also doubled the weight in the wheel barrow. I just never thought about the wheelbarrow being extra heavy. I did not realize I was making him work harder and straining his back.

Walter noticed the extra weight and the extra exertion he had to put into his work, but never said anything until after the work was done. He never complained. He just did the work. After the floor was poured he said, "We sure got that floor done quickly." I instantly realized what I had done when he told me that I had given him twice the weight to haul in place. We laughed but I felt badly, even when he graciously said he was glad I had done it because we then finished faster. That is why he was the boss of the job and I was the assistant.

The wooden frame building walls were erected. Over the wood frame corrugated steel walls inside and outside sandwiched pink insulation between. We added the insulation. As a result, I know how nasty and itchy that pink insulation can be. It gets into your clothing and you need to wash it off your skin and out of your clothing to get relief from the itchiness. But, there was no bathtub and no shower. We had to wait until everyone left the kitchen so we could get a good wash using basins and little bits of water. After a long day, a shower would have been so very welcome. There are pictures to show the finished building showing Bill, Harvie, Brownie, Walter and me. Walter made the fastener that you see on the door.

The diesel engines gave us the power to do the work. One engine, a red Waukesha Diesel with a Rolls Royce engine had to be workable and running allowing us electricity to work. It was not mounted on cement but sat on the ground. It would later be cleaned and moved to a cement floor.

The building was built around the working red Waukesha diesel with the Rolls Royce engine that had never been mounted on a cement floor and for years had sat on the ground. We poured cement all around it before it was moved out and I think put back in the same spot but now on a cement floor.

Walter cleaned a yellow Caterpillar Diesel and refurbished it. The last time it had been cleaned was 1935 some 48 years previous. This cleaning alone took several days. We made the cement floor in sections. We completed one half of the floor and the yellow Caterpillar was set into place, bolted to the floor and started to supply electricity before the red Waukesha was disconnected.

In these pictures, it is possible to see how the engine was pushed in and out on rails. These machines weigh about half a ton. Moving the machines into their location was a big job that involved using a tripod winch and pulley system, and a large front end loader. Once inside the engines were pushed and pried into place, using 2x4s and the muscle power of Walter, and Eugene a truck driver serendipitously there at the right time.

I helped hold screws and the metal sheeting in place for the walls. It was hard work. We would have hired someone to help but no one there wanted to work. Locals would come and stare but no one wanted to work. We did it ourselves.

Together we carried the plywood to the roof nailed it in place. I climbed to the roof using a ladder. Going up was ok, but the coming down from the roof onto the scaffolding I was afraid. I was not accustomed to the height. I could go from the ladder to the scaffolding and reverse with no problem. I did not mind being on the roof but the first step down from the roof to the scaffolding was scary. Walter would always help me with my footing. Walter always grabbed my ankles and guided my feet to the right place. I can still remember his thick strong hands and loving touch on my ankles as he carefully helped me off the roof.

The building looked quite nice inside and out when it was completed. The interesting piece of equipment on top of the building is a diesel muffler for the yellow Caterpillar diesel. Before we finished we painted the floor and all the trim outside and inside. Bill Bilenduke was very pleased with his new power house. It was the nicest building in the whole area. Well built, and new, it sat amidst a lot of old deteriorating buildings and shacks.

Cigarette in hand, Walter is pictured in the finished power house. He stands between the two working engines on a shiny clean floor with clean machines. Shortly after this picture was taken Walter, quit smoking. I was proud of him for doing so. This was then close to his last cigarette, and he was making his mind up to quit.

Harvey, Me, and Bill Bilenduke, stand in front of the finished building. This is one of the few pictures of Harvey. It is this Harvey, that was called to empty Milda's trap line. Brownie the dog stands in front of us. We were all happy the job was done.

We returned home after the job but were back a few more times to work on other jobs for Bill and Milda. Even as we moved from Manitoba to BC, we stopped here so Walter could do work on an ice machine. I drove the car and Walter drove the van.

The bill for parts for some of the work at Denbeigh Point was billed to a treaty First Nation band. It is not a particularly interesting bill other than the treaty number at the top. This was a detail one had to remember when working in the north. The bands did not pay tax.

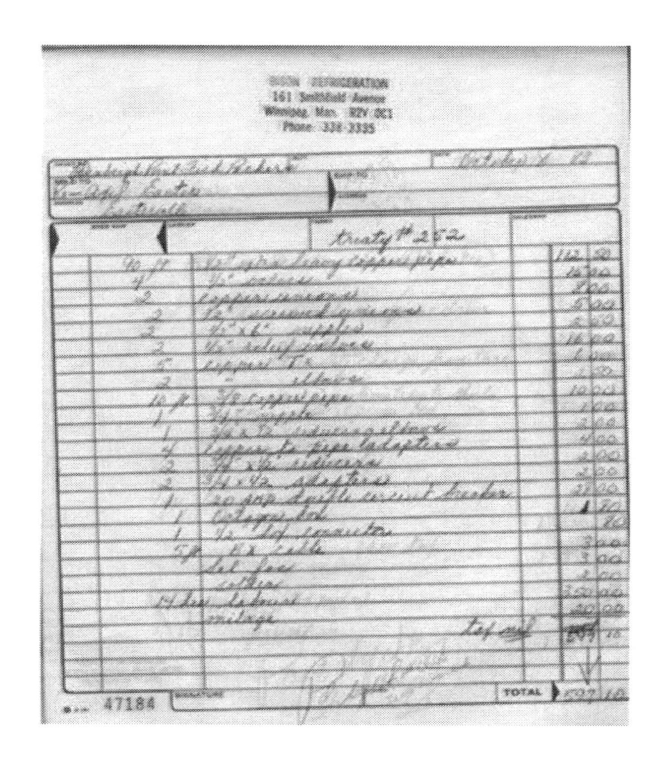

REFRIGERATION
161 Smithfield Avenue
Winnipeg, Man. R2V 0C1
Phone: 334-3335

Treaty #252

47184

TOTAL

The Bilendukes had no view of the lake from their house at Denbeigh Point yet they lived in a picturesque setting. When one walked to the yard and the fish plant one had a view of Lake Winnipegosis. The lakes are always beautiful in the north.

Cedar Lake in the summer had driftwood piled along the shore. Trunks and branches both weathered smooth.

Months later, in winter, the same spot is an ice fantasy as the logs are covered in ice. The wind blows in across the lake spraying water into the air coating the trees with ice. Ice coats everything near the lake until it is frozen over.

Another good and frequent customer in the same general area was Parker Burrell, in Dawson Bay, Manitoba. In many ways, the fisheries operations at Dawson Bay and Denbeigh Point, were similar. Both were on Lake Winnipegosis a strangely shaped lake. Both were fish buying operations, both had stores and both were operated by two brothers. There were differences too. Denbeigh Point had a bigger store, was a bigger location and about 5 miles from the main provincial highway, and there was no equivalent of Milda at Dawson Bay. We did not do as much work in the smaller Dawson Bay about a half mile from the road as we did at Denbeigh Point.

At the end of a winding gravel road, about a half mile from the highway Parker Burrell had his fish camp. This road was much better than the trail around stumps and rocks to Denbeigh Point.

Parker Burrell ran a small cramped store. In it, one could find the oddest and oldest things. In this store, some 30 years ago, I bought moccasin rubbers, and an enamel pan that I use to this day. Almost every Christmas I make fruit cake in this pan, and I use it throughout the year. The entrance to the store was an, unfinished porch that had not been insulated. There was no door. Swallows mud plastered a nest inside the porch, high up on the wooden wall. To enter the store one kept your head down to avoid the dive bombing swallows protecting their nest but it meant for an exciting entrance.

Parker Burrell was a nice fellow. His office was a little bit of a rustic disorganized mess. There were a lot of a papers, and piles of papers none of which were neatly arranged, spread around his desk. He sits in his office with a broken window surrounded by papers, files of papers in the cupboard behind him and more papers hung on the wall. He always paid his bills on time. Sometime after we moved to BC, he became an elected politician as a MLA in Manitoba.

Walter worked on ice machines in Parker Burrell's waterside fish shed below.

On one trip to Dawson Bay we had to stay over for a few days and were able to use the house belonging to Parker Burrell's brother and his wife who were away for a few days. We always had our own bedding with us in the van including pillows, sheets, pillowcases, and sleeping bags. We lay these on top of their bed so as not to cause extra work. On more than one occasion, we slept inside the van. Below is the house we were lucky enough to stay in at Dawson Bay. We enjoyed our time there but not as much as with the Bilendukes.

Walter knew I sometimes took notes about our trips. When I had time, I wrote sitting in the truck. I wrote letters to the boys, my sister Ruby, and other people, all while sitting in the truck. I never wrote when we were going down the highway because it was too bumpy, and Walter never wanted me writing, knitting, or crocheting if I were in the passenger seat because he was afraid the needles and pen were dangerous if he had to make a fast stop. I am pretty sure he also just wanted to make sure I was alert to our driving and talking to him so that he was alert and we were not getting lost.

July 5th 1981 I made these notes below:

These notes are being written so our children will know some of our experiences. The notes are intended to be rewritten properly later with additions and explanations.

"Good Harbor is about 40 miles of hard top road, and 10 miles of gravel and stone road full of holes, north of Winnipegosis. Upon arrival July 5, 1981, Good Harbour consists of about 25 or so cabins used mostly by fishermen during that season. Most of the cabins are painted a brilliant yellow and have painted black trim. The roofs are green. Some of the cabins are very tiny and may just hold a cot and a stove.

We used one that was an office. It was a fair sized building in comparison to the others.
Inside were two tiny bedrooms, a kitchen of not a bad size. The color inside was a startling. Every wall was bright orange and the ceilings were white. A plastic table cloth covered the table and it was orange and white. The floor linoleum was separating from the floor, and was buckled up and lumpy, and had a brown and white checkered pattern. This was startling but not all that bad in comparison to even more crude places we had stayed in.

As we arrived there was no place other than the floor to put our bedding. Walter had the key to a summer store house. In it was a bed we dismantled it. We piled the mattresses on to the roof of the van and the rest inside the van and took it across the road to our temporary house, the orange office.

Delightfully the fish shed had running water and a flush toilet. This was great as long as one did not have to answer the call of nature in the middle of the night as the fish shed was some 100 feet away. Going outside at night was not a good idea. The great outdoors at night was not as pleasant as it was in the day time. At night, it was a humming chorus of tiny, hungry, mosquitoes all waiting for lunch. There were so many that they could easily kill a person not properly covered. I never saw the likes of this in all my travels.

A ranch located in the bush is hard to imagine but there was one not too far away from Good Harbour. The cattle were nearly going mad from the number of flies and mosquitoes after them. We could hear them braying at night. The cattle would go to the lake for some protection from the bugs and from the intense heat at the time that was about 100 F.

Gwen, came with Lara and Trevor, to Onanole, near Clear Lake. I went to see them from
Good Harbour. Walter drove me to Duck Bay which is 4 or 5 miles away from Good Harbour. At Duck Bay a mostly First Nation community at the end of a road, I would catch a bus at 7 in the morning. We went the night before to buy the ticket. A huge, untidy, white woman, wearing red and white plaid pants was a ticket agent and she sold tickets from her house. She arrived about 8pm saying she had been visiting in Pine River. On asking for a ticket to Onanole she said she did not know how much it was for a ticket to Onanole so she sold me a ticket to Dauphin part way to Onanole. When I got to Dauphin I was to buy a ticket to Onanole.

At Good Harbour Walter is installing 5 ice machines for the fishermen who are impatient to get them working. The fishermen always wait to order equipment until it is needed the next day and then expect miracles regarding installation time. Last year we were here Walter was repairing ice machines. It is a fisherman's Co-op and everyone wanted to be boss. They were all giving orders that did not agree and it was difficult for Walter to know what needed to be done. Co-ops are fine but can be problematic if there is no clear leader. This year however things are different. Walter got two of the leading fishermen to sign a work order stating what work was to be done. With this document, Walter, could tell the other bosses who showed up to give conflicting instructions that they could just take off.

Walter looks tired. The long work hours are taking their toll. He is 64. Walter has one helper a First Nation man Raymond Flett. He seems to be nice man. I can not help much. I am just reading crocheting, cooking and making up the bills. I must carry water from the plant to the orange office and carry out the slop bucket. I try not to go out day or night for fear of being eaten by bugs.

At night, I hear a bird sounding like a whip-or-will makes a noise at night. Then I think maybe it is just some kind of owl. The crows start cawing at 5:30 Am. The fishermen must have trained them as wake up birds.

The fish here are mainly suckers and some pickerel. About 25 boats are in the harbour.
They look nice in a group. The owners are mixed racial, and ethnic backgrounds. Some are First Nation, and some are Caucasian, white men, perhaps these are also farmers. The boat below is returning to Good Harbour."

We travelled through the Peguis Reserve on the way to JackHead. I took the pictures below. The house is a neat house and the picture lets you see the rural setting and a nicely kept house.

Just past the house, we came to a fire in a field. The farmers had lost all their hay they had recently harvested. We wondered how the hay would catch fire. It seemed to us that it had to have had human involvement.

Anama Bay on Lake Winnipeg was a bit out of our way when our destination was Jackhead, but we just wanted to have a look at the place. The home below was in Anama Bay. As is typical in some places in the north the yard is littered with junk and trash.

The kids below were also in Anama Bay near Hwy 513. They came to say hello. It is a frontier like rustic location near the edge of the lake. Friendly visitors are not common, so our visit was unusual, and we were lucky to have them come with their curiosity to say hi.

Through the Peguis Reserve we travelled to Koostatak. The oiled gravel road comes to a forced junction quite near the water's edge. From this vantage point you can see, and perhaps get the feeling of the immense size of Lake Winnipeg, the last of glacial Lake Agassiz as it disappears into the horizon. It is 436 Km long, 24,510 square KM. Water drains into this lake from Alberta, Saskatchewan, Manitoba, Ontario, North Dakota and Minnesota.

Further south east of Anama Bay, and still on Lake Winnipeg, is Jackhead. It is not far from the road junction pictured above as road #224 comes to the water. At the village of Jackhead on the small fast flowing Jackhead river Walter did work for the fishing reserve. I was a bit worried about him going up the ladder as he was alone but could not help him. He was working on an ice machine and doing some wiring. The buildings were camped on the waters edge seen here at a high level close to flooding. Behind the boat is an elevated ramp leading upwards, perhaps to enable ice blocks to be more easily loaded into the buildings in the winter.

We were only here for a few hours. I do not remember if I thought of Alaska at the time. Now when I look at the pictures I can see similarities. Bethel, Alaska is about 700 miles closer to the North Pole, but both areas of fishing camps are low to the water, in bog areas, the river water is high in the area of the camp, and the First Nations are residents in an isolated harsher life style than are most residents further to the south.

Four Japanese tourists check things on the dock. The tourists had arrived in one of the boats. They were going to Hudson's Bay by boat. Interestingly the boat would be the one pictured facing us on the right. This is not a trip I would want to take in that type of boat hammered by the waves and wind. It would be an uncomfortable trip with days of body jolting bouncing over waves. The trip would be time spent surrounded by bugs that hug the shoreline for a hundred yards or more, and all this just to get to the end of Lake Winnipeg. It would be a dangerous trip and take longer if a wind came up. This lake is noted for wind storms. A bit of a breeze would chase away the bugs but at night, the tourists would be a buffet for the bugs even if well covered as they appear. We wondered if they realized what they intended to do. We never said anything as they had travelled a long way for experience.

On one of our trips north to Denbeigh Point, we decided to go and see the power dam at Grand Rapids. We had heard that others had gone and wanted to see it ourselves because it seemed interesting. Walter was interested to see inside and see the turbines. Taking highway # 6 north the picture below shows the approach to the dam. The road is built up over the low ground. Inside the machines were clean and colorful and the people showed us around and were nice and friendly.

We ventured into Ontario too. We went where work called us. The Precambrian Shield stretches across Northern Ontario making the geography similar to that of parts of Saskatchewan and Manitoba. We had a lot of work on the Precambrian Shield.

Windigo is a spiritually sounding name and an isolated place in North Western Ontario. Locals said Windigo means evil spirits. Evil spirits and isolation could combine to make for interesting events. In our time there, we never had any experiences that would make us think the place had any connection to any kind of spirits or was at all haunted. It was a tranquil place situated in remote beauty.

I seems that at some time in the past an epidemic had killed nearly everyone in the village. Their bodies were taken to a small island, and buried. The remaining residents all moved away from Windigo because it was a place of great sadness. They moved to Weagamow, an even more isolated place a bit further north without road access.

If Windigo had a different name previously I do not know. It seems reasonable to think people would not name a place where they were living after evil spirits, so perhaps the name came after the epidemic.

If one could drive straight to Windigo today Winnipeg, it would take over 15 hours. We did it in two days, stopping over at Pickle Lake, overnighting in a decent hotel. The road from Pickle Lake to Windigo was a good gravel road built up above the surrounding area, standing high above the land. Local gossip in the area told us that this road was to be part of a more northern road crossing of Canada and so the road was good. This part of the drive took five hours. There were no services such as gas stations, bathrooms, restaurants, on this road, and nothing at the end in Windigo. To be able to get back out we had to take with us extra gasoline in the van to fill our tank before we left. Bathrooms were the wilds of the bush. If the vehicle broke down, we were stuck and there was no telephone cell service.

Arriving at Windigo was like arriving absolutely nowhere. The road just plain ended, abruptly. One minute you are driving down a highway thinking you are going somewhere. The next minute you are at the end of the road having arrived at nowhere. The entire rest of civilization was just plain gone.
We were alone. It was silent. The air was pure, clean, fresh, and quiet. The last sign of recent human activity was 50 miles or so back down the road. We were isolated, and 100% alone.

It was as if civilization had ceased to exist; we were the last two humans to be alive, or the first two on a new alien planet. We had no two way radio and of course no cell phones. We had no way of contacting anyone. Our family did not know where we were. We were healthy, and happy in our adventure. We were not at all afraid.

A few authorities knew we would be there at some approximate time. Importantly we had the most comforting thought that we had brought enough extra gasoline to leave. The outside world can easily be forgotten, completely, in such a remote, isolated, and lonely place. We had brought a battery powered radio with us but the longer we stayed the less we bothered with the news and even listening to music decreased over time. The stresses of the outside world evaporated. Our focus became our immediate challenges, the jobs at hand, and enjoyment of each other's company.

In an area heavily treed with spruce trees, the road ends in a clearing with a central pile of gravel almost in the middle. The somewhat circular clearing has dense forest abruptly right to the edge except for the portion that is along the open water shores of Windigo Lake. As one stands in the clearing, the wide and open water draws one's eyes away from the solid wall of trees and into the lake.

Around the clearing's perimeter were some old, abandoned, run down, almost fallen down, trappers' cabins, of a sort that are distinctive because they are made from scavenged material, some barely standing and in a deteriorating state of deserted disrepair. Abandoned years before when the trappers and their families all got sick and died, it would have been a good place for ghosts and spirits to hide but we never heard any such stories. It is just since we were there to establish the icehouse that residents started to come back to Windigo. Walter's work restarted this community giving it a second life.

This quiet location changed quickly because Walter was erecting a building and supplies were flowing in. Float planes started to arrive, trucks arrived, and workers from Weagamow came to work with Walter bringing their families. Soon a place of no activity was becoming active for the first time in years. The end of the road now had occupants and life and was somewhere to arrive.

Not too long after arriving in Windigo, I wrote to my sister Ruby. I knew Ruby was ill before we left Winnipeg. I wanted her to have a letter. A pilot took my last letter to her and mailed it for me. I got word through another plane that Ruby was gravely ill. I arrived at Ruby's side before the letter and it did not arrive in time for her to read it.

I plane hopped out. First, to Weagamow, then to Sioux Lookout, then to Winnipeg, and then finally I arrived in
Edmonton. After the memorial for Ruby, I came back to Winnipeg. I worried about Walter while I was gone because I knew he would be really tired from work, and faced a 15 hour solo drive home. I was stressed. I could not be with both my husband and my dying sister. I felt I was needed in both places and wanted to be in both places. The impossibility of that was stressful and worrisome.

Walter had only stayed in Windigo a week or so after, I left. He worked long 18 hour days, cooked his own food, and managed the crew and bookkeeping. His drive home was a grueling long drive for him. He was worried about me and upset about Ruby. He arrived home played out and needed a few days resting before he could continue. Walter wanted to know the details of my trip and knew I had to be in Edmonton, and was glad I was one of those with her when she died.

Arriving home, I wanted to know details of the Windigo job, and what had happened and about the people in Windigo. Our few days together while Walter recovered allowed me to grieve, and accept the loss of Ruby. It was not really enough time.

The collection of odd pieces of wood, plastic, metal, and canvas stuck together by some means I do not know how, and pictured below, is actually a residence. Used building materials leaned up help to protect the inside from the wind. It is better than nothing but not by much. It looks like it might be part tent, with sheets of plywood, added bits of plastic, and scraps of whatever to finish it. The family lived here while the husband worked for Walter. They had not intended to build a log home and just used whatever they could find to block the wind. The family also had no building materials, nails, hammers, glue, or anything else to build a temporary home. It was a home slapped together with what was handy. I was glad not to have to live in something similar. Later I would visit this home with some cookies but did not go inside. Belongings, perhaps washing, hang high from a fallen tree.

On our way into Windigo, we passed many roadside areas with ripe wild blueberry patches. From the van, we could see the bush was just full of these intense flavored wild berries. Though common berries in the Canadian north, not every area has big blueberry patches, so we stopped and had a good look making a note of the location. Sun ripened wild blueberries pack a much bigger, bolder, and more pleasing flavor punch than the larger versions sold in the stores. Once you have had wild blueberries, the store bought ones always remain kind of a disappointment. It is easy to understand why bears love blueberries. We were excited to think of being able to pick from this area.

On one evening after work when the workers and families had arrived from Weagamow, we all climbed into The Beast for the short trip down the road to pick berries. Men, women, and children about eleven extra people all piled into the van and we went down the road about 5 minutes. Walter drove and took this picture of us. Everyone was so excited to be able to get the berries because they taste so great and are a real treat especially in isolated areas where taste treats are few. We had a great time.

The group was from Weagamow. Looking at their dress and demeanour one can imagine the hardships they faced living in the primitive cabins camping at Windigo for the summer. They were happy because when Walter arrived there was work for the men, money, income, and I know they were happy with the contact from the outside civilization from far away, and the relief from their own isolation. One can see in the picture that the people are dressed for practicality and warmth.

Later on, perhaps a week or so later, just Walter and I picked berries on a return trip into Windigo. The ground was still just covered in berries. Parking on the side of the road we eagerly walked just about 50 feet from the van and picked. We talked a bit certainly, and were not silent in the silence of the wilds. It seemed so peaceful. Sweet smelling air, the silence of the remote bush, and abundant berries made our stop very satisfying and enjoyable. The berry picking was superb and we became completely engrossed in what we were doing. Outside in the fall warmth of the sun we picked alone, so we thought.

On our way out looking at the ground, we were greatly surprised. Our spines tingled as fear and shock went through us pretty fast. We took this picture of the bear tracks in the ditch by the van placing the enamel saucepan close to show the size. We had not heard the bear. We never heard so much as a twig break. The bear had been there near us, but we never heard a sound. Clearly, the bear knew we were there. Had the tracks been there when we got out of the van to pick we would have not stayed. We took the picture got in the van and left. This shows you how close you can be to danger in the north and be unaware of it. We were lucky.

Using a blue Roll Book, I kept track of the hours the men worked. I still have it and it still has the price tag still on it. That makes me laugh at the cost comparison of the items then and now. I see that I paid $3.62, at Wilson Stationary. I recorded the hours the men worked in August, September, and October. The men all worked long hours 8, 9, and 10 hour days, every day. They were for the most part unskilled workers who worked hard for weeks. Walter always worked an hour longer, getting things ready for the team of workers. In October, he worked 11-14 hour days. We would walk from the icehouse to the trailer late at night but it would still be light out because the days were long.

This Windigo adventure was business for Bison Refrigeration and I needed to keep accurate records to forward to the Indian affairs officer Kai Kiakowski. Daily, Walter gave me the number of hours for each man. I entered this number into our records in this blue Roll book. The entries are pictured below. This is all handwritten as there were no personal computers or lap tops.

A family called this shack home. Outside the door is a pile of chopped wood, behind it a garbage pail, beside the door is a bottle of bleach. It is likely the mother chopped the wood and used the bleach on the clothing and floor.

I was only in the doorway of this cabin and I remember it had a wooden floor. She has bedding hanging on a line. The poverty is noted, by not only the rustic setting and cabin, but also in that, the bedding on the line is ripped and torn but still used and cared for. Wealthier people would have better bedding and perhaps a trailer to live in, but certainly not a house as this was a temporary living site.

One day I saw her outside, busy around a fallen tree. I watched. I could not see exactly what she was doing. She appeared to be hanging things on the branches of trees. After a while, I approached and observed more closely. She explained that she had gathered moss from the forest. She would cut and peal the moss from the fallen trees and from clumps on the ground. She was drying it in the branches of the fallen tree. It would be used as diapers for the baby. It was a traditional ecological type of diaper invented from necessity. Our store bought disposable diapers need to be as ecologically sound.

The little boy wearing the red sweater with the white and blue diamond pattern used to follow me around a lot and called me Kokum, the equivalent of grandma. I liked that and was glad to have him around me. One day his mother and I, and some other women, were out picking blueberries when the little guy stepped in a hornet's nest and was badly bitten on the legs. He cried of course. Immediately the women found clay and put that on the bites to reduce the pain by drawing out the stingers. I have had that same treatment and know it works.

For a while Stanley Matawapit the child pictured above, lived with his parents in a tent until they were able to get this log house into condition to live in. You can just barely see the white pointed end of a small tent up close to the log building on the left side of the picture. It is a huge improvement in life style but still rustic. I am glad I had better at the time; still it was not that much better.

While here the first year we stayed in a trailer. Luckily, for us, a Koval Transport truck from Pickle Lake hauled in a construction trailer the same day after we arrived and was part of our contract to go to Windigo. That is what we lived in. It did not leak, kept the wind away, gave us privacy, and was functional. Compared to the cabins we had luxury.

The differences between how the workers and families lived, and in what they lived, compared to our living arrangements, made me think "oh my". The differences were substantial between our rustic work camp trailer with a gas stove, and the workers outside fires, scavenged materials leaned together to form a shelter, and the ancient bug infested huts. Inside they slept on the hard floors while I slept on a bed.

I saw a child, sprawled out sleeping, certainly not on a mattress but perhaps on a coat or blanket remnant. These people knew they were coming to a camp style environment for the summer and prepared as they could. Still how they lived compared to how we lived bothered me, even though we certainly did not live luxuriously. I could cook and bake things in the oven and they could not. I had a washboard along and loaned it to them to wash clothes. I would try to help them out as much as I could. I invited them into the trailer and made tea and we drank from mugs, I gave the kids candy occasionally, and taught the children spelling.

This white trailer was pulled to the edge of the clearing right next to a pile of fallen trees and the dense bush. Gravel was put out the front to cover the ground of dirt and sticks. This was our home for 2 months. Propane tanks sat outside for the stove, but there was no propane heater. Luckily it was summer still mornings and evenings could be cool in this mobile tin shack.

Our wash line was strung between two tall sawhorses. My scrub board, yes, the one I talk about previously, that is down stairs, sits in the red plastic fish tub.The great advantage of life in the bush is there is no stale smog smell of the cities, and the night is quiet. Absolutely no traffic noise affronts the ears, and when the men quit working absolute silence wraps around you like a coat. There were no dogs and animals running around. When the sun was gone, the atmosphere was still and silent.

Bears could have passed through at night but we never saw evidence of them, or deer, skunks, raccoons, or any other animals. They were there but they never came to the clearing. You do not know what animals or how many animals are standing in the bush watching you when you are this isolated. It is not the same as living anywhere else. When the bush and wilderness are your immediate surroundings, they act as a barrier into another wilder world. In the picture below the trailer and civilization confronts the bush and wilderness.

In this remote area, strangers were a curiosity. I did not know the kids were there when I started to take the picture of the pile of stumps and trees next to the trailer. They played in the stumps and wanted to see what I was doing. There were not many things for kids to play with except nature. I was a new and interesting diversion. Though I was interested in their lives, it may be that I was more unusual to them as I was more in their civilization than they were in mine. The kids and younger women would touch my hair, as it was white and unusual for them to see this color. The youngest of the children did not speak English as well as the older kids of school age. It seems certain English was not their first language.

Life at Windigo in 1981 was rugged. There was no running water and no indoor plumbing in the camping shacks for the workers and their families, and no indoor plumbing for Walter and me either. We all used out houses.

Selma Crane, the young mother in the pictures below borrowed my washboard so she could do laundry, outside on a wooden bench using a washtub, and pails of water she carried from the lake. Pails of water are heavy and it was hard work for Selma. With the washboard, washing was easier because it could be done with one hand in the cold water rather than two hands in the cold water rubbing the garments back and forth between her hands. She might have also had to go to the lake to rub the clothing on a rock in the water. Having had to wash family clothes kneeling on rock in the lake when I had young children, I knew this washboard would be a significant aid to her.

A five gallon pail of clean water stands to the bottom right of the picture. She would have carried this about 50 feet from the lake. Carrying water that far, for washing and cooking, is a muscle building exercise, so Selma was not pampered or soft and was accustomed to hard work. Selma's husband worked with Walter, and Selma had hard work to look after the home life of the family. Selma scrubbed the clothes in the wash water using soap and the washboard, then dumped this water out and rinsed the clothing you can see folded and piled in the large pan beside where she works. She did this bending over a bench. There is an orange handled screwdriver under the bench something her kids likely played with. I wonder if it was one from Walter's work site as it is new. Kids may have taken it to play with.

I took this picture below of Selma Crane to show the rugged life at Windigo. She is a strong woman

making as good a life as possible for her family in a time of little wealth. Standing in the doorway soon after they had arrived Selma posed for me at their temporary home in an abandoned trappers shack. There are no neatly cut grass lawns, no sidewalks, nor stores, and no playgrounds. Stuff is scattered around there are no shelves, no cupboards and no storage areas. A tree stump rises from the ground up close to the shack and it looks like the root has been chipped for kindling wood. The ground is covered by branches and wood chips. The old trash remnant of an airtight heater stands outside, but there would be no place to store it either. The stovepipe comes out of the wall framed with scrap wood and a small split branch as the top part of the frame. The split branch did not match the other pieces of lumber but it was used out of necessity. It was likely like that for years.

An axe leans on the old tin heater and the wood logs are lying around. She has been splitting wood something that both men and women do in the north. It seems to me that observing native communities of the north women work very hard, did, and do most of the work. The men hunted, sometimes, but it was the women who utilized the hides, curing them and fabricating things from them, cooked, and had the responsibilities of the children no matter how many children there were in the family.

Michael's hair needed cutting. Selma had either seen the hair clippers I had with me or somehow knew that I cut Walter's hair. She asked if I would cut Michael's hair. She thought he would let me cut his hair because he liked me. She thought wrong. I let Michael hold and examine the clippers first. Then I began to cut his hair. I made a pass on one side of his head and that was the end of his cooperation. He no longer wanted his haircut. He had a big patch of hair missing. To complete the job Selma held his legs and his arms, while I had his head under my left arm. He still put up a fuss but we cut his hair. After the haircut, he was back to his normal self, calling me Kokum.

The plain, unfinished, rustic, inside of the shack was mostly empty. A child sleeps on a mattress on the floor. The walls are unpainted plywood and it might have been insulated, because it has inside walls. This was a more recent building of a winter trapper.

Denim jeans and rubber boots, are common for both adults and children watches Michael dressed warmly and wearing rubber boots. Waterproof rubber boots are popular footwear because they can be put off and on in a hurry, do not need laces, and are well suited to the rugged lives near lakes were the ground was sometimes damp.

Though it was summer, it was not particularly hot and with the breeze from the lake, kids had to be dressed warmly. Even I had a sweater handy when the wind blew. Michael came for a visit and is pictured on the steps into our trailer. He is dressed warmly and cleanly. Selma always tried to keep Michael looking neat and tidy.

At this time in the north, it was against the law to sell yeast to Indians. Stores could stock yeast but kept it out of sight. Vanilla was also not allowed to be open on shelves for sale. It was feared that the Indians/First Nations people would make home brew from the yeast. They had a history of making home brew and this was an attempt to stop that. The vanilla contained alcohol and there were fears it would be consumed straight out of the bottle. When I worked in a corner store in Winnipeg the vanilla was kept out of site, and we were not allowed to sell it to First Nation people. Any other race could buy vanilla and yeast.

I did not agree with the ban on yeast and vanilla. It ticked me off. I think the same now. The government allowed all kinds of bad and useless things to be sold to these Canadian citizens. The yeast stopped some from making alcohol, but the outsider bootlegger, businessmen, made sure that the Indians got the alcohol by selling it to them, and if necessary delivering it, skirting whatever regulations could be put in place. Bootleggers did not care about the related consequences of alcohol, and they readily made a lot of money selling alcohol to Indians. At the same time, the natives could also buy all kinds of sugary, junk food, and cigarettes, but were prohibited from making basic, simple bread. Was it a good law? The intent may have been good in that it wanted to prevent alcoholism, but it was a law that did not work and discriminated. It seems it was a law invented without much thought, and without concern for equality. It was a bad law.

One day a native not working with Walter showed up badly drunk wandering in from the road. I do not know how he got there. In his intoxicated state, he was an unwelcomed guest. The men locked him in a shack until he sobered up, and then somehow chased him away. I do not know how he left. Perhaps he left by boat. These people were making a statement. They were here to work and did not want alcohol present, interfering, and ruining lives.

I took yeast to Windigo because I made bread and buns. I could get it because I was not legally discriminated against. The smell of baking bread would go everywhere when I cooked. I would share the buns with the other families. I made a lot and gave it away.

The women at Windigo had never made bread because of course they could not get yeast and few knew how to make a bread starter. At Windigo, I taught the women how to make bread using our propane stove oven. They were all so pleased at being able to accomplish this. I was happy to be able to teach them. It was a pleasure and in taking this picture, I was happy too. We were a happy group of friends. I cannot now remember if we used all the yeast baking bread. If I had any, I was prohibited from giving any to my friends. I suspect we used up all the yeast. They could no longer make bread when I left.

Walter was there to erect a metal building for the diesel engines, and ice machines, and to build a dock. Walter would be back and forth between the two projects, directing, and showing people what to do next. I knew generally his plans, but was not part of the work. I took pictures to document the work. Mooring was needed for boats bringing fish, and for the airplanes taking the fish away. Trees were cut down and hauled to the lakeside. A cribbing was made and filled with rock. The rock kept the cribbing

in place on the floor of the lake and made a firm foundation. The finished Y shape permits more than one plane or boat to be tied into place and allows boats and planes to be tied up to limit wind interference. Along the left side is a white colored water line that ends in a corrugated round container at the point of the Y shape. From this container, clear water was taken for the ice machines. Now walking on the dock could be included in a leisure walk and people were happy.

Employing locals, a rare but pleasant opportunity, Walter built the metal building for the diesel engines and ice machines. After making a wooden frame, he made and poured cement for the floor. A few men, using 2x4 pried the diesel engine into place before starting the construction of the building. Power lines did not run to Windigo. The diesel engine would generate the electricity required. The metal sheeting for the outside was laid out on the ground with 2x4's placed on them to stop the sheeting from taking flight in the wind and flying into the lake or bush. The metal screws and bolts for the building had to be hidden from the local kids who found they were perfect ammunition for slingshots. The cost of the metal building was $13,000 but the band paid no tax. Making sure the screws and bolts were not lost became important because it would be a big effort to get more. The delay would be costly, so care was taken to protect the supply of bolts and screws.

The shot here shows the diesel fuel container sitting outside the unfinished engine room and that the cement flooring extends beyond the building. The diesel sits in place.

What happened to the gravel pile in the middle of the desolate clearing? It became part of the cement base for the building in a now active location.

The picture below shows the view greeting an airplane passenger arriving at Windigo. It looks fresh and new. Inside the airplane, the view and smell would have been entirely less pleasant. That view would have been of fresh fish in ice. The fish would have been picked up from elsewhere perhaps other lakes perhaps also from elsewhere on Windigo Lake, and brought to this plant and in through one of these doors.

The stack of red plastic tubs were used for fresh caught fish and ice. The fish seen below have been gutted, beheaded, and then packed in the tubs. Loaded on a dolly they are ready for the trip up the dock to the icehouse. No processing occurred here. The fish would be taken by truck elsewhere for processing. The fish in the red buckets appear to be both pickerel and trout both are very delicious. The fishermen would gut and head, the fish in their boats throwing the guts and heads back into the water.

The first load of fish going into the icehouse at Windigo Lake 1981 is pictured below. Eight boxes of about 75 – 100 pounds each are stacked on a dolly and two men are hauling them in, as Walter, in the white hard hat, watches the action. Note this is a community project. There is a child up close watching the action, something that would not happen in a large city or town.

Through the door in the first room, the fish were iced. The ice machines were placed on the upper floor. Fresh ice would be made and fall into a bin below. Snow shovels were used to distribute the ice in boxes and onto the fish. Once covered in ice the fish were stored and then transferred to a semitrailer and taken away for processing to Transcona, a suburb of Winnipeg. Processing in this case would mean filleting or steaking, scaling, boxing and freezing.

It was with great satisfaction we watched the first airplane arrive, and then as the first load of fish were dressed with ice from the newly installed new ice machines, and finally loaded into the back of this truck. A few weeks earlier, this had been only isolated, and lonely, crude, empty, deserted, clearing, and now it was a working facility.

The second year in Windigo Lake, the summer of 1982, our living arrangements were not quite as nice as the trailer we had the first year, and certainly not as bear resistant. Our quarters were more similar to the primitive homes of the workers. This year we lived in a shack tent, a hybrid structure that was part shack and part tent. The floor and part of the walls were wood like a cabin. A wood frame shaped the

roof but the roof is a canvas tent. That means it is less drafty than a tent and it is warmer than a tent, and there is a door rather than a tent flap.
Compared to a trailer a shack tent is primitive, but better than a tent on the ground, or living in the

back of the van though the van was better protection from bears. Certainly, it is better than the moldy dirty old abandoned shacks the workers used. The shack tent gave us a wonderful lakeside view and close proximity to pristine nature in a lovely setting. Vacationers pay big bucks for such an experience, and if I could have it again for a day, and only a day, I would enjoy it.

Ours was similar to but better than the flooded tent shacks seen in Alaska from YutBiat. Viewed looking towards the lake it is more picturesque than the reverse view from the lake inland because the back ground is more industrial with an array of uneven dirt, gravel, and equipment of all sorts.

In the one room shack tent, there was: no electricity, no fridge, no stove, no running water, no sink, no bathroom, no mirror, no radio, no windows, but Walter made us a plywood bed that we covered with foam. The foam made the hard
bed acceptable but not wonderfully comfortable. I tried to make certain when possible that we had nice fresh white sheets even in the roughest conditions. It was a way to remain civilized even in the frontier. We were nice and warm because we had the comforter and Walter's sleeping bag. It was peaceful and quiet at night. We were together and happy.

I propped the book I was reading so that the title could be seen and snapped a shot. I was reading the book Bush Trails. It was a story Walter and I could easily relate to as it was set in Canada's North. Gone were the luxuries of a simple kitchen we had in the trailer of the previous year. We had neither. I cooked on the airtight heater. These are heaters rather than stoves, and are not at all, designed for cooking. The top of the airtight heater is not level. The round lid is in the middle and sits above the rest of the top by about an inch. The top surface is not large and pots and pans are never too safe.

Airtight heaters heat up quickly. There is very little opportunity to regulate their heat and there are no cold spots. When the heater is hot, the whole thing is hot, including the top and the sides. Cooking with an airtight heater one does not always stand too close to it for too long, as your legs can burn. A small vent on the side near the bottom can regulate the amount of air on the fire and control the flame a bit, so that the whole thing is either hot or extremely hot. There is no chance to move things to the side, as there are no warm or cool spots on an airtight heater unless the whole thing is cold and not in use.

Our food was carried in with us in the van. I used a small fire and cooked basic things and mostly in a frying pan. We ate the likes of canned ham, Klick or Spam, bologna, wieners, fried potatoes, and using a small pot a few boiled vegetables such as, carrots, canned corn. Walter wanted anything that was food and there had to be some kind of meat. A lunch meal might be fried Klick and potatoes, and supper may have been bologna fried with boiled carrots and maybe corn. This was not the healthiest diet but it was necessary and temporary.

Walter made a small counter on which to keep a few supplies and the water bucket. We were the first to use the shack tent so it was still nice and clean. Rounds of logs served as chairs, night table, and doorstop. We kept the door open a lot, because it could get stuffy with the sun beating down and the canvas top emitted a smell in the heat. We had a rather friendly squirrel that would visit regularly through the open door.

I had been sitting on the edge of the bed when the squirrel came in, crumpled up the towel I had spread over the raw unpainted wood counter. I had to keep an eye on him so that he did no damage. There is the temptation to try to make squirrels and such into pets, but one has to watch them carefully as they are not predictable and take alarm easily and can bite.

In the back corner of the counter is the five-gallon water pail covered with a T-towel. This was nice fresh water from the spring down the road. You can also see the shack tent was not insulated and the door was a sheet of plywood with a hinge. This squirrel became interested in the belongings of a guest.

One of the nicest fellows we met on our travels was Kai Kiakowski. Kai had numerous stories to tell of his life in the north even though he was not all that old. He was the fisheries representative, or worked for Indian Affairs or a similar government body, in the area of Windigo.

He was a real nice and personable guy, but a terrible shot. I took this picture so I remember the process it took to get this bird. He and I were travelling out of Windigo on our way to Pickle Lake, in a truck owned perhaps by the fisheries department. The truck was known to be difficult to start and to sputter. After the truck engine was started one had to be concerned about keeping the engine going and not letting it stop because it might very well not start again for a time. Kai was driving. All of a sudden, he spotted a prairie chicken along the side of the road. To him that meant chicken dinner. He stopped the truck in the middle of the road. The motor immediately stopped. Instantly one wonders, if the truck will it start again, and are we stranded here in the middle of nowhere. The bird was only a few feet away. Kia grabbed a 22 rifle and shot at the bird. He missed. Twice. He scared the bird away. His chicken dinner flew to sit in a tall tree.

Kai got back in the truck, which luckily, and happily, started. Kia drove down the road a few yards, and aimed at the bird sitting up high in the tree. This time he shot it and threw it in the back of the truck to take home. We both laughed that it took him three shots at such a close distance. We were also amazed the truck started easily. At Pickle Lake, I caught a plane and left for Winnipeg and I guess Kai had prairie chicken for supper.

One day Kai came to Windigo around lunchtime, and had lunch with us. Into the shack tent, he brought his backpack that contained his lunch. On this day, the friendly squirrel came inside, looked around, and started to worry the knapsack. I was concerned the squirrel would damage the knapsack.

At the red arrow the inquisitive squirrel sits on Kai's knapsack intent on getting inside. He was after Kai's lunch perhaps. I wonder if the squirrel would have been so eager eat Kai's lunch had he realized that Kai's lunch was to be a distant relative of the squirrel, a cooked rat. Soon after I took the picture, I had to chase the squirrel away. In the back, a lidded frying pan sits on the airtight heater where I was to make lunch. The heater sits on a sheet of tin placed to catch sparks.

Kai had a great sense of humor and apparently so did his wife, Moira who had good job and was perhaps a nurse. They owned a truck that had a few challenges and unworkable parts. The windshield wipers were one feature that did not work. As a joke, Kai tied a rope to each blade in a loop, so that the passenger could pull alternately the wipers back and forth across the windshield. One day they drove through Sioux Lookout and purposely passed the hotel where they knew would be seen by people perhaps friends and neighbors. He drove the truck and encouraged Moira to pull the rope saying "pull Moira, pull". He only did it for a laugh. We never met Moira but I would like to meet her, as she must be as wonderful a person as Kai.

The families working at the plant were not well off. They were a long way from home living in a northern bush camp. Their home Weagamow was not accessible by road but still there were stores and a post office in the town. This community of workers was isolated. There was no road to it them home to Weagamow where they had homes and clothing. If they had extra clothing, it would not amount to much, perhaps an extra pair of pants, or coat, but not closets full as people in less isolated areas are accustomed to having. There were three adult women, their husbands, and several single men. Indian Affairs brought them to Windigo by air. That they needed more clothing was obvious.

Living in a remote area like this, away from every service, people could not easily go shopping for clothing even if they had the money to spend, and most of these people did not have money to spend.

In the first season at Windigo during a trip out to Winnipeg, I talked to my good friends and our neighbors about the need for clothing. Fanny Schniderman was our neighbor on one side. Fanny and her daughters Sandy Collerman, and Mickey Schniderman, got to work and got in touch with all their friends and collected 12 large plastic garbage bags crammed full of clothing. A mix of children's and women's clothing was collected in perhaps a week. The picture below shows Michael, Darren, Corrine, and Dennis standing outside the trailer in some new clothing. They were happy to have the picture taken in their new clothing.

I piled the garbage bags into The Beast on top of Walter's tools. We could barely see out of the back window as we drove down the road. The noise of the van subdued by the bags of clothing. The return trip took two days of driving and we overnighted in Pickle Lake. I wondered how I would distribute the clothing. I cannot recall exactly how I told the women to come check out the clothing, but I did, and the three of them arrived together.

I did not worry about setting up a display. I poured a bag or two onto the tables inside our trailer. The women were excited to get the clothing. The excitement of the scene was like that of a rummage sale. The women held up clothing to see sizes. They evaluated if someone in their family could wear it and passed them on with recommendations to one of the other two with a recommendation saying this should fit so and so. Articles of clothing went flying through the air from woman to woman. As soon as the pile of clothing decreased, I would put more on the tables emptying more bags. Soon all twelve bags were sorted through, divided up, and had new owners. It was a complete pleasure to be involved. The women were kind to each other thinking of their own and the others children. It made the effort worthwhile. Below the kids pose in their new clothing.

Georgina, her daughter Sheila and son Stanley Matawapt show their new clothing. It was like a fashion show and they all looked good in the new clothing. I took the picture inside their temporary shack house. After we left the second year, Sheila wrote asking if were to come back again and if we did, could we bring more clothing. Unfortunately, this letter is lost and regrettably, we did not go back again. Had we gone back for sure I would have taken more clothing with me. Nice clothing was difficult to get in remote areas. These great people were appreciative. I wish I had gone back again with more clothing for my friends.

In our travels, we visited a few places where I would not take clothing. In these places, the chiefs had nice big cars. Clothing and garbage were littered everywhere and people just drove over it all walked through or around it. There are some unhealthy places with frustrated people, but the people in Windigo were special, and I like, and miss them.

Windigo is no longer so isolated. It has grown and become a community. This area of the world is beautiful. It is a combination of rocks, slim trees, lakes, and wild animals. Much of the area is like the picture above where Walter is on a rock at water's edge, fishing.

On the drive into Windigo, we wanted to stop for water. Walter sampled some water and said it was not bad but I would not drink swamp water. Beaver Fever, an intestinal disorder could be had from drinking swamp water where the water is full of bugs. A few miles down the road, we came to a clearing with a few dead trees and lush under growth.

Near a culvert in the road we stopped. Although from a distance it did not look like there was a creek, it turned out that there was a lovely creek almost hiding from view. There was an active spring with beautiful clear water much nicer than the chemical blend we have in big cities like Surrey. Such pure water is something many people do not get to experience even in bottled water. These days, one has to travel away from urban areas to experience such water.

Deceivingly the creek looked as if it were perhaps a few inches deep. In fact, it was very deep and very clear. Walter could dip our 5-gallon pail easily into the water without touching the sandy bottom. We drank our fill using the basin I had bought earlier and still use to make Christmas cake. This December 2016, I used to mix the fruit, flour, and eggs for this year's cake, which will be slightly different from years previously as I sort of followed two differing recipes. It is a well travelled and well used basin.

For the first few days, we would come back to this site to get fresh spring water. We learned the spring was named Koval Springs after Alex Koval of Koval Transport fell into the spring when he would have learned of its deceiving depth. The water was beautifully fresh and very clear and worth the short drive to get away from the work site and to see something else.

Along this same road, closer to Pickle Lake is a small sawmill. This is a small perhaps single operator, sawmill. The standing timber in the area is mixed and not all has the girth necessary for a larger sawmill. Most of it is stunted bush. The mill would not be a constantly busy operation.

If we had to get supplies, such as food parts, building supplies, we would try to leave Windigo Lake early in the morning before sun up. This would allow us to get to town, shop, and get back to camp before it was too late in the evening. Evening travel would be in the dark, we would arrive in the dark and have to unload in the light of the headlights, and that made things cumbersome.

We always stopped to eat selecting what we could not have at the camp. It was a long trip. In Sioux Lookout, we stayed in this hotel, the same one Kai and Moira drove by in the rain pulling the rope tied to the windshield wipers.

On a trip into Windigo Lake in 1984, we stopped and Walter installed an air conditioner at the Four Winds Motel, in Savant Lake, Ontario. The picture below shows five men pulling the air conditioner up to the roof. They had used a rope and the ladders, as a guide to slide the unit up as they pulled. This was a job where I had nothing to do but wait, take pictures, make up the bill, and walk around town. Strangely, though we spent overnight in the hotel I never met or talked to anyone. This was an uncomplicated call but Walter did a few jobs for this place, fixing air conditioners in the bar, and dining room and ice machines etc. The final bill July 31, 1984, was $6,105.71

When our time came to leave Windigo and the area, we were glad to return to Winnipeg. The pleasures of civilized society a warm house and indoor plumbing greeted us. Those we left behind did not have the same awaiting them. They remained until the summer was over. Sometimes during our heavy summer busy season, we had a few days to recover before we left again to work elsewhere and make more friends. Other times we got a good night's sleep and were off again the next day.

Our trips with Bison Refrigeration were, on the whole, a very positive life experience. We travelled in Manitoba, Saskatchewan, and Ontario. We met many good people and only a few rascals. Nearly everyone we met became friends. Some had a lot of money, but you would not know it because they did not flaunt it. Others had almost no money, and that was obvious. Of course, our arrivals were for the most part anticipated with happiness. Always our presence was associated with some positive change Walter's talent was able to make to their lives. Not everyone could do the work, and of those that could do the work it was would be hard to find those who liked the adventure as we did.

Walter had a very diplomatic way of dealing with customers and people in general. One could say his public relations skills were front and center in his business dealings. He was a fair man. Walter always wanted to treat people fairly and equally and wanted to be treated fairly. He truly liked his work and the people he met. It showed. He made friends easily wherever he went. I was always confident that people would like him and we shared the same attitude. We greeted new people with the pleasure of making new friends at work.

Living conditions of the people we met varied greatly. Some lived in the woods, or close to the woods in shacks, barely surviving. Other people had the conveniences of heat and electricity as enjoyed by people in the closest big cities of Winnipeg, Regina, and Saskatoon.

Many times the frontier isolation was peaceful, but we always had the chance to come back to civilization and comfort. The people we met only rarely saw the hectic pace of places where multitudes lived. Isolated people accepted their lives that are not as comfortable and easy as are those in urban areas. For some it was a choice between living in poverty and remoteness or poverty in a city. The desire for peace and quiet led them to remoteness. Others had no choice. Still others did not even know they might have had a choice of where to live.

Do isolation and poverty build good character? I do not believe either are requirements for good character.

Are the people we met in these remote areas different from city folk? Yes of course.

Every experience shapes a person. The people we met travelling were different from the city people I live with now, because the northerners existed on the very edge. It is an edge where the frontier meets civilization. Daily they experienced a bit of both in their worlds. That makes them different. In many cases, their lives have not modernized at the rate of the rest of Canada. Not all locations were the same. Whether or not they lived without indoor running water, and bathrooms, electricity, central heating, proper flooring, and proper clothing depended upon where they lived. I am not convinced that doing without modern conveniences, and being poor makes you a better or worse person. It just makes life more difficult and gives you the opportunity to appreciate what you have. In remote areas, people can appreciate silence and quiet, where in comparison in the city, we are assaulted by noise all day long. Food is not as available in remote areas so finding it is sometimes more a personal joy, perhaps making the tranquility of berry picking more appreciated than the pleasures of finding food wrapped in a store.

I do not think poverty improves or worsens a person's character. Both rich and poor can be disagreeable. I am not sure but I think some of the crankiest people I have met are the richest. Poverty makes surviving more difficult and less comfortable.

Having experienced life in the North, I can say that I am glad I live where I do, and that I have become comfortable in the city. For myself, I can say that the isolation and frontier life has allowed me to appreciate better what comforts I have.

When Walter and I moved west to retire in Vancouver we knew our lives were changing and we would have to adapt. We did not regret leaving. We did not regret the life change. We did regret leaving our friends but we wanted to be near our sons, so we bit the bullet, and left. We knew our time together had changed us bringing us closer together to appreciate each other more than before. We would never be able to look at the comforts of the city without appreciating them. We would always know what life is like without them. We would always meet new people with the notion that we were just becoming friends.

We looked forward to a new life styles and new adventures. We were glad of our time working together, and we were ready together, to tackle a new period of our lives. I have to say, I wish we had started this book together earlier.

Winnipeg To Vancouver: Travels Of A New Kind

Since the time after we left Chilliwack when Walter was stationed there in the army, he and I had talked of moving back to BC. We liked the climate and beauty of the area. At the end of the war, we considered it but his parents were too demanding that he come back to Saskatchewan. Now as I look back it seems foolish to have listened to them and we would never have thought to be so interfering with our own sons. Things were different in those days. Had I the self confidence then, that I earned a few years later, I would have spoken up stronger. We would not go back to the isolation of the west and farming that neither of us liked. The circumstances eventually proved that we were not suited for such a life. Eventually we made a return to BC. We were both glad we finally made it back.

Walter was upset about Lyle leaving for BC because Walter had spent a lot of time away when the boys were growing up. Walter had hoped to be able to spend more time with Lyle. At the time, Walter and I thought that it was good for Lyle's future if he wanted to go and get a better job. We knew we would miss Lyle and we did. It was a hard separation. The time for the first of our sons to go quite far away seemed to come far too fast.

I was not in tears every time Lyle called, but Walter was teary. Lyle would call. Walter would talk to him for a few minutes and then hand me the phone. Walter would disappear into the bedroom for a half hour or so emerging after an emotional time. I worried about Lyle having enough money to travel. I hoped and worried that he would soon he would get work in BC. Shortly after arriving in Vancouver, Lyle had a job at Finning Tractor. Lyle was proving my worries unfounded.

About 4 months later David left Winnipeg for Vancouver. He and Lyle had discussed Vancouver and BC. Lyle was positive about the greater opportunities to be had on the west coast. David soon got a job in Vancouver. Meanwhile Sharon and Darcy stayed with us for a month before they flew to Vancouver. We missed David and his family too but we knew David had to leave Winnipeg to get work. When David phoned, Walter would again talk for a bit, then hand the phone to me, and disappear.

This left only Walter and I, and Glenn at home. I was working in a store with owner and good friend Leona Slotek. This small grocery store was close to the house and sold almost everything, sliced meat, cheese, milk canned goods, candy, cigarettes, paper towels and high on the top shelf toilet paper that I helped stack.

One fall day when I was not working, I sent Glenn then 18 or19 over to the store. He only had to walk four houses down the back lane and across the street to get there just far enough it seems for him to perhaps, become shy, or maybe embarrassed about buying toilet paper. He went in looked around and whether or not he saw it I do not know, but he came back empty handed and told me there was none and would not go back. I knew there was some and let him off the hook thinking it was better not to force him. Even years later he had to think about whether or not he saw any and the answer is he does not know. Raising 3 different boys there were different reactions. David and Lyle would not have gone in and made the purchase. As a young boy, David was far more talkative at a young age, learned to walk late, and was later delighted to get his hands greasy with tools. Lyle walked at 8 months much earlier than David walked. Lyle was more active, always walked very erect, did not like to get his hands dirty, and was a bit of neat freak. Glenn on the other hand was very shy until he was well into his teens.

When Walter and I worked in Alaska during the summer, I worked with Leona in the winter. Then Leona and her husband Nick sold the store and she moved to Thunder Bay. We were renting a house with and the address digits of the sign of the devil, 666 Cathedral Avenue. It was owned by the family of Lyle's former girlfriend Carla. Lyle and Carla were no longer a couple. The owners said they had family members wanting to live in the house and would like us to move. In a year of so the house was sold.

I began to look for places to purchase. I took Glenn along to look at one of the first houses. It was not far away and rented. This was not such a good experience. The house was rented to an elderly couple and was too small for our needs. The elderly lady inside was very upset that the house was being inspected. She was in tears and shaking. We felt as if her home were being taken away and that by looking we were part of the process that was upsetting her. We did not want to hurt her. We left quickly and made sure the agent knew and told her that we were not buying the home. We found a different place. We were under pressure to get the place and move in, as we had to be out of the house with the sign of the devil, and into a different place immediately as we had work elsewhere.

We moved to our own house about 15 minutes away. We purchased 161 Smithfield Avenue in West Kildonan. It had a better kitchen, a bigger living room, was a bigger house all round, and was right across the street from the Anglican Church St Martin's In the Field. In front of this house we stand with my brother Willie's wife Dorothy Fitzpatrick who was now remarried and a widow again. Her son Eldon took the picture.

We had terrific neighbors. Fanny Schniederman and her daughter Mickey lived on the West side and Jim and Dorothy Clark lived on the East Side. In the evenings, the neighbors would come from both sides to play games and Walter would make lunch of tea and cookies. We became close friends as well as neighbors.

In the above picture from a Christmas dinner in our basement. It did not matter that some followed the Jewish Religion and some Christian. We were respectful and fond of each other. We used our basement and in the back ground is my wringer washing machine. It eventually went to Denbeigh Point to the Bilenduke's as part of a big load of stuff. We had purchased a clothes dryer but I used this wringer machine. A more modern machine did not seem necessary at the time. I was not used to always having the best machines and was glad having a working machine I knew how to use.

Fanny's grandson Ari always had a big personality. We had many a good laugh over this lovable outspoken young man. He got a bull terrier dog, and took it over to show his other grandmother, Mrs Collerman, who made the error of speaking her mind and said the dog reminded her of a pig. Ari, about 6 years old was angered. Ari would not talk to his grandmother for a few months. When he came to show me the dog Fanny forewarned me, and like her, I never said what I thought of the dog, but said what a nice dog it seemed. I never said I thought his grandmother was right about the dog. He continued to talk to both Fanny and me.

Fanny's son in law was Howard Collerman, Ari's father. When his father died, his mother wanted to sell the house. Eldon was looking for a house at the time. Being the one that knew both of them I informed both sides and they made a deal right away. Both were happy.

By this time, Glenn had already moved to BC leaving us all alone in Winnipeg. We were lonely without our boys. Walter was still working on out of town jobs. Walter was finding it more and more difficult to do the out of town work. I began to suspect something was wrong with him because he would be so played out after a job. We began to slow things down and finally made the decision to move to BC in the summer of 1986. We spent a month in Vancouver and Walter made an ice crushing machine to be used to get bagged ice from a glacier.

The next year 1987, we moved to BC. We had bought the house in Winnipeg for less than we sold it for and made a bit of money. We drove from Winnipeg to Denbeigh Point, in May, and Walter did a job for a few days. From there we went to Saskatoon, and then Edmonton, and finally to Vancouver. I drove the car and Walter followed in the van. We kept our eye on each other all the way out. Lyle and Gwen met us in Chase and now we were three in procession with Lyle leading. We stayed with Lyle and Gwen when we first arrived in Vancouver, and eventually found the house on 104 Avenue.

Our furniture was all shipped to Polar Industries and we were in our own place Saturday, July 17, 1987. We were glad to be settling into our own place and to feel at home. On the Monday, I drove down the road and got a speeding ticket. It was the first one ever and only one so far. I was so ticked off with the officer because I did not see the sign and said to the office something like, "you would give your own mother a ticket wouldn't you", and he said his mother would not speed. He made an error with the ticket and had to go back to his car. When he returned, he said something like he had made an error and I said, "Don't we all". I would have liked to give him a ticket for his error. I drove for 42 years without a ticket.

When we bought the house on 104 Avenue because it was central to David and Glenn in Burnaby, Lyle in Surrey, and Polar Industries in Coquitlam, not too far from the hospital, close to a church, on a bus route, had a basement we could use to have family meals, was on a corner and easy to find, we liked the layout and Walter thought it was well built. At the time, it had a very plain yard with yellow dead grass and no flowers and empty window boxes. It was our intention to change that after we bought it.

We set to work to make the yard more attractive. While at 161 Smithfield in Winnipeg, we did not have many places to have flowers other than along the side of the house and in a small window box at the

front. This house was different. We had the location and the time to change things. Walter immediately dug up the soil for a flower garden and planted roses.

Glenn was staying here in the house studying and we were travelling. The workers on the roof asked what kind of tree was growing in the front yard. The men were talking about this spectacular sunflower. They found it hard to believe it was a sunflower so large. I do not know where the seed came from for the sunflower below. It was a huge plant well over 10ft and had over 75 blooms.

Once we moved to Surrey, we had numerous visitors. Family and friends came to stay. We were glad to have the room for them to stay with us. The visitors were always a pleasure. In between visitors from 1987 to 1992, Walter and I had a lot of fun driving into the Fraser Valley and exploring around. We drove to family events like my Brother Syd and Betty's 50th wedding anniversary. We drove back to Winnipeg weddings and to visit. It was nice to be able to see our old house. It was nice to visit with our dear friends that we missed, Jim and Dorothy Clark, Fanny and Micky Schniderman, the Collerman family, but we were glad to have moved to BC to be with our family.

Our trip to Syd and his wife Betty's 50th wedding anniversary in Pierceland was a time when luck was on our side. The anniversary was held in the community hall. It was a big affair and a lot of fun, held August 1, 1987. We drove through Edmonton. Thinking it was such a nice day we would stop and visit friends Syd and Gladys Wygle. I was driving. I fortunately missed the entrance to the motor home park. We turned around and had second thoughts about stopping for a visit as we felt we were a bit late. It turned out they were not home so we would not have been able to visit. We drove on to Pierceland. As we drove by the edge of Smoky Lake, we noticed people running to take things in from clothes racks and put things away in a hurry. We wondered about this but had no ready answer.

When we arrived in Pierceland, an excited Syd and Betty greeted us. They had spent the day wondering and worrying about our arrival. It turns out we were driving and narrowly avoiding a tornado. They were concerned and wondering if the big tornado would strike Pierceland 4 hours from Edmonton. Had we stopped to visit the Wygles we would have had a parked our car beside their home. The tornado hit that very trailer park hard. The home next to the Wiggles' was destroyed and had we stayed perhaps our car too. Over 20 people in Edmonton were killed in the storm and most of these were in the mobile home park that we did not stop to visit. It seemed we were lucky to have left as soon as we did.

At the wedding anniversary, we got our picture in the paper with the write up about Syd and Betty, though they called us just friends. I was pleased the article said I had been the bridesmaid and listed all their family. Fifty years earlier I wasn't interested in wearing a long dress because I thought they were sloppy, but really how many had I seen at that age and in that town? The answer is few. At the anniversary, I bought my own dress, and no, it was not a long one. Now I think long dresses are all right in the right place, and if I had to wear one I would now too and I might be glad it would cover up my not so stylish shoes that I now have to wear for my sore feet. I was never in a financial position to be too aware of the latest styles. I had to wear what was affordable and many times that was second hand clothes.

24 Tuesday, August 25, 1987 The Grand Centre-Cold Lake Sun

Taking their wedding vows seriously...

A Pierceland couple celebrated their 50th anniversary earlier this month

On Saturday, August 1, 1987, Mr. and Mrs. Sydney Baker celebrated their 50th Wedding Anniversary.

Present were their children Robert Baker and wife Joan of Saskatoon, Saskatchewan, Ronald Baker and wife Mathilda of Beacon Hill, Saskatchewan, Rita Dorner and husband Fred of Leipzig, Saskatchewan, Raymond Baker and wife Nadene of Fort McMurray, Alberta, Roger Baker and wife Irene of Whitecourt, Alberta, Roseanne Abele and husband Randy of Edmonton, Alberta, Ruth Lebedoff and husband Glen of Saskatoon, Saskatchewan.

Also present was the bridesmaid of 50 years ago, Sarah Sergius and all 22 grandchildren and 10 great grandchildren. Many friends and relatives attended. Also present was Betty's cousin Dave Rice and wife Esther of England.

Syd and Betty arrived at the celebration in a 1928 Dodge Coupe car driven by Ruth Lebedoff.

The master of ceremonies was Robert Baker and the toast to the couple was by Roger Baker. Gary Baker did the interviewing for the video tape and Glen Lebedoff did the taping.

Dale and Brenda Read, Sarah and Walter Sergius and David Corney sang some lovely songs.

David and Dorothy Corney composed a beautiful song for Syd and Betty, "Ode to Syd and Betty Baker". It was sung by David Corney accompanied by his guitar.

Grace was said by the Rev. Isaac Sawatzky and a delicious anniversary supper was held at the community hall in Pierceland. A beautiful anniversary wedding cake decorated by Shirley Grandner centered the head table.

Many beautiful cards, gifts and congratulatory messages were received by the Bakers.

Syd and Betty Baker were married August 22, 1937 at the McEvay farm in Pierceland by Rev. Deering.

Flanked by their friends, Mr. and Mrs. Sydney Baker pose for photo.

In 1989, Syd Baker unveiled this cairn to the memory of those who attended the Winnifred School that I attended. He was the only living student from the first class of 1914. Counting Syd and I, there were about 20-25 students from the school at the event. The cairn is in the schoolyard, but the school is now gone having been torn down. In the picture below I am on the left with my husband Walter, Syd age 86 and Betty Baker are on the right.

We made frequent trips back to Saskatchewan and Alberta for funerals in 1990. Trips for funerals became so frequent I finally never wanted to go to Edmonton again because when we did it was because someone was sick or had died. On our way back from my brother's Syd's funeral in 1990, we stopped to see Walter's youngest brother August. He was working on a field of our old farm driving a huge tractor with wheels as tall or taller than August with the front wheels being smaller. I do not remember the name of the tractor

but I remember it being big. It was a powerful and dangerous machine. We were there not more than half an hour and left for home. It was the last time we saw August alive.

In 1990 some of the roads along highway 5 were flooding. We were stopped by a train wreck on the road and had to spend two days in Revelstoke. It was another stroke of good fortune. Had we not been stopped we could have been at the wrong place at the right time. The odd thing about this visit to Revelstoke is that we had not intended to make it and luck was on our side. Upon leaving Revelstoke initially, Walter realized he had forgotten to put in his glaucoma preventing eye drops. We pulled over and waited a few minutes for his eyes adjust to the drops, and then started to drive again. Within that time, a truck passed us sitting on the edge of the road.

A short time later, perhaps 10 minutes, we started to drive down the road again. In a few minutes, the same truck that we noticed had passed us as we were stopped came towards us, flagged us down, and told us to go no further. There had just been a train wreck blocking the road. We felt lucky and had an edgy feeling wondering what our fate would have been if Walter had not needed to stop. Could we have been in the wreck? We were glad it was not meant to happen. Later when the road was being cleared, we took these pictures.

Staying two days in Revelstoke gave us the opportunity to look around the town. Interestingly we got to see a dam on the Columbia River, and were there at the right time to see them open the flood way and the first water of the day come gushing out.

It is a thrilling event and an amazing site. It makes a loud low noise and blasts out with great force and speed. Just downstream from the dam was a bear on a small green island. When the water was released from the dam, he was stranded. The water rose. His island got smaller. It was disappearing quite quickly. We wondered if the bear would drown, but he easily managed to swim easily to shore. So, that tells you that bear,s even small ones, are well muscled animals deserving respect.

We were back home from this trip only about an hour, and eating supper at Lyle and Gwen's, telling them of the dam and train wreck, when Walter's brother-in-law Peter Ternowski called to talk to Walter. His news was not good. Walter learned that his brother August had been killed.

August and Gabby had been doing something on the big tractor. Gabby was in the driver's seat. Like all farmer's wives she had spent hours driving a tractor. Farmwomen on the prairies are as skilled at driving tractor, as are men. August was standing beside the tractor but in front of the huge tractor wheels. I know there are parts in that area of such machines that sometimes needs to be adjusted. It is a location a few inches from the wheels. Something happened. This big tractor with the large wheels lurched forward. I do not know why but it happened. By the time, Gabby got her wits about her and got the tractor in reverse, it was too late. August was crushed perhaps twice.

Farm accidents like this, when the huge tractor wheels run over a farmer, are not unheard of, and always tragic. To be run over by the tractor wheels twice in an accident happens sometimes on farms. It is very tragic. How these things happen, no one knows, as the tension of the time blurs the event.

We did not finish our meals at Lyle and Gwen's. We rushed home to unpack, wash shower and repack and have a few hours of sleep in order to return to Golden Ridge and Pierceland. We were both upset and stressed. We left the next morning at 5AM. We drove all the way to Smokey Lake, Alberta, just north of Edmonton switching drivers and eating on the way, stopping only for gas and washroom breaks. It just did not feel real to either of us. It was real though. To lose two brothers in a short time was awful. We stayed with my sister in law Betty Baker, in Pierceland, as it is only about 25 miles away from Golden Ridge. The funeral was in Goodsoil and held in the Roman Catholic Church about three weeks after we had said goodbye to my brother Syd a few miles away. Syd was 86 and August 63.

Gaby, August's widow stayed on the farm, but I heard she was not used to managing the farm. She stayed on the farm for some time and then moved to Edmonton and remarried. Who could blame her for wanting to move to where she was less isolated. She never seemed to regret moving to the city and it is a feeling she shared with me when we talked when I again saw her a year later at our own celebration.

August 4, 1991, we had a big celebration. Four months later would be our 50th Wedding Anniversary. On, December 23, the actual date of our anniversary, we had a smaller celebration in the basement. We had the celebration earlier so that people could easily come to the event. We rented a large banquet room in a golf club overlooking the beautiful green fairways. We had a wonderful grand buffet with a lot of good food, salads, vegetables, barbequed and roast meats, and wonderful desserts, wine, an open bar and a four piece live band and speeches.

This lovely buffet with a lot of good food served outside on a terrace, was a lot different than the small intimate dinner we had when we were first married. We were aware of the differences 50 years had made not only in our ages and appearances but also in our good fortunes.

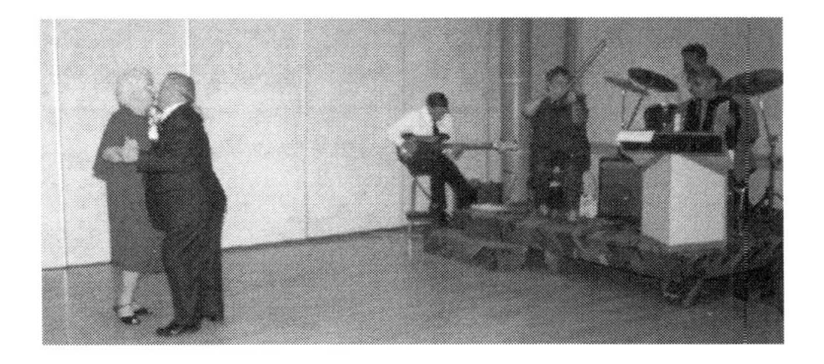

Walter and I had the first dance. I loved to dance with Walter and it felt as natural as breathing. When Walter and I had this first dance, it seemed like only yesterday we were courting and dancing. The party seemed to start a week early and lasted for a few days after the event. We never expected that. It was a wonderful surprise. We had old friends Syd and Gladys Wygle park their motor home in our yard. Syd and Walter had been friends since they were teenagers.

Guests travelled to the event from Manitoba, Saskatchewan, Alberta, and Vancouver Island. It was a big happy party. As a family, we all took part in the planning of the event. We had a dinner and a dance and speeches. Lyle was MC, and Glenn kept the event flowing. Walter's brother John came and his sister, Minnie came from Edmonton and spoke and danced. Minnie was quite funny and had people laughing. She reminded us that she cried when she knew her brother was getting married and in the end, was happy because she was now getting a sister. We felt like sisters until the day Minnie died. Betty Baker, my sister-in-law attended. My cousin Dave and wife Dorothy Corny travelled from Red Deer Alberta. Dorothy held the sheet of words while Dave played the guitar and sang a song he wrote for the celebration.

Our friends Jim and Dorothy Clark came from Winnipeg and stayed with Glenn. Nieces and nephews from both sides of our family attended. Our friends Syd and Gladys Wygle parked their motor home in our yard and visited for at least a week. From my school days 60 years earlier my friend Hazel Lacharity nee Laird caught a ferry from Nanaimo and attended. Hazel and I also lived together for a time in Chilliwack on Yale Road when Walter was in the army.

Letters of congratulations came from politicians like the Prime Minister, Premier, Mayor, etc. I have saved them and mounted them and every now and then, I look at them and remember.

We were proud of our family and friends, and so happy those who could attend did so. A wide range of people of all ages assembled. All, were friends in celebration. We were humbled.

At the end of congratulatory comments Walter and I rose to speak our thanks. Glenn insists this picture be included because he says it shows love. I know Walter was very emotional. Walter had spoken briefly and thanked everyone for attending. I was reading a few short remarks. It was much easier for me to speak than it was for Walter to speak. He was happy and thankful, and though I do not think I could find the words to say exactly what Walter was thinking in this picture, I know for sure he wasn't thinking of divorcing me the next day.

This picture we selected to be framed for our celebration. The picture was a surprise for our sons who did not know we were having it taken.

Walter and I posed with our three sons on the day of our Anniversary Party in 1991.

The first 2 years we were in BC, Walter worked at Polar Industries where he had a bench. He would go to work with Lyle. To start, I would call down every 4 hours to remind him to put in his eye drops. They soon told me they would remind him and I need not call. For only a short time perhaps a few months, he worked all day but he found it hard. I would then drive down and pick him up at 3 pm. He began to spend more time painting and was becoming good. We took a few short trips together to Vancouver Island and the interior of BC. It was a wonderful but too short a period.

When Walter got sick, he could have had much better attention. One of his doctors, a fellow who is now in jail, also taught our grandson judo. The doctor apparently was prosecuted for getting rid of one wife somehow, and hiring a person to kill his second wife. Glenn had a warden guided tour of a jail, and the warden pointed the doctor out as a controversial inmate and one that was a bit of a lazy arrogant man. The inmate was Walter's doctor. The doctor's ability with judo was well known so when the police decided to arrest him they came prepared and in numbers. The doctor was stopped on King George Blvd and surrounded by several police officers just in case he resisted arrest using his judo to escape.

Another doctor did not think anything was wrong with Walter but a repeat visit when a locum was there produced quick results, but it was too late. Walter quickly died from cancer August 8, 1992, ten days before his 74th birthday.

So, there I was, a widow. The man I loved and one person I had spent most of my life with, was gone. I was without the man I loved, again. This time he was not just away working. He would not come back, and I was not isolated. Still I felt alone, and grieved. I had to start over again. My sons were around but I was alone. When the house lights dimmed at night, I was alone. It was not something I liked to start, but have become used to it.

Over the last few months of Walter's life, I could see he was not well and I came to expect the worst. It did not make it any easier. Walter and I did so much together. Now alone, I knew I must go on. I did not want to die, but I did not want to be without Walter either.

I knew Walter would want me to embrace life without him, and remembering him, I do embrace life. That is how I began to go forward. It took me a while to be able to live on my own. The first year of everything, every celebration, every event, was the hardest. Even now with Walter gone more than 20 years, it is hard to attend events without Walter, because without him these events are not so much fun. I am used to it now. I do not like it, but I am used to it. I loved Walter then and still do.

About a month later, my great niece had a party in Penticton. I went with Lyle and Gwen. I was glad to be there because it was a happy event and people were enjoying themselves. I liked the music but did not think I should be dancing because people would think badly of me. Lyle came and insisted I dance with him. I did. I felt strange, but I was not about to wear widow's weeds. It would have been great to be dancing with Walter, but I danced with our son instead.

I had always wanted to go to England. When the opportunity came after a few months to go on a tour to England that Glenn was leading he insisted I go. It was leaving for England in winter when it is rainy and gloomy in Surrey, and he thought the change would do me good. The rest of my family thought it was a great idea. I was the only one thinking I should not be going. I was unsure of many things at the time. In the end, I completely enjoyed the trip. Eventually, I travelled to England four times. The first two times I went with the tours Glenn organized, then I went with a friend, and lastly, Glenn and I went alone.

The first time was the most exciting because I never thought I would ever travel across the sea and because I found relatives. My nephew Gary and his wife Laura Sager were also on the trip. To start there was just the hope of a possibility to meet long lost relatives and a chance to see the historic sites of England.

We had two days in London. Taking a bus north, we stopped at Oxford, and Windsor Castle. We had lunch in a wonderful teahouse in Oxford where the server's dresses and aprons were styled from at least 50 years earlier making this tea more interesting. We travelled north, and walked through Warwick Castle museum and stayed the night in the Shakespeare Inn, which was over 450 years old. The floors were irregular, the hall floors went up and down, and to enter some of the rooms, one had to step down into the room, while other room entrances were level. The halls once straight and level now twisted and went up and down.

The group had a tour of Cadbury's chocolate factory. Glenn and I spent more time reading the signs than the rest of the group and were left behind and separated. The plant manager came along and found us still enjoying the displays all by ourselves and then gave us a private tour of the place and gave us loads of candies. We felt we had the best tour. The tour visited Ann Hathaway's cottage and ended the day in Birmingham. Coventry Cathedral, sitting in the shell of the old cathedral that was destroyed in the bombing of the Second World War was beautiful and a place we visited it a few days later.

Years earlier, my brother Syd and his wife Betty had gone to England and got the address of Albert and Joan Corney. When in London we called, and arranged to take the train from Birmingham to Rotherham. I went with Gary, Laura, and Glenn. Albert and his seeing-eye dog met us at the train station. We visited for a few hours establishing our relationship. We were second cousins. We were all apprehensive about meeting people we did not know, learning how we were related and hoping people would get along.

However, any apprehensions were unwarranted perhaps as we had a great time and really liked each other and were both glad to have found relatives. It felt good to find relatives in England.
I was happy. Syd would also have enjoyed the new found relatives.

I remembered that my brother Syd had been christened in St Peter's Church, in Conisbrough, not far from Albert and Joan's house. Albert, Joan, and their youngest son took us there and I took this picture of the font Syd was christened in about 89 years earlier. I was thrilled to be able to have this tangible connection

to my family history. I had never been in such an old church. The elation of being in historical family surroundings collided with the joy of meeting new family made for a terrific feeling.
Later on, the same day we caught the later train back to Birmingham. I was very excited about having met relatives. The whole episode was something I never would have even considered could ever have happened a year earlier. I reflected how happy my mother would have been to know I had met relatives from her side of the family. I had to tell myself I was not dreaming it was so wonderful.

This short trip made in apprehension began a great relationship. Within the year, Albert and Joan came to visit me in Surrey, a trip they would make twice. After Albert died, Joan came alone.

We stayed in a very grand hotel in Birmingham. The rooms were large. The ceilings and windows were tall. Gary and Laura strung up lines in their room and washed clothes in the Jacuzzi tub. I met people from the tour and it was a good time to be with family and new friends from Canada. Travelling abroad it is a good feeling to be able to see familiar faces now and then amidst the excitement of the new and unexplored. When the rest of the tour went home, Gary and I stayed on longer going south of London to Portsmouth on the train. I was now feeling more confident with the world without Walter. Travelling with Gary was a pleasure.

Portsmouth was the port from which my dad's two brothers went to sea. Even though I had not met them, it was great to see a place my parents had told me about when I was younger. I eagerly looked at every naval building and display imagining my uncles having been there. We spent two nights in a bed and breakfast across from the train station facing the sea. The lobby had a trunk rescued from the sea. Our room had a broken drafty window. Gary made a special effort to tell the owners it was broken and they said they would see to it. However, a year later I stayed in the same room with Gwen. The window was not yet fixed. They were a bit embarrassed when I brought the subject up. I guess maybe many people told them the same thing and they just never got around to it.

Gary had to stop at many pubs to have a beer. He said it was so that he wanted to make sure his aunt had a cup of tea and did not get tired. I did have a sore knee, but it was Gary needing a rest and a drink, that
caused us to stop, and not his older aunt. We enjoyed teasing each other and exploring and got to see a lot of different pubs.

To get from Portsmouth on the south coast, to Dover also on the south coast, by train, one has to take a long route back north through London. In Dover, we were able to go through Dover Castle where from the top we looked across the sea towards France in the winds.

The first trip was so good I decided to go again. On my second trip to England my daughter-in-law, Gwen came along and so did Frank Mesich, Glenn's partner. When the tour left for home, Gwen and I went north. I went to see Albert and Joan, while Gwen went north to Scotland to see her long time pen pal. Albert, Joan, and I went to visit relatives. Joan did the driving. I appreciated the ride, but Joan had a lead foot. She knew the roads and drove what we might consider aggressively. It was a bit scary especially since I kept thinking the traffic was on the wrong side of the road. Some of the roads were so narrow only one car could use it at a time. Sometimes the hedges brushed up against the car and we had to make abrupt stops. Had we gone up and down more hills it would have been like the one and only roller coaster ride I have ever had, in Winnipeg, with Glenn. As it was, we were thrown around a bit in the car with sudden stops and quick movements. However, this just added to the excitement of the trip. We went to York visit Albert's brother and wife, Jim and Pauline.

Chepstow Castle built on the Wye River and Bristol Channel was enchanting. Nothing I had ever seen before was as old. It was like something out of a movie one never expects to see. It was a thrilling to be in Chepstow Castle.

A few days later walking around London and I got food poisoning from some chicken in a fast food restaurant. I was sick all night and all next day on the way to Swindon where Gwen and I stayed with her mother's pen pal. Although no relation, her last name was Baker. The next day I was feeling better and Mr Baker drove us to Portsmouth and left us to continue our journeys. The Bakers were very good to me but I could not eat the chicken supper they offered.

Gwen and I travelled together south to Dover. It was too windy to climb to the top of the castle. We were told, "You will be blown to France up there". Underneath the castle are a series of tunnels and rooms used by Winston Churchill as his war office. I did not know of their existence. From these rooms, plans were made that affected my early married life by stationing Walter in Chilliwack. One gets an eerie feeling to be where the plans that won the war were directed by significantly important people of recent history.

A few years later, I felt brave enough to go to Britain without my family. At first, I would not consider it but Glenn bolstered my confidence and I believed him. Beatrice Robie, someone that I had known from age 9 when we had met in Pierceland, decided to go with me. It was 1995. I was 72 and Beatrice was 70. Beatrice wanted to look around where her mother had originated. Her father had been an orphan and she had no information about his background, but she knew her mother came from the Cumbria in west England. I could easily relate to her yearning to know more. Wanting to know more of my parent's background, where they lived in England I understood her desires. Beatrice's kids wanted her to go on the trip. This was Beatrice's first trip overseas and we were excited to do it together. Age was not going to be an impediment.

Prestige

6766 Jubilee Avenue
Burnaby, B.C. V5H 3G8
Fax: (604) 434-2110
Tel: (604) 434-2111

INVOICE № 1248

MRS SARAH SERGIUS
TEL: 581-0960

DEPART: 04 MAY 95 - 25 MAY 95 ** ZANIA
VANCOUVER TO LONDON - RAIL

Ticket Number(s) & Airline(s)	Passengers	Base	Tax	GST	TOTAL
018 6341 357 769+2 CANADIAN	MRS S. SERGIUS	$818.00	50.00	22.12	$ 890.12
018 6341 357 770+3 CANADIAN	MRS B. ROBIE	818.00	50.00	22.12	890.12
8 DAY BRITRAIL FLEXI-PASS	$305.00 X 2	610.00	N/A	N/A	610.00
[illegible] T.I.C. COMPREHENSIVE	INS. SARAH	89.00	N/A	N/A	89.00
[illegible] T.I.C. COMPREHENSIVE	INS. ROBIE	38.00	N/A	N/A	38.00
BRITAIN [illegible]	$275 x2		N/A	N/A	550.00

INSURANCE	FORM OF PAYMENT	TOTAL	$3,[illegible]7.24
ACCEPTED: CANCELLATION ☑ / COMPREHENSIVE ☑ / MEDICAL ONLY ☐	CA 5191 4300 0432 2134 / SARAH SERGIUS $2398.24 / + 550.00	Deposit Balance	[illegible]
		LESS DISCOUNT	-127.00
DECLINED:	CASH/CHEQUE/CREDIT CARD	TOTAL	[illegible]

Thank You $2,940.24

I caught the plane in Vancouver and Beatrice boarded in Edmonton. Beatrice was not accustomed to travel and brought too many bags for two arms. Since I had my bag on wheels, I was able to help carry things. I was bigger and stronger than Beatrice. Our first night was in a hotel in London, and the next night with a distant relative Cheryl Corney a librarian in London.

The new underground English Channel Crossing, “the Chunnel”, had just opened a few months before we arrived. Such an opportunity could not be missed. We caught a tour to France. In 20 minutes, we were in France. The train was fast and the seats and cars were all nice and new. We left from Waterloo Station. busker below playing a piccolo, or a tin flute, was part of the Paris street scene.

We did not have all that much time to explore and the streets were so packed with people. I had to keep a close eye on Beatrice so she did not wander and get lost as she sometimes did. The crowds were a surprise and it would be easy to lose someone in the crowds. I would not go again unless I knew the weather report ahead of time and could avoid some of the crowds.

Returning to London, we spent one more night with the gracious Cheryl, and caught a train north to Rotherham to visit Albert and Joan Corney. After a short visit, we left by train going to the Cumbria area, but sadly never found any of Beatrice’s relatives. It was a letdown. We had little to go on and that made searching difficult. Still, Beatrice was happy just to see where her mother had grown up.

Taking the train north to Scotland, we went to Edinburgh. The castle looms as a very large presence as the train rounds a corner. Beatrice was at times prone to take naps and was napping leaning against the window as the castle came into view. As I look back now I think, she was having some problems with her health, and her memory even then. She would fall into a deep sleep and miss a lot of scenery. Frequently I would nudge her to wake her up when some special scenery was out the window. Usually she would look out the window. This time she awoke in a daze turned towards me and said "what?" We soon got her straightened out looking through the window and she was pleased not to have missed seeing at least part of the castle. She was beginning to forget things. I think Beatrice just forgot she was at the window and just needed to look out to be entertained.

At the train station in Kirkaldy, Scotland, we met Jim Davidson. Jim was a family friend. I had met him on my first trip to England. Jim is a tall good looking man who many think looks like Sean Connery of James Bond fame. Of course, he is better looking than Sean Connery and such a gentleman. Jim is a good sport and has a great sense of humor. We had plenty of good laughs. From the train station we went to Glasgow to pick up Frank.

We paid for a car rental and Jim graciously drove, and thus we got a superb private tour of parts of Scotland. The four of us made good company and enjoyed our trip, Frank and Jim in the front seat and Beatrice and I in the back. By car, we travelled to the northern tip of the Isle of Skye, looped around the island and back to Edinburgh. It is a rugged and interesting part of the world made more interesting by Jim. The Isle of Skye is hilly with smaller farms, stone buildings, and small creeks. Flat land is not plentiful. Below is a picture typical of the area.

The Edinburgh Castle tour takes at least a couple of hours. After the tour of the castle, we went to a department store and I bought Glenn a statue of a running Cairn terrier, a Scottish breed of dog he breeds, and the statue was more special because it was also purchased in Scotland.

The Isle of Skye is a rustic beauty. The rocky nature of the island is part of life and very beautiful. The rock can drop dramatically straight down many feet or have rocky sloping beaches. Stone fences and stone homes abound. Driving through the countryside, we came across these cattle walking down the road. We had to wait for them to move, they owned the road. Here you can see the rough nature of the countryside. It reminded me of my days on the farm and I thought of the time I was frightened when the cattle surrounded our farmhouse. The Isle of Skye, as nice as it is, did not make me want to emigrate. I could see why some from there would want to come to Canada where farming and life might be easier.

I have been afraid of cattle all my life, even when I had to take care of them because they are not to be trusted. To get a good picture of the native highland cattle, because they are different breed than I had known all my life, I approached this well fenced cow and took this picture so that I could remember the size and horns of the beasts.

Further, along the road we saw a string of dead birds hanging on the wire fence. They are hung on the fence to chase other similar birds away from the crops. I leaned over on a protected stand to take this picture of the Isle of Skye coastline in 1995.

Loch Lomond was a place I never dreamed I would see. As a child, I had heard the song, " On The Bonnie Bonnie Banks of Loch Lomond" played from a cylinder disc, and I had played the song on the accordion many times. I heard the song in my head as we approached. It was a thrill to be there. When we arrived, I was surprised to see the town named Luss. I had never heard of Luss, and it was not mentioned in the song, but of course why would it be. It was great to be there and we took a good boat ride but a thunderstorm came up, and we just went around in a loop. Still I was able to see what a wonderful place it is and that it is deserving of a song.

Frank is on the left, then Beatrice, Jim and me. We are on a boat on Loch Lomond with thunder clouds above our heads. Just after this, we got into the car and drove off as it rained. In a short time, it stopped and we made it to Mallaig to board a car ferry to the Isle of Skye and up the east coast to Flodigary.

We stayed in the wonderful Flodigary Hotel and our room in the portion called Flora Macdonald's cottage. Outside in the evening a piper played until sunset.

The next morning was the beginning a memorable event. At the time, it was more stressful than funny. We did not know Beatrice was beginning to forget a lot of things and was not just acting daft. Frank and Jim were in the front seats and Beatrice in I were in the back. Beatrice elbowed me and pointed at her chest, and whispered that she had forgotten it. Too embarrassed to talk she could only whisper, "I forgot it." I did not know what she was talking about but knew it was a sensitive topic. I whispered to ask if she had forgotten her artificial breast. She had. Jim, the ever gracious, driver, knew something was going on so he asked. Eventually I had to tell Jim that Beatrice thought she had forgotten her artificial breast back at the hotel. We stopped the car. Beatrice searched the suitcase, but since Jim was standing around and because Beatrice was too embarrassed to let Jim see inside her suitcase, her search was superficial and quick. She did not want a man to see her suitcase open. We drove 20 miles back to the motel. Beatrice raced in ahead of me. When I entered the room, Beatrice had taken the entire room apart looking in drawers, under the bed, and in the bathroom. Looking in furniture drawers was a sure sign of her frustration because we had not used the drawers being there only one night. She had every sheet on the floor with the pillowcases and towels but could not find it. She was standing in the room in tears.

Of course, when we searched the suitcase again without Jim or Frank around we found it immediately. Beatrice was then even more embarrassed. Jim and Frank knew what she had forgotten, and knew she was too embarrassed to look in her suitcase properly. That we had wasted time going back when we need not have done so was not a big cause for concern for the rest of us, but Beatrice was feeling badly. However, Jim played the hero solving the situation using humor. Onward, upon getting back into the car, and after every stop, whether to look at something, or eat, or have tea, Jim would turn around and say in his strong Scottish accent: “Well gaurlls, do you have all your paarrts?” We would all laugh and it made it fun. I think perhaps that it was funnier then, and in person, than it is printed here.

Jim was always able to add a great deal of commentary to every part of the journey. He truly was a remarkable tour guide. He made our trip better all round. However, we did need to find something to tease him about to make things even. Later Jim was the source of our humor.

The opportunity arose with a visit to a large home museum. It started with Jim parking in a place he felt was correct. It was not correct. He was not allowed to park there. In a few minutes, the guards told him he had to go move his car and could not park where the cone was on the parking lot. Jim did go and move his car but was not too happy about in a sort of playful way. The security guard, and Jim, had a little discussion about it, as Jim did not want to have to move his car, but the security guard was not accustomed to having to negotiate with someone who did not want to move the car perhaps felt challenged. Jim made his point that he thought his choice of parking spot was warranted perhaps because we three were seniors, and resumed the tour. A few minutes later back in the museum, Jim leaned to examine a display in more detail. His clothing touched the display case setting off the alarm. A commotion followed. Bells were ringing. Guards came running. Had someone had tried to steal something? Jim did not realize that he was the center of the commotion and was looking around as bewildered as the rest of us.

When it was clear it was his error, he was embarrassed that it was his fault. Everyone ended up staring at him as if he had done some horrible wrong, but he was feeling innocent. The guard said something to Jim akin to “oh, so it is you again”. From then on, we were able to tease him about where he was parking and keeping his paarrts away from the displays. It worked out beautifully as if Jim had orchestrated it to make Beatrice feel better.

South west of Flodigary, following the shoreline road, we wandered through small roads and to Dunvegan Castle, where for £3.60 we were able to stroll around the castle and grounds.

Scotland has plenty of rocks. Between Inverary, and the Isle of Skye we marvelled at this quite unusual river cutting its way amongst the rocks. It is a sample of the rugged beauty of Scotland.

Crofters houses built of stone are scattered around Scotland. Their stone walls and thatched roofs are a distinctive look. Built hundreds of years ago, many are still lived in. They look interesting but are nothing I would want to live in. They appear small and cramped and not all that tall inside. I wonder if they are damp and about their ventilation.

We left the wonderful laughter and companionship of Jim and Frank in Edinburgh boarding a train to London, where we stayed in the Scotland Hotel at a good rate of $100 for the room. Perhaps the vacation was just long enough as I think Beatrice needed a rest. At breakfast, the next morning Beatrice went to the buffet but returning sat somewhere else rather than with her purse and me. We laughed about it at the time but I was concerned. I am glad I had this trip with my friend while she could enjoy it. After our return home, we talked on the phone several times, I could witness her forgetfulness growing, and in 2 years or so after the trip, she died.

The next year I returned to England, landing at Heathrow this time with Glenn. We stayed in the same Kensington area hotel, The Jury's Kensington. We had an interesting meeting with a professional that did Ancestor Research to help find families. Her magazine ad said she could research ancestors and provide contacts. She said her husband was a member of the House of Lords and that if we mentioned his name when we went to the House of Lords he would give us a tour. We did not do that. We did not believe her and began to think she was pretending. She was not entirely believable and more mercenarily minded than was appropriate. We felt she was a con artist. She appeared wearing rather worn clothing for a woman whose husband was in the House of Lords. I paid her for what work she had done or claimed to have done; including giving us a name of a woman who she said lived near York, and had a box of papers.

Supposedly, this woman with the box of papers had looked after the daughter-in-law of my dad's youngest sister Emily Baker. The box lady claimed to have lived next door to Emily Baker in Thirsk, west of York.

Calling this woman to arrange to get the box proved useless. Each time she had some excuse each time preventing a meeting. She had to do this or that, or go to a funeral, and had too many reasons why we could not meet. She said no Baker had ever shown any interest and never came to ask for anything. We felt certain she wanted money for the papers. She would have had to keep these papers for over 40 years. That seemed like an unreasonable thing to do, when the papers, and pictures, were not from her family or personal. We doubted the legitimacy of the story. Had we believed her, I would have paid the price and bought the papers. We felt she too was a fake, and never got the box of papers.

Leaving London, we went north to visit Joan and Albert in Rotherham. They had been to visit us and I had driven them to Saskatoon around. Albert was glad to find relatives. It was a joyous meeting when we arrived. On the first day, Albert and Joan took us to visit some relatives and Sherwood Forest about an hour drive. We visited Albert's brother Jim and Elsie Robinson my shirt- tale second cousin on the Corney side of the family. Elsie was a small friendly, sincere woman and seemed kind hearted.

Flo, a rather flirtatious and gregarious woman was also a cousin on the Corney side. Her husband Charles was a nice fellow. Flo enjoyed teasing and flirting with Glenn. She floated into harmless teasing flirtation so easily, it was as if she were a professional. Elsie, and Flo and Charles lived in Doncaster. Sadly, Elsie, Flo, and Charles all died within two years. I was very glad to have met them. In the picture Glenn took for me are, from the left Joan and Albert Corney, Flo Osborne, me, and then Charles Osborne, in the yard of Flo and Charles. It was a delightful and fun afternoon visit.

We only stayed one night with Albert and Joan because Joan became suddenly moody. Crankily she left the room saying she had to pack for a vacation they were to take on a bus in two days' time. Albert was embarrassed and it was awkward. Clearly, we did not know about some issue. We left very early the next morning feeling rather disliked, unwelcome, hurt, and offended. We would have left immediately had we a place to stay and it was earlier in the day but this was evening. It was a terrible restless night, without much sleep, as we felt so unwanted. Still in a few months, Albert and Joan were at my house for two weeks, and did so twice, and then Joan came on her own. We never really understood what was going on, but it upset us at the time. Whatever it was it passed and we did not let it ruin the relationship.

We were tired on our trip to York where we called a couple with the names Geraldine and Toni Baker.

I think Toni was an administrator at college or university. I had their contact number through the ancestry search from the woman in London. It is possible that they were related but we never determined this for sure. I still think they are related on my father's side of the family tree. Together we looked for names on gravestones in the churchyards.

These pictures were taken in June 1997, in Braithwaite Church yard.

Toni Baker's grandparents were James William Baker, and Esther Ann Baker.

My father's sister Emily was a Mrs George Ackroid. This stone could be for some his ancestors as it is in the same area. In the picture below, the top of the stone says:

> *"Sacred to the memory of Ann, the wife of Joseph Ackroid, who departed this life July 22, 1825, aged 53 years. Also above Joseph Ackroid, who died April 7, 1834 aged 61 years."*

The tombstone following seems like it must belong to an ancestor of mine. I have not yet had time to research it but perhaps it will be done in the future. I include the picture here because someone, someday, may find it useful.

After meeting with Geraldine and Toni Baker, we met Jim Davidson and rented a car. Jim was again a wonderful tour guide and driver. We drove to York, and met Jim Corney the brother of Albert, in a pub and had a great chat and then went on to do some tourist sites like a tour of a Viking village and viewing of a Roman road and wall, under York minster, and through the countryside and home.

Tick Hill Castle, was a place where my mother had worked as a chambermaid. It was a name that always had a romantic far away never tangible quality. Seeing Tick Hill Castle was always a dream I never imagined I would get to realize. When at last it happened there was a strange and emotional feeling to be in a place where my mother had worked. It was also a great feeling to be able to be there and know Mam had been there too. I was so excited to be able to find it. I know Glenn was excited too. I was wishing my mother would be there to see it now. I thought how great it would be to be able to tell her we were at Tick Hill. It was a dream come true to be at Tick Hill. I had no idea what it would look like and when I saw it I was happy.

I am standing at a side door to Tick Hill. Glenn took the picture. He said he wanted to see a picture of his mother at the door of a place he had heard her talk of so many times, answering his questions.

The young girl seated in both pictures, is my mother Harriet Corney. Two cousins and sisters are standing. First picture it is Polly Jenkins and in the second it is Sarah Ellen Jenkins. All 3 worked at Tick Hill.

The original Tick Hill Castle was destroyed by Oliver Cromwell. The present day grand house made from the stones of the original castle. It retains the name Tick Hill Castle. There are remnants of the original building and parts of the castle wall still intact. It was being refurbished when we visited but still we could walk around the grounds.

Tick Hill was a place Mam talked about quite a lot and told me stories of her time there. She had for a few days dusted around money left on a dresser by one of the daughters of the estate owner. She would dust around it, move it, dust under it, and keep going. It happened so many times she went to the woman of the house, the girl's mother, and told her about it. The mother said that her daughter was testing to see if Mom would take it and went on to say," Now that you have told me about it go take it." I do not remember if Mom took the money or not.

Mam was the youngest girl of the staff. She was perhaps the most daring too and that helped to create a situation that scared her pretty badly. In the bowels of the building among old staircases, and doors into abandoned little used rooms, and a tunnel that went to rooms underground from a bigger older building, a group of girls descended and opened a door. Mom said as the door opened she could see wine racks and many cobwebs. She stepped through the door. Immediately her work mates closed the door, locked it behind her, and ran away.

She was left in the dark for about a half hour. The fearful imagination of a young girl took over in the smelly and dark place. Certainly, spiders and other awful creatures with large teeth and slime were surely waiting to eat her up. When she was eventually let out, she was greatly relieved. She said it was the time in her life when she was most afraid.

Tick Hill has been built in stages as indicated by the different colors of the building. I would like to go in someday but I am not sure if that is possible. I would like to see where my mother dusted skulls on the mantelpiece whistling through their eye and nose holes. The place is rented to a couple from Vancouver, BC, and their son lives in it. He is not too keen to participate in the traditional open days, when the grounds and possibly the house or part of the house are open to the public.

Here I sit in a meadow of blue lupines on the way to Calgary with Glenn. While he went to dog shows, I visited family. I made a few short summer trips with Gary and Laura and her mother to Vancouver Island.

I certainly enjoyed my travels, with Walter in Canada and those I made with family and friends abroad. Everywhere, and every experience, is interesting. In everyplace, all the time, there are people waiting to be friends. I wish I had been able to do more of them with Walter and my siblings.

Parties and Retirement: Life in Surrey

I have had 93 birthdays so far, and the last few have been some of the best. Lately I have had a lot more parties to celebrate age than I did when I was younger. In the early days, after we were married my birthday just seemed to slip by, as we were too busy. I have been given several great cards, and though I would save them for a few months, and sometimes years, eventually, after years of being kept, they nearly all were tossed. I appreciated getting good wishes, but well, a card is a card.

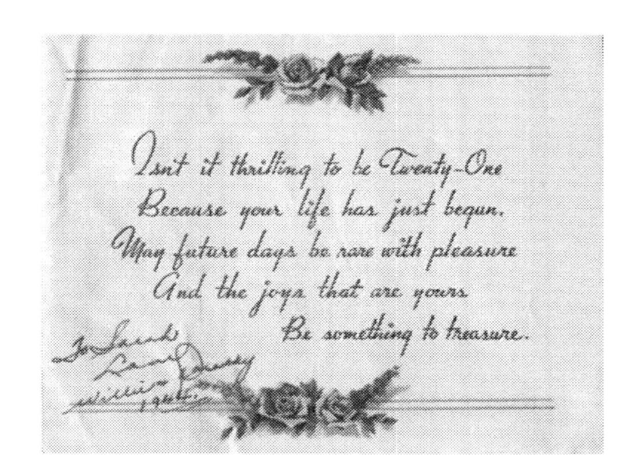

My 21st birthday card from my brother Willie and his wife Dorothy is an exception. Somehow, I managed to save it for the last 70+ years.

It is different from birthday cards today in that the shape is different. It opens like a book as cards do today, but it is only half the height, about 4 inches. It is not too mushy and neither is it a joke. The front and inside are copied below so you can see an example of an old style birthday card.

My 74th birthday party was at my son Glenn's house. I have had cakes before to mark the day but this was the first party. This was the first of many that Glenn has organized for me. I felt honored people went to such effort to celebrate in my birthday.

When I turned 75 we went to a fine buffet dinner at a hotel.

On my 80th birthday, we had great celebrations in two places. After church, we had a lunch outside in the church yard under tents and as the rain let off it allowed us to eat and celebrate. I was especially glad to able to celebrate with church friends. Kathy Holmes, a friend of Glenn's came over to prepare the food. This was the first of a few times Kathy was there to help celebrate. Kathy had all the food ready as we came from church and my sons attended church.

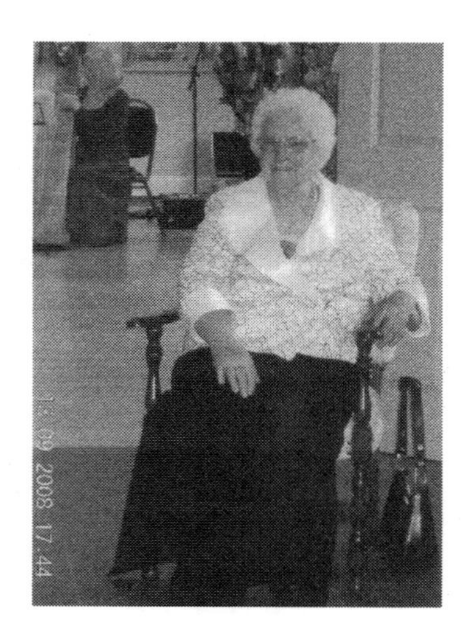

The day just seemed to get better and warmer. That evening we celebrated with a barbeque dinner and squeezed 56 people into the basement to eat using narrow church tables.

Squeezed in as we were, it made an intimate and fun party, and encouraged people to chat while they ate though not everyone knew each other. After dinner, rather than the usual speeches, each one had the opportunity to speak. Each person was introduced to everyone else. The stories and greetings were personal, from the heart and everyone appreciated being able to share. In this small enclosed space, everyone could hear and no one was too shy to speak up. I felt honored and truly happy with so many nice remembrances and thoughts from so many people who have been part of my life for a long time. I cannot remember what I said after everyone had spoken, but I know I had to have said how honored and truly happy I was that I was able to celebrate with so many special people. My sons did the cooking outside, and Kathy and Gwen and Laura worked inside. Relatives came from everywhere and it was a good party.

The biggest party I have had to date has been my 85th birthday party. Maureen Bodie, a friend of Glenn's, played the harp as people arrived and I greeted them at the top of the stairs. The picture below shows us both seated. It was early on as people arrive because I greeted all 100+ people standing at the top of the stairs I was so happy to see them all arrive and I do not have my corsage. I had two. The first corsage did not last. All the great hugs crushed it flat as a pancake. The second one looked pretty.

Glenn again corralled his friends to help cater. Kathy Holmes, Lloyd Sung and Frank all worked very hard and Glenn is lucky to have them as friends. I sure appreciated the effort they went to on my behalf. There were plenty of raves about the mashed potatoes. Many people have asked for the recipe both at this party and later at my 90th. So many wanted this recipe for these home cooked potatoes but I just could not give it out easily. This recipe has been a guarded family secret that combines talent and a special technique. Home cooking techniques are sometimes like that. People do not always give them away. Recipes are given but one ingredient or technique is omitted so it is not an exact duplicate. I too, never wanted to reveal this one. I saved it to tell you all now. It has been a secret for some time but I want to make sure the technique is not lost and is handed on. I will make sure I include every ingredient and technique. Ok here it is. The potatoes came frozen in bags from Ricky's restaurant and were a combination of instant and regular potatoes to which Kathy added big gobs of butter. Ha ha.
My 85th birthday featured a fabulous and delicious cake made by my great niece Alison Abele, now married to Thierry. She made and decorated a truly fabulous cake. It was a work of art to see and tasted great. She added sparklers.

Using a cart Alison wheeled the cake through the crowd as people sang Happy Birthday and then had to sing For She's A Jolly Good Fellow to give enough time so everyone could see this spectacular creation. The tall sparklers on the cake lit up the room like a hay fire. There were plenty of oohs and awes over Alison's beautiful creation and it was delicious. With all the sparklers and candles, lighting up a dark room like bonfire it may have been that people were oohing and awing over the fact that the building had not caught fire as well as the spectacle and the chance to taste the great cake.

Everyone was able to have time at the microphone to speak. There so many warm wishes and some pretty funny stories. I hired a country singer. He played music and people were able to get up and dance. It was a great evening with family and friends. It ran throughout the weekend and family brought treats to eat with tea that was always ready.

I made a speech after the cake and everyone had a chance to speak. I meant the words as much then as I do now when I read them again. Our world is enriched, the highs of life accentuated, and the lows of life moderated by the love and support of those we love and who love us. I thought I would cry when everyone clapped vigorously and then rose to applaud. As then, I thank you all.

For my 90th birthday party it was much the same. This time my great niece Cherisse made and decorated the cake. It was another controlled fire. The sparklers were lit and the cake wheeled through the crowd and it was wondrous the automatic sprinklers did not come on. Glenn corralled his friends to help cook and play music. Kathy, Frank, Lloyd, and Glenn dressed in wigs and sang a song; I'm Sarah with an H I Am. I hired Heart and Soul, two accordion players to play an assortment of music. It added a bit of warm ambiance to the night. They played softly and people talked, and laughed and had a good time.
It was a good party with family and friends, a smaller party as some good friends and family had died. As I age, that happens. I wonder now as I write if I will have a 95th but certainly intend on having one. I am pleased to have my nephews, nieces and all my family and friends attending.

This 90th birthday was made special because two days before the event David and Jean Wilcock arrived from England. They were second cousins on my mother's Corney family side. They came and stayed with me for two weeks. During that time, a relative they had been in contact with came up from Denver to visit for a couple of days. We travelled around to see some of the local sights and did a lot of talking.

My father never had a grave marker. For a long time, we did not know where he was buried. Bob Baker spoke at the party and presented me with a picture of the grave marker that Ruth Lebedoff organized her brothers and sisters and had placed on their grandfather's grave. It was a great birthday present and I am pleased to know he has a proper grave marker. It was an emotional moment.

Birthdays and anniversaries can sometimes make you think and reflect on your life. I have done so with my birthdays. The same is true of our wedding anniversary. In 1990 as our 50th Wedding Anniversary approached, we were living in Surrey. Walter and I thought how different our lives were from the days before our marriage. At both times, we anticipated the event and began to plan it and that we were in love. There were similarities. Now family would be around and that it would be a happy emotional time. Huge differences and other factors were also at play.

In 1941, I did not really know if I would soon be a war widow. Would my new husband be killed in action? Would we ever have a family? How long would it be before Walter went overseas? Would I be a good wife? Would religion mar the celebrations?

After 2 years of marriage, I had new questions. Would I raise my new son alone? Would the war ever end? We faced many unanswered questions along with everyone else in our generation. It was an awful time of stressful upheaval.

Originally, outside religious pressure was a factor in our lives. This ceased to be an irritant when we moved away from the religiously split area where we lived. The intent of the Roman Catholic Church was to force us to become Roman Catholic through social pressure. Jehovah Witness followers came to the house also with quite a lot of intent to convert us but did not dispute our marriage.

On one occasion while living on the farm a Jehovah Witness man or couple came to the back door. They tended to be pests caring more about getting their message of indoctrination out than they cared for the lives of the people they were pestering. One could easily see through the house from that door to near the front door where Walter was fiddling with a tube radio squeaking and making a noise. Of course, Walter had enough of the pestering and playfully ignored the door. I had to answer the door and Walter made the radio squeak even more while the man was trying to make me afraid of eternal hell pushing our necessity to convert to save ourselves. Only 144,000 were going to be saved. We had to act immediately. I was tiring of the religious pull from both sides and with Walter's making the radio squeak and squawk. Finally, I reacted and told the fellow that if it came to pass and only 144,000 were to be saved that I would rather be dead because he would have one hell of a mess and smell to clean up with the rest of us all dead. I cannot actually remember if it made any difference to the number of visits, we had but it ended that visit.

Fifty years later as we planned a celebration the church of our choice was close. We enjoyed the fellowship. Certainly now, we were considered married by everyone. Our family was close and we had weathered the storm of a world war and had shared a life together. In fifty years, life changes people and in over 90 years you change a lot more. The social, economic, environmental, and psychological pressures are factors in life and shape our personalities. I look at myself and although I am a far different person than I was when I was married, I can also see similarities between myself as a young bride and myself now.

I was never a complete push over easily pushed around. I was certainly agreeable and wanted to make friends. As a young bride, I did not speak my mind as much as I might now. That helped me get along with my in-laws rather quickly. I never argued with them. I imagine at the time Walter's choice of British background bride may have caused at least concern because our cultures were so different.

As a young girl, I had the seeds of self confidence and reliance that life ripened and nurtured. I am not going to lie and say I always knew where I was going and why. I didn't. I can say I had an inner instinct to protect my family. I worked hard to make sure I gave them the encouragement and protection that I could. I gave my husband my love and tried to be a good wife. I guess sometimes I succeeded and sometimes I failed. Still after 50 years we were together. I feel I must have succeeded more than I failed.

In the 50 years there were some years that were not all that nice, and in fact, they were down, right hard, and awful. Some things I wish had not happened and some things I wish had happened. For example, I wish we had never gone to the farm, and I wish we had stayed in BC after the war.

When I first met Walter, I never knew him to take a drink. Yet within a few short years after leaving the farm and going north to Lac La Ronge, he became a different man due to two main influences. First, he spent a lot of time away from home and in isolated communities. Looking back, his experience was like a kind of sensory or social deprivation, because he was away from me, and his family, working long exhausting hours. His working life was horrible with a lot of isolation. That changes personalities and makes them into different beings. He became bushed. Had we stayed in BC after the war, I am sure this would not have happened.

Alcohol can sneak into a life and take over. Alcohol makes at first just subtle intermittent changes. Soon the changes become the new normal. Alcohol was the second influence that altered Walter's life and then mine. It was a dark period and Walter struggled. I did what I could to help him and he realized he needed to address the issue to be his true self.

I saw alcohol affect my father and saw how it changed him. I know now alcohol worried me. I understood why I did not really know my own father when I saw him a few years later. I remember how awkward, and unsure I was to recognize him and even how to decide it if was him, and whether or not I wanted to recognize him. I saw how awkward it made him feel, and how unsure he was to recognize and meet his own daughter. I saw how he knew it changed his life. I understand that even more now. I now know my dad did change. He had plans for the future. In that brief possible meeting, neither of expected, confusion stole a possible momentous of reunion. Was it really him? Then he died. Certainly, alcohol abuse stole a husband from my mother. It stole family from my father. I recognized when evil alcohol was stealing my husband.

When drinking, Walter was not the man I married. I forgave the mental and physical humiliations. It was however a bad time. Some years were worse than others were, and the whole episode lasted for about 20 years off and on.

I was not a drinker, yet I was again trapped by alcohol, backed into a corner by a beast in a bottle, or more appropriately many beasts in many bottles. At times, I was at a loss of what to do and did not know where to turn. I did get intermittent help from clergy for a short time. Alcohol can only be beaten with sustained effort and it took a while to get that effort.

I could not rely upon expertise and insight to fight the influence alcohol had on Walter. I had none. He had none either. At first, I was confused and so was he. I had only the power of flight, to run to hide, my love to give, and my support for a man I knew was different from the demon that he would become when drinking. In the end, the strong, good, man, that I married beat alcohol. Alcohol caused Walter great embarrassment, employment, and heartbreak. It was not easy for either of us. It was actually really, really, hard. Still he did win. When a good man overcomes adversity to win and deliver goodness that makes him a hero. Walter did beat it just like, he later beat smoking. It was his struggle but it affected others and he knew it. I rejoice in his victory. I ask you to as well.

I do not want to dwell on this part of the hardships of life making Walter into a horrible, bad man. He was not. I did not love an ogre. I have to include it to be honest because it affected me and I believe affected my family. If I were to leave it out, many people would know I had lied by omission. What then would be the value of my work in this book? Certainly, it would be of less value, and in truth, you would all find it less interesting to read. Truthfully, it was something many of you already knew about anyway. That is why it is just a small part near the end of this book. That cursed alcohol. It happened. It hurt. We cried. We got over it because we loved each other. Life went on, and I still love Walter.

So, when Walter and I began to see the possibility that we would make 50 years of marriage we had already faced a few dark days together and overcome the usual family life problems that were not unique to us but affected us in our own ways. We were closer than ever. I loved Walter and he loved me and we were both glad to have each other. We were quite happy to consider the notion of an anniversary celebration. Our family began to talk about having a celebration. It quickly took shape.

Walter and I took a few wonderful trips after the party. We toured Vancouver Island in two different trips. Touring the south of the island and saw Point No Point and returned home to celebrate Walter's 73rd birthday at Lyle's place. A bit later, we explored the north of the island and returned to celebrate my 68th birthday at Glenn's. A day or so later we went to see the town of the famous Ma Murray, or Margret Murray in Lillooet, B C. We had written her a letter one time. We were pleased when the famous lady answered. She simply turned our letter over and used it to scratch a few lines of reply. We were happy we saw the house where she and her husband had lived.

From the time, we moved to Vancouver, Walter never drove a vehicle alone other than the one time we drove both vehicles to get licences. He always had me with him when he drove. In the last few years before he died, driving was different than it had been in the many years before. Having a need to go to the hardware store or some other place Walter would come into the house and say something like, "we need to go here or there". I would stop whatever I was doing and go with him mostly as a passenger to local places. I am sure he felt some assurance that he was not alone and it was more fun to go together. We enjoyed doing things together. Our day trips to the valley had us sharing the driving.

Walter would paint pictures in the basement. He saw a few TV shows about painting, and taught himself how to paint. While downstairs painting, he seemed to listen to me moving around upstairs, and if I sounded busy doing something he left me to work on my own. If I were playing the organ or accordion, he would sometimes call up telling me what to play. As soon as I was no longer making noise, he would ask me to come downstairs. I would take my knitting or crochet projects downstairs and sit while he was painting.

One Valentine's Day I commented I had not received my valentine. Sometime later, he came up from downstairs. He gave me the valentine he had painted and it is still hung on the wall upstairs.

Walter started to be tired. We went to doctors but nothing seemed conclusive. In retrospect, nothing could have been done to save Walter, but he would have had more time to prepare for death, or perhaps worry about it. He rapidly became tired, and in pain. Doctors seemed to dismiss his symptoms.

The last while, he slept on the floor in the living room. The hard floor did not hurt his chest. Walter had cancer throughout his body. Walter died the morning of August 8, 1992; I was in the room holding his hand as was Glenn and our niece Laura. From then I had to start another life with Walter away again, but now he was not coming back. That is a lot harder than it sounds.

It is tough when you lose your partner. One knows that you have to carry on living alone. I had a lot of support from my family and St Helen's Church. Soon after we joined St Helen's church members had invited me before to join the ACW. I had not joined because it would mean leaving Walter alone at night and he did not like to be left alone. I wanted to spend time with him while I could. After he died, I joined and was grateful for the love and support of good people. I also joined Bible study classes at St Helen's Anglican Church.

I had been going to Bible study classes at the United Church in the daytime while Walter worked at Polar Industries. For the year or so that the church hall was being renovated we had ACW meetings in my basement and Bible study meetings in kitchen. ACW Christmas dinners in the basement were nice and filled the house. I set the tables and had the tables all ready decorated for the dinners. My niece Laura Sager made the white tablecloths that we used many, many, times and, she gave me a large set of 4 x 4 inch mirrors to reflect the light. Each place setting had a mirror and a candle. In a darkened room starting from one candle we passed the flame to our neighbor and made a Christmas wish. It took a few minutes but it made for good feelings and good bonding.

We had many family dinners in the basement when Walter was alive. He made these large tables so we could celebrate together. We celebrated everyone's birthday as well as holidays with a big get together. Always there was 20 plus people. Relatives and friends all crammed together to eat and talk. Most of the time everyone helped by bringing food.

After Walter died, several people thought I should sell my house and go live in an apartment. Then I had breast cancer and did not want to do anything until I handled that. Some might speculate that the cancer perhaps came from the stress I felt after losing Walter and adjusting to a new life. I cannot say if that is true, but I can say it was hard and perhaps there is a link between the events. However, I have not sold my house and moved. I like where I live. Someday I will have to move and then I will do so. As for now, to this day, going in and out of the house, and up the stairs have helped me to continue doing stairs and keeping me active. When we finish this book, I intend to get outside, and continue knitting and crocheting.

I have continued to work in and for the church as I can. In 1998 St Helen's Anglican Church honored me the following certificate of appreciation. It was the first for being myself and I accepted this with humbleness.

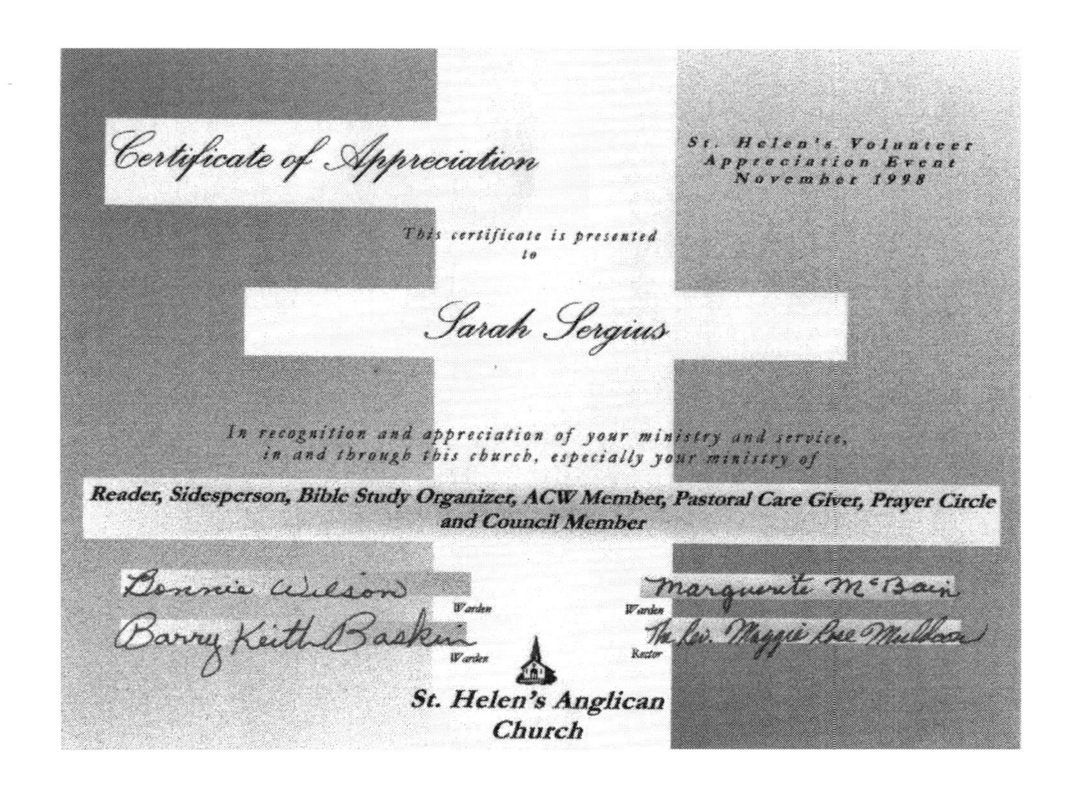

Certificate of Appreciation

St. Helen's Volunteer Appreciation Event
November 1998

This certificate is presented to

Sarah Sergius

In recognition and appreciation of your ministry and service, in and through this church, especially your ministry of

Reader, Sidesperson, Bible Study Organizer, ACW Member, Pastoral Care Giver, Prayer Circle and Council Member

Bonnie Wilson, Warden
Marguerite McBain, Warden
Barry Keith Baskin, Warden
Rector

St. Helen's Anglican Church

In 2013 I was honored again. I was made a member of the Order of the Diocese of New Westminster:

"in thanks giving for and grateful acknowledgment of outstanding ministry and devotion to God within the
Anglican church of Canada."

This was a big event in my life. I was honored in public before a large crowd for being myself. It makes one feel very humble. I stood in front of hundreds and they knew me for myself. During a special service in a full Christ Church Cathedral in Vancouver, the Archbishop and Primate of The Anglican Church of Canada read individual citations.

The primate individually hung the medallion around our necks, which I am reminded to wear at some church events and, presented a group of us each with a certificate. A copy below but it is not entirely correct, as I never served as a leader in the choir at St Helen's, I did in Lac La Ronge.

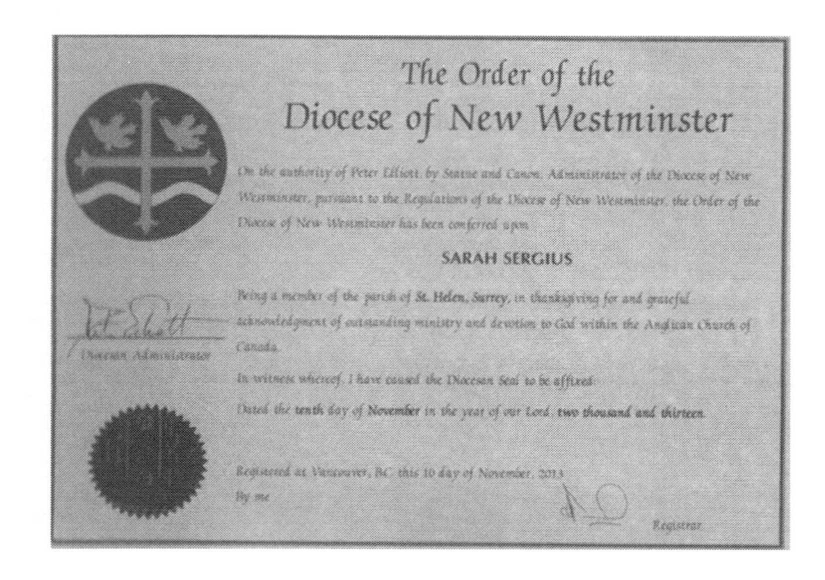

The Order of the
Diocese of New Westminster

On the authority of Peter Elliott, by Statute and Canon, Administrator of the Diocese of New Westminster, pursuant to the Regulations of the Diocese of New Westminster, the Order of the Diocese of New Westminster has been conferred upon

SARAH SERGIUS

Being a member of the parish of **St. Helen, Surrey,** *in thanksgiving for and grateful acknowledgment of outstanding ministry and devotion to God within the Anglican Church of Canada.*

In witness whereof, I have caused the Diocesan Seal to be affixed.

Dated the **tenth** *day of* **November** *in the year of our Lord,* **two thousand and thirteen.**

Diocesan Administrator

Registered at Vancouver, BC this 10 day of November, 2013
By me

Registrar

Citation for

Mrs. Sarah Sergius

upon the presentation of
the Order of the Diocese of New Westminster 2013

The introduction of the recipient read by the Warden of the Order at the service:

Sarah is an example of someone constantly walking her faith with grace and love. Her work is often informal and frequently unsung. She has a gift for turning strangers into family between the opening hymn and the Eucharist.

The Citation as recorded in the Permanent Register of the Order.

It is not so much Sarah's positions and terms of service that Sarah is being recognized for as it is her constant example of someone walking her faith with grace and love, being always willing to assist in all ventures while maintaining a positive attitude. Since joining the parish of St. Helen, Surrey, in 1987 Sarah has served as a leader in the choir, with the Anglican Church Women, as a sidesperson/greeter, as a member of the Prayer Circle and in organizing a monthly Seniors' Lunch. She served as trustee (1999-2001) and as Warden (2000-2001) during a particularly challenging time in the life of St. Helen's. During renovations of the church hall, she invited both the ACW and Seniors' Lunch into her home for their regular meetings. She has been frequently found in the kitchen making sure coffee and tea were ready and doing the dishes after parish events. Her hospitality to new members and visitors is immediate and deep – she turns strangers into family between the opening hymn and the Eucharist. Sarah is one of those church members whose work is often informal and frequently unsung, but without whom the life and ministry of the parish would be significantly diminished.

We had a group picture in the Anglican Church Journal paper on pages 10 and 11, January of 2014, and my name was listed with a few words, on page 13. After the ceremony, there were light refreshments. I was pleased some of my family could attend and we went out for supper.

With the help of Cindy, my housekeeper, found relatives in England. I pay for the use of Ancestory.ca and Cindy searches for me. Cindy has found a few relatives we did not know existed. Some are in the US, some in Australia, and but most in England. I am hoping that through the saliva genetic DNA samples submitted to Ancestory.ca that not only will our family learn more about itself but that we will keep and expand our connections. I look forward to learning more about our family.

Perhaps the DNA samples and this book help you to connect and to understand one woman's life, and to know and appreciate your own lives better as a result of having read of these pages.

I always seem too busy. Yes, things take me longer to do and my feet hurt. I guess, after this long a life, many things could hurt. I do not have a bucket list, but I plan to travel a bit. For as long as I can, I want to remain active doing things, and when I cannot do things I want to die. For all those who have called me friend, I am grateful to have had you as friends. To all those who have called me Cousin, Grandma, Aunt or Great Aunt or Great, Great, Aunt, I can honestly say I am delighted to be able to talk with you and share your lives. It is a pleasure to know you. I am glad to have had you around and appreciate your attention. I am glad to have had three sons to love. I thank Glenn for helping with this book. I thank Frank for cooking while we worked on the book. Lastly, I thank Walter. He changed and enriched my life and I still love him.

Made in the USA
Columbia, SC
13 June 2017